Cash for College's™
WRITE IT RIGHT

Other books by Cynthia Ruiz McKee
and Phillip C. McKee Jr.

CASH FOR COLLEGE™, REVISED EDITION

Cash for College's™
WRITE IT RIGHT

How to Write the Essay They'll Love and Get the Cash You Need

CYNTHIA RUIZ MCKEE
AND PHILLIP C. MCKEE JR.

Quill

A HARPERRESOURCE BOOK
An Imprint of HarperCollins*Publishers*

HarperCollins books may be purchased for educational, business, or sales promotional use. For information please write: Special Markets Department, HarperCollins Publishers, Inc., 10 East 53rd Street, New York, NY 10022.

FIRST EDITION

Designed by: Stratford Publishing Services

Library of Congress Cataloging-in-Publication Data
McKee, Cynthia Ruiz.
   Cash for College's write it right: how to write the essay they'll love and get the cash you need / Cynthia Ruiz McKee and Phillip C. McKee Jr. — 1st ed.
       p. cm. — (A HarperResource book)
   Includes index.
   ISBN 0-688-17108-7 (alk. paper)
   1. College applications—United States.   2. Universities and colleges — United States — Admission.   3. Exposition (Rhetoric)   I. Title: Write it right.   II. McKee, Phillip C.   III. Title.   IV. HarperResource book.
LB2351.52.U6 M36 2000
378.1′616—dc21   00-039703

00 01 02 03 04   10 9 8 7 6 5 4 3 2 1

DEDICATION

We dedicate this book to four people who have influenced our lives and the writing of this book.

The first is Emma Merritt, writer, teacher, and friend. You taught us more about writing than we ever thought possible. You were the consummate professional, always ready to help and willing to listen. There were so many times, as we wrote this book, when we wanted to call you and share an anecdote. We miss you.

The second is Doctor Allan H. Chaney, Cynthia's professor, mentor, and friend. You taught her to have the courage of her convictions and how to identify, catch, and milk poisonous snakes. You're that rare individual who'd take under your wing any dunderhead who was up for a challenge.

The third is Izaak Martinez, our nephew. You challenge us to keep up with you. It amazes us that as a seventeen-year-old, you can already write circles around us. It won't surprise us to one day see a book published with you as the author.

The fourth is our son, Phillip C. McKee III. You were the impetus for our starting our journey on the road to helping students worldwide. You've affected the lives of thousands, and you've only just begun.

ACKNOWLEDGMENTS

As always, there are many people whom we want to thank for helping us get this book published. The first is Toni Sciarra, our editor and friend. The next person is Associate Editor Katharine Cluverius. These two ladies came together as a "dynamic duo" who could e-mail reminders with a single click, fax instructions without blinking an eye, and send parts or all of the manuscript by overnight delivery with a mere leap from their desks. Never once did they utter a scream for help or of anguish when they opened a package we'd sent containing plastic spiders and cockroaches for that special morning or afternoon surprise. Your assistance, guidance, suggestions, and humor kept us going through those times when it seemed this book would never get finished.

Thanks to Sheri Townsley, Joyce Trutter-Briggs, Danny Campos, Dave Peterson, Tommy Beacham, and Michael Russo for letting us whine, moan, and vent our frustration as we agonized over this manuscript.

Last, but most certainly not least, thanks to the students whose essays we use in this book, the students we've helped in the past, and the students we'll help in the future.

CONTENTS

BEFORE YOU BEGIN THIS BOOK

Welcome to **Cash for College's**™ **Write It Right**. We wrote this book in response to the many requests we received from students and parents for more information on writing essays and on other aspects of the college and scholarship application process. It can be used by students from seventh grade through graduate/professional school, parents, English teachers, other educators, and counselors.

Write It Right will give you insight into what admissions and scholarship committees are looking for in an essay. It will also help prepare you for standardized exams, such as the Texas Academic Skills Program (TASP), which Texas students must take before entering public colleges and universities in that state (unless they have completed three semester credit hours of college-level classes before 1989 or achieve a certain SAT, ACT, or TAAS score).

After you've read the book and completed your essays, you might want to consider using our critique service (see the special offer at the end of this book) and mail a copy of your essay to us. Please enclose a self-addressed, stamped envelope with the essay. We won't write the essay for you, but we might be able to provide suggestions that will make your essay stronger. Make sure you include a copy of the question or assigned essay topic and any specific guidelines.

We welcome your evaluation of this book. We always enjoy hearing from students and parents who are going through the scholarship and college application process. You can contact us in a variety of ways:

Cynthia Ruíz McKee and Phillip C. McKee Jr.
1633 Babcock Road, PMB 425
San Antonio, TX 78229-4725
Tel: (210) 614-5919
Fax: (210) 614-5937
E-mail: mckee@cashforcollege.com
Web site: http://www.cashforcollege.com

Good luck and happy writing!

PART I

Essentials for Excellent Essays

CHAPTER 1

___ GETTING READY TO WRITE ___

Where does a person start when getting ready to write? Many people think they must be inspired to write. Professional writers will tell you that "getting inspired" is baloney. If you make your living by writing, the most important ways to get ready to write are sitting your rear in a chair and putting pencil to paper—or, with the new technology, putting fingers to a keyboard.

Once you've done all those little things you "must do" before starting, such as sharpening all your pencils, turning on the radio or turning off the radio, and so on, you can do one of two things. You can just jump in with both feet (figuratively speaking) and start writing, or you can answer four basic questions.

_____ FOUR QUESTIONS TO ASK YOURSELF _____

1. *Who's* going to read what you've written?
2. *What* are you writing?
3. *When* and *where* are you writing it?
4. *Why* are you writing this assignment?

WHO?

Who's going to read what you've written? Are you writing to your parents, in your diary, to a professor, or to a scholarship committee? This question is closely related to what and why you're writing. You must consider the expectations, level of interest, and level of understanding of the person or persons who will read what you're writing. If you're just writing to your parents about the great time you're having at camp, you primarily have to assure them that their money was well spent in sending you to camp. On the other hand, if you are trying to convince the members of a scholarship committee that they should invest scholarship money in you,

you might write a completely different type of essay.

If you're writing an essay for a scholarship sponsored by the Daughters of the American Revolution, the essay will be vastly different from a scholarship essay you might write for the local Optimist Club. One organization is run by a group of women dedicated to preserving history. The other organization is made up of upwardly mobile, businessmen. What you emphasize in each essay therefore will be quite different.

WHAT?

What are you writing? The assignments in this book are designed to help you write an essay that could get you free cash for college or may enable you to get into the college of your choice. Of course, there are many types of essays. An opinion essay will be different from an essay written for a scholarship committee.

WHEN AND WHERE?

When and where are you writing this essay? Are you at home, preparing to write an essay that will determine whether you'll be able to attend college in the fall? Are you in a classroom, writing an essay for a portion of a standardized test? Will you be meeting the people on the committee who will be evaluating your essay? Do you know if they do their reading and evaluating individually or as a group? You must consider the situation in which your essay will be read.

WHY?

Why are you writing this assignment? In this book, most of your assignments will be to write essays concerning your goals: educational, professional, short-term, or long-term. Knowing why you're writing establishes the relationship between you, the writer, and the reader or committee member. Are you writing a letter to your parents from camp? Or are you writing a letter to your parents to defend your decision to change majors or even schools? Your letter about camp will be informal, maybe even funny, while a letter telling your parents you've decided to transfer to another college would be much more serious. An essay written for an English class will be vastly different from a letter to the editor at a newspaper.

ALSO BEAR IN MIND

You must keep those four questions in mind when you are writing any type of paper or essay. Maintaining a constant awareness of who, what, when, where, and why will make your writing more effective. You don't want to shift your topic (start with one topic and then go off on a different tangent), change your natural tone (for example, trying to impress people by using highly technical terms), or introduce a conflict between tone and topic (for example, writing about how the death of a friend affected your perspective on life, but ending the essay with a joke). If your essay has any of these problems, your reader will question the reasoning behind your presentation.

Once you've answered these four questions, you can proceed to the next phase of your assessment. Will the assignment require any research? If you're writing a paper on the economic impact of the Civil War on the South, you'll need to do some research. If you're writing an essay on what you expect to get out of a college education, you must do some personal reflection, but you don't necessarily have to do much research. Completing the Personal Questionnaire in Chapter Four will help you get an idea of some issues you might want to discuss in a personal essay.

STRUCTURE

If you're writing anything longer than one paragraph, you must get your thoughts in order. If you're taking the writing portion of a standardized test, such as the SAT II or Texas Academic Skills Program (TASP), your essay needs to be at least three to four paragraphs long. The test grader will be assessing whether you can put your thoughts in logical order. A well-constructed essay must consist of more than one paragraph, because you will be discussing more than just one thought or idea on a topic.

Each paragraph should develop one idea or central point. The first paragraph should start with a topic sentence, which you should be able to derive from the assigned topic or essay question. Each sentence in the paragraph should build upon the one before to support the main point of the paragraph. Think of the paragraph as a jigsaw puzzle and of the sentences as puzzle pieces that fit together to present the complete picture of your topic. If you find that you have two main points or ideas in a paragraph, you need to rework or edit that paragraph into two paragraphs or remove the second point.

CLARITY OF THOUGHT

Your ideas must be clear. If you write circles around a point and never quite reach the point, the reader has no idea what you're trying to say. When you take a picture with a camera, you must first focus (unless it's an automatic function of the camera). If not, the final result will be a blurred image. Essays are no different. You must present a clear picture of your points; otherwise, your reader can't follow your thoughts.

Are you ready to begin? Well, don't start writing yet. There are a few other important items to be aware of before you actually start writing. Keep reading.

CHAPTER 2

CREATING AN OUTLINE

To write a well-organized essay that's more than one paragraph in length, you must make an outline. Don't groan. Outlines are easy. An outline for an essay isn't quite as formal as outlines you may have submitted at school. Yes, you may use standard outline format—Roman numerals, letters, and numbers—but it isn't necessary. A simple outline delineates a beginning, middle, and end for your essay in terms as general or as specific as you wish. No one will see or grade your outline, but we can assure you that a committee member will know whether or not you've organized your thoughts. An essay that is hastily written the night before it's due generally reeks of disorganization. Do yourself a favor and make an outline.

Once you start writing, you may think of new ideas you want to add to the essay. You might want to revise your outline or just jot down ideas in the margins of your outline. It can be useful simply to write a phrase or a sentence about how you will organize your essay, as Rachel does in the following example:

EXAMPLE: Rachel is prepared for her exam. She's gotten plenty of rest and has brought four sharpened pencils to class. She studied the night before and was able to review during an unexpected, but welcome, study time in her previous class. The test contains four sections. The first three sections consist of true-or-false, multiple-choice, and fill-in-the-blank statements. The fourth section is a thought-provoking essay, "Evaluate the need to continue the use of animals in medical research."

Rachel quickly outlines the points she wants to make:

1. Ninety-five percent of all animals used are rodents.
2. All animals receive humane treatment before, during, and after procedures.
3. Computer simulation and cell culture cannot replace a living specimen.
4. A countless number of advances have been achieved because of animal-based medical research (blood transfusions, anesthesia, pain killers, antibiotics, insulin, cure for polio, vaccines, chemotherapy, CPR, coronary bypass surgery, etc.).

Rachel's outline is complete. Her essay will have four paragraphs, one for each of these four key points.

Rachel didn't use Roman numerals or do any fancy diagramming or mapping in her outline, although she could have chosen to do so. When you're taking a test, such as the PSAT, SAT, SAT II, or TASP, your time is limited. You don't have time to waste trying to get your outline to "look" nice. Only you will see the outline. Your essay, on the other hand, must deliver the best content possible.

CONSTRUCTING A GOOD OUTLINE

It's not always easy to focus your thoughts. Many of you may view an essay assignment as an ordeal, and you may just want to get it out of the way. We don't want you to view an essay as an obstacle but rather as a means to an end. Here's some help in coming up with your outlines.

We're going to start by asking you some questions. Most scholarship and college admissions essays ask you to write about your goals. Though we want you to concentrate on your goals, we also want you to be aware of how you decided on those goals. Someone or some event probably influenced you in one way or another. These realizations will enrich your essay. Outline how you might answer the following questions. Below each question are some suggestions for how you might respond and examples of other students' responses.

Is there a person whom you look up to as a role model?

This person might or might not be famous. You might want to write about a grandparent, parent, brother, sister, aunt, uncle, or teacher, or someone in business, the media, or the arts. You might choose to discuss why you admire Oprah, Bill Gates, or Winston Churchill. You might decide to write about how your grandmother always expected the very best from you.

Is there an event that affected your life in some way?

The event doesn't have to have been a major awakening. It might be a volunteer activity that touched your life, or even a hobby. It might involve the person you just wrote about in the previous question or it might not. If the two are related, that's acceptable. You might want to write about what you learned from being class president, student council president, or chairperson for a schoolwide food drive. You might want to describe the time you visited your grandparent in the hospital and how difficult it was to accept that your grandparent was dying and there wasn't anything doctors could do to cure him or her. Perhaps because of this experience you've decided to become a medical researcher, hoping to find cures for diseases so that no one else will go through what you and your family did.

What do you hope to accomplish while you're in high school?

If you're in middle school or high school, you may be asked to write about the goals you want to accomplish while in high school, such as maintaining a good grade point average (GPA), improving SAT or ACT scores, joining certain clubs or student council, participating in a sport, participating in a volunteer activity, getting a job to save money to buy a car, selecting a college and gaining admittance, and even winning scholarships. You don't have to list your goals for each year.

If you're in middle school, write about what you want to accomplish over the course of your years in high school, not year by year.

If you're a high school senior, write about what you hope to accomplish during senior year.

If you're already out of high school, you need to write about what you hope to accomplish during the current academic year. Those goals might include getting into college, selecting a major, or applying to and winning scholarships. This section of the essay might be one paragraph or several paragraphs long. The length will be determined by how many things you want to accomplish.

What do you hope to accomplish while you're in college?

Do you hope to select a major, study abroad, or participate in an internship? Do you want to obtain an associate's, bachelor's, master's, doctorate, or professional degree? Depending on which degree you have in mind, you might be writing about your goals over the next two years or about your plans for the next ten or more years. Once again, list your goals not for each year but for all of them combined. This section of your essay might consist of one paragraph or several paragraphs.

Once all of your education is complete, what do you hope to accomplish?

Don't take the easy way out and write that you want "to be a success." What does being a success mean to you? Does it entail having a challenging job, starting a business, having a home, having a family, or traveling?

Your goals reflect who you are and what you want from life. Discussion of life goals can be an important part of your essay. Not all goals have to be academic. Consider the following:

Get a job during summers
Buy a car
Refurbish a car
Get a job and gain experience
Start own business, perhaps home-based
Do volunteer work

QUESTIONS TO PONDER

Here are three questions to think about when preparing your goals outline:

1. What do you hope to accomplish while you're in high school?
2. What do you hope to accomplish while you're in college?
3. Once all of your education is complete, what do you hope to accomplish?

SAMPLE OUTLINES

1. Goals for current year
   a. Help out in community
   b. Win state basketball championship
   c. Get accepted to in-state, public university
2. Goals for college years
   a. Select a major
   b. Study abroad
   c. Earn money or scholarships to help pay for college
3. Long-range professional goals
   a. Become a successful engineer
   b. Use skills to help community
   c. Establish own architectural engineering firm

I. Introduction on importance of goals
II. Past goals
   A. What they were
      1. Become a movie star
      2. Become a famous dancer
   B. What influenced them
      1. Television
      2. Competition winners

III. Present realistic goals
   A. What they are
      1. Graduation
      2. Success in college
   B. What influenced them
      1. Family
         a. Parents
         b. Brother/sister/other relatives
      2. Present successful college graduates
         a. Brother/sister/other relatives
         b. Friends

Finish high school
Get into college
Get bachelor's degree
Work on master's degree
Get into law school
Get married and possibly have children
Own my home
Establish my law firm
Travel as much as possible

GETTING STARTED

Now that you have the rudiments of an outline, the easiest way for you to begin your essay is to just start writing, beginning with the first point in your outline. Get your thoughts down on paper.

Always work from your outline. If you do, your reader will recognize that it has sound structure and will be able to tell that you prepared well for the task of writing an essay.

You don't want to be the student whose essay is so poorly written that the reader will say in amazement, "Can you believe what this student wrote?" You don't want to be remembered for that reason. You want to be the student who submits an essay the reader wants to hold onto and read to anyone who'll listen. That is an essay a reader will remember and that will go on to win scholarship money or admission to college.

What's important is that you're prepared to write. Once you're prepared, just do it. Write down a sentence. Maybe you'll keep it and maybe you won't. Most writers know they might throw out those first few words, sentences, paragraphs, or even pages. What you choose to say in your essay is ultimately your decision. After all, this is your essay.

Several years ago, when Cynthia began writing a historical family saga, she just started writing. The first chapter she wrote has remained basically unchanged, but its placement within the story has changed. She just needed to start. Once she began writing and the characters evolved, she went back and added earlier chapters. That first chapter became chapter two, then three, then five, then eight. Now it's chapter twelve. Writing a book takes much more time and planning than writing a 500-word essay, so these changes occurred over a year or so. You don't have that much time when you're writing an essay, but you also won't need it.

Just jot down your thoughts in a simple outline and start writing. If you have to copy your essay over again for neatness, so what? If copying over an essay will allow you to attend the college of your choice or means that you win scholarship money, then do it. That's all there is to it. Don't waste time trying to come up with reasons why you shouldn't or can't do it. There won't be any good reasons. Writing gets easier once you get started. So get started!

CHAPTER 3

_____ WHAT DO THEY WANT? _____

In this book, you'll be practicing writing essays that may be read by scholarship selection committee members, college admissions committee members, or standardized test graders. You must convince whoever is reading your essays that you're the best candidate to receive a scholarship, be admitted to their college or university, or pass the writing portion of a standardized test. How do you do that? Well, basically all of these readers are looking for the same things. The following is a list of items to remember—the list is not in order of importance, because all of them are important.

_____ WHAT THEY WANT _____

What are selection committee members and standardized test graders looking for in an essay?

BREVITY

They want you to be concise. They want you to get to the point. Use the least number of words possible to express yourself. If you can use five words instead of ten, do so.

EXAMPLE:

At the present time we are experiencing precipitation.	Eight words	Wordy
It's raining right now.	Four words	Better
It's raining.	Two words	Good

The third sentence is direct and to the point. It's a better sentence than the first because it's shorter, describes the situation as effectively, and doesn't make you sound like a meteorologist.

Brevity can be applied to choosing words, not just writing sentences. Consider:

numerous	_many_
remainder	_rest_
sufficient	_enough_
initial	_first_
attempt	_try_
referred to as	_called_
facilitiate	_ease_
implement	_do_
for the purpose of	_for_
very tired	_exhausted_
very happy	_excited_
very sad	_despondent_

Don't be tempted to add phrases that aren't needed just to add to your word count. Overwriting makes you sound pompous. Here are some phrases you should avoid:

I might add	Just add it.
It should be pointed out	Point it out.
I feel	Who else would feel it? It's your essay.
I think	Who else would think it? It's your essay.

unexpected accident	All accidents are unexpected.
in my opinion	Why would you give us someone else's opinion?
personal friend	What other kind of friend is there?

EXAMPLE:

| I think that setting goals is important. | Seven words |
| Setting goals is important. | Four words |

The second sentence is direct and to the point. The reader knows you're the person making the statement. *I think that* is therefore redundant.

CONTENT

What you say and how you say it are crucial. In shorter essays, what you *don't* say is as important as what you do say. Each word should move your ideas forward.

HONESTY

You can only be yourself in an essay. Never read someone else's essay and try to make it your own. Don't imitate someone else's writing style or copy someone's ideas. Never pass off someone else's experience as if it happened to you. Not only is it dishonest but the reader will also be able to spot the change in writing style.

Another good rule of thumb to follow is advice a lawyer would give a client about to serve as a witness: Answer only what's asked.

EXAMPLE: If you're asked to write about a role model and you've always considered Bill Gates a role model, say so. He saw a need in the computer industry and worked hard to corner the market. Bill Gates is truly a visionary. If, on the other hand, you view Bill Gates as a role model because he has 90 billion dollars, you might not want to mention the ninety billion reasons you consider Bill Gates a role model. Although there's nothing wrong with appreciating success and what money

can buy, you don't want to emphasize it in an essay if you're asking for financial assistance.

SINCERITY

Don't write something just because you think others want you to. An essay should inform a committee member who you are, what your goals are, what choices you've made, and why. Many students who are considering health-related careers may write that they want to attend medical school, nursing school, dental school, or other medical training, and then open a free clinic to provide good medical care to lower-income families. That idea is wonderful, but the reader (generally several years older and wiser than the writer) is probably thinking that by the time the student finishes his or her medical training, the student is going to need a free clinic because the student will probably have many years' worth of debt to repay.

Committee members know students are looking at the future through rose-colored glasses. We advise you to clean the lenses from time to time and take a long, responsible, and objective view of your goals. If you truly feel that your goals are reachable with long-term planning, then say so. Cynthia's mentor, Dr. Allan H. Chaney, after years of putting up with her erasing right answers to make them wrong answers, taught her to have the courage of her convictions. Don't be afraid to state your goals and dreams, but be ready to defend them and prepare yourself to accomplish them.

VIBRANCE

Let your personality shine through your words. Show your enthusiasm. Get excited about what you're writing. But don't use exclamation points at the end of all of your sentences. Don't use gimmicks to get attention, such as fluorescent yellow paper. The attention you get from these tactics isn't the type of attention you want. Learn to use words effectively to convey your thoughts and capture positive attention.

THOUGHT/PREPARATION

Even in a timed situation, you should take a few minutes to think before you write. Consider what your goals are. Make an outline (see Chapter Two). Then begin to write.

ORGANIZATION

As noted above, make an outline to help you organize your thoughts. You must demonstrate that you're able to think logically and have prepared yourself to write the essay.

SELF-AWARENESS AND SELF-MOTIVATION

Who are you? What makes you tick? Why did you choose this major, school, or activity? Why should the committee member choose you?

CAREER AWARENESS

If you've researched what it takes to pursue your chosen career, your knowledge will show in your essays. This point hearkens back to several previous points. You want to demonstrate that you've prepared yourself for your future, not just for writing this essay. Are you considering law school? That will take seven years: four undergraduate years and three years in law school. Don't write that you want to be a lawyer in four years. It's not ordinarily possible. If you don't have a career in mind, be honest. Let the committee member know that while you're in college you want to learn more about yourself, your talents and interests, and find out what you're going to do with your life. There's nothing wrong with that approach.

CLARIFICATION

An essay should clarify a weakness without making excuses. Do you have a solid, strong grade point average (GPA), yet you haven't scored as well as you'd like on standardized tests? Do you normally score well on standardized tests but did poorly on this crucial one for a specific reason? Perhaps you were involved in a car accident the night before. You weren't injured, but you stayed at the hospital with the person who was injured. You might have been sleepy when you went to take the test, and your mind was on the person still in the hospital. Thus, you didn't do well. Such a scenario would need to be explained.

Perhaps you've got a great GPA, but you've never been able to join school clubs. With one or both parents working, there's no one to care for your younger brothers and sisters, which means that you have to go straight home to take care of them. Taking care of siblings is a family responsibility, not a job, even if you are being paid to do it. You should explain this situation as well.

Keep in mind you don't always have to clarify everything in each essay you write. For example, if you're writing an essay for the American Mensa Education and Research Foundation, the assigned topic is simple: "Write a 550-word essay on your goals." They don't require a detailed application. Therefore, they don't know your GPA, SAT or ACT score, your financial need, or anything else, for that matter. In this case, you don't have to justify a less-than-stellar SAT score, because it's not a criterion for selection.

ORIGINALITY

You might want to consider humor, poetry, or writing your essay in the form of a recipe. An essay titled "A Recipe for Success," could include ingredients and directions, such as "one cup of determination, a pinch of obstinance, mix vigorously, and whisk to a froth." You would, of course, include specific quantities and qualities (for example, good grades, awards, and extracurricular activities) that you possess. It's all about leaving a lasting impression.

If you use humor, be careful. Don't just crack a joke to try to be funny. Humor isn't appropriate in a serious essay. You must consider the assigned topic and decide if it's something that can be explained with humor. If you have to add "ha ha" after an anecdote, it's not funny. Take it out.

If you've chosen to relate a humorous incident, have someone else read it. Just make sure the person you choose to read your essay wasn't present during the incident you're relating. If the incident occurred at home, don't get a parent or sibling to read it. If the incident occurred at school, don't have a teacher or friend who may have been present during the incident read it. You need an objective opinion. Watch the person's face as he or she reads your essay. Does the person smile, snicker, giggle? If your essay is read with a straight face, it isn't funny. Choose another topic. Start over. Don't use that essay. There are times when humor can be misinterpreted as having "an attitude."

If you're inclined toward poetry, you might want to consider writing an essay in the form of a poem. Don't force it, or it will appear contrived. However, if it comes to you naturally, poetry is an effective way to get a committee member's attention. If you're entering a writing competition, you may not be able to substitute poetry for prose, but you might use this form for scholarship or college application essays.

CORRECT SPELLING

It's important to check and double-check your spelling. Whether you type or handwrite your essay, you must pay attention to detail. It shows that you care.

GOOD GRAMMAR

If you're using a computer, don't just run Spell Check. You should also run Grammar Check. You might have transposed letters, writing "saw" instead of "was" or "from" instead of "form." You may have used a word incorrectly, for example, using "your" instead of "you're" or "their" rather than "there." Spell Check won't catch these errors. You don't want such mistakes in an essay. Don't assume that Grammar Check is always correct, either. After all, your computer is only a machine. Get another person to proofread your essay. You might have dropped a word you meant to insert. Each time you read it, your mind sees the word although it's not there. Another person will catch this type of error.

PROPER FORMAT AND NEATNESS

What does your essay look like? Is it neat? Did you follow the correct format, indenting your paragraphs? Did you use so much Liquid Paper that the paper bends backward? Perhaps you were instructed to handwrite the essay, but as you wrote it a bit of ink got on the outside of your palm, which resulted in your leaving tracks all over the page. If this happens, you have one choice: rewrite it.

Your essay must look appropriate. It must reflect you at your best. Would you attend your prom looking as if you were going to clean the garage? Of course not. You'd spend hours looking for the right outfit. You'd have your hair cut or styled. You'd spend more time in the shower than usual. You'd work hard to make sure that everything was as close to perfect as possible. That's what you have to do with your essays. The reason is simple. There's much more on the line regarding your essays for college admission and scholarships than there is regarding the prom. Do what it takes to put your best foot forward. If you do, you'll never regret this decision.

_____ DOS AND DON'TS _____

When writing your essay,

DO

1. Answer the question that's been asked.
2. Follow all the suggestions in this chapter.
3. Be concise. Get to the point.

4. Be honest. Don't try to be someone you're not. Discuss qualities you possess, not ones you wish you had.
5. Do the best job possible. Don't wait until the night before it's due to write it.
6. Keep your essay focused. Don't try to mention everything you're interested in or have

done. Choose one experience, incident, or person to concentrate on in your essay.

7. Be specific. Mention what you've learned, not just that you learned "a lot." Give examples of what you learned.

DON'T

1. Second-guess the committee and write what you think they want to read. Never, ever write, "I know you want me to . . . ," because you have no idea exactly what any committee expects you to say.
2. Send an addendum to your essay. Don't send a second package trying to change or update what you've already sent. It will look as though you didn't think things through the first time.
3. Send a videotape.
4. Send a sample of your work, such as instrumental or vocal music on an audiotape, artwork, articles, essays, short stories, or poetry. The essay itself is a sample of your work.
5. Ramble on.
6. Quote others in your essay. It's great that you know what others say, but scholarship or college admissions committee members want to know your thoughts, not what Benjamin Franklin, Martin Luther King, Jr., or Betty Crocker may have said. One quote might be suitable if it had a direct effect on your life in some way. Otherwise, don't quote others. Quoting more than one person is overwhelmingly the wrong approach to take.

7. Turn down writing an optional essay. If you're given any opportunity to provide more information, take it. It could mean the difference between getting into a college or being rejected, or winning free cash for college or having to pay for it yourself.
8. Use flattery. It looks as though you're "kissing up" to the committee. The colleges and universities already know how good they are and how they mold students into leaders.
9. State the obvious. There's no need to discuss how much you love the school, its location, its size, or its appearance. Why would you be applying to that school if you didn't like it?
10. Indicate that a school is your "safety" or back-up school.
11. Write that you're going to college because you don't know what to do with your life and you don't want to get a job.
12. Try to be cute. This can easily turn a committee member against you.
13. Be evasive. If there's something you need to admit and explain, do it. Stand up for what you believe in. Remember to have the courage of your convictions.
14. Lie about your grades, your experiences, your opinions, or anything else. Lies can come back to haunt you.
15. Use footnotes. This isn't a research paper.
16. Use a bibliography. Unless you are asked to write about a book or magazine article you've recently read, there isn't any reason to discuss it in an essay about you—unless you wrote it.

TOPICS TO AVOID

Although an essay should express your beliefs, your ideas, and your personality, there are some topics you should avoid. Although the following topics may be important to you, they don't have any place in a college admission or scholarship essay:

Romantic relationships
Views on drugs or alcohol
Opinions about sex or other moral issues
Political beliefs
Religious beliefs
Views on current events (from abortion to disarmament)

It doesn't matter how much you've learned from forming your religious or political beliefs or from choosing a boyfriend or girlfriend, don't use these as essay topics for scholarships or college admission applications.

The only time you would address a problem such as teen crime or teen pregnancy would be if you're directed to write on that particular topic. An essay assignment might be to select what you think is the worst problem facing teenagers today and what you might do to help work toward a solution. If presented with this assignment, you must then discuss teen crime, alcohol or drug abuse, teen pregnancy, or any one of countless other problems.

Write on these topics only if you're asked to answer a specific question or select such a topic. Otherwise, choose a topic that centers on something positive, such as defining success, or why setting goals is important.

CHAPTER 4

_ GETTING TO KNOW YOURSELF _

If you were taking a history, government, or economics course and were assigned to write about an event in history, you would have to do some research in order to write the essay. In this case, colleges, universities, and scholarship committees are asking you to write about yourself, and it may seem as if there's nowhere to turn. This chapter will help you do some personal research in order to write a convincing essay. It's also a useful way to write essays and keep track of what you've written and what you haven't.

_ EXERCISES THAT WILL HELP YOU RESEARCH YOURSELF _

EXERCISE 1

We want you to look at who you are and put your discoveries into words. We want you to select three words that you think describe you, but from three different viewpoints:

1. How would you describe yourself in one word? We're not talking about your physical description. We don't want to know that you're tall, short, blond, brunette, brown-eyed, or left-handed. We're talking about how you see yourself and how others might see you.
2. How would an adult describe you in one word? This time, consider how a parent, a teacher, or someone you admire would describe you. How do you think he or she views you? Use a different word from the one you used to describe yourself.
3. How would your best friend describe you in one word? Use your imagination. Have fun leafing through a thesaurus or a dictionary. If you're stumped on what words to choose,

here are some you might consider. Do any of these apply to you?

aggressive	friendly
attentive	helpful
bold	honest
cheerful	hopeful
clever	idealistic
compassionate	industrious
confident	influential
cooperative	insightful
courageous	inspiring
daring	intelligent
dauntless	intense
dependable	intuitive
determined	kind
dreamer	leader
dynamic	lively
eager	motivated
earnest	opinionated
energetic	optimistic
enthusiastic	patient
ethical	persistent
fearless	risk-taker

scrupulous tenacious
shrewd tender
sincere tolerant
smart trustworthy
spirited understanding
strong-willed virtuous
stubborn visionary
supportive warm
sympathetic zealous

EXERCISE 2

Describe yourself in one or two sentences. Who are you? To give you two examples of how you might respond, we wrote sentences for this exercise.

CYNTHIA'S SENTENCES: I'm a forty-eight-year-old Hispanic female who, generally, won't take no for an answer. As a writer and educational consultant, I empower students to fulfill their potential, hopes, and dreams.

(After I wrote these two sentences, I was intrigued that I didn't mention that I am disabled. Then I realized why I didn't. I don't think of myself as disabled. Yet to give a clear picture of who I am, I should have included that word.)

PHIL'S SENTENCES: I'm a forty-eight-year-old man who started on a new career path ten years ago, and found that success and happiness are what you make of them. Because my new career entails working with young people, I find it fulfilling and invigorating.

EXERCISE 3

Regardless of what grade you're in, what do you want to accomplish in the time you have in high school? This information can be put in sentence form or organized as a list. It should include both academic and nonacademic goals.

EXERCISE 4

What do you want to accomplish in college? This information can be in sentence or list form. It can include, for example, selecting a major, studying abroad for a year, internships, and nonacademic goals.

EXERCISE 5

What do you want from life? Don't just say you want to be successful. What does being successful mean to you? Your list may include working for a Fortune 500 company, owning your own business, traveling, getting married and starting a family, or having a home, a stock portfolio, or a summer home.

EXERCISE 6

Has there been a person whom you've considered a role model or who has affected your life? This could be a person you've known all your life or someone you've never met. In a sentence or two, write who the person is and how he or she has affected your life.

EXERCISE 7

Has a particular event or experience affected your life in some way? In a sentence or two, briefly write about an event or experience that has affected your life and that you learned from.

VOILÀ

Can you believe it? You've just composed an informal outline. You also have no excuse about where to start when you begin writing your essay. You have three key words, one or two sentences, and information about your goals for high school, college, and beyond. Remember, committee members want to know who you are. Using these items in your essay will give readers insight into the wonderful person you are and hope to become.

Though we say you can use your three key words in your essay, we don't mean literally. For example, if you chose the words "leader, motivated, and optimistic," you shouldn't write: **I've always thought of myself as an optimistic and motivated leader.** That would be the easy way out. You want to describe situations and events that bring to mind these words. Here's one such description:

> **One experience that was especially important to me was the school Thanksgiving Food Drive. The student who was appointed Chairperson moved out of town and left our school and the committee floundered. I knew that many families facing hard times would be disappointed if the food wasn't collected. I stepped in, challenged the various school club leaders to see which club could collect the most food, and arranged bake sales to cover the cost of purchasing specific items. I knew that our student body could meet the challenge. They just needed someone to tell them what, how, and when to do certain tasks.**

You've now shown, not told, the reader that you're an optimistic, motivated leader. This is a much better way of describing these qualities without sounding arrogant.

When you're explaining who you are, remember, "Show, don't tell." For instance, suppose you're applying to a college which might be a stretch for you academically. Your performance has been consistent, but not as academically strong as the average student at that school. Don't just state in your essay, "I know I can do it." Otherwise, the first question that might pop into a committee member's mind is, "Then why didn't you do it while you were in high school?"

We'd like to suggest a different approach. To show a committee that you believe in your ability to accomplish a difficult task, relate a story that shows this confidence. Perhaps during your freshman year you tried out for the swim team but didn't make it. The coach gave you a critique explaining why you didn't make the team. You were determined that next year you were going to make the team, and you developed a strategy to improve your skills. You spent more hours at the pool than the swim team members did. You practiced, practiced, and then practiced some more. The following year, you not only made the team but won more meets than any other member. That's why you know you can face and master a challenge you wish to take on. An essay that spells this out will effectively *show* who you are and why you're the best choice for college admission, a scholarship, or both.

PERSONAL QUESTIONNAIRE

This questionnaire is designed to give you the opportunity to get to know yourself, making you aware of things that might be important to mention in an essay. On a separate sheet of paper, answer each question using as few words as possible, yet providing as much information as possible. It's all right to skip a question and then go back to it.

1. Where were you born?
2. Where were you raised?
3. How many brothers or sisters do you have?
4. Do you ask your family for advice? If so, what do you ask about?
5. Has anyone ever asked you for advice? If so, what do they ask you about?

6. Are you close to your aunts, uncles, cousins, grandparents, or other relatives?
7. What is your ethnicity?
8. What do you know about the culture of your ancestors?
9. Would you like to know more about the culture of your ancestors?
10. Has your ethnicity or gender influenced who you are? If so, how?
11. If your ancestors spoke a different language, do you speak it?
12. Would you like to know that language?
13. Are you neat, or are you a slob?
14. Are you musical?
15. What instrument(s) do you play?

16. Are you a vocalist or singer?
17. What kind of music do you enjoy?
18. What do you do with your free time?
19. What are your hobbies?
20. Do you enjoy attending school or college?
21. What teacher or professor do you respect most? Why?
22. What teacher or professor has most influenced you? Why?
23. What's your favorite class or subject? Why?
24. Would you like to go away to college? Why?
25. Would you like to go to a large or small college or university? Why?
26. What career are you sure you don't want to pursue?
27. What career would you like to pursue? Why?
28. When did you become interested in this field of interest?
29. How did you learn about your field of interest (for example, from a friend of the family, class work, reading, independent study, or employment)?
30. What major(s) are you considering? Why?
31. Do you know if the college(s) you are thinking about attending offer(s) that major?
32. What one or two things have you done or accomplished that you are proud of? Why?
33. What one or two things have you done or accomplished that you would change? How? Why?
34. What event or experience will you never forget? Why?
35. What event has had the biggest effect on your life? Why?
36. Do you have an item from childhood you still treasure and hope always to have?
37. Why are you special? What makes you unique?
38. Have you ever been or tried to be someone's hero or role model? Why do you think that is?
39. What would you be willing to do to become someone's hero or role model?
40. Have you ever had an idea for a new invention or tool, improved on a tool or product, composed a song or dance, or written a play, short story, book, or movie? Describe it.
41. What have you learned from a teacher, professor, or class that has helped you grow?
42. What have you learned from school or work (for example, leadership skills, management or organizational skills, or listening skills) that has helped you grow?
43. Have you ever been taught something in school that you don't believe?
44. What obstacles or hardships (for example, financial, familial, physical) have you faced and overcome?
45. What characteristics (for example, integrity, determination, or compassion) do you have that will help you succeed in your field?
46. Why should a scholarship or college admissions committee choose you over someone else?
47. What are you doing now and what are you planning to do in the future to "give back" to your community?
48. Is there anything you should explain about yourself or your performance (such as, good grades but low standardized test scores; low GPA, which is now improving; or not much school or community involvement)?
49. Have you ever traveled to or visited a place you'd like to visit again? Why?
50. Have you ever traveled to or visited a place you never want to visit again? Why?
51. Is there a place you've always dreamed of visiting?
52. Have you ever had an argument or said something harmful to someone and not had the opportunity to apologize or set things straight with that person and wished that you had?
53. Pretend it's your ten-year high school reunion. What would you like to tell your high school friends that you've done in those ten years?
54. Pretend it's your twenty-fifth-year college reunion. What would you like to tell your college friends that you've done in those twenty-five years?

55. Pretend you're retiring from your future career. What would you like the people you've worked with to say about you?

56. Pretend your life is over. What would you like the person who writes your eulogy to say about you?

_____ YOU'RE ON YOUR WAY TO WRITING YOUR ESSAY _____

Once you have identified your key words, personal characteristics, and goals, you can use them in various combinations to make the process of writing your essays more efficient, adapting your essays to meet different subject and length requirements as needed.

In Appendix C, we've provided two Essay Tracking Charts. The first chart helps you keep track of which essays you've written and those you still need to write. The second chart tracks which essays and combinations of essays you've sent out, and those yet to be sent out. This book is all about making writing essays and applying for college and scholarships as easy as possible.

You are now closer to being able to write dynamic essays that will linger in a committee member's mind long after he or she reads your essay. The next chapter will help you consider other characteristics about yourself that you might want to write about.

CHAPTER 5

___ SAMPLE ESSAY QUESTIONS ___

The following is a list of essay questions or topics commonly used by college, university, and scholarship applications. In some cases, we've included the name of the scholarship, college, or university that might have asked that particular question in the past.

Though Chapter Nine gives you specific writing assignments, you might want to try writing on some of these topics, especially if you're considering applying to one of the scholarships, colleges, or universities mentioned.

COMMON TOPICS AND QUESTIONS FOR ___ SCHOLARSHIP AND COLLEGE ADMISSIONS ESSAYS ___

1. Describe your short-term and long-term goals.
2. Describe an experience that has deeply influenced your development.
3. Tell us about a person who has influenced you in some way, whether by showing you the need to set goals or by being a mentor, or describe someone who was there when you needed a friend.
4. How have your background and upbringing influenced your personal development and outlook?
5. Describe what you're like, using information about your most significant accomplishments.
6. Choose a book (or books) that you have read on your own (not as a school assignment) that has affected you deeply and explain why.
7. Make up a question that is personally relevant to you and answer it.

8. Describe how you have demonstrated leadership both in and out of school.
9. How have you prepared yourself to be a successful student, and how are you choosing the best school for your needs? (Oklahoma State University)
10. Write an essay that conveys to the reader a sense of who you are. Possible topics: an experience that shaped your life, circumstances of your upbringing, the way you see the world—the people in it, events great and small, everyday life—or any personal theme that appeals to your imagination. (Columbia University)
11. Write an essay describing in detail an achievement, experience, some special interest, or anything else that would help the Committee on Admission know you better. (Tulane University)
12. The Admissions Committee welcomes comments from you that would help us

to know your son or daughter better. (Tulane—Optional Parent's Statement)

13. Describe yourself. What qualities do you like most and/or least about yourself? What do you hope to accomplish during the four years in college? (Hobart and William Smith Colleges)

14. Write your own recommendation for admission or an excerpt from your autobiography. (Hobart and William Smith Colleges)

15. If you could travel through time and interview any historical figures, who would you choose, what would you ask, and why? (Centenary College of Louisiana)

16. Tell us about what you would love to study, and how that choice, if it became reality, would change your life.

17. In 1,200 words or less, write a true, first-person story about an experience that changed you. It need not be highly dramatic or unusual, but it should demonstrate how faith in God has made a difference in your life. (Guideposts Essay Writing Competition)

18. Make a statement of your plans as they relate to your educational and career objectives and true goals.

19. Describe how athletics and education have affected your life. (Hooked on Sports—FootAction USA Scholarship Application)

20. Explain your Christian faith and how you anticipate it will be influenced by attending ORU. (Oral Roberts University)

21. Write an essay of no more than 500 words on any subject that interests you. (Boston University)

22. Discuss how your system of values would help you succeed as a Baylor student and throughout your lifetime. (Baylor University)

23. Outside your family, who has been your greatest teacher? How and what did he or she teach you? Give us an idea of this person's qualities and talents and tell us what made him or her worthy of emulation. Be sure to include specifics regarding your interaction with the person, giving us as complete a picture as possible. A character sketch is fine, but a short narrative or other essay style is also appropriate. (Amherst College)

24. Choose one: What social or political issue most concerns you and why? (Agnes Scott College)

25. What has been the most significant event in your life? (Agnes Scott College)

26. What cultural work (literature, art, music, or dance) has had a significant effect on your life? (Agnes Scott College)

TIMED ESSAYS

The following questions and topics have been presented in the past as essay writing assignments on standardized tests. In order to duplicate the actual testing conditions, you should choose a quiet spot that has a desk or table. Don't write while lying on the floor. Even if that's your favorite way to write, you won't be allowed to do it during the test. There should also be no music, radio, or television playing in the background. They won't be permitted during the test. You'll want to have some sort of timer to stand in for the person at the front of the room who'll be proctoring the exam.

You will be allotted only sixty minutes in which to consider:

Who's going to read what you've written?
What are you writing?
When and *where* are you writing it?
Why are you writing this assignment?

You will also need to construct a simple outline. It will help you remember all the points you wish to make, in logical order. You will need to write a rough draft. You will then need to make any changes, corrections, deletions, and other edits necessary to create your final draft.

Do not under any circumstances turn in a one-paragraph essay. If you've constructed an outline, each of those points, ideas, or topics should be addressed in separate paragraphs. An essay *can-*

not be one paragraph in length. Only a paragraph can be one paragraph in length. An essay must present several ideas, one per paragraph.

Remember, you have only sixty minutes to complete your essay.

SAMPLE QUESTIONS FROM THE TEXAS ACADEMIC SKILLS PROGRAM (TASP)

1. Write an essay in which you present your views on how to handle litter in your community.
2. Write an essay in which you discuss why you are entering college and what you expect from a college degree.
3. States today observe Dr. Martin Luther King Jr.'s birthday because of his contributions to the Civil Rights movement of the sixties. However, observance of this holiday still causes controversy. Write an essay, to be read by a peer who has recently immigrated to this country, explaining the various sides of the issue.
4. Because of increased crime involving teenagers at area malls and other places of activity, local city councils have recently proposed curfews. Write an essay, to be read by the city council and concerned citizens, approving or disapproving of the proposed curfews for teenagers.
5. As a teenager in today's society, what do you consider to be the worst problem facing teenagers and why? What steps would you suggest a community take to begin eliminating that problem?

SAMPLE QUESTIONS FOR PERSONAL STATEMENTS, GRADUATE/PROFESSIONAL SCHOOL LEVEL

Here are some sample topics for personal statements required for application to graduate or professional schools. These topics and questions are different from those encountered by under- graduate students. You may attention to the topics posed programs to which you're intereste

1. What ten items would you choose along on a solo space flight and wh (Wharton School at the University of Pennsylvania)
2. Describe a situation in your life where you challenged the majority or traditional thoughts of the group. What impact did you have on the group? (Wharton School at the University of Pennsylvania)
3. What is the world's greatest problem? Why? (Wharton School at the University of Pennsylvania)
4. I wish the admissions committee had asked me . . . (Kellogg Graduate School of Management)
5. People may be surprised when they learn that I . . . (Kellogg Graduate School of Management)
6. Describe a risk you have taken, adversity you have overcome, or obstacles you have encountered that influenced who you are today. (University of Chicago)
7. How would you characterize the effect of your contributions to the groups or organizations in which you have participated? (Yale University)
8. Describe the characteristics of an exceptional manager using an example of someone whom you have observed or with whom you have worked. How has his or her management style influenced you? (Amos Tuck School of Business at Dartmouth)
9. Discuss a personal failure: In what ways were you disappointed in yourself, and what did you learn from the experience? (Columbia University)
10. The year is 2010 and the annual edition of *Who's Who* includes your biography. What does it say, beginning from the time you completed your next degree? (University of Michigan)
11. You are the manager of a product line that has, since its introduction ten years ago, been extremely popular with consumers

and very profitable for your firm. However, your research team has advised you in confidence of a long-term study, recently completed, that shows the product may lead to health problems in consumers five to ten years after they purchase it. Therefore, it is probable that some consumers are already experiencing problems, perhaps even unknowingly. But due to its increased competition in the rest of your company's industry, the company will be forced to close down a part of its operation—leading to widespread layoffs—unless it continues to manufacture and market this product. You have full authority over the future plans for it. What are the issues facing the company, and how would you approach the situation? (University of Michigan)

12. Why are you and this school well-matched? (This or a similar question is asked by many schools.)

13. Write an essay describing the areas of law that interest you most and explain your reasons for seeking a graduate degree in law. Provide additional information you believe should be taken into account by the Committee on Graduate Admission. (Tulane Law School)

14. Submit a personal statement which will give the admissions committee a sense of you as a person and as a potential student and graduate of Harvard Law School. Do not write what you think committee members want to read. (Harvard Law School)

15. We want to know who you are. Instead of asking you to recount information we can read in other parts of your application, we want you to show us who you are by using your creativity. Imagine you've gone on a cruise. The cruise ship begins to sink; you're able to grab ten items you had on the trip. You are now stranded on a deserted island. What would those ten items be and what would you do? Your essay should be approximately 1,000 words in length. (This or a similar question is asked by many schools.)

16. Describe the setting in which you envision conducting your medical career. Also include how and why you think this setting would help fulfill your interests related to the practice of medicine. (This or a similar question is asked by many schools.)

CHAPTER 6

SAMPLE ESSAYS

The following fourteen sample essays were written by a variety of students vying for scholarships or for admission to colleges or universities. These essays should serve only as examples. We cannot stress strongly enough that to use any part or all of any of these essays would be plagiarism. Not only would using these essays be a violation of trust, but they don't describe you. These essays describe other students. Some of the information in these essays, including names and places, has been changed to protect the students' anonymity.

As you read these essays, ask yourself, "What did I learn about this student?" Although you may not learn whether the student is tall, short, male, female, athletic, nonathletic, blond, or brunette, you will have the unique opportunity of seeing into these students' lives. Take the time to read these essays, evaluate them, and, most of all, enjoy them.

There are times when you can reuse an essay on different applications, but it isn't always safe to do so, as we discuss in Chapter One. The following essay was used to answer two different questions posed by two different universities. This essay does a good job of providing the information requested in both cases.

SAMPLE ESSAY 1

Topic A: In 250 words or less, discuss one or two activities that have meant the most to you during your secondary school years.

Topic B: Describe how you have demonstrated leadership both in and out of school.

During my high school years there have been two activities which have meant a great deal to me and which serve as examples of my leadership ability. One is the Student Council Presidency and the other is my volunteer work at a local nursing home. They've both contributed significantly to my development.

The Student Council Presidency is a wonderful learning experience. I've always assumed the leadership role in classroom group activities, but these roles don't entail true leadership. As Student

Council President, I'm the leader who sets the agenda, who can make binding policy decisions, and who affects the voting of the council by the simplest variations in speech. The powers that our Student Council Constitution gave me brought great responsibility. From this post I learned the value of hard work and of setting a good example.

My volunteer work also helped develop my character. My primary duty at the nursing home is to walk with an elderly woman who requires exercise. While there, I also visit with the other residents. Having been influenced by the Hispanic tradition of respecting and revering my elders, it warms my heart to see their eyes light up at my approach. They enjoy my visits because I have time to just sit and listen to their stories. In my own little way, I make their last years that much more enjoyable. This volunteer work has made me a compassionate individual who is more attuned to the needs of others.

When both experiences are combined, they join to make me a better person; a person more capable of compassion and handling responsibility.

SAMPLE ESSAY 2

Topic: Briefly describe your short-term and long-term goals.

Goals are one of the most important parts of a person's life, and yet as a teenager they're the last thing you want to think about. So when I came across this essay question, I found myself thinking about what was deep inside me. "What are my short- and long-range goals?" I asked myself. Here is the answer I found.

In the short term, my goals are simple. I want to get into a good college and get a bachelor's degree in economics. Then I want to continue on and get my master's and my doctorate. Of course, somehow I have to pay for this, so another short-range goal is to get adequate financial aid. All of these are stepping stones to higher things.

For long-range goals, I have several choices. One is that I would like to receive a position in the private sector as an economist or I'd like to become a professor of economics at a university. In the end, I hope to become a well-known authority and advise heads of state on economic policy or even run for office. All the while I hope for the usual things such as a wife, children, house, etc. To some, these goals may seem odd and simplistic, but they're what I wish for from deep inside me.

SAMPLE ESSAY 3

Topic: Pick the one experience that has most influenced your development, and briefly describe how it has done so.

The activity which has most influenced my development has been my volunteer work at a nursing home. When I'm there, my primary duty is to walk with an elderly woman who requires exercise but who has osteoporosis and dizzy spells. I also visit with the other residents and listen to their stories. It creates immense personal satisfaction for me when I see their eyes light up at my approach. They know that I'm someone who will listen to their stories, and they enjoy talking. It makes me feel good to know that I've made their last years just that much more pleasant. This experience has made me a more compassionate individual. I value the time at the nursing home because of this.

SAMPLE ESSAY 4

Topic: Write a short note telling your future college roommate what to expect from you in the coming year.

Dear Future Roommate,

When it comes to housekeeping I'm a bit of a slob, so expect a little mess. I don't play music very loud, although you may not like my taste in music. I mostly listen to classical or big band music, but I do listen to a few modern groups. When I'm working, I don't like to be interrupted at all. I am usually drinking a non-alcoholic beverage. I am a non-smoker. I'm an evening person who stays up late to work on things, but I also sleep late. The good thing is that I'm very flexible about things. Well, that's essentially me.

_____ SAMPLE ESSAY 5 _____

Topic: In 250 words or less, choose a book or books that have affected you deeply, and explain why.

Recently, I reread two books and in them I found meaning I had missed the first time. Those books were *1984* and *Brave New World*. When I first read them they had been nothing but stories. When I read them again, they were more than stories; they were biting social commentaries. The books told of two societies with totalitarian governments.

1984 showed a government that controlled through terror and violence, yet the regime enjoyed wide popular support. Many individuals didn't know what was going on and were happy to have their lives controlled. Others believed it was all for the best and that the government was doing good. Only a few were against the government, and these were dealt with promptly. This situation has already existed, most notably in Nazi Germany.

Brave New World depicted a society which had rigid genetic classes but which controlled society by making life so enjoyable that hardly anyone wanted to rebel. However, it was just as repressive as the society in *1984*.

That was what scared me about both novels. It would be so easy for modern Americans to become members of societies such as those. These books taught me to appreciate every single right protected by our Constitution. They taught me to be wary of those advocating the limiting of a right for the good of society. They taught me how to be a good citizen.

_____ SAMPLE ESSAY 6 _____

Topic: What is the most stimulating book or article (other than those you have read for school assignments) that you have read in the last six months? Why do you think it was stimulating?

The most stimulating article I have read in the past six months was "Japanese Tract Rankles Americans" in the November 20 edition of *Insight*. This article dealt with the contents of a book called "The Japan that Can Say 'No'," written by Akio Morita, founder of the Sony Corporation, and

Shintaro Ishihara, an ultra-nationalist politician; and the subsequent reactions when a pirated version surfaced in the United States.

The book, according to the article, boiled down to the idea that Japan holds complete economic and technological supremacy in the world and could therefore say no to the United States and world demands. The article also stated that Sony Corporation never intended that the book be read outside of Japan. To say the least, there were some violent reactions in the United States. The article, quite frankly, outraged me. It also made me more interested in our economic relations with Japan and has prompted me to read more on the topic.

_____ SAMPLE ESSAY 7 _____

Topic: Discuss one or two academic interests or out-of-class activities that have meant the most to you.

One interest of mine that has transcended the boundary between academic and out-of-class activities is my violin. I originally began taking private violin lessons at the age of seven. At that age it was a task which had to be done, not enjoyed. I quit after several years of lessons and didn't resume lessons until this year. I found that I had room in my schedule for one more class, and Orchestra was offered that period. I returned to the violin, and now it holds meaning. Every note is a shade of emotion, every piece of music a creation of feelings. I am able to see a beauty to which I was blind before. I now appreciate art and music much more, and I enjoy playing my violin.

_____ SAMPLE ESSAY 8 _____

Topic: Describe what you are like, using information about your most significant accomplishments. Include extracurricular and community activities, awards, hobbies, primary interests, volunteer work, and employment, as well as future plans and goals.

My major extracurricular activity has been to participate annually in regional science fairs and in Junior Academy of Science competitions. I was able to participate in these competitions because for the last three summers I have interned at a medical research laboratory. My projects have not only expanded my knowledge and that of others, but they have also allowed me to participate at the State Science Fair and at State Junior Academy competitions.

In my sophomore year I was Class Parliamentarian and a Student Council Representative. In my junior year, I was Student Council Treasurer, and I am Student Council President this year. Under my guidance, the Council has attempted to create institutions, such as a student store, which will help to increase student involvement.

Throughout my high school years, I have organized and supported projects which have encouraged school spirit; such as being co-founder and editor of the school newspaper, which has evolved into a journalism class. I have also founded and am Vice President of the school's Bowling Club, which has expanded into a district-wide league. These activities, and my exposure to economics class, have led me to pursue a career in what I perceive to be one of the driving forces of our society: economics.

I have always been interested in the great events of history, especially in the mass movements which have changed the fate of nations and molded our political view. I wish to understand the forces that shape our daily lives, as well as the ones which mold the destinies of our nation's industries and those of the entire world. I wish to understand all of this, not only in its present state but also in its historical context. This will probably require study in areas outside of economics alongside the traditional studies and unrelated courses, but this extra work is welcome and anticipated because of my hunger for knowledge.

To relax after work and school, I have several hobbies. My favorite is to exercise my imagination with creative writing. It invigorates me to create a character from scratch and to define his personality by his words and actions. I also enjoy paper modeling. Paper modeling is just like other types of modeling except that instead of wood or plaster, you're cutting, folding and pasting together paper. I can make planes, boats, buildings and even birds with paper. Finally, if I just don't feel like moving, it's nice just to sit back and read a good book while I listen to classical music. I prefer reading science-fiction, fantasy, and mystery.

I also find the time to spend a few hours, every weekend, at a local nursing home. I visit with the residents, take some on walks and try to brighten the lives of a few elderly people.

My short-term goals are simple. I want to get into a good college and get a bachelor's degree in economics. Then I want to continue on and get my master's and my doctorate.

For long-range goals I have several choices. I would like to hold a position in the private sector as an economist, or I'd like to become a professor of economics at a university. In the end, I hope to become a well-known authority and advise heads of state on economic policy or even run for office. All the while I hope for the usual things such as a wife, children, house, etc. To some, these goals may seem odd and simplistic, but they are what I wish for from deep inside me.

This essay may have made me sound almost angelic, but let me set the record straight. I enjoy going out with my friends and often I make minor sacrifices in other areas, such as house cleaning duties, so that I can. That, in brief, is a summary of my major activities. I hope it has been informative, or at least entertaining!

SAMPLE ESSAY 9

Topic: We live in a complex and everchanging society, yet our family heritage and tradition allow certain values to be maintained. How has your background influenced your personal development and outlook? Is there something special about you as a person you would like the committee to know? Support your statement with experiences you have had.

When I was a small child, the part of my Hispanic background which influenced me most was the concept of the extended family and family loyalty. Most children are lucky if they know their uncles and aunts. Because of my Hispanic tradition, I not only know my aunts and uncles, but also my great-aunts, second and third cousins, and many more.

Whenever trouble surfaced, there were many arms to fall back on for support. This family loyalty and the continuity between generations has helped me adjust to changes in my environment due to my mother's increasing physical disability and due to the death of my grandfather. The loyalty I've found in my family has spread into my friendships and made those friendships much closer. I value my heritage and what it has contributed to my life and my personality.

Even though only my mother is Hispanic, I know that I have a heritage rich with legends, such as Don Pedrito Jaramillo and La Llorona; a culture based on a civilization hundreds of years old; and a language whose words carry feelings that can't possibly be conveyed in translation.

Being Hispanic is as much a part of me as being a male, or being an American. That heritage will always be part of my conscious and unconscious mind. That heritage will follow me as I move on to college and grow into adulthood. It will always be a part of me that no one can take away.

—————————————— SAMPLE ESSAY 10 ——————————————

Topic: Make up a question that is personally relevant to you, state it clearly, and answer it. Feel free to use your imagination.

What is success? Success is an abstract term, yet many of us strive for it with a single-minded determination. People fight for success so hard that it drives many to their graves, or, even worse, to living nightmares of substance abuse. It is the driving force in our lives, yet we don't know exactly what it is.

How should we define success? For any normal animal or plant species, it would be survival, but for man it is different. We are thinking animals living in a highly developed, materialistic society. In that context, even survival takes on an ambiguous meaning. Survival could mean breaking even financially or making a meager profit. Survival could also take on its literal meaning of staying alive, or it could mean maintaining one's lifestyle. The definition of survival is different for each of us because we are all individuals.

It's the same with success. Because we're all individuals with different personalities, success means something different to each of us. In a society where yearly income is so important, it is reassuring and comforting to a teenager to discover that success is a unique phenomenon for everyone. Here we are trying to set out our life-time goals and adults keep reminding us of the average yearly income of various professions. This just confuses us about the meaning of success. When we discover that success is measured by our personal satisfaction with our life, then we can truly set realistic goals. The definition of success is therefore unique for each of us. We, as individuals, are the only ones who must find satisfaction in our own success.

—————————— SAMPLE ESSAY 11 ——————————

Topic: We hope you'll use your essay to help us understand your thoughts and feelings about what's important to you. Name three people whom you admire and respect or who changed your view of life in a deep and significant way.

Three people whom I admire and respect would be my maternal grandfather, my mother, and my middle school history teacher.

I admired my grandfather for many reasons. The first was respectability. He not only deserved respect, he earned and commanded respect from all people. The second reason was loyalty. He was loyal to his country by serving it in the Navy for thirty years. He was loyal to his family and friends as well.

When I was 11 years old, my grandfather died. It started out like any other day. Grandpa had driven me to school and I told him I had remembered the coupons. We'd planned to get hamburgers after school the day before, but I'd forgotten the coupons. I remembered them that day and we were going to go out to eat together. Little did I know that when I hugged him and told him goodbye that morning, it would be the last time I would see him alive.

My day at school was going by fast. I couldn't wait to go get hamburgers with Grandpa. Then, a little before noon, my parents came to pick me up. I thought they were taking me out to lunch. Once I was in the car they told me Grandpa had died. He'd gotten home and had had a heart attack. I couldn't believe what they were telling me. I kept thinking he would show up and it would all be fine. He never showed up. Grandpa had always told me not to cry at his funeral, so when the time came, I sat there holding in my emotions. I didn't cry for him until months later when I finally accepted that he was dead.

I had never really faced death until that moment. Death had always come to obscure relatives who I didn't know. Now death had taken my Grandpa, who had raised me, who loved me and cherished me. I can't fully describe the emotions that flowed through me. It finally dawned on me that our life on earth is a finite span of time. Grandpa had accomplished much in his lifetime and I saw then that in the short stretch of years I was destined to live through, I needed to accomplish much as well. I finally became motivated to succeed. Even now when I do something, I want to succeed not only for myself, but for my Grandpa. He taught me many things during his life and in death he taught me how to work.

When my mother was three months old, she caught polio. That disease has handicapped her all of her life. Despite it, she struggled and got a college education. Her physical handicap hasn't stopped her from getting involved in numerous groups, such as the Polio Survivors Support Group, and three local and one national writers groups, or from being a City Council appointed member of the Animal Control Advisory Board.

She currently is working part-time as a Research Associate in a medical school. This part-time endeavor will soon cease, as her doctors have strongly advised her to stop working. As an alternative, she has turned to writing. She has published many nonfiction articles and is working on a novel.

Now she is suffering from Post-Polio Muscle Syndrome, which means she is facing further neuromuscular deterioration. Everyday tasks are becoming tiresome or impossible and with these restrictions come frustrations.

It is hard to see one you love slowly getting worse. Especially when they refuse your help. I understand she wants to be independent, but it hurts to see her tire from trying. From her struggle I am drawing strength. She has shown me the value of trying. She has shown me that one must never quit because the more the obstacles, the sweeter the victory. She has implanted within me a drive to succeed that is so powerful it can knock down walls. My mother has become a role model for me.

My mother is a very special woman, no matter what the circumstances. I know that if I ever have a problem, I can come to her and she will force me to rise to the occasion. She has done so much to shape my life. This is why I respect and admire my mother.

Finally, I admire my middle school history teacher. He took me under his wing and taught me the importance of history and the humanities. He never accepted second-best from anyone and was always willing to help his students become more efficient. Never once did he tolerate dishonesty or a lack of integrity in anyone, and he stood up for his ideals no matter what the consequences.

He had an indomitable fighting spirit which especially manifested itself in the end. In my sophomore year, he was diagnosed as having leukemia. He never stopped fighting, but after fighting the Nazis, the North Koreans, and years of unruly students, he finally found an adversary he couldn't beat. He taught me the value of spirit, honesty, integrity and efficiency. I admire the way he lived.

I admire all of these people because they are/were true to themselves, each one epitomizing virtuous characteristics or qualities. I try to emulate them in my everyday life so I might be a better person.

SAMPLE ESSAY 12

Topic: We want to know who you are. Instead of asking you to recount information we can read in other parts of your application, we want you to show us who you are by using your creativity. Imagine you've gone on a cruise. The cruise ship begins to sink; you're able to grab ten items you took with you on the trip. You are now stranded on a deserted island. What would those ten items be and what would you do? Your essay should be approximately 1,000 words in length.

I wake to the sound of water lapping nearby. I can feel the warmth of the sun on my back. Where am I? I open my eyes. I'm on a beach. Marks in the sand indicate that I must have dragged myself out of the sea. I can hear birds chirping in the distant trees. What's happened?

In my befuddled state it takes a few minutes to remember the cruise, the sinking ship, the screaming, the pushing. I'd been on a lifeboat, but when another person tried to climb on I fell out and no one noticed. I was wearing a life vest and was able to grab a deck chair as it floated by. That chair must have saved my life and brought me here. But where was here?

I stand and make my way further from the water's edge. Down the beach I can see the deck chair. I snicker as I think that at least I'll have something to sit on. I realize I'm clutching a bag in my left hand, the bag into which I was hurriedly ramming items as the alarm shrilled onboard the sinking cruise ship.

I sink to the warm sand. I open the bag and dump the contents on the ground. The first thing I notice are my reading glasses glittering in the sand. Next to my glasses is my organizer. At least I'll know which appointments I'm missing. There's the novel I'd brought to read on the trip; although it's waterlogged, it's readable. I'd had the presence of mind to bring my newly refilled prescription bottle of sleeping pills. It's comforting to know I'll be able to sleep for at least 90 days. I'd also grabbed my manicure set in its leather zippered case. The case was somewhat the worse for wear, but I'd be able to stay well groomed. I'd thrown in a small box of the Whitman chocolates I always carry with me. Ripping the cellophane and opening the box, I discover that the chocolates didn't survive the ocean water. Oh well, I'd been wanting to try to cut my chocolate intake for a while. Now's as good a time as any.

My journal is among the jumble, but it too is waterlogged and the entries I'd made are unreadable. I'm not sure what I was thinking as I grabbed my valuables but there was also a plastic bag filled with tea bags and Equal. I could make a cup of tea, if I'd only thought to bring a tea pot, a stove, and a portable generator with me. Fortunately, my obsession with re-sealable plastic bags paid off. I'd also included a plastic bag filled with my favorite granola bars. I'll have to eat them sparingly until I find out where I am and determine the odds of being rescued. The last item I'd shoved into my bag was my travel alarm clock. What was I thinking? Of course, now I'll know exactly when I'm missing those appointments listed in my organizer. I put the clock up to my ear, but hear no ticking. What I do hear is water sloshing around inside. So much for knowing what time it is.

Though I know there are many pressing matters to attend to, I can't help thinking that my bagful of items reflects who I am. I'm an obsessive, workaholic, chocaholic, insomniac who tries to relax by reading, and who tries to counter her sweet tooth by using Equal in her beverages. If there were ever a time to make changes to my personality this is it. There won't be anyone to offend as I go through chocolate withdrawal.

So much for meandering thoughts. Putting all the items back into the bag, I look left and right. This might be an island, but I haven't had time to walk the coastline. First I have to make some sort of shelter. Though it's warm now, it might be cold at night and a shelter would also provide some respite from the unrelenting sun. Second, I'll find a source of fresh water. Then I'll look to see if there are any wild fruits, berries, or nuts to eat. Those granola bars will only last so long. I also have to find some large rocks, so I can write HELP in the sand for airplanes that might fly by. I also want to find some dried firewood and kindling to start a fire. The fire could be seen at night by passing boats and planes, while the smoke could be seen during the day. A fire will also keep me warm at night, as well as keep any predators at bay. I might even be able to read by firelight. I'll have to get the fire going before the sun goes down, if I'm going to use the glass in my reading glasses to start a fire.

With a plan of action in mind, I go to work. I'd always thought that time was money, but now time means survival. The sun is directly overhead. I have about seven, maybe eight hours in which to do as much as I possibly can. Whatever doesn't get done today, I'll do tomorrow. Maybe I'll be lucky and round the bend to find a resort with all the comforts of home. Unfortunately, there's a greater chance that around the bend will be more of the same: one of the cleanest, whitest beaches I've ever seen.

As I begin walking down the beach, I realize something. Just before I'd left on the cruise, I'd thought I'd give anything to find enough hours in the day to allow me to rest. I guess the saying is true: Be careful what you wish for, because you just may get it.

This essay is 961 words in length. The essay did its job. Using a creative and humorous approach, the student was able to inform as well as entertain. Anyone, including committee members, who reads this essay will remember the student and know much more about her than if she'd just written, "My goals are . . ."

_____ SAMPLE ESSAY 13 _____

Topic: Describe, in 150 words or less, your ultimate educational goal. Be creative. Tell us about what you would love to study, and how that choice, if it became a reality, would change your life. Essays will be judged based on their relevance to subject, sincerity, clarity of expression, passion, and originality.
   (This student presented her story in the form of poetry, which was an acceptable form. Had the student presented it in prose, the story wouldn't have been as effective, and probably would have been much longer.)

At 6:45 the night arrives.

The sun goes down and darkens the skies.

Time for an act of violence to take place.

Time for another person to be erased.

At 10:30 I lay down in my bed,

Praying to God I won't be shot dead.

Not knowing what the night has in store,

I began to pray once more.

At 1:25 I hear ten gun shots.

Then I hear my cousin scream before he drops.

Scared to death, I crawl to my mother.

Scared for my life, I run to see about my little brother.

At 1:39 I see my cousin in a pool of blood.

I cry as I fall to my knees in mud.

I rock him in my arms and tell him he'll be okay.

But I guess I was wrong because he died the next day.

This is why I gotta have a dream.

Though this essay doesn't reveal the student's educational or career goal, it doesn't have to. The reader realizes this student's goal must be to get out of the environment in which she lives. If she wants to survive, she must get an education and perhaps try to bring change to her neighborhood.

We believe that this was an award-winning essay. Yet, this student chose not to submit this essay to a competition. It might have won something. It might have provided her with the financial assistance to accomplish her dream. She didn't enter the competition, so she didn't win. It's that simple. If you enter, you have a chance. If you don't enter, you WON'T win.

SAMPLE ESSAY 14

Topic: Through your application, we want to get to know you as well as we can. We ask that you use this opportunity to tell us something about yourself that would help us gain a sense of who you are, how you think, and what issues and ideas interest you the most. Your statement should be completed in your own handwriting.

My father was born in Detroit, Michigan; *mi mama nacio en Buenos Aires, Argentina.* I was born in Chicago as Xochitl Marie. Over the past eleven years, I've attended nine different schools in five states. Sometimes, I wonder where I fit in.

When I spoke only *español,* I used to travel to Argentina every winter with my grandparents to visit *mi familia.* When my parents came for me I cried because I didn't want to leave. I couldn't leave so freely once I started kindergarten in Chicago. In the mornings I went to a private school, and in the afternoons, I attended a public school.

At the private school, it was common for kids to have large houses like Tammy's with the indoor pool. No one knew I spoke Spanish, but I fit in. At the private school, I was "Marie." The public school had mainly Hispanic and African-American students. I was "So-chi," and part Hispanic, so I fit in. I excelled in both schools.

In third grade, I switched to a public school in the inner city. Classes were taught in Spanish and English. Though most of my classmates were poor and were either Puerto Rican or African-American, I fit in. At the inner-city school, I was "Sos-chitl."

When I was in the fifth grade, my mother became superintendent of schools in Kansas City, Missouri. There I attended Coolidge Elementary. Other than Daniel, who was African-American, I was the only person in my class of a different ethnicity, but my aunts Mary and Peggy lived in Missouri and I loved having them nearby. I entertained my friends by speaking Spanish. My teachers expected schoolwork of a quality befitting "the superintendent's daughter," and I delivered. I fit in. In Missouri, I was "Mary."

By seventh grade, my mother was appointed superintendent in Houston, Texas. At Madison Middle School I was the only non-Mexican-American, but I was part Hispanic. Things were described as "*mas* hot," or "*mas* gross." Madison was in the middle of the projects, so we couldn't wear team logos because of their gang significance. Some of my classmates didn't have the support systems needed to succeed, yet I fit in. My standards exceeded the expectations for "the daughter of the superintendent."

At Travis High School we carried mesh backpacks so kids couldn't conceal weapons. Again I lived up to the title of "superintendent's daughter." There was pressure on me to be perfect, and at times, I felt my only identity was, "our superintendent's daughter." I was reminded that if I slipped up, it would not be Xochitl, but "the superintendent's daughter" making the mistake. I mastered the smile, the handshake, and the obligatory, "It was nice to meet you." I knew that when you saw your friends in the hall you said, "Hey, dawg?" or "What's up, my sista," so I fit in. In Texas I was "Sos."

Spending Junior year away gave me a chance to search for who I was beyond "the boss's daughter." I spent the fall semester in New York, with affluent, predominantly white, private school kids. I was one of only two Hispanics. Between classes you said, "What's up, babe?" or "Hi, hon." We discussed issues and learned because we wanted to. The classes were demanding but I was energized by this new-found intellectual stimulation and I eventually fit in. No one cared that I was a superintendent's daughter. Ironically, while away from my familiar Mexican-American school in Texas, I felt a renewed pride in my Latina-ness. This surfaced after reading *Drown,* by Junot Diaz, and a book of poems by Pablo Neruda.

I spent the next semester at a private school in Maine, another school of mostly advantaged kids, but again, I fit in. My hunger for learning continued to be revived, along with a growing pride at being different. My spirits rose when I went to Spanish class or spoke to my mom on the phone and heard the Spanish words coming out of my mouth. With my Maine friends I'd say, "mad tired" or "mad tough." I felt my White and Hispanic heritages blending. I accepted that I was a superintendent's daughter. At the New York and Maine schools, I was "So-chi."

It's a struggle, needing to belong to a community of friends and also wanting to be independent and a high achiever. I've evolved in different environments without changing my overall being. I adapt, I adjust, I accommodate. I'm part White and part Hispanic. I am a superintendent's daughter, but I am and will be much more. I am "So-chi, So-chi Marie, Sos-chitl, Mary, Sos, and Xochitl."

BE UNIQUE

The preceding essays give a clear picture of who the students are. The reader has been allowed into their lives. All of the essays are different and the approaches are different, because each student is unique.

That's exactly what you have to do: be unique. Think about what you've just read and decide what you want committee members to know about you. If you're not sure how to proceed, you might want to take advantage of our Essay ER, in the Special Offer at the end of the book. The entire purpose of this book is to make sure you know how to approach and write essays for scholarships and college admission. Sometimes writing a stand-out essay takes a bit more time and effort, but the result can definitely be worthwhile.

CHAPTER 7

CREATIVE NAGGING 101: ___ SPECIAL TIPS FOR PARENTS ___

As a parent or any concerned adult, it's important for you to know how to help a student write a strong essay for a scholarship or college application.

Before beginning this chapter, you might want to read Chapters One through Six in order to understand what students need to know about writing essays. Keep one thing in mind as you read: you may have the best intentions of helping a student, but the student must be the one who writes the essay. You can critique it. You can correct errors. You can suggest that words or phrases be moved or removed. *You cannot write the essay.*

Whether you critique a student's essay or we critique a student's essay, the student has the last word on what is submitted. The essay must sound like the student and contain the students' ideas. All anyone can do is suggest how a student can more clearly and effectively say what he or she wants to say.

There may be times when the student chooses to write an essay in a way you may not agree with. There isn't anything you can do or say to change that. We can assure you that when we critique an essay and provide guidance or advice about how to strengthen an essay it's because, as scholarship committee members, we know what we need to see in a winning essay. We hope that by reading this book, you'll learn to critique an essay the same way.

If you'd like us to critique your student's essay, please follow the directions we provide in the Special Offer at the end of the book. Please don't fax us the essay after it has been written or typed on the application. By that time it's too late to make changes, and it will make the application look messy.

___ TO WRITE OR NOT TO WRITE ___

How do you know when a student has selected the right topic? That's a tough question to answer. There is no set rule. Each essay and each student must be considered separately. Your role is not to select the topic, but to help the student think before writing. For example, when students are asked to write about an event that has meant a great deal to them, they have a vast array of subjects from which to choose. Where do they start? It can help to have them answer some basic questions:

1. Did the event change how the student behaves or thinks?
2. Did the event cause the student to change a major aspect of his or her personality?
3. Did the event bolster the student's self-image?
4. Did the event cause the student to have a major effect on someone else's life?
5. Did the event help the student understand something never before considered about himself or herself?

If the essay topic is to select a role model or a person whom they feel had an effect on their lives, students once again need to think about the topic before starting to write. The person could be someone they know (a parent, grandparent, or teacher), or someone they've never met but have always tried to emulate (a U.S. president, Louis Pasteur, or Madame Curie). Have them answer the following questions:

1. Did the person change how the student behaves or thinks?
2. Did the person cause the student to change a major aspect of his or her personality?
3. Did the person bolster the student's self-image?
4. Did the person cause the student to make a major effect on someone else's life?
5. Did the person help the student understand something never before considered about himself or herself?
6. Did the person introduce the student to a subject area or career he or she hopes to pursue?
7. Did the person inspire the student in choosing a particular college or major?
8. Did the person challenge the student to do his or her best at all times?

BEFORE THEY START WRITING

Before students begin writing, you might want to give them some help on starting their essay. The fastest, easiest, surest way to get a reader's attention is to tell a story. Ask them to think about one of their favorite books of fiction. Good fiction is a good story. The stories they relate must be true, but just like fiction, their stories must be interesting and memorable.

Whenever possible, a student writing about his or her goals should refer to any past experiences or individuals who influenced those goals. Urge students to be as specific as possible. They should carefully analyze what they're writing and be sure that they include *who, what, when,* and *where,* as well as *how* and *why* in their essay. Only they can explain why they made a specific choice or how an event affected them.

As students prepare to write about their goals, they should ask themselves:

1. Why did I choose that particular college or university?
2. Why did I choose that particular career?
3. Do I want to work with children or adults?
4. Why do I want to start my own business?
5. How did I decide that I want to be a physical therapist (or whatever)?

Even if students aren't quite sure what they might major in, they nearly always have some ideas. Have them ask themselves:

1. What *don't* I want to do as a career?
2. Do I want a health-related career?
3. Do I want to work in law enforcement?
4. Do I want to work in science/math/engineering/teaching, etc.?
5. Do I want to work independently, or do I prefer to work in a group?
6. Am I considering a career in which I'll work with numbers, computers, or people?

Remind students to touch on the subject of community service. They should mention any volunteer work they're doing now or are about to start, as well as volunteer work they plan to do in the future.

The committee needs to know what makes a student tick, and how that student is different from the other applicants. Students shouldn't brag or sound as if they're shouting their achievements from a mountain top, but they should clearly and honestly describe how an accomplishment made a difference in their lives. What the student chooses to write in an essay is a strong reflection of the student's personality and priorities.

Make sure the student's essay is always positive. The essay should never highlight a negative. Perhaps a student wasn't focused as a freshman, but by junior year she came to her senses and started trying to improve her grades. The student's grades will be listed on her transcript for all to see.

She need not focus excessively on the issue. She could simply note, "I'm more focused now and am working hard to improve my class standing."

At times, students agonize over their essays. Getting them to write is harder than extracting wisdom teeth. Unfortunately, it's easy to pick out an agonized essay. There have been times when we want to tell students they should just start over, but we don't ever want to undermine a student's confidence.

Let students know that you have faith in their ability to do the job. As you correct a rough draft, always find something positive to remark on. We know from experience that sometimes this is difficult, but it's not impossible.

Instead of marking corrections in red all over the essay and having it appear to be bleeding to death, we begin by providing positive, gentle criticism. You might want to comment on:

1. The student's ability to use sensory tags in describing an event.
2. The student's clarity in stating what he or she learned, instead of just saying, "I learned a lot."
3. One phrase in the essay that no one else could have written.
4. The student's having chosen a particularly interesting topic.
5. The fact that it's the beginning of a good story.

Once the student has an idea of what's needed in an essay, the next draft is usually a bit better. In the second or third draft, you can focus on those areas you might have wanted on first impulse to delete altogether.

There has only been one time when we provided a rather harsh critique. A student submitted an essay for us to critique, along with the assigned topic. Though the essay was strong and effective, it didn't answer the assigned topic. The first paragraph made a great start, but then the student veered off on a tangent. Because we could see that the student was a strong and confident writer, we felt it was constructive to tell the student to keep the first paragraph and toss the remainder of the 500-word essay. Once nudged in the right direction, the student did an excellent job on the essay.

Each student is different and each essay is different. As a parent or a concerned adult, you must judge how much to critique an essay. Your sensitivity to the student's needs and level of confidence are crucial. You never want to discourage a student from wanting to write, even if it means wading through text that you suspect will have to be removed or altered later.

Whatever you do, don't reenact General Sherman's march through Georgia and slash and burn the entire essay. Instead, your critique should be much like a parent's gentle touch on a fevered brow. Make subtle suggestions as you prod the student in the right direction. Though it might take several drafts to get the desired result, it's better than stopping the entire writing process.

PART II

It's Your Turn to Write

CHAPTER 8

_ BEFORE YOU START WRITING _

Sometimes the hardest part of writing an essay is knowing how to begin. To help you figure out how to begin, we want to ask you a question. Which do you remember longer, a homework assignment in your least favorite class, or the gossip you heard in the hallway six months ago? That's an easy answer: the gossip. The reason is because the gossip is about a person you might know or at least know about. It might be true and it's definitely interesting.

You want committee members to feel as if they know you. The surest way to get a reader's attention is to tell a story. Think about all those books of fiction you've read. They're nothing more than stories. The difference will be that your story must be true, but just like those books of fiction, your story must be memorable, and most of all it must be interesting.

Your essay assignment may be to discuss your goals, but you need to begin your essay with a story. Think of a person who has affected your life, influenced you, or whom you think of as a mentor. This person might be famous or not, alive or dead, someone you've met or someone you haven't met but whom you know about. Your role model could be a grandparent, parent, brother, sister, aunt, uncle, teacher, or someone in business, the media, or in the arts. You might choose to discuss how you admire the geography teacher who made the subject come alive in such a way that you almost felt the cold air nipping at your nose when she discussed the Himalayas or almost heard parrots squawking while she discussed the rain forests along the Amazon River. You might decide to write about the middle school principal who provided you with challenges, opportunities,

and encouragement, and helped you realize that someone believed in you. Take a moment to jot down a few thoughts about your role model. Just write down a few thoughts. Don't write the essay. You're working on your outline. You'll start writing your essay in a few minutes.

When you've finished jotting down some thoughts about the person you've chosen, think about an event or accomplishment that affected your life. You might want to describe a hobby or a time when you were challenged by an assignment, task, goal, or a fear.

A few years ago, a student wrote an excellent essay on her fear of the dark when she was five years old. Your first inclination may be to wonder how being afraid of the dark has to do with getting into a college or receiving a scholarship. You would be wrong. Written effectively, as that essay was, committee members could see who she was and what made her different from other students. In her concluding paragraph, she compared her fear of the dark, which was no more than her fear of the unknown, to the unknown she would be facing in college. Just as she conquered her fear of the dark at age five, she knew she would meet the challenges that would arise during her years in college. Her essay was extremely effective. The story was also compelling. Who couldn't relate to a childhood fear? We've all had them.

Now we want you to make a list of your goals, but in a certain order. Start with the goals you've set for yourself during your current educational level (high school or college). The next section should cover those goals you have set for yourself after you've finished your education. The time period might be three years from now or twelve years from now. It all depends on your goals and where you are in your education.

Throughout the goals section of your essay, you need to include information about the volunteer work in which you're involved. When discussing your high school goals, include a sentence or two, such as, "I want to continue my volunteer work with the homeless (or Habitat for Humanity, food drives, clothing drives, illiteracy, or children)." When you're writing about your college goals, you might want to mention, "While in college, I'd like to change the focus of my volunteer work to include environmental issues (or battered women, or making sports camps available to underprivileged kids, or other areas of interest)." When discussing your long-term plans, if you're considering having a family, you might want to insert, "I will encourage my family to continue with volunteer work, so they can learn the joys of giving of their time, talent, and energy." You want to impress upon a committee that you want to succeed, but also help others along the way.

Sometimes a question or topic will require that you link your essay on goals with your essay on your experience or your essay on your role model, or both of them. The transitions between essays need not be awkward. Just start with your short-term goals, in other words, those goals you hope to accomplish while in high school and college. In the next paragraph, discuss your long-term goals, those goals you hope to accomplish at some point within your lifetime. In the final paragraph, discuss how the lessons you learned from your experience or role model help you accomplish those goals.

Your story is important because it gives the committee a glimpse into your life, but what you learned from that story is much more important. Even if you choose to write about something as simple as a hobby, if you learned something from that experience or endeavor, it's worth writing about.

What happens when the topic or question has nothing to do with a specific experience or role model? It could be that the assigned topic is no more than: Who are you? Your task then is to give the committee member the opportunity to see you and the differences between you and every other applicant.

To highlight the difference between showing and telling, we're going to provide two examples of essays answering the same question. The first version will tell the reader who the student is, and the second version will show the student. Which version is the most memorable and gives you a better idea of who the student is?

Essay Topic A: Who are you?

TELLING

I am a graduating high school senior. I work two days a week and weekends. I hope to attend the University of (fill in your preferred in-state school) in the fall.

I have always enjoyed (insert your choice: math, science, business, or working with: my hands, numbers, computers, animals, children, etc.). In college I plan to major in (fill in a major or area, if you have one) and I know I can do it.

After I graduate from college, I want to be successful in my chosen career. I want to be able to travel and spend time with my family and friends. I also want to encourage my children to do volunteer work and learn the joy of helping others.

SHOWING

As I walk out of my high school, it takes a mere second to find my car, not just any car—my car. My gaze lingers on the length of the 1964 black Chevy Impala with fire engine red upholstery. With a click of a button, the doors unlock. I reach for the door handle, but I don't just yank it open. No. I allow my fingers to caress the warm door handle and gently open the door. No one thought I could bring the clunker this car had been back to life. It took me all summer and three additional months, but I completely refurbished it.

Though my car doesn't have that new car smell, I couldn't be happier with it. I wipe away the nonexistent dust on the supple upholstery of the dash board. As much as I'd like to sit here and enjoy the car, I must hurry. I'm on my way to work. I work two afternoons a week and weekends. My job helps pay for the car insurance and for next year's tuition.

I don't know where I'll attend college next year or what I'll eventually major in, but it doesn't matter. I view attending college as a learning experience. I want to know more about several areas of interest I currently have, such as: automobile design, computer science, and business, but I also want to learn more about my talents, strong points, and other interests.

I'm confident that I'll be able to achieve my goals and overcome whatever obstacles may present themselves in college. No one thought I could refurbish that rusty, old Chevy Impala I'd bought for $300, but I could see it was a diamond in the rough. One day in the future, I hope that everyone who knows me will realize that I'm as multi-faceted as a diamond and all will be dazzled by my successes.

Essay Topic B: Describe an event that has affected your life.

TELLING

During my high school career I've been actively involved in several sports, but baseball is my favorite. I'll never forget THE BIG GAME. During that game I learned more about myself than I ever thought possible. I've always been goal-oriented, but if it hadn't been for that game I don't know if I could have accomplished all my goals.

SHOWING

"Crack!"There's no other sound quite like the one a wooden bat makes when it comes in contact with a hard ball. At the moment of impact the crowd went wild. It was the bottom of the ninth, two outs, and two men on base. Our team was up by one point. My heart was beating so hard I thought it would burst out of my chest. As the ball reached the apex of its climb, I knew it would come down just about in the middle between me and Mike, the right fielder. Mike was a good player, but never got the attention he deserved because he always thought about the team first and himself second. In the split second when I knew where it would fall, I decided I would give the ball to Mike.

Mike caught the ball. We won the game and Mike's name was included in the story in the city newspaper. Though I could have made the catch and gotten all the attention, it was Mike's turn. That decision made me realize that it's not always about "me." Sometimes it's about the good of another person.

The second versions of both sample essays are longer than the first versions, but they're also more interesting and realistic. In the first sample, the reader understands why the student has chosen to work. The reader knows that when the student puts his mind to a task he wants to accomplish, he can and will do it. The student presented his character traits through the story about his car, which was true, interesting, and memorable. Which version did you prefer reading? Which would you remember if you're reading hundreds, maybe thousands, of application essays?

_____ USING SENSORY TAGS TO TELL A VIVID STORY _____

Whatever your topic, you must write it in story form. You want to write your story as a memory you're sharing with the reader, in this case the committee members. You want your memory to be vivid, to come alive on the page. You want the reader to connect with your story. The way to "hook" a reader with your story is to engage all of the reader's senses, so he feels almost as if he is having the experience himself.

As you're going through your day, a memory might suddenly surface. Why did that happen? The memory surfaced because of a sensory tag—something you saw, heard, touched, tasted, or smelled brought the memory to the surface. As an example, if you've ever visited an elementary school, even one you didn't attend as a child, you may find yourself wanting to go stand in line somewhere and say the Pledge of Allegiance. The reason for this is because of what you see, hear, smell, feel, and taste. You can smell the cafeteria food, hear the children chattering, feel the construction paper on any bulletin board, and just about taste the chalk dust floating in the air. Those sensations immediately transport you to your elementary school days.

Don't just tell the reader in your essay that you were involved in a car accident. You want to show the reader what happened. What did you hear, see, feel, taste, and/or smell? A few years ago, in one of our workshops, a student's first attempt at writing about his car accident wasn't vivid enough. It was the quietest car accident in history. With a few nudges in the right direction, the second draft had the screeching of tires, the thump of the impact, the jostling, the breaking of glass, and the wailing of sirens of arriving EMS units. All these tags were needed to bring the reader into the story. After all, who hasn't been involved in, seen, or heard a car accident? Those tags made the essay come alive, and be interesting and memorable. We've included this student's essay and the adaptations he used in several applications (essays 53 to 55). That essay made it possible for the student to be offered admission to several top-tier schools and receive thousands of dollars in scholarships.

Every time you write something, ask yourself, who, what, when, where, why, how, and lastly, what senses were involved? Many students will start an essay with: "When I was a child . . ." Generally, the committee member who reads that essay will be older than the student and will in all likelihood think that even at eighteen, you are a child. Be specific. Change the sentence to, "When I was five years old . . ." Be specific. Be vivid. Above all, be yourself.

CHAPTER 9

WRITING ASSIGNMENTS

Now it's your turn. We have five more exercises, just for you. This is where you'll use the outline you created in the previous exercises.

SENSORY TAGS

As you consider how to begin your experience or role model essay, think about what made this event or person stand out in your mind. When an event or person is particularly memorable, there are certain "triggers" that instantly evoke that memory—perhaps a scent, a song, or a taste. You hear a song and remember a certain dance with that special someone. You smell a certain brand of cologne or perfume and you remember that first crush or kiss. The scent of rain or freshly mown grass might make you remember a picnic with your family.

When you write your story, engage the reader's senses to help him or her vividly experience your memory. Don't just write that you went to the hospital to visit a relative. Describe the smells, the sights, and the sounds that were going on around you. A hospital has a distinctive odor—that of alcohol and cleanser. Describe the sound the nurses' or doctors' shoes make on the floor. Open yourself to your memory and think about everything. Were dinner trays banging and clanging? Were there static-filled announcements over the intercom? Was it summer or winter? If it was summer, don't just tell us it was hot. What month was it? How hot was it? Were you in Brattleboro, Vermont, or Houston, Texas? A summer day in Brattleboro is different from a summer day in Houston. The same is true of a winter day in Chicago or in Miami.

Are you describing the unforgettable memory of when you narrated a play or took part in a talent show? Your name was announced, and you froze. How did your throat feel? Were your hands sweaty? Was your heart pounding in your ears? Did you feel a cold drop of sweat travel slowly down your spine?

ON YOUR MARK, GET SET, GO!

Assignment 1: We want you to tell us a story. Refer to your outline from Exercise 7 in Chapter Four, which details an experience from which you learned something. This should be a rough draft. Don't worry about spelling or grammar. Don't worry about precise word count. You can strike through words, and add arrows to move words, sentences, and even paragraphs. Remember to use all your senses in describing everything that's happening in your story. Remember to include what you learned from this experience. If you don't know where or how to start, try: "I'll never forget the day when . . ." The essay should be approximately 1,000 words (no less than 500 words and no more than 1,500 words).

Assignment 2: Now write a story about your role model using the simple outline you created in Exercise 6 in Chapter Four. Just as in the previous exercise, don't worry about writing perfectly. What did you learn from this person? If you don't know where or how to start, try: "I'll never forget . . ." Your essay should be approximately 1,000 words (no less than 500 words and no more than 1,200 words). The essay should discuss someone you view as a role model and why.

Assignment 3: Write a short essay on your high school, college, and long-term professional and life goals. Refer to the outline you developed in Exercises 1 through 3 in Chapter Four. Try to keep the essay to three paragraphs in length. The goals portion of an essay is generally the shortest, at approximately 200 words in length.

As you write your rough drafts and then the finished essay, check off the appropriate line in the Essay Tracking Chart 1 in Appendix C. You're going to need these essays for your college/university and scholarship applications. You may as well write them now and have them ready.

Be as specific as possible in your essays. Be sure you're answering the questions who, what, when, and where. Don't forget how and why, too. Only you can explain why you made a specific choice or how some event affected you. Why did you choose to apply to a particular college or university? Why did you choose a specific career? Do you want to work with kids or adults? Why do you want to start your own business? How did it happen that you decided you wanted to be a physical therapist?

Even if you're not quite sure what your major will be, do you have some ideas? Do you want a health-related career? Do you want to work independently? Are you considering a career where you will work with plants, animals, children, or adults? If you don't have a clue about what you want to do with your life or what you'd select as a major, you might want to take the opposite approach. What *don't* you want to do? Though you may not know what you want, most people know what they don't want. By excluding what you don't want to do, you've now narrowed the field of choices about what you might want to do.

In your essay, remember to touch on the subject of community service. You might mention any volunteer work you're doing now or you're about to start, as well as what you anticipate or plan to do in the future. (If your experience or role model essay deals with volunteer service, you need not refer to other volunteer service.) The reference need be no more than one or two sentences, but you definitely want to mention it. The following are a few examples of how to mention volunteer work in just about any essay:

> While in high school, I'll continue to work with the homeless [or the environment, being a mentor to elementary school children, or any other area of interest].

> While in college, I'd like to volunteer at a local food bank [battered women's shelter, or any other organization or area of interest].

> Once I have children of my own, I will get them involved with volunteering, in order to help them experience the joy of helping someone in need.

The only time you wouldn't insert a reference about volunteer work would be in an essay on a specific topic, such as on patriotism, problems facing teenagers, or what would you do if you were stranded on an island (yes, some committees really ask this).

When you've finished writing about your experience or role model, you must close with a paragraph that ties up all the loose ends. Think of your essay as a present. You wouldn't wrap it up in special paper and pretty ribbon without putting a bow on it. Your last paragraph should be your bow. It should refer to your opening text without repeating it. You might want to say,

> Because my grandfather taught me to believe in myself and to set goals, I know I'll be able to accomplish any task I must face.

Or you might wrap up your essay by saying,

> Just as I faced what I thought was an impossible task as a child [or whatever], I'm now ready to face the unknown challenges in my future.

Your essay isn't written in granite. Committee members know that as you change, so will your goals. That is expected. Don't agonize over any essay. Just write about what you're presently anticipating as your goals. No one is going to come after you if you change your mind. As you experience all that life has to offer and take college classes that expose you to new ideas and careers, you will learn more about yourself. You may discover talents and interests you never knew you had.

MAKING SEVERAL ESSAYS FROM ONE ESSAY

After you've written the two 1,000-word essays, cut each one down to 500 words, and then again down to 200 words. You now have six separate essays. There will be times when you can combine your essays.

Assignment 4: When you've finished Assignment 2, add what you've written in Assignment 3 to the end of your experience essay. Then write a concluding paragraph on how you know you'll be able to accomplish your goals because of this experience. The resulting essay should be approximately 1,000 to 1,500 words.

Assignment 5: When you've finished Assignment 2, add what you've written in Assignment 3 to the end of your role model essay. Then write a concluding paragraph on how you know you'll be able to accomplish your goals because of your role model. The resulting essay should be approximately 1,000 words to 1,500 words.

TO CUT OR NOT TO CUT

If you think writing a shorter essay is easier than writing a long one, think again. Condensing your thoughts into 200 words from 1,000 words is difficult. In this case, what you *don't say* is just as important as what you *do say,* as the following essay and the shorter version of it show.

Long Version

My entire life has been devoted to learning. I love to learn. Children are quite innocent and, unlike adults, all they know is truth, black and white. They have a curiosity that is unfaltering and an undaunted determination. I have held onto those qualities throughout my life. This curiosity and search for truth help me as I explore the science fields. I have the personality and dedication to succeed in the biological and environmental sciences. That is my goal.

I have always wanted to work with animals and help the environment. I want to be instrumental in solving problems in ways that will be beneficial to all. The answers to all our problems concerning the effect of "human progress" on nature are out there, someone just needs to find them. That person could be me. I have that dedication and am willing to work hard to accomplish my goals.

I am steadfast in my beliefs and will attend college somewhere—somehow. I intend to increase my knowledge and understanding so that I can be beneficial to society. Although I do wish to have a family, my career path is clear: to help mankind make amends for its destruction and inhumane acts toward animals and the environment. It's a slow process that might take generations, but someone must continue the work that others have started.

I can do this with a degree in environmental science, forestry, or perhaps veterinary medicine. I wish to work in the National Forestry Service to help protect the natural habitats that still remain. I would like to do field research and pursue my interest in animal behavior. We must protect those creatures that share our planet and the habitats they live in. There are many animals that are endangered. Not only do they need to be protected, but so do other animals so they won't become endangered as well. It's easier to prevent something than to go back and correct it.

I have a strong sense of duty when it comes to the betterment of our world. For humans to progress any further, we must first heal the world in which we live in and make it better place for all. When we can finally coexist with all the creatures in harmony, we deserve to be called humane. My lifelong dream and goal is not to be famous for solving environmental problems, but to start a legacy that others will follow in the protection of our natural treasures.

In the past two years of high school, I've been involved in many community activities. As a member of a veterinary Explorer Post, I've volunteered at the San Antonio Cat Show, where I helped the judges and cleaned cages between events. I played in the church orchestra, helped with the church's blood drive and gave blood. I also participated in a 30-hour fast. During this event, we had sponsors who pledged money for each hour we fasted. This money was then sent to third world countries. The Explorers went on a scavenger hunt to collect canned goods, which we gave to a local food bank. We then volunteered at the Samm Shelter for several hours. For the last two summers, I've worked for the City of San Antonio, Parks and Recreation as a lifeguard, instructor candidate, and a water safety instructor. I'm responsible for teaching swim lessons, water aerobics, and water safety. My duties have also included cleaning the pools, decks, and grounds; pool maintenance; chemical adding and analysis; paperwork for supplies and chemical information; bather surveillance and rescue; as well as first aid. We have employee exercises which involve laps, technique practice, and mock rescues and emergencies. I also baby-sit for friends and relatives and tutor my friends during the school year. I do this mainly to help out so my friends and their siblings will pass their classes and be eligible for extracurricular activities. From cat shows to tutoring, I enjoy it all. I love to learn new things and love to help others learn something new. Seeing their progress and understanding is so rewarding when I know that I taught them.

Though it's descriptive and informative, this essay is 687 words in length. The student wanted to use this story for the Tylenol Scholarship Competition (worth $10,000), but the essay for this competition can only be 200 words in length. This essay is three times longer than it needs to be. With a snip here and a slash there, the essay can be cut down to 145 words. There's still room in the shortened version for her to mention the expected educational costs and why she needs financial assistance.

SHORTENED VERSION

I've always wanted to work with animals and help the environment, perhaps with a degree in environmental science, forestry, or perhaps veterinary medicine. The answers to our environmental problems concerning the effect of "human progress" on nature are out there, someone just needs to find them. That person could be me. I hope to work in the National Forestry Service to help protect the natural habitats that still remain. I'd like to do field research in animal behavior.

In the past two years of high school, I've been involved in a wide variety of community activities. The activities have all been rewarding and provided many different types of responsibilities. From band, cat shows and life guarding to tutoring, I've enjoyed it all. I thrill at learning new things and enjoy helping others learn something new.

I'm steadfast in my beliefs and will attend college somewhere—somehow.

WATCH YOUR WORD COUNT

When you count the words of your essay, you need to count every single word. Some teachers instruct you to count only words longer than three letters. But in the real world of real word counts, all words count. If you have a number (age, date, or dollar amount) in your essay, it's counted as a word. If you are working on a computer, have your computer count the words. It will do it appropriately. Just make sure you don't have a title on your essay, or it will be included in the computer's word count.

A student once commented to us that having to count words like *a, an, is, it,* and *the* and still write an essay that stayed within the word count was going to limit her creativity. Our response was quick and to the point: "Try to write an essay without a, an, is, it, the, etc., and see how creative you can be." ALL words count.

If a committee specifies a 200 word count, then you can't submit an essay of more than 200 words. You can have less, but not more. If a word count of between 500 and 800 words is specified, the essay must be in that range. If you are instructed to place the essay in a certain space or page, you must do so. Our son wrote an essay that had to fit in a certain space, but when we typed a practice version on a copy of the form, the essay didn't fit. Not wanting to cut words, we tried lowering the font size. It still didn't fit. Keep in mind that you should never use a font smaller than 10 points. We widened the margins. It still

didn't fit. We decreased the space between each line. It still didn't fit. There was only one option. We went back to a 12-point font with one space between lines. We then took it to a photocopier, reduced the size until it fit in the space, and glued it on the application.

Today's word processing programs have the ability to make it fit in whatever space you specify. These programs will decrease font size, line spacing, and margin spacing until the text fits. Modern technology is wonderful.

If there is no limit on word count or on the number of pages that can be added, write approximately 1,000 to 1,200 words. Strictly limit yourself to 1,200 words. Once we read an essay of 5,000 words; we thought it would never end. Chances are good that there isn't anything you've done that is so interesting and complex that 5,000 words would be required to describe it. In the case of the 5,000-word essay, the student took the assigned topic literally: relate what you've been doing since graduation. The essay began: "The next morning I got up, had a glass of orange juice . . ." That wasn't the assignment. The student should have written about his first job after graduation, his duties, and what he learned from the experience.

Now start writing. Who knows? You just might enjoy writing your essays now that you have an idea what to write about and how to write them. Good luck.

CHAPTER 10

HOW TO EDIT YOUR ESSAY

EDITING ROUND ONE

Congratulations. You've written your essay. Now you must edit what you've written. As writers, we know that you may feel that every word you write is a pearl and precious, worth more than the paper it's written on. Pearls are wonderful, but one beautiful strand is more valuable than many strands of poor quality. Overkill never works. Choose your words carefully. Unfortunately, editing and revising can be painful. There will be times when you must cut words, sentences, even paragraphs. Editing and revising is a lot like exercising. It can be difficult at first, but it gets easier the more you do it. Besides, with editing, you probably won't sweat (or at least much) and you won't be sore the next day. Moreover, you can save what you've cut and you may be able to use it in another essay.

The first revision of your essay should be done by you, the writer. You must be objective and not think that every word you've written is a pearl. That kind of attitude won't improve your writing. You need to assess your work as if you were a member of the scholarship or admissions committee. You might want to take a few days break—or at least an hour if you're on a deadline—from what you've written in order to be able to view it with a fresh eye. This is one more reason why it's a good idea to write your essay well ahead of the deadline.

There are professional proofreader's marks that you could use to edit your essay, but unless you plan on pursuing a career in writing or publishing, there isn't any real reason for you to learn them. Make up your own editing system. As long as you understand your edits, you'll make the appropriate correction.

Here are some of the questions you should ask yourself about what you've written:

If I were speaking aloud, is this the way I would tell my story, explain my situation and goals, or defend my opinion?

Your essay must always sound like you. Read your essay aloud. Listen to yourself. Is that the way you talk? Your essay must sound as if you're talking to the committee member, using correct grammar, of course (we'll discuss that in Round Three).

Did you use contractions?

There is a gap between you, the writer, and the unknown reader. The two of you don't know anything about each other. Your essay must bridge that gap, the distance between you and the committee member. Writing an overly formal essay, one without contractions (such as don't, won't, aren't, and more), only widens the distance. Contractions provide the bridge. When we talk, we use contractions. If an essay must sound like you, then you should use contractions. Many well-meaning teachers will remove contractions from students' writing. If you ask a teacher to proofread your essays and he or she indicates that you should remove your contractions, thank the teacher for the critique, but don't remove the contractions.

Does each paragraph flow into the next one?

Each paragraph should contain only one topic or thought. The last sentence of a paragraph should lead into the topic of the next paragraph.

If you want a good example of how to do this, you might want to look at a favorite book, especially a work of fiction. Notice how each paragraph leads into the next, but of particular interest is the last paragraph of a chapter. The last sentence of the last paragraph of a chapter will compel you to read the next chapter. Similarly, you want to hold the committee members' attention from beginning to end.

Are related paragraphs close to each other?

Suppose you're writing about an event or experience that influenced your goals, to be followed by a discussion of your current, short-term and long-term goals. When you finish your story and begin to write about your goals, discuss your current goals first, then your short-term goals, and finally, your long-term goals. This structure is logical, unfolding from the present into the future, clearly delineating your goals to the reader. Reading your essay shouldn't feel like watching a tennis match, crossing back and forth, back and forth through time.

Are you explaining yourself fully to the reader, or do you need to clarify an incident or include a detail that wasn't originally in your essay?

For example, don't write about the time someone was near death in the hospital and never let the reader know whether the person survived. Don't refer to an accident without relating who was involved, the type of accident it was, and the outcome.

EDITING ROUND TWO

1. Does each sentence clearly explain what you wanted to say?
2. Does each sentence in a paragraph flow logically into the next one?
3. Are there any redundant sentences in your essay?
4. Is the essay within the specified word count?

When word count is crucial, there are two words that might be deleted: *that* and *had*.

EXAMPLE 1: You must be objective and not think that every word you've written is a pearl.

You must be objective and not think every word you've written is a pearl.

The deletion of the word *that* didn't change the meaning of the sentence. If the meaning of your sentence changes when you delete words, put them back in. Otherwise, you can safely delete them and cut the word count. Two words that should never be used are the words *very* and *really*. Both are weak words. The presence of either word often signals where an essay can be made more vivid. Consider these examples:

I was very happy.

Happiness doesn't have degrees. You're either happy or you're not. If you're more than happy, you're "ecstatic" or "thrilled" or "exhilarated." These are more descriptive than "very happy."

I was very sad.

Sadness doesn't have degrees. If you're more than sad, you're "despondent" or "desolate" or "in despair."

I was really tired.

If you're more than tired, you're "exhausted."

By omitting the words *very* and *really* you reduce your word count, but more important, you use words more creatively and effectively. Learn to listen to yourself and analyze the quality words you use.

If your essay is too short, reread your essay objectively. Are there topics you might be able to expand? Did you give enough description and detail?

5. Is your point of view consistent? For example, if your essay began with "I," did it also end with "I" (and not "you")? It would be incorrect to say, "I love my literature class—you always feel challenged by the teacher." It is correct to say, "I love my literature class—I always feel challenged by the teacher."

6. Is the tense consistent?

7. Is there sentence variety in each paragraph? Don't start each sentence with the same word or with words having the same ending (such as "ing").

8. Are you using two words where one would do? Consider the following sentence:

   It is very difficult to understand why we allow there to be hunger in this world.

   The first "it" doesn't really refer to anything. Then there's that pesky "very." The word *this* preceding "world" makes it sound as if the writer has experience in other worlds. Where else would hunger occur, if not on Earth? Here's a more economical way to write the same sentence:

   The existence of hunger is unacceptable.

   The second sentence offers the same information, but does so in six words rather than sixteen.

9. Did you use the active voice, rather than passive voice, whenever possible? Passive voice: **The college I attend will be chosen by me.** Active voice: **I will choose which college to attend.**

10. Did you overuse any word or phrase? Are there words you use as crutches? These include *you know, like, I would think, I believe, I feel,* and *in my opinion.* Whose opinion could it possibly be but yours? Why would you be writing about someone else's opinion? The committee wants your thoughts, not someone else's.

    Removing these words will make for a tighter, shorter essay. One phrase to avoid at all costs is "To be honest . . ." This phrase could make a committee member wonder whether other parts in the essay are untrue. Why did you specify that this particular statement was the truth? Were the rest of your statements lies? Don't use this phrase in your essay.

11. Have you used clichés (for example, "dark as night," "bright as the sun," or "straight as an arrow")? Everyone uses these images. Try to find your own new images to use.

12. Have you overused adverbs, adjectives, and other descriptors?

13. Did you tie up all the loose ends at the end of your essay? Remember that present you spent hours searching for, the one we mentioned in Chapter Nine? Did you put a bow on the present? Put a bow, though not literally, on your essay.

14. Does the true you shine through? Don't try to sound like someone else. It won't work.

EDITING ROUND THREE

Now, proofread one more time, this time checking for errors in spelling, typos, punctuation, indentations, numbering, underlining, and capitalization. Don't just use your computer's Spell Check to check spelling. If you've written "to" when it should be "too," then the word is wrong, but Spell Check won't catch it, since there is such a word as *to.* The same is true with the words *was* and *saw, form* and *from,* and many more. Be careful.

Be sure to check what isn't there as well as what is. The mind is a wonderful thing. If you meant to say something, the mind will insert the word in the text even though you may have omitted it. At this stage, you might want to have someone else proofread your essay. Ask your parents, your English teacher, or an English tutor to proofread your essay. If you know a writer, ask if he or she would consider reading your essay. Just be sure that an outside reader checks for clarity, grammar, and other errors, but doesn't pressure you to write the essay their way, or worse, rewrite it for you.

How does the essay look? Are there smudges? Did you put your name at the top of the page?

Ask yourself, Would I go to the prom dressed as if I were going to clean out the garage or take a quick trip to the mall? Of course not. You would spend hours finding the right tuxedo or prom dress, hours getting your hair done or cut, and still more hours bathing, shaving, or putting on makeup.

All that effort, for an occasion that lasts all of a few hours. Yet, many students don't want to retype or rewrite an essay that could result in their getting into college or receiving a scholarship. The extra attention paid to detail could pay off. Don't jeopardize the fate of your application by not paying attention to detail.

Do whatever it takes to make a good impression. You only have one chance to get a committee member's attention. Give your essays and applications the attention they deserve. We believe in you. We know you can do it.

PART III

Essay Makeovers

EDITING SAMPLE ESSAYS

This section presents 114 essays that have been written by students ranging from middle school through graduate school and from ages twelve through fifty. Since parents sometimes are required to write an essay of their own, we've also included two such examples. We've changed the essays slightly to disguise the writers' identities. With these sample essays you can get an idea of how to present your essay by showing, not telling, select which of your life's stories to write about, and practice your editing skills. We've found it's much easier to learn how to edit when you edit someone else's writing. A critiqued, edited version immediately follows the original version, along with explanations of why we recommended the proposed changes.

You may photocopy these essays in order to edit them without writing in the book. You may want to try editing the same essay several times. All of the essays have been printed double-spaced to provide enough room for you to make your edits.

Keep in mind that an essay could need many improvements, may require only one or two minor changes, or need no fixes at all. Although this chapter includes many complete essays, a few are excerpts from longer essays. We chose to use excerpts because doing so allowed us to include a larger variety of essays, writing styles, and suggestions on ways to improve problem areas. Our editing suggestions illustrate how to make a weak essay strong, and a strong essay stronger. There are often several ways to improve a given sentence or paragraph in an essay. As a rule of thumb, we always try to make as few changes as possible to maintain the student's own voice and style of writing.

When a topic or question isn't included at the start of the essay, it's because the essay itself clearly delineates the topic. Generally, the students were writing about their goals, a role model, or an important experience.

SAMPLE ESSAYS AND THEIR MAKEOVERS

Essay 1: Write a brief essay on a topic of your choice.

Success is judged in our society by the earning of an individual. However, I feel that an individual should be judged on the individual's happiness and their accomplishments. Goals lead us to our success. There are three types of goals. The first is the one year goal; next, is the five year goal; lastly, is the ten year goal.

My success will truly be predicted on my striving for my goals. One key ingredient in planning one's goals is that the goals should always be attainable. One year goals should be the most important to the planner, because you can change your mind about your profession while you are young. Five year goals should also be important but not as important. Ten year goals are only used, so that there can be a general direction for one's career.

Essay 1—Makeover: The first sentence is a generalization, which can be softened by inserting the word "sometimes." Though the author of this essay must ultimately decide how best to express his idea, in the second paragraph, we suggest retaining the first sentence and deleting the rest of the paragraph. The first sentence could then be used as a lead-in to the student's descriptions of several personal and professional goals.

sometimes   *s*

Success is judged in our society by the earning of an individual. However, I feel that an individual

by his/her

should be judged ~~on the individual's~~ happiness and ~~their~~ accomplishments. Goals lead us to our

[Delete the last two sentences. There are many types of goals.]

success. [~~There are three types of goals. The first is the one year goal; next, is the five year goal;~~

~~lastly, is the ten year goal.~~]

My success will depend on how aggressively I strive for my goals. [~~One key ingredient in~~

~~planning one's goals is that the goals should always be attainable. One year goals should be the~~

~~most important to the planner, because you can change your mind about your profession while you~~

~~are young. Five year goals should also be important but not as important. Ten year goals are only~~

~~used, so that there can be a general direction for one's career.~~]

Essay 2: Write a brief essay about your goals.

I have learned more about myself than one could imagine throughout the time I've been a senior.

Just learning that I am ambitious, responsible, and creative. I know one goal already. This goal is to

go to college and to be successful therein. Once accomplishing this goal, many more come into

play. Such goals include: making as goof of friends as I had in high school: continuing activities such

as the ones that I have previously been involved in: and most importantly, being happy with this

new stage in my life. One last goal that I hope to achieve is to find out what I really want to do as a

career for the rest of my life. All these goals are going to make me a successful student and person

throughout my next year.

Essay 2—Makeover: There were quite a few changes needed to strengthen this essay.

I've   *during senior year*   *I*   *have*   *d.*
~~I have~~ learned more about myself than ~~one~~ could imagine ~~throughout the time I've been a senior.~~

                                       I want
~~Just learning that I am ambitious, responsible, and creative. I know one goal already.~~ ~~This goal is~~ to

                       I've accomplished   *goals*
go to college and ~~to~~ be successful. ~~therein.~~ Once ~~accomplishing~~ this goal, many more come into

    These   *continuing to make d*   *like*   *have*   *;*
play. ~~Such goals~~ include: ~~making as goof~~ of friends as I ~~had~~ in high school/ continuing activities such

[Give examples.]   *I've*   *,*
as the ones that ~~I have~~ previously been involved in/ and most importantly, being happy with this

[What stage? Completing high school?]
new stage in my life. One last goal that I hope to achieve is to find out what I ~~really~~ want to do

   with   *of*   *help me focus on my successful*
~~as a career for~~ the rest of my life. All these goals are going to ~~make me a successful student and~~

development as a student and as a person throughout my college years.
~~person throughout my next year.~~

Essay 3: Write an essay of 300 words or less that answers the question "How do you plan to make your mark on society?"

To paraphrase a famous quote, twenty years from now it will not matter what shoes you wore, how you did your hair, or even whom you hung out with. What matters is what you did with your life, and whom it has affected. One day I hope to be able to hold my head up high and be proud of what I have done and who I have touched.

In 6th grade, my teacher used strategies that made learning exciting. I was challenged by the curriculum, but her creative ways of teaching made it easier to learn and impacting enough to be remembered to this day. Since then I have wanted to bring a similar experience to other children's lives. After going to college, majoring in special education with a minor in mathematics, I hope to teach hearing-impaired children and prepare them for life. I also hope to education children that are not hearing-impaired in signing and to communicate better with children that are. I hope that when I become a teacher I can think of original and creative ways to teach and help students fully understand the curriculum. They need guidance and support and I want to provide it for them.

I hope that all the students that I teach will remember me for helping make high school a little easier, having made learning fun, and knowing someone cared and supported them in everything they did. Impacting the life of children is the mark I hope to make on society.

Essay 3—Makeover: At 221 words, this essay is within the required word length, but it needs a few changes.

To paraphrase a famous quote, twenty years from now it ~~will not~~ *won't* matter what shoes you wore, how you did your hair, or even whom you hung out with. What matters *will* is what you did with your life, and whom it has ~~impacted.~~ *affected* One day I hope to be able to hold my head up high and be proud of what ~~I have~~ *I've* done and ~~who I have~~ *the lives I've* touched.

In ~~6th~~ *sixth* grade, my teacher used strategies that made learning exciting. I was challenged by the curriculum, but her creative ways of teaching made ~~it~~ *the material* easier to learn and ~~impacting enough to be~~ ~~remembered~~ *memorable* to this day. Since then ~~I have~~ *I've* wanted to bring a similar experience to other children's lives. After going to college, majoring in special education with a minor in mathematics, I hope to ~~teach hearing-impaired children and prepare them for life.~~ I also hope to ~~education~~ *teach hearing* children ~~that~~ ~~are not hearing-impaired in signing and to~~ *so they can* communicate better with children ~~that are.~~ *hearing-impaired .* ~~I hope that~~ ~~when I become a teacher I can think of~~ *I want to use* original and creative ways to teach and help students fully understand the curriculum. ~~They need~~ *I'll provide the* guidance and support ~~and I want to provide it for them.~~ *they need.*

[Try to avoid starting a lot of sentences with the word "I."]

~~I~~ *My* hope *is* that all the students ~~that~~ I teach will remember ~~me for~~ *whom* helping make ~~high~~ school ~~a little~~ *that I* easier, ~~having~~ *ed* made learning fun, and ~~knowing someone~~ cared ~~and supported them in everything~~ *about them.* *My mark on society* *will be having an effect on children's lives.* ~~they did. Impacting the life of children is the mark I hope to make on society.~~

Essay 4: Write a brief essay about yourself.

Getting to college is a task in itself. However, graduating from there with a good, high degree is equally as important. In the next five years I hope to have gained a great deal of knowledge in college. A very important goal for me to set is that I use the education I have received in college to its fullest potential. I strongly believe that to give of yourself is rewarding. In turn, I have selflessly dedicated numerous hours in doing community service, here in San Antonio. I have gone to a couple of centers here for the retired elderly. Not only have I done community service, but I have also volunteered my time to help others out academically. I have tutored kids in math, English, and science. By doing so, I believe they will go on to display examples of leadership and become goal-oriented, as well.

Essay 4—Makeover:

into [Replace "to" with "into"; otherwise it sounds as if traveling to the college is a task.]
Getting ~~to~~ college is a task in itself. However, graduating ~~from there with a good, high degree~~ is

I'll
equally as important. ~~In the next five years I hope to~~ have gained a great deal of knowledge in

In the years after I graduate, I want to
college. ~~A very important goal for me to set is that I~~ use the education I ~~have~~ received in college to its fullest potential.

Giving of one's time and talents   *I've*
~~I strongly believe that to give of yourself~~ is rewarding. ~~In turn, I have selflessly~~ dedicated

to   [The reader assumes it's where you live.]
numerous hours ~~in doing~~ community service. ~~here in San Antonio. I have gone to a couple of~~

~~centers here for the retired elderly. Not only have I done community service, but I have also~~

~~volunteered my time to help others out academically.~~ I have tutored kids in math, English, and

I hope that I've helped them
science. ~~By doing so, I believe~~ They will go on to display ~~examples of~~ leadership and become goal-oriented, as well.

Essay 5: In a brief essay, please tell us who you are.

In the past, I've made a lot of mistakes and in result, I have gotten in a lot of trouble or felt real guilty because of my actions, but in the next couple of years, I will have to take control of my life and make decisions that will depend on my future. As a senior, graduation is the main thing on my mind everyday that I attend school, because I am having to worry about my attitude towards school and overall, school itself.

A lot of times when I plan things, it sometimes doesn't work out, but I learn from my mistakes. If I'm out of school in ten years from now, I hope to work at a clinic and help kids or young adults with their problems. I've always wanted to work with kids.

I know that in ten years I will have reached many of my most important career and personal goals. Ten years from now, I will be an independent person who has made a difference in the lives of others. By doing so, I will have learned about myself and about others. I hope that through my experiences and my personal efforts, I will have achieved success, and most importantly I will have helped others through my actions.

Essay 5—Makeover: An essay written for college admission or for a possible scholarship needs to be positive and upbeat. This student was much too negative. Much was deleted, making the result more positive.

[Delete; too negative.]
~~In the past, I've made a lot of mistakes and in result, I have gotten in a lot of trouble or felt real~~

I'll   [The future
~~guilty because of my actions, but~~ in the next couple of years, ~~I will have to~~ take control of my life

can't affect the present.]   *affect*   *my*   *goal.*
and make decisions that will ~~depend on~~ my future. As a senior, graduation is the main ~~thing on my~~

[Delete; too negative.]
~~mind.~~ everyday that I attend school, because I am having to worry about my attitude towards

~~school and overall, school itself.~~

[Delete; too negative.]
~~A lot of times when I plan things, it sometimes doesn't work out, but I learn from my mistakes.~~

be working   *helping children*

~~If I'm out of school in~~ Ten years from now, I hope to ~~work~~ at a clinic and ~~help kids~~ or young adults

children.

with their problems. I've always wanted to work with ~~kids.~~

~~I know that in ten years I will have reached many of my most important career and personal~~

[Already said.]   *I'll*   *who's*   [How?]

~~goals. Ten years from now,~~ I ~~will~~ be an independent person ~~who has~~ made a difference in the lives

In   *I'll*   *Through*

of others. ~~By~~ doing so, ~~I will~~ have learned about myself and about others. ~~I hope that through~~ my

I'll

experiences and my personal efforts, ~~I will~~ have achieved success, and most importantly ~~I will~~ have

helped others through my actions. [How? Be specific.]

Essay 6: Write a brief essay on your goals.

I believe experience is the key to maturity. From the day we are born to the day we graduate, we are exposed to many activities. It is through these activities that we get to know ourselves better. While we are on this journey, we come upon a roadblock, a time when we must sit down and plan out the rest of our lives. This is the time where we set forth our goals.

I would like to become a doctor that specializes in the nose, throat, and ears. Based on my short-term goals, I will then plan my long-term goals for the future which are I would like to finish graduate school and after I would like to have my own clinic and also be financially stable.

Essay 6—Makeover:

E   *we're*   *,*

~~I believe~~ ~~e~~xperience is the key to maturity. From the day ~~we are~~ born ~~to the day we graduate,~~

we're   *T*   *experiences,*

~~we are~~ exposed to many activities. ~~It is~~ ~~t~~hrough these ~~activities that~~ we get to know ourselves

[Unnecessary]   *When*   *pause, evaluate,*

better. ~~While we are on this journey,~~ we come upon a roadblock, ~~a time when~~ we must ~~sit down~~

how we'll proceed. Those roadblocks prepare us for achieving our goals.

and plan ~~out the rest of our lives. This is the time where we set forth our goals.~~

I would like to become ~~a doctor that specializes in the nose, throat, and ears. Based on my~~ *an ear, nose, and throat specialist.* [Why? You might want to relate a story that explains your interest in this specialty.] ~~short-term goals, I will then plan my long-term goals for the future which are I would like to~~ *After I* finish ~~graduate~~ *medical* school, ~~and after I would like to have my own clinic~~ *I want to have a thriving private practice* and ~~also~~ be financially stable.

Essay 7: In 500 words or less, share your views on how your religion has affected you and who you are.

I am not going to lie and say that I am the greatest Christian alive, and that I should be selected for the scholarship because I am the best and only model catholic. I don't think that is why I should be selected, because I know I am not the best, and most perfect catholic. None of us are. I feel I should be selected because I am one of the most eager and determined Catholics.

I often find my self lost in a world of questions and disbelief, and I try to understand and cope with what God has given us. It is hard, but I do the best I can. Being in God's love and life is something I strive to be apart of every day, and not one day goes by when I want to just quit, but then I know I would be loosing the greatest award of all, God.

So if the question is why do I feel I should win the award, it's not because I am the best, but because I try to be the best I can, and I don't give up on the person who can solve everything. God.

My effort at trying to keep into God's teachings brings me new challenges everyday. Mind boggling questions, and time consuming answers. I try everything I can knowing that it may bring me one step closer to God.

Giving food to the needy and adopting a family at Christmas are just a few of the things I try to do. Also help giving out school supplies to the less fortunate during the beginning of the school year. Even though I know this may not be much, I pace my self and do a little at a time.

I do all this while I am involved in JROTC, and drama. I have participated in a school production, and I am an officer in my schools JROTC program. I was on the school drill team for two years, and won many first, second, and third place trophies with them.

I maintain a A-B avg. , and have not missed the Honor Roll once since my years at Holy Angels Catholic High School. I was accepted into Honors Religion and Honors Spanish classes. I have also been accepted into Advanced placement English. I love reading and writing.

My plans for the future change, and I sometimes think I know what I want. Yet with the rapid change of the world my decisions are not always certain.

I am certain I will attend college, not only for a better education, but for a better person in me. One thing is for sure, and that is God is and always will be in my future. I can't imagine my life with out the challenge of striving for God's kingdom. For that is what life is. He is everything and does everything. He gave me this opportunity with you. For that I thank him, and also thank you.

Essay 7—Makeover: Normally, religion isn't an appropriate topic for an essay, but this essay was being written for an essay competition offered by a religious organization. Thus the topic is acceptable. The original essay was 498 words in length and wasn't clearly focused. The opening paragraph was a bit negative. With a few minor changes, deletions, and additions, the essay is direct and to-the-point and 420 words in length. The essay is now stronger and ready to go.

I'm not going to try to convince you that I'm   living
~~I am not going to lie and say that I am~~ the greatest Christian ~~alive~~, and that I should be selected

                                        I'm   *C*   *My goal is to strive to be the*
for the scholarship because ~~I am~~ the best and only model ¢atholic. ~~I don't think that is why I should~~

best person I can be by following Christ's example and living by God's teachings.   [Move this
~~be selected, because I know I am not the best, and most perfect catholic. None of us are. [I feel I~~

sentence to next paragraph.]
~~should be selected because I am one of the most eager and determined Catholics.]~~

          myself
I often find ~~my self~~ lost in a world of questions and disbelief,/ ~~and~~ I try to understand and cope

                              It's
with what God has given us. ~~It is~~ hard, but I do the best I can. Being in God's love and life is

          toward   *for a few seconds don't*
something I strive ~~to be apart of~~ every day, and not one day goes by when I want to ~~just~~ quit, but

remember I'd be losing   *reward*   :
then I ~~know I would be loosing~~ the greatest ~~award~~ of all~~/~~ God.

I always strive to do the best I can. I don't give up on the only One who can solve everything.
~~So if the question is why do I feel I should win the award, it's not because I am the best, but~~

~~because I try to be the best I can, and I don't give up on the person who can solve everything. God.~~

Every day my efforts at trying to live within God's teachings bring   *and mind-*
~~My effort at trying to keep into God's teachings brings~~ me new challenges ~~everyday. Mind~~

boggling   .   ,   *it'll*
~~boggling~~ questions~~/ and time consuming answers.~~ I try everything I can knowing ~~that it may~~ bring

me one step closer to God.

I've always tried to help others by participating in food drives for the needy, adopting a family
~~Giving food to the needy and adopting a family at Christmas are just a few of the things I try to~~

at Christmas, and at the beginning of each school year collecting and distributing school
~~do. Also help giving out school supplies to the less fortunate during the beginning of the school~~

supplies to students who are less fortunate.   *I do what I can with my time and resources.*
~~year.~~ Even though I know this may not be much, ~~I pace my self and do a little at a time.~~

As an officer in the Junior Reserve Officer Training Corps (JROTC), I'm able to serve as an
~~I do all this while I am involved in JROTC, and drama. I have participated in a school production,~~

example to my peers and younger students.
~~and I am an officer in my schools JROTC program.~~ I was on the school drill team for two years, and

have   -   -   -   .   [We're all three dimensional.]
won many first, second, and third place trophies ~~with them. Since no one should be one-~~

[Student added this sentence in the second draft.]
~~dimensional,~~ *I'm also active in drama and participated in a school production.*

My proudest academic achievement is having maintained an A-B average in all
~~I maintain a A-B avg. , and have not missed the Honor Roll once since~~ my years at Holy Angels

[Don't include information that can be found on a transcript.]
Catholic High School. ~~I was accepted into Honors Religion and Honors Spanish classes. I have also~~

The world comes alive for me through
~~been accepted into Advanced placement English. I love~~ reading and writing.

as I change. Sometimes I   *career to pursue, yet*
My plans for the future change~~/ and I sometimes~~ think I know what ~~I want. Yet~~ with the rapid

changes occurring in our world,   *must be constantly revised.*
~~change of the world~~ my decisions ~~are not always certain.~~

Attending college will allow me to attain a higher education and to become a more educated,
~~I am certain I will attend college, not only for a better education, but for a better person in me.~~

well-rounded, and compassionate person.
~~One thing is for sure, and that is~~ God is and always will be in my future. I can't imagine my life

without   *Kingdom. After all, that's what life is all about.*
~~with out~~ the challenge of striving for God's ~~kingdom. For that is what life is. He is everything and~~

With your help, I'll be one step closer in doing my best for God.
~~does everything. He gave me this opportunity with you. For that I thank him, and also thank you.~~

Essay 8: Write a brief essay on your educational and career goals.

Goals can also be defined as dreams. They allow one's imagination to expand. Throughout time one sets different goals and tries hard to accomplish them. Even though sometimes they may not come true, trying to achieve it becomes the goal. In my life I've had several goals, from childhood to present day to future goals that have allowed me to open up my shell.

As a child I had an imagination with no boundaries and wanted to become everything I'd see. My all time goal was to become a moviestar and win numerous Oscars. I would watch TV and hope that one day it would be me on TV being saved by Superman. I concluded that if that didn't work, I would become a dancer. Finally, my mind was running wild, but slowly realized that these goals were changing and becoming more realistic.

As time changed so did my childhood unrealistic goals. As I high school student I now have other goals set to accomplish. First, is to graduate. After six years, it is getting closer and closer. I see that my brothers and sisters did it and therefore so can I. Second, is to do successfully in College. I look at people that were at one time in my shoes and are now doing very well in their studies. As a result of this, I see myself striving to achieve these two significant goals.

Fifteen years from now my goals would somewhat be similar to those of highschool. To begin with my first goal would be to have a job that I really enjoy doing. I don't mind if it pays minimum wage, so long as I feel good inside. Next, is to be a positive role model to my children. I want them to be able to trust me and run to me whenever they need me. After all the influences I have gotten, I want to be able to influence others as well. People such as my family and some members of my community. Thus, I feel that along my journey people have helped me reach my goals and therefore I want to help others reach theirs.

Essay 8—Makeover:

Goals can also be defined as dreams. They allow one's imagination to expand. Throughout ~~time~~ *life* one sets different goals and tries hard to accomplish them. Even though sometimes ~~they~~ *dreams* may not come true, trying to achieve ~~it~~ *them* becomes the goal. ~~In my life~~ I've had several goals ~~from childhood to present day to future goals~~ that have allowed me to ~~open up~~ *come out of* my shell. [What shell? Are you introverted? This needs more explanation.]

As a child I had an imagination ~~with no~~ *without* boundaries and ~~wanted to become everything I'd see.~~ *was constantly changing my goals.* My ~~all time~~ *ultimate* goal was to become a movie star and win numerous Oscars. ~~I would~~ *I'd* watch TV and hope that one day it would be me on TV being saved by Superman. I concluded that if that didn't work, ~~I would~~ *I'd* become a dancer. ~~Finally, my mind was running wild, but slowly realized that these~~ *Slowly, as I got older, my* goals ~~were changing and becoming~~ *became* more realistic.

[Redundant-same as previous sentence.] ~~As time changed so did my childhood unrealistic goals.~~ As ~~I~~ *a* high school student I now have other goals ~~set~~ to accomplish. ~~First,~~ *My first goal* is to graduate. After six years, [Why six years? It takes four years to complete high school.] ~~It is~~ *it's* getting closer and closer. I ~~see that~~ *watched* my brothers and sisters ~~did it~~ *do* and ~~therefore so can I.~~ *I know I can, too.* ~~Second,~~ *My second goal* is to ~~do successfully in College. I look at people that were at one time in my shoes and are now doing very well in their studies.~~ *successfully complete college. I've seen students who were doing poorly academically turn themselves around.* As a result ~~of this,~~ I see myself ~~striving to achieve~~ *accomplishing* these two significant goals.

[Unclear, delete.] ~~Fifteen years from now my goals would somewhat be similar to those of high school. To begin with~~ *After college graduation,* my first goal would be to have a career ~~that~~ I really enjoy. ~~I don't mind if it pays minimum wage, so long as I feel good inside.~~ [Never say this.] ~~Next,~~ *My next goal would be* is to be a positive role model to my children. I want them to be able to trust me and ~~run~~ *come* to me whenever they need ~~me.~~ *help.* ~~After all the influences I have gotten, I want to be able to influence others as well. People such as my~~ *My* family and some members of my *have been good role models for me and I want to be the same for others.*

community ~~Thus, I feel that along my journey people have helped me reach my goals and therefore~~
      ^

~~I want to help others reach theirs.~~

Essay 9: Write a brief essay on your goals.

I am a senior in high school. Right now I am ranked at fourty seventh out of about two hundred and eighty-two. That puts me at about the top sixteen percent of my class.

I plan on attending a university that has a Professional Golf Management curriculum. When I graduate, I will have a bachelor's degree in business administration and marketing with a Professional Golf Association status. This will enable me to attain my career goals, which include running a golf course and teaching golf professionally. But most of all I would like to introduce the underprivileged children to the game of golf. Perhaps I could inspire a kid to reach for higher goals through the game of golf, the same way I did.

Essay 9—Makeover: This essay just needed some minor adjustments.

I'm   I'm   forty-   approximately
~~I am~~ a senior in high school. Right now ~~I am~~ ranked ~~at fourty~~ seventh out of ~~about~~ two hundred
      ^   ^   ^   ^

                              in
and eighty -~~two.~~ That puts me ~~at about~~ the top sixteen percent of my class.
            ^   ^

                                          P   g   m
I plan on attending a university that has a ₱rofessional ₲olf ₥anagement curriculum. When I
                                          ^   ^   ^

      I'll
graduate, ~~I will~~ have a bachelor's degree in business administration and marketing with a
      ^

                          certification.
Professional Golf Association ~~status.~~ This will enable me to attain my career goals, which include
                          ^

                                                    M   ,   I'd
running a golf course and teaching golf professionally. ~~But~~ most of all ~~I would~~ like to introduce ~~the~~
                                                    ^   ^   ^

                                                    child
underprivileged children to the game of golf. Perhaps I could inspire a ~~kid~~ to reach for higher goals
                                                    ^

            as my father inspired me to do.
through the game of golf, ~~the same way I did.~~
            ^

Essay 10: What are your goals?

What a goal is is generally the same to me as the person next to me. What it means differs immensely from my neighbor's opinion to mine. I have so many goals to attain that I tend to forget how much time I have to achieve them.

Besides that I have recently become very interested in liberal arts. Likewise, I hope to get involved with a non profit organizations. One that deals with animals or with AIDS. The reason I chose these two things is because I am particularly interested in AIDS and I am the biggest animal lover.

I might be making the wrong impression on you and thus you might think of me as someone who aspires too much. I intend to continue my studies so that through them I will accomplish my ultimate goal to become a doctor.

Essay 10—Makeover: The last sentence in the second paragraph is not a good explanation of this student's choices and interests. Why does she love animals? Why is she interested in AIDS? Does she know someone who has AIDS? Has she volunteered at a hospice for AIDS patients? Does she want to do AIDS research?

[Delete—this is understood.]
~~What a goal is is generally the same to me as the person next to me. What it means differs immensely from my neighbor's opinion to mine.~~ I have so many goals to attain that I tend to forget

little [Use "little," not "much." "Much" implies that you have a lot of time.]
how ~~much~~ time I have to achieve them.

a [Why? How?]
~~Besides that~~ I ~~have~~ recently become ~~very~~ interested in liberal arts. ~~Likewise,~~ I hope to get

, preferably one
involved with a nonprofit organizations. ~~One~~ that deals with animals or with AIDS. ~~The reason~~ I

areas [Explain why you're interested in animals and AIDS.]
chose these two ~~things is~~ because ~~I am particularly interested in AIDS and I am the biggest animal lover.~~

[Delete—sounds as if you're trying to butter up the committee. There's nothing wrong with
~~I might be making the wrong impression on you and thus you might think of me as someone~~

wanting to achieve.]
~~who aspires too much.~~ I intend to ~~continue my studies so that through them I will~~ accomplish my

ultimate goal/ to become a doctor.

Essay 11: Write a brief essay (100 to 200 words) on your goals.

Our goals are what drive us to work, to strive, and to compete. With them, we have something to look forward to, something to dream of. Without them, we become careless and unconcerned with our futures. Both short-term and long-term goals provide us with determination and ambition.

My goals for the near future involve my development as a high school student and a citizen. This summer, I plan to enhance my education by attending as many summer schools and programs as I can fit into three short months. In the next school year, I would like to join the Interact Club and Executive Student Council. I plan to become a team member of Varsity Volleyball, and in working towards this goal, I have joined a city volleyball league to better my abilities. Outside of school, I would like to participate in a wide variety of volunteer services, because I learned this year the value of service, although I regret to say that I had to be done through school requirements. These are the goals I hope to reach in the coming year, and I plan to continue them throughout my high school years.

Essay 11—Makeover: At 198 words, the original essay is within the word count, but needed several changes to strengthen it. The resulting essay is 167 words in length.

Our goals are what drive us to work, to strive, and to compete. With them, we have something to
look forward to, something to dream ~~of.~~ *about* Without them, we become careless and unconcerned ~~with~~ *about*

our futures. Both short-term and long-term goals provide us with determination and ambition.

My goals for the near future involve my development as a high school student and a citizen. This

I'll continue
summer, ~~I plan~~ to enhance my education by attending as many summer schools and programs as I

can fit into three short months. In the next school year, ~~I would~~ *I'd* like to join the Interact Club and

[In the U.S., we use the word "toward." The U.K. uses "towards."]

Executive Student Council. I plan to become a team member of Varsity Volleyball, and in working

towards this goal, ~~I have~~ *I've* joined a city volleyball league to ~~better~~ *improve* my ~~abilities.~~ *skills* Outside of school, I

~~would like~~ *plan* [How? Be specific.] to participate in a wide variety of volunteer services, ~~because I learned this year the~~ [Delete—why you started is irrelevant.]

~~value of service, although I regret to say that I had to be done through school requirements.~~ These

are the goals I hope to reach in the coming year, and I plan to continue them throughout my high

school years.

Essay 12: Write a short biography of 200 words or less stating special interests, career goals, reasons for pursuing higher education, and any other pertinent information. (Vikki Carr Scholarship)

Special interests include reading, volleyball, and being involved with the community and my church.

Career goals are to receive a position in public education as an Administrator in Education or Professor in Mathematics at a University.

My parents and teachers have taught me to achieve a high education. I would like to teach that to everyone especially Hispanics. Statistics prove MY HERITAGE has lagged. behind other ethics when it comes to education. The struggle I see in the Hispanic communities gives me the strength to over come any obstacle in pursuing a higher education in the end I would like to have made a difference in young people's lives to be successful, academically as I have been

I thank my parents for guiding and supporting me through school. Their help, dedication, and most of all encouragement have always been there. I am very proud to say that I will be the first in my family to attend a University. As a child my parents planted a special seed in me about school, following my dreams, and more critically attending college. I feel parents should plant a special seed in their children from the very beginning.

Essay 12—Makeover: This essay had several problems. The first two sentences don't seem connected to the essay. The student wanted to use the image of planting a seed as a metaphor, but needed to integrate it into the entire essay. With just a few changes, the essay came together nicely. Many of the sentences were moved and merged, so only the final version is provided.

Much like gardeners, from the moment of my birth, my parents lovingly tended me and implanted the burning desire to succeed. Hispanics academically lag behind other ethnicities. Therefore, I want to cultivate students to overcome any obstacles they may encounter in attaining a higher education.

As a child, my parents planted a special seed in me to follow my dreams and attend college. Their smiles and tears of joy were the rain that fed my inner growth. Their encouragement and positive reinforcement were the fertilizer ~~which~~ *that* allowed my roots to reach out to new experiences in which to participate, such as in volleyball, being involved with my community and church, and my abiding interest in reading. Through my parents' influence I've formulated the career goals of one day being either an administrator within the public school sector, or ~~as~~ *being* a mathematics professor at the college level.

Through their tender nurturing, my parents ~~were~~ *provided* the guiding framework for my growth. I will be the first generation in my family to obtain a postsecondary education, and one day ~~I will~~ *I'll* have a garden filled with young minds and bodies so that I can make a positive difference in their lives.

Essay 13: Write an essay of approximately 500 words about your goals.

When I read this question, I thought, "Is this a joke?" I thought scholarship essays were supposed to be hard." Well, I have to talk, er, write for approximately 500 wrods, so here goes. Well my goals number many, I have a basketball goal in my backyard, a soccer goal in the park, and a mini-goal in my room. Oh my God, sorry, this is *goals,* as in life. Sorry about the "is this a joke?" joke. It's not so easy anymore, goals are something serious, they control your life, actually, they are life.

I can't believe there's just one more year left, then I'm off to college. I remember being a freshman and hearing seniors complain about how time flies. For this coming year, I have a few set goals. First of all, I want to successfully complete all my college applications and hopefully get accepted to a college. After getting accepted, I would like to hang in there for the final drastic months of this next year and pass all my courses. If I do pass all my course, it will lead to the accomplishment of my final goal, to graduate. It is not going to be easy, it takes hard work and determination, that I always hear about. Besides that, it will take the planning and organization of time to help me in the struggle they call the senior year. I'd sum up, my first year goal is graduate and get accepted to college.

If I do accomplish these first goals which I can, then comes the next set of goals, which aren't so short-term. Throughout the next five years, I hope to be all I can be and more in college. I do not want to take college lightly and fail to realize that this is the last and final step on to that wild rollercoaster ride they call life. I plan to work harder than hard in college, and really get something out of it. What I plan to get out of it is an idea of what direction my life will go in, and a sense of accomplishment. In the course of the next five years, what my basic goal is to get something out of my college years, not just intelligence and knowledge, but the wisdom and experience it takes to make it after college.

After college, that's when the goals that will make up my life come in. In the next 10 years, I will grow, but not in the physical sense of the word "grow", in the mental sense. Hope to be prepared after graduating from high school and college. One basic goals I have is to start a small family that I can have. I want to have the time to be able to give pay my dues to the community I grew up in. When I feel I have the time, I want to come back to my roots, and try to help in the movement that will increase the education one can receive in this town, but most importantly, decrease the ignorance people have. My home town need help, and the help starts when one person does their share to help. Whether I help with donations, or with actual time and effort, I will help. Hopefully, I will be able to personally help the youth in their struggle for education, but if not I will figure out a way to help. The bottom line is, I want to come back and help, an that is my main goal for the next 10 years.

I hope to do success, and I hope I do have the time to help. Actually, I will succeed, and I will have the time to help. Life is not about making money or having fun, it's about the satisfaction of accomplishing your goals. Satisfaction for me will come the day I accomplish my final goal, to make a difference. For now, I will try my hardest, believe me I will. I will take one day at a time and focus on the daily goals that will help me succeed in also conquering the big picture. Life is the bit picture.

Essay 13—Makeover: This student was trying to be funny and just sounds flakey. At 696 words, it was also too long, so the entire first paragraph was deleted. The resulting essay is 306 words in length.

~~When I read this question, I thought, "Is this a joke?" I thought scholarship essays were supposed to be hard." Well, I have to talk, er, write for approximately 500 wrods, so here goes. Well my goals number many, I have a basketball goal in my backyard, a soccer goal in the park, and a mini-goal in my room. Oh my God, sorry, this is *goals,* as in life. Sorry about the "is this a joke?" joke. It's not so easy anymore, goals are something serious, they control your life, actually, they are life.~~

I can't believe there's just one more year left, then I'm off to college. I remember being a freshman and hearing seniors complain about how time flies. For this coming year, ~~I have a few~~ *I've set* set goals. ~~First of all,~~ I want to successfully complete all my college applications and ~~hopefully get~~ *be the college of my choice.* *I'll continue to maintain or improve my grades and* accepted to ~~a college. After getting accepted, I would like to hang in there for the final drastic~~ *SAT scores, leading to graduation in the spring.* [This next sentence is a bit negative–delete it.] ~~months of this next year and pass all my courses. If I do pass all my course, it will lead to the~~ *It's* ~~accomplishment of my final goal, to graduate. It is not going to be easy~~/ *.It'll , planning,* it takes hard work and *but can do it.* [This has been said–delete.] determination, ~~that I always hear about. Besides that, it will take the planning and organization of time to help me in the struggle they call the senior year. I'd sum up, my first year goal is graduate and get accepted to college.~~

After
If I ~~do~~ accomplish these ~~first~~ goals ~~, which I can, then comes the next set of goals, which aren't so~~

~~short-term.~~ *over* Throughout the next five years, I hope to ~~be all I can be and more~~ *maximize my success* in college. I ~~do not~~ *plan*

~~want~~ to take college ~~lightly~~ *seriously* and ~~fail to~~ realize ~~that this is the last and final step on to that~~ *my potential so that I'll be prepared for the* wild

roller coaster ~~rollercoaster ride they call life. I plan to work harder than hard in college, and really get something~~ *of life after college.*

~~out of it.~~ What I plan to ~~get out of it is an idea of what~~ *find* direction ~~my~~ *my* life ~~will go in, and a sense of~~ *in* , gain experience, and feel a

sense of accomplishment. ~~accomplishment. In the course of the next five years, what my basic goal is to get something out of~~

~~my college years, not just intelligence and knowledge, but~~ *I hope to gain* the wisdom ~~and experience~~ it takes to

make it after college.

~~After college, that's when the goals that will make up my life come in.~~ In the next ten years, ~~I will~~

~~grow, but not in the physical sense of the word "grow", in the mental sense. Hope to be prepared~~

~~after graduating from high school and college.~~ One basic ~~goals~~ I ~~have~~ *hope* is to start a ~~small~~ family ~~that I~~ *, and I plan*

~~can have.~~ I want to ~~have~~ *take* the time ~~to be able~~ to give ~~pay my dues~~ *back* to the community I grew up in.

[Delete—unflattering.]
~~When I feel I have the time,~~ I want to come back to my roots, ~~and~~ try to ~~help in the movement that~~ *improve the local educational system,*

~~will increase the education one can receive in this town,~~ *and,* ~~but~~ most importantly, decrease the

~~ignorance~~ *needs* ~~people have.~~ My hometown ~~need~~ help, and the help starts when one person does ~~their~~ *his or her*

share to help. ~~Whether I help with~~ *Through* donations, ~~or with actual~~ *of* time and effort, ~~I will help. Hopefully, I~~ *I'll be there for the youth*

of my hometown. [Delete the rest. It's redundant.]
~~will be able to personally help the youth in their struggle for education, but if not I will figure out a~~

~~way to help. The bottom line is, I want to come back and help, an that is my main goal for the next~~

~~10 years.~~

[Delete—redundant.]
~~I hope to do success, and I hope I do have the time to help. Actually, I will succeed, and I will~~

~~have the time to help.~~ Life ~~is not~~ *isn't* about making money or having fun; it's about the satisfaction of

accomplishing your goals. Satisfaction for me will come the day I accomplish my final goal; to make

I'll

a difference. ~~For now, I will~~ try my hardest/ ~~believe me I will.~~ ~~I will~~ take one day at a time and focus

to reach that final goal.

on the daily goals that will help me ~~succeed in also conquering the big picture. Life is the bit~~

~~picture.~~

Essay 14: Write a brief essay on your goals.

I remember one year, I had successfully played a very difficult piece of music at a recital, nonetheless, another girl had decided to perform that same piece at the next competition. I was determined to play the best I could. I practiced for hours until I reached perfection. At the recital I played perfectly and was very pleased with myself. Then the other girl played. She did not play as well because she did not understand the dedication and commitment that was required to accomplish ones goals. The valuable lesson I have used and lived by throughout my life. Through piano I have come to realize the dedication and commitment required to successfully accomplish my goals and dreams. I have also pursued this commitment and dedication as a violinist. My accomplishments as a violinist is as gratifying as my successes as a pianist.

Essay 14—Makeover: This essay was about her expertise on the piano. To insert information about the violin takes the focus out of the essay. Never feel you have to include your entire history in an essay. Essays for scholarships and college admission should give just a focused glimpse into your life.

O

~~I remember~~ one year, I ~~had~~ successfully played a ~~very~~ difficult piece of music at a recital/

Another student

~~nonetheless, another girl had~~ decided to perform that same piece at the next competition. I was

determined to play the best I could. I practiced for hours until I reached perfection. At the recital I

didn't

played perfectly and was ~~very~~ pleased with myself. Then the other girl played. She ~~did not~~ play as

didn't

well because she ~~did not~~ understand the dedication and commitment ~~that was~~ required to accomplish one's goals. ~~The valuable lesson I have~~ *I've* used ~~and lived by throughout my life. Through~~ *this valuable lesson*

~~piano I have come~~ *that* to realize the dedication and commitment required to ~~successfully~~ accomplish *are* [No one can unsuccessfully accomplish a task—redundant.]

[Don't insert another topic. It takes the essay out of focus.]
my goals and dreams. ~~I have also pursued this commitment and dedication as a violinist. My~~

~~accomplishments as a violinist is as gratifying as my successes as a pianist.~~

Essay 15: Write a brief essay (100 to 200 words) on your goals as they relate to your education, career, and future plans. (Tylenol)

I was in the control booth with the station's newest intern who was putting the tapes in the right order. The undergraduate had already searched the wire for scores and interesting national and state-wide stories to enhance tonight's show.

"After the commercial, we'll hear from Izaak Martinez with Eyewitness Sports," the anchor said. I had one minute to make sure my makeup wasn't obvious, get to my seat, and clip my microphone in place, all the while making jokes with my colleagues.

Sitting in my chair at the news desk, I put my notes in order. I took a moment to remember my intern days right here at KENS-TV. It had seemed a dream come true. I was able to spend time with sportscasters who I'd listened to for years. I'd worked alongside producers and reporters and learned how to put together tidbits of information into interesting stories.

"Here's Izaak Martinez with tonight's sports," my fellow anchor announced turning toward me.

"Good evening, tonight I want to start with a story about long-time resident, local legend, and retired Spurs center, David Robinson. This clip shows David with inner-city kids in a sports camp he conducts nationwide. I caught up to him in Harlingen before he left to go to the next camp in Detroit."

The monitor breaks to a clip of a high school gymnasium. A semi-circle of kids ranging in age from about eight to twelve watch enraptured as David talks to them about the importance of teamwork.

"David, what would you say was your greatest accomplishment?" I asked.

"It would have to be seeing the faces of these kids as they prepare to begin working toward possible athletic careers," he answered candidly.

"You mean to say that winning five NBA Championship title rings in your career isn't in first place?"

"Let's put it this way," David said grinning from ear to ear. "They both run neck and neck for first place," he says with a chuckle, giving the camera that wholesome grin for which he's noted.

"Your son, a midshipman at Annapolis, your alma mater, is with you on this trip, isn't he?" I asked.

"That's right. Whenever he's on vacation, he comes with me," David answered like the proud father he is.

"I still remember when you had him in your arms after your first NBA Championship win," I said, feeling my age. The camera moves to another corner of the gym where David's son is working with rows of kids who are running through drills.

This is what I want to learn and how I want to build toward my future and reach my dreams. The internship in which I've been participating has already provided an incredible opportunity to learn from the best in that area of journalism—sports, in which I am most interested. I want to learn as much as I can so that when I attend college, I'll be at the head of the pack.

Essay 15—Makeover: This was a strong essay, but it's too long. Something had to be cut, without disrupting the student's vivid account.

[Unnecessary—delete.]
~~I was in the control booth with the station's newest intern who was putting the tapes in the right order. The undergraduate had already searched the wire for scores and interesting national and state-wide stories to enhance tonight's show.~~

"After the commercial, we'll hear from Izaak Martinez with Eyewitness Sports," the anchor said. I

get my notes in order.

had one minute to ~~make sure my makeup wasn't obvious, get to my seat, and clip my microphone~~

~~in place, all the while making jokes with my colleagues.~~

[Though this is interesting, it's unnecessary—delete.]

~~Sitting in my chair at the news desk, I put my notes in order. I took a moment to remember my~~

~~intern days right here at KENS-TV. It had seemed a dream come true. I was able to spend time with~~

~~sportscasters who I'd listened to for years. I'd worked alongside producers and reporters and~~

~~learned how to put together tidbits of information into interesting stories.~~

"Here's Izaak Martinez with tonight's sports," ~~my fellow anchor announced turning toward me.~~

"Good evening, Tonight I want to start with a story about long-time resident, local legend, and

retired Spurs center, David Robinson. This clip shows David with inner-city kids in a sports camp he

conducts nationwide. I caught up to him in Harlingen before he left to go to the next camp in

Detroit."

[Unnecessary—delete.]

~~The monitor breaks to a clip of a high school gymnasium. A semi-circle of kids ranging in age~~

~~from about eight to twelve watch enraptured as David talks to them about the importance of~~

~~teamwork.~~

"David, what would you say was your greatest accomplishment?" I asked.

"It would have to be seeing the faces of these kids as they prepare to begin working toward

possible athletic careers," he answered candidly.

"You mean to say that winning five NBA Championship title rings in your career isn't in first

place?"

"Let's put it this way," David said grinning from ear to ear. "They both run neck and neck for first

said

place," he says with a chuckle, ~~giving the camera that wholesome grin for which he's noted.~~

~~"Your son, a midshipman at Annapolis, your alma mater, is with you on this trip, isn't he?" I asked.~~

~~"That's right. Whenever he's on vacation, he comes with me," David answered like the proud~~

~~father he is.~~

~~"I still remember when you had him in your arms after your first NBA Championship win," I said,~~

~~feeling my age. The camera moves to another corner of the gym where David's son is working with~~

~~rows of kids who are running through drills.~~

As a journalism major in college, I plan to learn as much as I can and participate in internships
~~This is what I want to learn and how I want to build toward my future and reach my dreams. The~~
^
every summer. One day, I'll be a print and broadcast journalist.
~~internship in which I've been participating has already provided an incredible opportunity to learn~~
^
~~from the best in that area of journalism—sports, in which I am most interested. I want to learn as~~

~~much as I can so that when I attend college, I'll be at the head of the pack.~~

Essay 16: Write a statement that indicates how the scholarship will help you attain your education and career goals.

I am the single mother of two boys and interested in becoming a COTA (Certified Occupational Therapist Assistant). For the past three years I have been able to manage a full time job while attending college part time.

I enjoy working as an Occupational Therapist Technician providing therapy to the chronic schizophrenic population at the State Hospital. There is a severe shortage of COTAs at this hospital and elsewhere in the town, which encouraged me to pursue this field of study.

I took all the prerequisites and corequisites I applied for the Occupational Therapy Assistant Program at St. Philip's College in San Antonio to which I was accepted. The program started this Fall of 1995 and ends the Spring of 1997.

One of the criteria to be accepted in this program is the willingness to go to school on a full time basis. At this point I still continue working full time to be able to provide for my children and make ends meet, as I do not have any other means of support. Trying to balance the roles of mother, provider, and student has became very stressful.

I certainly believe that with your assistance I will be able to stand on my feet and focus on

my education. I will be under less stress and will be able to provide a better life and education for

my sons.

Essay 16—Makeover: This student could have included her goals once she becomes a COTA. She also could comment on whether she wants to continue working at the State Hospital.

I'm   *am* [How did you become interested?]
~~I am~~ the single mother of two boys and interested in becoming a ~~COTA~~ (Certified Occupational

       (COTA).   *I've*   -
Therapist Assistant). For the past three years ~~I have~~ been able to manage a full time job while

attending college part-time.

     providing therapy   [For how long?]
I enjoy ~~working~~ as an Occupational Therapist Technician ~~providing therapy~~ to the chronic

       Knowing there's
schizophrenic population at the State Hospital. ~~There is~~ a severe shortage of COTAs at this hospital

      I feel confident this career will provide me with job security.
and elsewhere in ~~the~~ town, ~~which encouraged me to pursue this field of study~~.

completed   *,*
I ~~took~~ all the prerequisites ~~and corequisites~~ I applied for the Occupational Therapy Assistant

       , and was   *in*
Program at St. Philip's College in San Antonio ~~to which I was~~ accepted. The program started ~~this~~

Fall ~~of~~ 1995 and ends ~~the~~ Spring ~~of~~ 1997.

     for acceptance to   *attend*   -
One of the criteria ~~to be accepted in~~ this program is the willingness to ~~go to~~ school on a full time
Unfortunately, at   *must*
basis. ~~At~~ this point, I ~~still~~ continue working full-time to be able to provide for my children and make

     don't   *source*   *income*
ends meet, as I ~~do not~~ have any other ~~means~~ of ~~support~~. Trying to balance the roles of mother,

     become
provider, and student has ~~became very~~ stressful.

     With   *I'll*   *economically*
~~I certainly believe that with~~ your assistance, ~~I will~~ be able to stand on my feet and focus on

     I'll
my education. ~~I will~~ be under less stress and will be able to provide a better life and education for

my sons.

Essay 17: Write about an experience that you feel has influenced your development or goals. The essay should be no more than 500 words in length.

Patience is a virtue. Working at the Outlet Dress Store has taught me that. I was hired at the Outlet Dress Store more than a year and a half ago. Before having a retail job, I never knew the meaning of patience. In the business field, I believe if you don't have patience, then you won't get too far.

I was recently promoted to floor supervisor. I am the youngest employee there and I was the one chosen. This tells me that I am a hard worker and I am committed to my responsibilities. Although being promoted has placed more responsibilities on myself, patience will help me through the times if I don't get something right and need to try again. I am now faced with more paperwork, opening and closing the store and making sure the store runs okay when I am the one in charge.

Having the job at the Outlet Dress Store has taught me many things. Working with people, dealing with money, organization and most of all, making customers happy. All of this had made my mind up to major in business management. I plan to have my own business in the future. I have not decided what kind of business I would like to open yet. I believe that business management will help me in figuring out how to run a business of my own and all the other responsibilities that come along with it. I know through all that I do, patience will help me succeed to greater achievements in my life.

Essay 17—Makeover: The original 258-word essay tells the information; it doesn't show it. After a short discussion, the student rewrote the essay. The longer version is 413 words in length, but it gets the reader's attention.

"Do you have this in my size?" the overweight woman asked. In one hand she ~~was holding out~~ *held* a red dress with polka dots, and in the other, a pile of dresses.

"Your size?" I repeated. I wanted to ask her if her size was somewhere around 20, but kept my thoughts to myself.

"I wear a size 10, sometimes a 12," she said, staring me straight in the eye in a challenging manner.

"I think we just might have your size," I said. I quickly grabbed a 12, 16, and a 20, but didn't make an issue of it. "The dressing room is over there."

"Thank you, dear. Here, I'm not taking these," the woman said, handing me the dresses. *S*ome were ill-hung, others inside-out, and some weren't on hangers.

I kept a smile on my face as I watched her go into the dressing room. Helping her save face about her size was part of my job. Who was I to question her self-image? Besides, her self-image was great.

Patience is a virtue. Working at the Outlet Dress Store has taught me that. I ~~was hired~~ *started working* at the Outlet Dress Store more than a year and a half ago. Before having a retail job, I never knew the meaning of patience. ~~In the business field, I believe if~~ *If* you don't have patience, ~~then~~ you won't get *in business* too far.

Though I'm one of the youngest employees, I was recently promoted to floor supervisor. ~~I am the youngest employee there and I was the one chosen. This tells me that I am~~ *My boss obviously thinks I'm* a hard worker ~~and I am~~ , committed to my responsibilities. ~~Although~~ *B*eing promoted has placed more responsibilities on ~~myself~~ *my shoulders, but* patience will help me through ~~the times~~ *If* ~~if~~ I don't get something right ~~and need to try again~~ *, I try again.* ~~I am now faced with more paperwork,~~ *Paper is now a constant part of my life. I'm responsible for* opening and closing the store and making sure the store runs okay when ~~I am the one~~ *I'm* in charge.

Having the job at the Outlet Dress Store has taught me many things. ~~Working~~ *W*orking with people, *, such as how to w* dealing with money, organization, and most of all, making customers happy. ~~All of this had made my mind up~~ *All of these experiences have influenced my decision* to major in business management. ~~I plan to have~~ *One day, I hope to open* my own business ~~in the future~~. ~~I have not decided what kind of business~~ *haven't* ~~I would like to open yet~~ *, but I'm sure that in time I'll know what's right for me.* ~~I believe that business management will~~ *Business*

management will provide the foundation of knowing how to start and run a business
~~help me in figuring out how to run a business of my own~~ and all the other responsibilities that
^
                              Through all that I do in college and beyond,   *achieve my goals.*
come along with it. ~~I know through all that I do,~~ patience will help me ~~succeed to greater~~
^   ^

~~achievements in my life.~~

Essay 18: Write a first-person story (no more than 1,200 words) about a memorable or moving experience you have had. Stories must be your true personal experience.

I'd like to hope that everyone has at least one life changing experience, which would bring out the best in him or her. It all started my freshman year in high school. My mom remarried and all of us relocated to our new home in San Diego. As circumstances would have it I was new once more. Trying to make new friends was becoming a difficult task. All through my previous school years I had moved a total of seven times. Smiling and talking to my new classmates was just natural. High School is just a different world. I had some okay days at school and some bad days. I knew I just had to get through it. I can recall almost every night, when I would cry myself to sleep asking God "why"? And that famous age old question why me?

Months went by it was all so confusing. It was my mother who encouraged me to join the pep squad she felt it would be a wonderful way of meet and make friends. I did hesitate at first, you could say I was feeling insecure. All I wanted was to be with my friend's back home. However, I did join and at first felt out of place. Until one day, after school, while waiting for the rest of the Pep Squaders to arrive I met Sharon. She was the first girl in Pep Squad that I actually could relate with. We talked and laughed about all things going on, and found out about all our hobbies that we shared. We've been the best of friends since then. I thought to myself, "Maybe high school won't be so bad after all." After our newfound friendship, Sharon started inviting me to attend her Sunday night youth group services at her church. My parents were noticing a difference in me, and were glad to see me smiling again. I believe God answered my questions and prayers when I met Sharon. I think he knew that she would bring me closer to him and closer to my true purpose in life.

Essay 18—Makeover: This essay needed a new beginning. The original essay was telling not showing, and didn't capture the reader's attention. The new version is 938 words in length. The student also added new information about her involvement with the church youth group.

My footsteps echoed in the huge hallway. A new family. A new school. A new city. New friends to make. It wasn't the first time. Throughout my previous school years I'd moved a total of seven times. Smiling and talking to new classmates was difficult. There would be good days and bad days. Every night, I'd cry myself to sleep asking God, "Why?" and "Why me?"

Months went by and I still felt like an outsider.

"I think you should join Pep Squad," my mother suggested.

"Pep Squad? Are you crazy? Pep Squad is for the popular kids," I argued. The thought of even walking into the meeting room made my knees quiver.

"How are you going to meet anyone if you don't make an effort?" my mom argued right back. I didn't have an ~~argument.~~ *answer* My mother was right, whether I wanted to admit it or not.

"According to this flyer, tomorrow is Pep Day for all freshmen. You can go sign up for Pep Squad in the auditorium," my mother ~~explained using a rhetoric voice.~~ *stated.*

At school the next day, I stood perfectly still in the hallway. I could only hear the conversation I'd had with my mother. What was I thinking? This was the Pep Squad. Sure, I'd always liked to dance, but that was different. I did that with my friends, for laughs. I really missed my friends back home. I wouldn't fit in. They'd probably all laugh at me.

Just then three girls approached and stopped at the door. They looked me up and down and then went in. As the last one entered, she turned around and said, "Are you coming in?" Her voice didn't sound as if she were laughing. It actually sounded welcoming. I walked into the room and took the first empty seat, keeping my eyes focused on the stage where the director stood.

"Hi, my name is Sharon," a friendly voice said from the seat next to me.

"My name is Amanda," I answered, timidly looking at her. Sharon was thin, with soft, wavy brown hair, and brownish-hazel eyes that looked warm and comforting. We talked and laughed among the crowd of giggling girls for the next forty-five minutes. I couldn't help thinking that maybe high school wouldn't be so bad after all.

We've been the best of friends since then. Sharon ~~started~~ invit*ed* me to attend her Sunday night youth group at her church. Within a visit or two, my parents were noticing a difference in me, and were glad to see me smiling again. God answered my questions and prayers when I met Sharon. He knew she would bring me closer to Him and closer to my true purpose in life.

The day I entered St. Matthew's United Methodist Church with Sharon I felt I belonged there. Everyone was friendly. It was great. I learned so much about God and myself. Each day my understanding of God's purpose in my life was becoming clearer. The summer of 1997 brought the annual Mission Service Project. I couldn't wait to go on the trip.

As the van arrived in Mission, Texas, I noticed that the bright morning sun I'd always thought of as being warm seemed harsh today as it fell on the dilapidated house. The humble, run-down house was home to six migrant farm workers. I was appalled to learn that this hardworking family lived in such a tiny space in conditions that would horrify my friends and family. The tiny house needed a lot of help*,* and that's why we were there. The Mission Service Project brought a team of volunteers together to repair and rebuild homes, helping families in need.

For five days we worked nonstop under the scorching sun, painting, fixing, spackling, and *doing* anything else that needed to be done. I'd never thought that people in the United States could live in such poor conditions. The poverty was unbelievable. I began to examine my own life and priorities. Never once did the migrant family blame God for their misfortune. Instead they were grateful for everything they were given.

Our group built the foundation for a new room that would provide the extra living space the family so badly needed. We fixed the roof, making it leak-proof and sturdy. I knew I would miss the family's enthusiasm. They would eagerly greet us each morning. It was as if we were family who had come to visit for the holidays.

On our last day in Mission, I heard the mother crying. Thinking she needed comforting, I asked her what was wrong and how I could help.

"I'm crying because I'm so happy," she said. "God sent you to help us."

I took a long hard look around me and my eyes were opened. Those things I'd always thought of as necessities: my own phone, a computer, nice clothes, and money to pay for whatever I wanted were all really luxuries. This family had virtually nothing and were thankful for the help we'd extended to them.

That week-long project was a turning point in my life. I was able to make a difference in a needy family's home and, most of all, in their hearts—just as Sharon had made a difference in my life. There will always be a place in my heart for anyone who may feel there is no hope. Even when things get tough, I know it could always be worse and that there are always people who have it worse. Those days at Mission I helped a family with their battle and together we won the war. With God by my side, all things are possible.

Essay 19: In 1,200 words or less, write a true, first-person story about an experience that changed you. It need not be highly dramatic or unusual, but it should demonstrate how faith in God has made a difference in your life.

Imagine yourself with rushing water all around, bouncing off rocks and the constant crashing sound as it goes down the mountainside. If you look up or down, all you can see is the side of the mountain and the sound of the water as it pounds down towards the bottom. If you look to the sides, you see tall pines and aspens all around. You can see mountainsides all around with no peak in sight. In the midst of all this chaos is complete peace. In the midst of all the never-ending scenery, you're overwhelmed by the complete beauty. You can feel the presence of the Holy Spirit. The only thing you can think about is, "Wow! God has an awesome taste in art work!"

That is the exact place, the exact feelings, and the exact thoughts that I had when I saw all of that. I was so amazed at everything, and that wasn't even the best part. At first, when I walked over the "cascading waterfall," I wanted to find a spot where I could complete the journal activity I was given. Everywhere I looked to sit was wet. Finally I spotted a group of trees arranged in a triangle in the middle of the water. They had debris caught on them and it appeared to be the only dry place available. I jumped to the center of the debris carefully. I didn't have an extra pair of clothes with me and the water was coming from melted snow, so it wouldn't have been fun to get wet. When I was sure it was stable, I sat down and enjoyed the beautiful scenery. As I sat there in the midst of the rushing water, I got my first chance to really listen to God. I sat there for over two hours listening and watching the water. I don't think I even wrote a single sentence in my journal, but I didn't care. When I finally looked at my watch, I was fifteen minutes late. We were only supposed to be gone an hour and forty-five minutes. So I got up and ran up to the hiking trail and back to the vans. As we were leaving Rocky Mountain National Park, I was very quiet. I was still listening. People said they talked to me, but I didn't hear any of them.

When we got back to the place where we were staying, the leaders gave us some free time. So I went outside, sat on a big rock, and did some more listening. After sitting there for a little while I decided to talk back. That was the first time prayer had meant anything to me or much less, made sense. I have been raised Catholic, so my parents have taught me many prayers. We'd say them together every night, but they didn't mean much to me. When I decided to talk back, sitting on the rock, the light in my head finally came on. I found that for me, prayer was just a conversation with God and it was my way to talk directly with Him. After I had finished talking, I listened some more. But when it was time for dinner, I had to go back inside. I walked back with a feeling of peace and a sense of overwhelming joy that consumed my body and soul. I walked back inside "high" on God and my faith.

As days went on after my initial "high," I thought my life could never get better. But time after time, I was proved wrong. Every time I prayed for something, God showed me the right answer.

Each time I followed what he said was right, things would get better. For a while, my faith only strengthened. But every once in a while I felt it leveling off, or even getting weaker, all I had to do was remember listening to the water and the peace it gave me. That allowed me to get my faith back on track and moving up again.

That event will always remain vivid in my mind. Nothing could compare to the beautiful waterfall down the mountainside. It's beauty and ambiance will drive my faith for many years to come. But more importantly, the understanding about prayer will serve me my entire lifetime.

Essay 19—Makeover: With just a few changes, this strong essay became even stronger.

Imagine yourself ~~with~~ *surrounded by* rushing water ~~all around~~, bouncing off rocks and ~~the constant~~ crashing ~~sound as it goes~~ down the mountainside. If you look up or down, all you can see is the side of the mountain ~~and~~ *. All you can hear is* the sound of the water as it pounds down towards the bottom. ~~If you look to the sides, you see~~ *T*all pines and aspens ~~all around.~~ *cover the mountain. There are* ~~You can see~~ mountainsides all around *,* with no peak in sight. In the midst of all this chaos is ~~complete~~ peace. In the midst of ~~all~~ the never-ending scenery, you're overwhelmed by the complete beauty. You can feel the presence of the Holy Spirit. The only thing you can think ~~about~~ is, "Wow! God has ~~an~~ awesome taste in art work!"

~~That is the exact place,~~ *Those are* the exact feelings and ~~the exact~~ *ly the* thoughts ~~that~~ I had when I saw ~~all of that.~~ *that scene.* I was so amazed ~~at~~ *by* everything, and that wasn't even the best part. ~~At first, when~~ *As* I walked over the "cascading waterfall," I ~~wanted~~ *tried* to find a spot where I could complete the journal activity I was ~~given.~~ *assigned.* Everywhere I looked to sit was wet. Finally I spotted a group of trees arranged in a triangle in the middle of the water. ~~They had~~ *D*ebris *had* caught on them and it appeared to be the only dry place available. I ~~carefully~~ jumped to the center of the debris *carefully*. I didn't have ~~an~~ extra ~~pair of~~ clothes with me ~~and the water was coming from melted snow~~, so it wouldn't have been fun to get wet.   [New paragraph.]

When I was sure ~~it~~ *the "seat"* was stable, I sat down and enjoyed the beautiful scenery. As I sat there in the midst of the rushing water, I got my first chance to really listen to God. I sat there for over two hours, listening and watching the water. I ~~don't think I even wrote~~ *didn't write* a single sentence in my journal, but I didn't care. When I finally looked at my watch, I was fifteen minutes late/ *for meeting my fellow hikers.* We were only supposed to be gone an hour and forty-five minutes. ~~So~~ *Reluctantly,* I got up and ran up to the hiking trail ~~and~~ back to the vans. As we were leaving Rocky Mountain National Park, I ~~was very~~ *wasn't just* quiet/ *, I was serene.* I was still listening. People said they talked to me, but I didn't hear any of them.

When we got back to the place where we were staying, the leaders gave us some free time. ~~So~~ I went outside, sat on a big rock, and ~~did~~ some more ~~listening.~~ *listened.* After sitting there for a little while I decided to talk back. That was the first time prayer had meant anything to me ~~or~~ *,* much less, made sense. I ~~have been~~ *was* raised Catholic, so my parents ~~have~~ *had* taught me many prayers. We'd say them together every night, but they didn't mean much to me. When I decided to talk back, sitting on the rock, the light in my head finally came on. ~~I found that for me, prayer was just~~ *Prayer turned out to be* a conversation with God ~~and it~~ *. I* was my way ~~to~~ *of* talk~~~~ *ing* directly with Him. After ~~I had~~ *I'd* finished talking, I listened some more. But when it was time for dinner, I had to go back inside. I walked back with a feeling of peace and a sense of overwhelming joy that consumed my body and soul. I walked ~~back~~ inside "high" on God and my faith.

As days ~~went on~~ *passed* after my initial "high," I thought my life could never get better. But time after time, I was proved wrong. Every time I prayed for ~~something~~ *direction*, God showed me the right answer. Each time I followed ~~what he said was right~~ *His lead and will*, things would get better. For a while, my faith only strengthened. ~~But every once in a while I felt it~~ *There are times I feel my faith* leveling off, or even getting weaker/ *. All I have* ~~all I had~~ to do ~~was~~ *is* remember listening to the water and the peace it gave me. That ~~allowed~~ *memory allows* me to get my faith back on track and moving up again.

day on the mountain   *will ever*
That ~~event~~ will always remain vivid in my mind. Nothing ~~could~~ compare to the beautiful

Its
waterfall down the mountainside. ~~It's~~ beauty and ambiance will drive my faith for many years to

I found that day
come. But more importantly, the understanding about prayer will serve me my entire lifetime.

Essay 20: In 1,200 words or less, write a true, first-person story about an experience that changed you. It need not be highly dramatic or unusual, but it should demonstrate how faith in God has made a difference in your life.

It was a cold, wet, storming night in May. I was helping my dad, a photographer, with a wedding like I always did on Saturday. We were on our way to the reception. The street was dimly lit and the rain was pouring down so hard that we couldn't see three feet in front of our faces. All of a sudden, we drove right into a 6-foot deep ocean of water. I was horrified. I couldn't help but scream in fear. This was not supposed to happen tonight. We were suppose to make it safely to the reception in one piece. As the car continued to float, we prayed that it would make it across and we'd be safe, but we were not that fortunate. Water started flooding the floor of our hunter green Suburban. My dad decided to call 9-1-1, but instead we somehow called my mother. All she got to hear was "Daddy, I am scared there is water coming in" and then the phone disconnected. I knew that 911 would not be long before the whole car was underwater. As my mother sat back at our safe, dry house not knowing what to do and panicking, I was also packing; our car was now halfway underwater.

"Roll down your window," my father instructed me. I did as I was told. I was then told that once out of the car I was to get on top and wait for someone to come and get us. As we both swam out of the car, me first and them him, we turned around to get on top of the car, but it was no longer to be seen. Water had filled the entire car and it was now somewhere at the bottom of the huge lake we were now floating in. We started to swim for our lives. I was on my dad's back just like a koala climbs a tree.

The current was strong and our clothes were weighing us down. After swimming for what seemed like an eternity, probably no more than twenty-five feet, we reached solid land. I was crying so hard that I could have started my own flood. I knew that I was safe now but no matter what I wanted to cry. I needed to cry.

We began walking back to the main street to find some form of civilization. We flagged down a white car that was headed straight for the same terrifying experience that we had just gone through. I don't know how they saw us with all the rain pouring down, but they stopped.

"What's wrong?" they asked. We explained what happed to us. We warned them not to go any further down the road.

"Here, get in the car," they said. They drove us to a nearby coffee house. As we got out of the car we thanked them for their kindness. We then headed in to the coffee house.

The people at the coffee house were very nice to us. We first tried to call home to tell mom that we were all right, but all the phone lines were out of order. The people at the coffee shop offered me the dry clothes off their backs. As stubborn as I am I refused to take them. I was still crying. What was wrong with me? I was in a dry building with people who I had never met, and would never see again, offering me the very clothes that they were wearing. We were stayed at the coffee house for about three hours. After ten hot chocolates, and a ton of people being extremely nice to me, I finally stopped crying. I finally changed into some t-shirts and sweatshirts that the coffee house sold. I looked like the biggest dork to walk the face of the planet. I was wearing a long-sleeve t-shirt with a sweatshirt over it for a shirt and I was wearing numerous long sleeve shirts as pants by just sticking my legs in the arm holes and then tying them around my waist. We called home to let mom know that we were all right and then called a friend of the family to come get us. He was unable to come until the rain died down.

We got home safely that night. Our car was totaled, my father's camera equipment was ruined, and yet the film, which had been in his pocket while swimming could still be developed and the memories of the wedding we had photographed were miraculously saved.

I learned a lot that night. I learned not to take life for granted, and live your life to the fullest. You never know what tomorrow will bring. Without God's help, I could not be relating this story. God is always with us. If you have faith and believe in Him, He will help carry you through the toughest times in your life. He is like your Father. He provides you shelter, love, and helps you when you need it. I know that God was with my father and me that night.

Essay 20—Makeover: This was a good essay, but it needed a few minor changes.

It was a cold, wet, storming night in May. *(Saturday)* I was helping my dad, a photographer, with a wedding *(As always)* ~~like I always did on Saturday.~~ We were on our way to the reception. The street was dimly lit and the rain was pouring ~~down~~ so hard ~~that~~ *[Rain only pours down.]* we couldn't see three feet in front of ~~our faces.~~ *(us.)* All of a sudden, we drove right into a six-foot deep ocean of water. I ~~was~~ *(screamed,)* horrified. ~~I couldn't help but scream in fear.~~ This ~~was not~~ *(wasn't)* supposed to happen tonight. We were suppose ~~,~~ *(, not)* to make it safely to the reception ~~in one piece.~~ *(d)* As the car ~~continued~~ *(started)* to float, we prayed ~~that it would make it across and~~ *[Across what?]* we'd be safe, but we ~~were not~~ *(weren't)* that fortunate. Water started flooding the floor of our ~~hunter green~~ *[The color of the car is irrelevant here.]* Suburban. My dad ~~decided~~ *(tried)* to call 9-1-1, but ~~instead we~~ *(on his cell phone)* *(hit the wrong button and)* somehow called my mother. ~~All she got to hear was~~ *[At that moment, you couldn't know exactly what your mother heard.]* "Daddy, ~~I am~~ *(I'm)* scared ~~there is~~ *(, there's)* water coming in*(,")* *(I said, just before)* ~~and then~~ the phone disconnected. *[New paragraph.]*

At the rate the water was pouring in, the car would be underwater before EMS arrived. ~~I knew that 911 would not be long before the whole car was underwater. As my mother~~ *[You had no way of knowing what your mother was thinking.]* By this time, the car was halfway underwater and panic was ricocheting in all directions ~~sat back at our safe, dry house not knowing what to do and panicking, I was also packing;~~ within my mind. What must my mother be thinking right now? I wondered. ~~our car was now halfway underwater.~~

"Roll down your window," my father instructed me. I did as I was told. *(He told me to get out)* ~~I was then~~ *(and climb on top of the car to)* ~~told that once out of the car I was to get on top and~~ *(help)* wait for someone to ~~come and get~~ us.

I went through first and my dad followed.

As we ~~both~~ swam ~~out of the car, me first and them him~~, we turned ~~around to get on top of~~ *to look for* the car,

but it was ~~no longer to be seen. Water had filled the entire car and it was now~~ somewhere

and *which had originally been a low-lying road.*

at the bottom of the huge lake we were now floating in. We started to swim for our lives.

tired and clutched *cub.*

I was ~~on~~ my dad's back ~~just~~ like a koala ~~climbs a tree.~~

It felt as if we'd been swimming

The current was strong and our clothes were weighing us down. ~~After swimming for what~~

[Twenty-five feet is a distance, so it
should be compared to another distance, not to time.]

at least ten Olympic-sized pools, but was *when*

~~seemed like an eternity,~~ probably no more than twenty-five feet, we reached solid land. I was crying

Though *,*

so hard that I could have started my own flood. I knew ~~that~~ I was safe ~~now but no matter what~~ I

wanted to cry. I needed to cry.

who would venture out in this storm.

We began walking back to the main street to find some form of civilization. We flagged down a

we'd

white car that was headed straight for the same terrifying experience ~~that we had~~ just gone

through the downpour,

through. I don't know how they saw us ~~with all the rain pouring down,~~ but they stopped.

had happened

"What's wrong?" they asked. We explained what ~~happed~~ to us. We warned them not to go any

further down the road.

G

"Here, ~~g~~et in the car," they said. They drove us to a nearby coffee house. ~~As we got out of the car~~

W *and headed toward the lights.*

~~w~~e thanked them for their kindness. ~~We then headed in to the coffee house.~~

M

~~The people at the coffee house were very nice to us.~~ We ~~first~~ tried to call home to tell ~~m~~om

The people at the coffee house gave new meaning to the word hospitality.

~~that~~ we were all right, but all the phone lines were out of order. ~~The people at the coffee~~

They *I wasn't ready for their kindness and* *.*

~~shop~~ offered me the dry clothes off their backs. ~~As stubborn as I am I refused to take them.~~

safe *I'd*

I was still crying. What was wrong with me? I was in a dry building with people who ~~I had~~

probably *and they were*

never met, and would never see again, offering me the ~~very~~ clothes ~~that~~ they were

wearing. [New paragraph.]

We ~~were~~ stayed at the coffee house for about three hours. After ten hot chocolates, and

countless   [Ton refers to weight, not a number.]

~~a ton of~~ people being extremely nice to me, I finally stopped crying. I ~~finally~~ changed into

a dry t-shirt   *had for sale*   [Dork is slang. Use a vivid metaphor.]

~~some t-shirts~~ and sweatshirts that the coffee house ~~sold.~~ *I felt as conspicuous as a prickly pear* ~~I looked like the biggest dork to walk~~

cactus in the middle of an English rose garden.

~~the face of the planet. I was wearing a long-sleeve t-shirt with a sweatshirt over it for a shirt~~

          A couple of shirts were serving   *through*   *sleeves*

~~and I was wearing numerous long sleeve shirts~~ as pants by ~~just~~ sticking my legs ~~in~~ the ~~arm holes~~

          the shirt

and then tying ~~them~~ around my waist.

     [New paragraph.]
     When the phone lines were repaired, we   .   *We*

~~We~~ called home to let Mom know that we were all right ~~and then~~ called a friend of the family to

pick us up, but he

~~come get us.~~ He was unable to come until the rain died down.

                    and took inventory.

We got home safely that night/ Our car was totaled, my father's camera equipment was ruined,

          my father's   *he was*   ,

and yet the film, which had been in ~~his~~ pocket while swimming could still be developed and the

images   *we'd*

~~memories~~ of the wedding ~~we had~~ photographed were miraculously saved.

                                        to

I learned a lot that night. I learned not to take life for granted, and live ~~your~~ life to the fullest. You

                                   w   *n't*

never know what tomorrow will bring. Without God's help, I ¢ould ~~not~~ be relating this story. God

was and

is always with us. If you have faith and believe in Him, He will help carry you through the toughest

          our   *strength*   *we*

times in your life. He is ~~like your~~ Father. He provides ~~you~~ shelter, love, and ~~helps you~~ when ~~you~~

                    and will always watch over us.

need it. ~~I know that~~ God was with my father and me that night/

Essay 21: In 1,000 words or less, write about a person or an experience that has had an effect on your life.

The moment that we are born into this world of chaos and beauty, we face a journey that we

must travel. This journey is called life. It is up to each individual to determine the way in which he

or she will travel. Will you walk or will you run? Will you push yourself and encourage others, or will you dwell on the pain, losing hope and thus giving up? Then there are those who sit on the sidelines. They make little headway themselves, yet they criticize those who are trying. For these people, I think Bob Moward put it quite cleverly when he said, "You can't make footprints in the sands of time if you're sitting on your butt. And who wants to make buttprints in the sands of time?" Anne Frank put it another way: "The final forming of a person's character lies in their own hands." My father seemed to have a quiet, insightful understanding of the strength and heart we are called to put into our journeys. He embodied honesty, integrity, wisdom, and compassion in all areas of his life.

I sat in the metal folding chair, my entire body uncomfortable in its cold, hard surroundings, strangely symbolic of the feeling in my soul. I watched the string quartet, my mind pondering the emotions of the instrumentalists. What losses had they suffered? What were the pains of their hearts? They had not known my father well, yet, perhaps they had lost someone close to them. Then the music would flow from their hearts, just as the slow, mournful melody flowed from mine. I fought the tears, determined to be strong for my mother. Then I lost the battle. Tears poured down as my dad's friend walked down the aisle and placed the sign in front of the urn, leaning it against the wooden oak box. "Bubba's Place," it read. "No!" my soul cried out. "My father lives on! He lives in my, in my sister, in my mother." Yet it pulled me to reality. I would no longer be able to laugh at his jokes or to help him plant a garden. He would not be there to walk me down the aisle. And though I realize now that his spirit will always be with me, my flesh, the human aspect of my being, wanted him to be in the flesh with me. I made my way to the doors and then outside. I walked around the church, my eyes a sea of sorrow and pain, my chest a heaving earthquake of loss, and my voice quietly crying out, "Daddy." It was obvious that I had lost my father. Yet, more importantly, I have found strength, love, and integrity in myself. In this epiphany, I had just defeated the statement: "I lost my father." He lives in me, and in this, I have won the battle. I will continue to laugh at his jokes when I am reminded of them. I am also planting a garden of life with my father constantly guiding me. I can feel his touch, and he will be there, smiling, when I walk down the aisle.

As we race through the journey of life, we may become fatigued and sore, yet this exhaustion is the way in which we grow. Our muscles are ripped so that they may grow larger and stronger. Such is what happened to the muscles of my soul. Now I have not only the strength, but also the desire, to reach out and touch the lives of others. "Life's most persistent and urgent question is: What are you doing for others?" (-Martin Luther King, Jr.) I want to be able, at any point, to look at my life and have a never-ending answer to this question. I want to show the same compassion for others as my father did. Such compassion and good will for others brings joy to my heart. As Lilian Gichler Watson said, "Happiness is not in having or being; it is in doing."

I also seek to be honest, just as my father was. I have an honest and true love for God and his children. This is the fuel that keeps me going. I realize the best way to live a life is with integrity. I have learned this through my father's guidance. With his inspiration, I can glorify God and reach others.

The sum of my thoughts and actions and the connections therein can be described as wisdom. I seek wisdom in a longing for right actions and right thought and for one to be the same as the other. I want to take action. I do not want to be hypocritical, but instead I want to see that path which God has chosen for me. My thoughts should be of how to live this path which God has chosen for me. My thoughts should be of how to live this path, this journey, to the fullest. I seek knowledge to help me in this trek, a knowledge that comes from God and which gently guides me. Certainly, I will make mistakes, but I pray I will have the strength and wisdom to learn and laugh, and to move one. "They are the strong who can laugh at themselves and cry for others." (-Kobi Yamada)

Some may say that I lost my father, or that John Allen Smith passed away. And though I miss him, I see something different. He lives on not only in me, but in ways which permeate the lives of all whom he touched—ways that cannot always be fully explained. He has helped us to realize the strength and heart we must put into our individual journeys as well as the journey that we all make together. "Believe in yourself! Have faith in your abilities. Remind yourself that God is with you and nothing can defeat you." -Norman Vincent Peale

Essay 21—Makeover: This is an excellent essay and a touching tribute to this student's father, but the essay contains too many quotations. In this type of essay, even one quote is too much. Though it's great to be well-read, the purpose of an essay is to allow college admission and scholarship committee members to get to know your opinions, not others'. We've made a few changes and removed all the quotes. At 785 words, the result is a stronger, tighter view into the student's personality and opinions.

The moment that ~~we are~~ *we're* born into this world of chaos and beauty, we face a journey that we must travel. This journey is called life. ~~It is~~ *It's* up to each individual to determine the way in which he or she will travel. Will you walk or will you run? Will you push yourself and encourage others, or ~~will you~~ dwell on the pain, losing hope and ~~thus~~ giving up? Then there are those who sit on the sidelines. They make little headway themselves, yet they criticize those ~~who are~~ *who're* trying. ~~For these people, I think Bob Moward put it quite cleverly when he said, "You can't make footprints in the sands of time if you're sitting on your butt. And who wants to make buttprints in the sands of time?" Anne Frank put it another way: "The final forming of a person's character lies in their own hands."~~ My father ~~seemed to have~~ *had* a quiet, insightful understanding of the strength and heart ~~we are~~ *we're* called to put into our journeys. He embodied honesty, integrity, wisdom, and compassion in all areas of his life.

I sat in the metal folding chair, my entire body uncomfortable in ~~its~~ *these* cold, hard surroundings, strangely symbolic of the feeling in my soul. I watched the string quartet, ~~my mind~~ pondering the emotions of the instrumentalists. What losses had they suffered? What were the pains of their hearts? They ~~had not~~ *hadn't* known my father well, yet, perhaps ~~they had~~ *they'd* lost someone close to them. Then the music would flow from their hearts, just as the slow, mournful melody flowed from mine. I fought the tears, determined to be strong for my mother. ~~Then~~ I lost the battle. Tears poured down as my dad's friend walked down the aisle and placed ~~the~~ *a* sign in front of the urn, leaning it against the wooden oak box. "Bubba's Place," it read. "No!" my soul cried out. "My father lives on! He lives

e — *that sign* — *wouldn't*
in my, in my sister, in my mother." Yet it pulled me to reality. I ~~would no longer~~ be able to laugh at

my father's — *wouldn't*
~~his~~ jokes or to help him plant a garden. He ~~would not~~ be there to walk me down the aisle. ~~And~~

T
~~t~~hough ~~I realize now that~~ his spirit will always be with me, my flesh, the human aspect of my being,

wanted him to be in the flesh with me. [New paragraph.]

I made my way to the doors and then outside. I walked around the church, my eyes a sea of

sorrow and pain, my chest a heaving earthquake of loss, and my voice quietly crying out, "Daddy."

I'd
It was obvious that ~~I had~~ lost my father. Yet, more importantly, I ~~have~~ found strength, love, and

having
integrity in myself. In this epiphany, I ~~had just~~ defeated the statement: "I lost my father." He lives in

I've — *I'll* — *I'm*
me, and in this, ~~I have~~ won the battle. ~~I will~~ continue to laugh at his jokes when ~~I am~~ reminded of

I'm
them. ~~I am~~ also planting a garden ~~of life~~ with my father constantly guiding me. I can feel his touch,

he'll
and ~~he will~~ be there, smiling, when I walk down the aisle.

through
As we race through the journey of life, we may become fatigued and sore, yet this exhaustion ~~is~~

That's
~~the way in which~~ we grow. Our muscles are ripped so that they may grow larger and stronger.
~~Such is~~ what happened to the muscles of my soul. Now I have ~~not only~~ the strength, but also the

not only
desire to reach out and touch the lives of others. ~~"Life's most persistent and urgent question is:~~

~~What are you doing for others?" (Martin Luther King, Jr.)~~ I want to be able, at any point, to look at

know I've helped others.
my life and ~~have a never-ending answer to this question.~~ I want to show the same compassion for

that — *Feeling* — *toward*
others ~~as~~ my father did. ~~Such~~ compassion and good will ~~for~~ others brings joy to my heart.

~~As Lilian Gichler Watson said, "Happiness is not in having or being; it is in doing."~~

H
I also seek to be honest, just as my father was. I have an honest and true love for God and ~~his~~

T
children. This is the fuel that keeps me going. ~~I realize~~ the best way to live a life is with integrity.

I've
~~I have~~ learned this through my father's guidance. With his inspiration, I can glorify God and reach

others.

The sum of my thoughts and actions ~~and the connections therein~~ can be described as wisdom. I
seek wisdom ~~in a longing for~~ _through_ right actions and right thought and for one to be the same as the
other. I want to take action. I ~~do not~~ _don't_ want to be hypocritical_:_ ~~but~~ _I_ instead I want to see ~~that~~ _the_ path
~~which~~ _that_ God has chosen for me. My thoughts should be of how to live this path, this journey, to the
fullest. I seek knowledge to help me in this trek, a knowledge that comes from God and ~~which~~
gently guides me. ~~Certainly, I will~~ _I'll certainly_ make mistakes, but I pray ~~I will~~ _I'll_ have the strength and wisdom to
learn and laugh, and to move one. ~~"They are the strong who can laugh at themselves and cry for~~
~~others." (-Kobi Yamada)~~

Some may say that I lost my father, or that John Allen Smith passed away. And though I miss him, I
see something different. He lives on not only in me, but in ways which permeate the lives of all _also_
~~whom~~ he touched—ways that ~~cannot~~ _can't_ always be fully explained. ~~He has~~ _He's_ helped us to realize the
strength and heart we must put into our individual journeys as well as the journey that we all make
together. ~~"Believe in yourself! Have faith in your abilities. Remind yourself that God is with you and~~
~~nothing can defeat you."-Norman Vincent Peale~~

Essay 22: Write a brief essay on an experience that made a difference in your life.

National Affairs are not what an average high school student is concerned with. Out of the
average I found a program I participates in this last year a melting pot of other students like me
who felt that issues such as a balanced budget, the environment, affirmative action, the arts, and
criminal punishment were important. For me the the YMCA's Youth and Government Program for
me, exposed many areas that I wouldn't have considered otherwise as critical to our nation and the
world. I was given the opportunity to participate in well-rounded controlled debate, leadership,
sportsmanship, faith, and knowledge with students from all over the United States. The conference
wasn't held by an authoritive adult but by the participating students. To add to the experience, the
conference was held in Black Mountain, North Carolina, among the Blue Ridge Mountains. The

serenity and peacefulness of the mountains helped participants to settle in and be comfortable away from home so they could concentrate on their proposals. Each proposal is passed on to a different committee but by the end of the assembly, it didn't matter if one's proposal hadn't passed one was too busy supporting another proposal that had. The Blue Ridge experience allowed me to become familiar with various backgrounds, upbringings, and cultures from all over the nation. It was then that I could truly appreciate the differences and similarities between us. Meeting and becoming friends with someone that lives 2000 miles away and being able to share everything from political views to mutual interests was a true testament to the breaking of boundaries. One of those boundaries was competitiveness. The author of each proposal so believed in his idea that he created some heated debate. Supporters and opponents were equally as involved in debate along with the authors as well to prompt fresh and intelligent debate. That kind of competition is what made the conference so enriching and stimulating. One of the experiences I enjoyed most was climbing the Blue Ridge Mountain. The mountain stood at 3000 feet and I thought climbing it would be a walk in the park. I was wrong. Only an eighth of the way up I became weak and was about to give up. I slowed to the end of the pack where I met a student from Tennessee who would not let me quit. He pushed me to the top of the world. Youth and Government among other things has taught me to be more aggressive in my beliefs, and has given me a greater ability to listen to others. I believe the greatest gift anyone can have the gift of an open ear. Listening can create new insight for one, a view which they might have never known. Since my national affairs experience, as a person I have become much more passionate about my work and about people. It would be impossible to forget about Blue Ridge not only because I plan to be back in the coming year but rather all the skills and maturity that I continue to practice everyday and that I hope to pass on.

Essay 22—Makeover: This essay underwent major changes. We suggested the student open the essay with a more personal account of the climb. Though the sentence: "I feel the sharp, crisp coldness in my lungs" was vivid, it could have gone a step further: "The sharp, crisp coldness pierces my lungs like shards of glass."

[Delete—used at end of paragraph.]

~~What am I doing here?~~ I ~~not only~~ see each breath I take as it becomes a cloud of mist in front of me. ~~but I can~~ feel the sharp, crisp coldness in my lungs. It's still dark. I'm sleepy. What am I doing here?

Now I understand why this "walk" is mandatory. No one in their right mind would volunteer. At least I'm not the only person who seems to be sleepwalking. It's five-thirty in the morning. I should be in bed.

Yesterday afternoon this mountain didn't look as high. In fact, I vaguely remember thinking it was going to be a walk in the park. I just heard someone say it's 3,000 feet high. I think they must have meant 30,000 feet high!

At least I'm not the only person ~~whose~~ *who's* making grunting noises. The only thing you can hear is ~~us~~ *our* breathing, the rocks that slide when our feet hit the ground, and the leaves rustling from the faint air movement. There are no bird noises to be heard. ~~They~~ *Birds* have enough sense to wait for the sun to rise before leaving their nests. Oh, to be a bird at this ~~very~~ moment.

When I started this climb, I was near the front of the group. I've slowed down. Now I'm in the middle half. At this rate, I'll probably be the last person to reach the top, but I will make it. That's why I'm here.

National Affairs ~~are not~~ *isn't* what ~~an~~ *the* average high school student ~~is~~ *might be* concerned with, *yet it's one of* ~~Out of the~~ *my consuming interests.* ~~average I found a program I participates in~~ *This* ~~this~~ *Tp*, *I participated in a program where I found* last year ~~a melting pot of~~ other students ~~like me~~ *also* who felt that issues such as a balanced budget, the environment, affirmative action, the arts, and criminal punishment were important. ~~For me the~~ *The* the YMCA's Youth and Government Program ~~for~~ ~~me,~~ *me to some* exposed ~~many~~ areas that I ~~wouldn't~~ *might not* have considered ~~otherwise~~ *otherwise* as critical to our nation and the world.

[Moved from the original first paragraph.]

The conference wasn't held by an authoritative adult but by us, the participating students. I ~~was given the opportunity to participate~~ *joined* in well-rounded controlled debate, leadership, *s learned about*

and   *shared*
sportsmanship, faith, and knowledge with students from all over the United States.

[Moved to beginning of paragraph.]
[~~The conferencewasn't held by an authoritive adult but by the participating students.~~] To add to

the experience, the conference was held in Black Mountain, North Carolina, among the Blue Ridge

Mountains. ~~The serenity and peacefulness of the mountains helped participants to settle in and be~~

~~comfortable away from home so they could concentrate on their proposals. Each proposal is~~

~~passed on to a different committee but by the end of the assembly, it didn't matter if one's proposal~~

~~hadn't passed one was too busy supporting another proposal that had.~~

exposed
The Blue Ridge experience allowed me to ~~become familiar with various backgrounds,~~

and ideas
~~upbringings, and~~ cultures from all over the nation. It was then that I could truly appreciate the

[Moved to end of this paragraph.]
differences and similarities between us. [~~Meeting and becoming friends with someone that lives~~

It
~~2000 miles away and being able to share everything from political views to mutual interests~~] was a

true testament to the breaking of boundaries to meet and become friends with students who live

2000 miles away and find out that we share everything from political views to mutual interests.

Students submitted   s   on a variety of
One of those boundaries was competitiveness. ~~The author of each proposal so believed in his~~
issues. Each proposal was passed to a different committee. By the end of assembly, it didn't
~~idea that he created some heated debate. Supporters and opponents were equally as involved in~~
matter if one's own proposal hadn't been voted in because each of us was too busy supporting
~~debate along with the authors as well to prompt fresh and intelligent debate. That kind of~~
another proposal which had passed. The author of each proposal so believed in his or her idea
~~competition is what made the conference so enriching and stimulating. One of the experiences I~~
that he or she created some heated debate. Supporters and opponents were equally
~~enjoyed most was climbing the Blue Ridge Mountain. The mountain stood at 3000 feet and I~~
involved in debate with the author, prompting fresh and intelligent discussion. That kind of
~~thought climbing it would be a walk in the park. I was wrong. Only an eighth of the way up I~~
competition is what made the conference so enriching and stimulating.
~~became weak and was about to give up. I slowed to the end of the pack where I met a student from~~

~~Tennessee who would not let me quit. He pushed me to the top of the world.~~

The   Program   have the courage of my convictions,   assertive
Youth and Government ~~among other things~~ has taught me to be more ~~aggressive~~ in my beliefs,
to be better able   T   give or receive is
and ~~has given me a greater ability~~ to listen to others. ~~I believe~~ the greatest gift anyone can ~~have the~~

and mind.   *about*   *one*   *never*

gift of an open ear/ Listening can create new insight ~~for one,~~ a view ~~which they~~ might have

considered.

~~never known.~~

  brief encounter with   *,*   *I've*   *and compassionate*

Since my national affairs ~~experience, as a person I have~~ become much more passionate about my

[Sentence added in the final draft.]

work and about people. *The arduous task of climbing the mountain was meant to symbolize my*

                                I'll never

doing whatever it takes to reach my current and future goals. ~~It would be impossible to~~ forget

my   *experience, and*   *hope*   *return. Next year I'll come with*

~~about~~ Blue Ridge ~~not only because~~ I plan to ~~be back in the coming year but rather all the~~ skills and

       I learned here at the Youth and Government Proram, skills I use every day

maturity ~~that I continue to practice everyday~~ and ~~that I~~ hope to pass on.

Essay 23: Write a brief essay about an event that affected your life.

For the past six years I have attended the Laredo Trail Ride. My dad, stepmom, and friends of ours also attend. It's always been fun and everybody treats each other like family.

Since I was thirteen, the past three years I have competed for Queen. There has never been very many girls who compete so usually you get it the first year. When I wasn't chosen queen I was very upset and didn't understand why. I thought maybe it was because there were four other girls running for queen with me. My dad and friends all felt sorry for me. I finally got over it and the following year I ran again. Now I'm sixteen and this past year I received runner up and I was very excited and proud of myself that I didn't give up.

Essay 23—Makeover: With some major changes, this essay became stronger.

                     I've participated in

For the past six years ~~I have attended~~ the San Antonio Trail Ride. My dad, stepmom, and friends

of ours also attend. It's always been fun and everybody treats each other like family.

           For   *, from the age of thirteen, I've*   *of the Trail Ride.*

~~Since I was thirteen,~~ the past three years ~~I have~~ competed for Queen/ ~~There has never been very~~

~~many girls who compete so usually you get it the first year. When I wasn't chosen queen I was very~~

~~upset and didn't understand why. I thought maybe it was because there were four other girls~~
Each time I wasn't chosen, I buried my disappointment and decided to keep trying.
~~running for queen with me. My dad and friends all felt sorry for me. I finally got over it and the~~
^
                               This year, at age sixteen,   *so*
~~following year I ran again. Now I'm sixteen and this past year~~ I received runner up and I was ~~very~~
                                       ^
        because
excited and proud of myself ~~that~~ I didn't give up.
                           ^

Essay 24: Share an experience that had an effect on your life. Your essay should be no longer than one double-spaced page.

It was December 20, 1989. All I could hear was the humming of the tires on the cold asphalt road. My mom and I were on the highway making the move from Dallas to San Antonio. I wasn't sure how fast we were traveling because at eight years old, I couldn't see the dash on the Camaro, much less over the dash. The radio wasn't on due to the anxiety inside the car. Though the move was necessary because of my dad's job transfer, all of my friends in Dallas would miss me as much as I'd miss them. The trip seemed to last forever. All I could think about was all of the times I'd spent with my friends at school, on the playground, chasing each other playing tag, and all the birthday parties we'd shared. I was moving almost 300 miles away from my friends I'd made since pre-school. The 300 miles might as well be 3,000 or 300,000 because to my eight-year old mind I may as well have moved to the moon. All the way from Dallas to our new house in San Antonio, I kept asking my mom over and over, "Are we there yet?" Like most kids I never thought about what my new house might look like.

Finally after four hours and thirty minutes in the car we arrived in the big city of San Antonio, Texas. I could almost feel the vibes of our new house. "We must be close," I thought. "Let's go take a look inside," my mom said as the Camaro came to a stop in our driveway. Getting out of the car was always difficult because the door was probably three times heavier than I was. I grabbed the chrome door handle and used my feet to forcefully push the door outward. As one of my feet hit the pavement it felt great to be on sturdy, safe, unmoving ground. Then it hit me, I was going to have to build a strong friendship with someone who lived on my street or on the street behind me. Through my thoughts I could hear my mom's tennis shoes walking across the hollow garage. It was eerie how her steps seemed to echo forever. The big white door swung open and my mom stepped through the enormous doorway. I followed, sprinting quickly to keep my little feet and legs up with her longer strides. The house had a familiar smell of Windex and rug shampoo.

A lump formed in my throat as loneliness and isolation seized my tender little heart in an icy death grip. Somehow I'd have to build a new friendship and hope it lasted for a long time. I had so many memories of the Dallas house that it was going to be difficult to leave it behind. From inside my room at the old house, I could glance out the window and see a lake just across the street and behind someone's house. The distance between San Antonio and Dallas was too great to continue my childhood friendships.

When it was time for me to go to my first day of first grade I was ready to make some new friends. I met my neighbor at the bus stop. He let me sit with him on the bus and that's how we started getting to know each other better. During the next few months in San Antonio I started new friendships that are still continuing and building stronger to this day.

I envision my transition from high school to college to be as successful as my move from Dallas to San Antonio was ten years ago. In college and beyond, I will continue to grow and learn for the rest of my life.

Essay 24—Makeover: This was a good essay, but the sentences weren't smooth enough. The final draft fits on one single-spaced page.

[Moved from second sentence.]
All I could hear was the humming of the tires on the cold asphalt road. It was

December 29, 1989, and I was eight years old.
~~It was December 20, 1989.~~ My mom and I were on the highway making the move from Dallas to
^
San Antonio. ~~I wasn't sure how fast we were traveling because at eight years old, I couldn't see the~~

~~dash on the Camaro, much less over the dash. The radio wasn't on due to the anxiety inside the car.~~
`[Moved to beginning`
`of paragraph.]`
~~All I could hear was the humming of the tires on the cold asphalt road.~~ Though the move was

necessary because of my dad's job transfer, all of my friends in Dallas would miss me as much as I'd

miss them. ~~The trip seemed to last forever.~~ All I could think about was all of the times I'd spent with

my friends at school, on the playground, ~~chasing each other~~ playing tag, and all the birthday parties

we'd shared. I was moving almost 300 miles away from ~~my~~ friends I'd _had_ ~~made~~ since _preschool_ ~~pre-school~~. The
                                                                            ^   ^

300 miles might as well _have been_ ~~be~~ 3,000 or 300,000 _;_ ~~because to my eight-year-old mind~~ I may as well have
                             ^   ^
                  The trip seemed to last forever.
moved to the moon. All the way from Dallas to our new house in San Antonio, I kept asking my
          ^

                                    `[Don't generalize. You don't know what most kids would think.]`
mom over and over, "Are we there yet?" ~~Like most kids~~ I never thought about what my new house

might look like.

          _,_
    Finally after four hours and thirty minutes in the car _,_ we arrived in the big city of San Antonio,
          ^   ^

Texas. I could almost feel the vibes of our new house. "We must be close," I thought. `[New paragraph.]`

    "Let's go take a look inside," my mom said as the Camaro came to a stop in our driveway.

~~Getting out of the car was always difficult because the door was probably three times heavier~~

~~than I was.~~ `[New paragraph.]`

    I grabbed the chrome door handle and used my feet to forcefully push the door outward.
`[Delete-sounds as if`
`your foot fell off.]`   _,_
~~As one of my feet hit the pavement~~ It felt great to be on sturdy, safe, unmoving ground. ~~Then it hit~~
                                        ^

~~me, I was going to have to build a strong friendship with someone who lived on my street or on~~
                                             the squeak of   _as she ed through_
~~the street behind me. Through my thoughts~~ I could hear my mom's tennis shoes walking ~~across~~
^   ^   ^
        empty
the ~~hollow~~ garage. It was eerie how her steps seemed to echo forever. The big white door swung
        ^

open and my mom stepped through the enormous doorway. I followed, sprinting quickly to
catch
~~keep my little feet and legs~~ up with her longer strides. The house was empty but there was a
^
              _;_
familiar smell a mixture of Windex, rug shampoo, and paint.
          ^

    As I walked to my room, a   _. It hit me._
    A lump formed in my throat as loneliness and isolation seized my tender little heart ~~in an icy~~
    ^   ^ ^

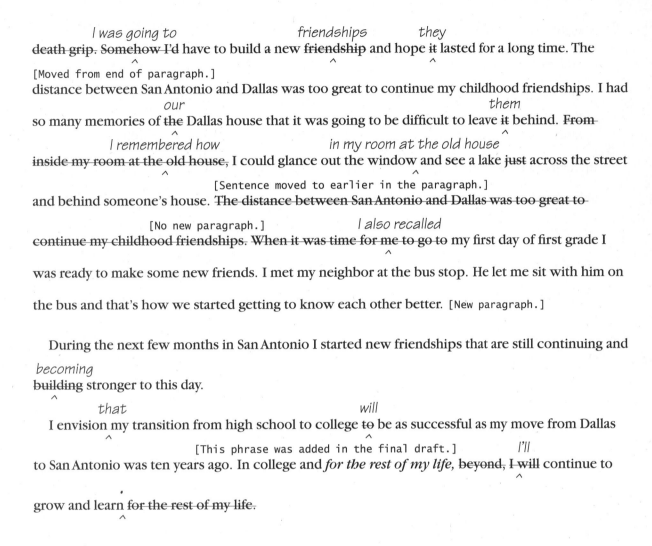

death grip. Somehow I'd have to build a new friendship and hope it lasted for a long time. The
I was going to *friendships* *they*
[Moved from end of paragraph.]
distance between San Antonio and Dallas was too great to continue my childhood friendships. I had
so many memories of the Dallas house that it was going to be difficult to leave it behind. From
our *them*
inside my room at the old house, I could glance out the window and see a lake just across the street
I remembered how *in my room at the old house*
[Sentence moved to earlier in the paragraph.]
and behind someone's house. The distance between San Antonio and Dallas was too great to
[No new paragraph.] *I also recalled*
continue my childhood friendships. When it was time for me to go to my first day of first grade I

was ready to make some new friends. I met my neighbor at the bus stop. He let me sit with him on

the bus and that's how we started getting to know each other better. [New paragraph.]

During the next few months in San Antonio I started new friendships that are still continuing and
becoming
building stronger to this day.
that *will*
I envision my transition from high school to college to be as successful as my move from Dallas
[This phrase was added in the final draft.] *I'll*
to San Antonio was ten years ago. In college and *for the rest of my life,* beyond, I will continue to

grow and learn for the rest of my life.

Essay 25: Describe and evaluate one experience that significantly influenced your academic interests. The experience might be a high school course, a job, a relationship, or an extracurricular activity. Be sure to explain how this experience led to the goals you now have set for yourself and why you think the academic program for which you are applying will help you reach those goals.

Fourteen freshmen at the International School of the Americas sat in various positions at

individual computers in a large old classroom who's walls were painted robin's egg blue, The Blue

Room. Our project, called The Olympic Project, which we had to accept, involved gathering as

much diversified information about our chosen city within a country, Vienna, Austria, as we could in

order to convince the Olympic Committee to chose it for the next Olympic Games. Some students

had to research the infrastructure of our country; others had to address the facilities already available as well as those facilities that would need to be added to the various sites. Still others had to address the cost of hosting these games as well as the aftereffect of the games on our chosen country. The computers before us held all the answers if only we could get them to talk to us.

Since I was five years old I had noticed a talent that I seemed to have regarding the understanding of how to maneuver throughout computers. As I progressed through school I was able to sit in front of a computer program that I knew nothing about and within 30 minutes be able to understand how it worked and to use it in depth. However, I never really used this ability for a specific purpose. Then in that Blue Room for the first time I could connect my talent and genuine interest in computers with our team's need to produce a composite of information for a presentation. My knowledge of computers and our teamwork proved very productive. Throughout the duration of working on our project we were successful at finding all of our information we needed about our country. We were able to convince but were not as successful as another group, which presented after we did. The other country won because their terrain and climate were proper conditions needed for the Olympic games. As a result of the Olympic Project, all of the individuals in my group learned in depth knowledge about our country. All of the other groups would present in front of the whole freshman class so that all students would learn about each other countries. It was a huge success for everyone and we all had a great time dressing up as people would dress within our country we were presenting.

From that Olympic Project in the Blue Room evolved my goal, which is to learn to appreciate and welcome the challenge of learning even more about the applications of the computer in a productive field such as computer science. The University of Texas School of Natural Sciences is nationally recognized as a leader in the field of computer science and its applications in many fields closely related to computers. I am certain this program would indeed help me to achieve my goals.

Essay 25—Makeover

Fourteen freshmen at the International School of the Americas sat in various positions at individual computers in a large old classroom ~~who's~~ *with* walls ~~were~~ *that* painted robin's egg blue, ~~The Blue~~ *known as t* he Blue

[No reason to admit you were forced.]

Room. Our project, called The Olympic Project, ~~which we had to accept,~~ involved gathering as much ~~diversified~~ information ~~about our chosen city within a country,~~ *on* Vienna, Austria, as we could in order to convince the Olympic Committee to ~~chose~~ *choose* it for the next Olympic Games. Some students ~~had to~~ research *ed* the infrastructure of our country; others ~~had to~~ address *ed* the facilities already available as well as those facilities that would need to be ~~added to the various sites.~~ *built.* Still others ~~had to~~ address *ed* the cost of hosting these games as well as the aftereffect *s* of the games on ~~our chosen country.~~ *the city* The computers before us held all the answers if only we could get them to talk to us.

~~Since I was five years old I had~~ *From the age of five, I'd* ~~noticed a talent that I seemed to have regarding the~~ *an innate* understanding of how to ~~maneuver throughout~~ *operate* computers. As I progressed through school I was able to ~~sit in front of a~~ *understand, within thirty minutes,* computer program that ~~I knew~~ *I'd known* nothing about ~~and within 30 minutes be able to understand how it worked and to use it in depth.~~ However, I never really used this ability for a specific purpose. ~~Then in that Blue Room~~ *Now,* for the first time I could connect my talent and genuine interest in computers with our team's need to produce a composite of information for a presentation. [New paragraph.]

My knowledge of computers and our teamwork proved ~~very~~ productive. ~~Throughout the duration of working on our project~~ *W* e were successful ~~at~~ *in* finding all of ~~our~~ *the* information we needed ~~about our country.~~ We were able to convince the committee, but ~~were~~ not as successful *ly* as another group, which presented after we did. The other country won because ~~their~~ *its* terrain and climate ~~were proper~~ *offered the* conditions needed for the Olympic games. [New paragraph.]

As a result of the Olympic Project *,* all of the individuals in my group learned ~~in~~ *in-*depth knowledge
about ~~our country/~~ *the* ~~All of the other~~ *we represented. Each* groups ~~would present in front of~~ *presented its project to* the ~~whole~~ freshman class so
that all ~~students would learn~~ *we learned* about ~~each~~ other countries. It was a huge success for everyone and
we ~~all~~ had a great time dressing up as ~~people would dress within~~ *citizens of* our country ~~we were presenting~~*.*

From that Olympic Project in the Blue Room evolved my goal, which is to learn to appreciate and

welcome the challenge of learning even more about ~~the applications of the computer in a~~

~~productive field such as~~ computer science. ~~The University of Texas School of Natural Sciences is~~
[Delete—the university knows this, and it sounds as if
you're trying to flatter them.]
~~nationally recognized as a leader in the field of computer science and its applications in many fields~~
~~closely related to computers.~~ ~~I am~~ *I'm* certain ~~this~~ *your computer science* program would ~~indeed~~ help me to achieve my goals.

Essay 26: Describe and evaluate one experience that significantly influenced your academic interests. The experience might be a high school course, a job, a relationship, or an extracurricular activity. Be sure to explain how this experience led to the goals you now have set for yourself and why you think the academic program for which you are applying will help you reach those goals.

It was my fourth and final day of rotation in the labor and delivery room at Methodist Hospital.

Over the past four days, I hadn't seen anything that I was overly excited about. I was disappointed

and having second thoughts about signing up for this clinical rotation class. I was twenty miles

from school, and hour before anyone else even had to be at school.

As I stood at the nurse's desk, I stared at the dry erase board, and memorized the patients names,

doctors, and how many children they had previously, and how dilated they were. I watched the

medical students rush in the rooms, and heard screams of pain, right before the soundproof door

was shut, once again slamming any possibility of witnessing the miracle of life. As I stood there, I

mentioned to the nurses that this is where I had been born sixteen years before and that I was

delivered by Dr. Thompson. Surprised, the nurse told me to look to my left and there in the flesh,

was the man, who had brought me into the world.

Sharon, one of the nurses, asked what school I went to and what I wanted to do in life. She told me most high school students don't get to see deliveries because the staff doesn't think they are interested or mature enough. She said she saw something different in me and she then promised to get me into see at least one delivery before my rotation was over.

At last, the opportunity arrived. Everything was frantic, I felt so lost. The nurse's had already gone to the operating room, and last minute, it was okayed by the parents that I could witness their personal moment. I was verbally directed to where the operating room was and encouraged to run to get there. I found it with no problems. I stood on my toes in order to see in the little window on the door. Even with my limited medical background. I knew I couldn't just barge into the small cramped room with no protection on, for mine and the patients sake. I knew I had to get someone's attention, because I knew it had already begun. The nurse saw me and peeked her head outside the door and pointed me in the direction to where the gown was and face mask. I sprinted over there and looked at the rows of boxes with all this fancy protective items. I grabbed a jumpsuit, a size too big, a mouth cover that had a huge clear plastic part that protected my eyes and hesitantly grabbed booties to cover my white Nike shoes. I was so afraid I didn't have on the correct things and I wouldn't be allowed to see what I had been wanting to see so desperately. I slowly pushed open the doors to huge amount of noise. Automatically I looked at the mother who had the father right by her head. Surprisingly she was awake and didn't seem to be in too much pain. Right under her chest she had a huge screen made of a sheet to block her sight of where three doctors were working. I then focused on her lower abdominal, and noticed that they had just made a slit through the top layer of skin, but it wasn't bleeding. Then the nurse had just brought in the heated baby bed, and gently guided me closer hoping that I could see better. I was right there with the doctors, who were having surprisingly light hearted conversations about the Boston Celtics. They made another slit with the scapal, this time deeper. I couldn't believe how small the incision was, length wise. I kept thinking how is a human being going to fit through that . It started bleeding perfusely, one nurse opened a package of towels, and begun handing them to the doctor, which he would stick in to her abdominal cavity. On the final slit, everything opened up I expected to her the baby crying, but I couldn't. They stuck their hands into this woman and made another incision. That was the most incredible part, all this amniotic fluid rushed out making it clear to be seen a little head full of hair. One doctor reached in and pulled on the head even the head was out and the neck was even with the incision, the baby wasn't making a sound. I was scared and had chills all up and down. I had no idea what was going on around me. They pulled a little more and got him completely out. Then the sound I had been praying for, the soft endearing cry of the child who had just entered the world delivered by cesarean section. At that moment, getting up early for so long for my clinical rotation class finally had rewarded me.

The first-hand experience of the miracles and hardships in the medical field convinced me this it where my life's path would lead me. My immediate goals include attending a well-rounded, well-respected university of choice. I want to remain actively involved in leadership positions and organizations both on and off campus. Along with continuing my community service. After graduating with a bachelor's degree, I plan to continue my education and obtain advanced degrees to broaden my opportunities.

Since that day in the delivery room, I have taken every opportunity to acquire more information about this field. This occupation will require an unbelievable amount of my time, energy, discipline, compromise, and above all devotion, but I know I am up to the challenge.

I always try to be and do the best I can in whatever I do, and this includes the field of study I choose. I want to leave no stones unturned along my journey toward the top of my profession and through my life.

Essay 26—Makeover: This essay really started in the middle of the fourth paragraph. The student rewrote the essay starting from that point. This is the result, with minor corrections.

I sprinted ~~over there and looked at~~ *to* the rows of boxes ~~with all this fancy protective items.~~ I

grabbed a jumpsuit, a size too big, a mouth cover that had a huge clear plastic part that protected

my eyes and ~~hesitantly grabbed~~ booties to cover my white Nike ~~shoes.~~ *s.* I was ~~so~~ afraid I didn't have

desperately hoped
on the correct things and ~~I~~ wouldn't be allowed to see what I ~~had been wanting~~ to see ~~so~~

hesitantly
~~desperately.~~ I slowly pushed ~~open~~ the doors ~~to huge amount of noise. Automatically I looked at the~~
seemed to be talking.   *The mother*   *surprisingly*
~~mother who had the father right by her head. Surprisingly~~ she was awake and didn't seem to be in

A sheet stretched across her at chest level, blocking her view of everything going
too much pain. ~~Right under her chest she had a huge screen made of a sheet to block her sight of~~
on at the foot of the table. Nothing blocked my view. [New paragraph.]
~~where three doctors were working. I then focused on her lower abdominal, and noticed that they~~
The doctor   *along her lower abdomen*   *A*   *wheeled*
~~had just~~ made a slit through the top layer of skin, but it wasn't bleeding. ~~Then the nurse had just~~
                a   *pushed*   *to the table.*   *Now*
~~brought~~ in the heated baby bed, and gently ~~guided~~ me closer ~~hoping that I could see better.~~ I was
at the doctor's elbow. The   *a*   *-*
~~right there with the~~ doctors ~~who~~ were having ~~surprisingly~~ light hearted conversations about the
                Another   *was made,*
Boston Celtics. ~~They made another~~ slit ~~with the scapal,~~ this time deeper. I couldn't believe how
                            How was   *, even a tiny one,*   *?*
small the incision ~~was~~ ~~length wise. I kept thinking how is~~ a human being going to fit through that
Now the incision was   profusely. A   *handed*
~~It started~~ bleeding ~~perfusely,~~ one nurse opened a package of towels, and ~~begun handing~~
                    to place in the patient's   *As he made the next*
them to the doctor, ~~which he would stick in to her~~ abdominal cavity. ~~On the final~~ slit, everything
        . I held my breath, expecting to hear a baby's cry, but I heard nothing. The doctor
opened up ~~I expected to her the baby crying, but I couldn't. They stuck their hands into this~~
stuck his hand into the woman's abdomen and made another cut.   *The*
~~woman and made another incision. That was the most incredible part, all this~~ amniotic
            . I could see
fluid rushed out ~~making it clear to be seen~~ a little head full of hair. One doctor reached
gently, yet firmly,   *. Then*   *, but*
in and pulled on the head ~~even~~ the head was out ~~and the neck was even with the incision,~~ the

Chills ran up and down my body. *didn't have an*

baby wasn't making a sound. ~~I was scared and had chills all up and down.~~ I had ~~no~~ idea of what

, except that everyone was moving, talking, and doing their job.

was going on ~~around me.~~

The doctor *the baby was* *The only* *could hear, the one I'd been praying*

~~They~~ pulled a little more and ~~got him completely~~ out. ~~Then the~~ sound I ~~had been~~

to hear, was *,*

~~praying for,~~ the soft endearing cry of the child who had just entered the world delivered by

C

⊄esarean section. ~~At that moment, getting up early for so long for my clinical~~ rotation ~~class finally~~

~~had rewarded me.~~

[Added in final draft.]
At that moment, being twenty miles away from school, an hour before anyone else even had

to be at school, seemed inconsequential. The clinical rotation class had presented me with a

memory I'll cherish, even on days or nights that seem endless.

This *that is*

~~The~~ first-hand experience of the miracles and hardships in the medical field convinced me this ~~it~~

will *college and remaining*

where my life's path ~~would~~ lead me. My immediate goals include attending ~~a well-rounded, well-~~

I also want to continue participating in

~~respected university of choice. I want to remain~~ actively involved in leadership positions and

organizations both on and off campus. ~~Along with continuing my~~ community service. After

obtaining *will*

~~graduating with~~ a bachelor's degree, I ~~plan to~~ continue my education and ~~obtain advanced degrees~~

experiences and *as*

to broaden my opportunities/ I pursue a medical career.

I've

Since that day in the delivery room, ~~I have~~ taken every opportunity to acquire more information

A medical career

about this field. ~~This occupation~~ will require an unbelievable amount of ~~my~~ time, energy, discipline,

I'm

compromise, and above all devotion, but I know ~~I am~~ up to the challenge. I always try to be and do

the best I can in whatever I do, and this includes the field of study I choose. I want to leave no

on

stones unturned ~~along~~ my journey toward the top of my profession and through my life.

Essay 27: Write an essay on an experience that affected your life.

In my hometown, one of the biggest events of the year is the County Fair. For many years this has been of the happiest events in my life until last summer. It was late August with a cool crisp win blowing. Several friends and I had just arrived at the Fair and were waiting to begin a fun filled evening. Little did any of us know but that night would turn out to be the worst in all of our lives.

Essay 27—Makeover: Never foreshadow the outcome of an event you're describing. Foreshadowing undermines the effect of the story you're telling.

~In my hometown, one~ *One* of the biggest events of the year is the County Fair *in my hometown*. ~For many years this~ *This* has been *one* of the happiest events in my life until last summer. It was late August ~with~ *— but there was* a cool crisp wind *,* blowing. Several friends and I had just arrived at the Fair and were waiting to begin a fun filled evening. ~Little did any of us know but that night would turn out to be the worst in all of our lives.~

Essay 28: Write a brief essay (100 to 200 words) on your goals as they relate to your education, career, and future plans. (Tylenol)

I am seventeen with a variety of choices still to be decided and to discover more of my own hidden talents. Education has always been an important priority in my family and after high school, attending college would be the next chapter in my life. I know that having an education is a necessity in today's society.

Having a talent in the field of mathematics, I can pursue a career in this field possibly in accounting, business, or finance.

Animals have been a part of my life and I am interested in helping these creatures possibly through veterinary medicine. Several areas are open to people with veterinary training, such as research, meat inspection, specialized medicines for animals. It may be beneficial to utilize my mathematics skills in research to assist in safeguarding animals and human life. Various careers are open to me through large corporations, business, industry, through diagnostic products, drugs, disease control, advertising, sale and management. Veterinarians even have a place in the aerospace field.

As a volunteer at a local hospital, I am aware of the needs of those who suffer ill health. I enjoyed working with the friendly and caring nurses who being comfort to others. My future may be in the area of nursing or doctoring human beings.

I plan to take advantage of all opportunities that are presented to me in deciding on a career that will enable me to be a self-sufficient, contributing member to society.

Essay 28—Makeover: At 242 words in length, the essay is too long. It also gives too much information.

I'm ~~I am~~ seventeen with a variety of choices still to be decided and to discover *talents* . ~~more of my own hidden talents.~~ Education has always been an important priority in my family and after high school *, completing* attending college would be the next chapter in my life. I know that having an education is a necessity in today's society.

[Added in final draft.]
There are several career paths I could follow. Having a talent in the field of mathematics, I can *possibly* [No new paragraph.] pursue a career in ~~this field possibly in~~ accounting, business, or finance. Animals have been a part of I'm possibly my life and ~~I am~~ interested in helping these creatures ~~possibly~~ through veterinary medicine.

[Delete—there's no reason to include anything that doesn't provide insight into who you are. ~~Several areas are open to people with veterinary training, such as research, meat inspection,~~ This information sounds like a career brochure.]
~~specialized medicines for animals. It may be beneficial to utilize my mathematics skills in research to assist in safeguarding animals and human life. Various careers are open to me through large corporations, business, industry, through diagnostic products, drugs, disease control, advertising, sale and management. Veterinarians even have a place in the aerospace field.~~
I'm
As a volunteer at a local hospital, ~~I am~~ aware of the needs of those who suffer ill health. I enjoyed

working with the friendly and caring nurses who b*r*ing comfort to others. My future may be in the

area of nursing or doctoring human beings.

I plan to take advantage of all opportunities that are presented to me in deciding on a career that

will enable me to be a self-sufficient, contributing member *of* ~~to~~ society.

Essay 29: Write a brief essay (100 to 200 words) on your goals as they relate to your education, career, and future plans. (Tylenol)

In the future, I hope to continue my high achievements and follow through with my goals in the

educational field to be the most successful person that I can with my abilities. One of my first

career goals is to go through the steps of receiving a degree in either elementary or secondary

education. I also plan to pursue a Master's degree in Education that will help me to further my

career, possibly in Administration. I have always enjoyed working with children and I hope to

inspire their lives as other teachers have done for me. The pattern of a teacher helping children

want to learn can continue for all times and I hope to be interwoven into that pattern.

Essay 29—Makeover: This essay needed to read more smoothly. The student added to the last sentence, but it read awkwardly. With some minor changes, and the use of a metaphor, the essay came together.

I'll   *striving toward achieving*
In the future, ~~I hope to~~ continue ~~my high achievements and follow through with~~ my goals in the
     . `[Redundant—implicit in previous statement.]`
educational field ~~to be the most successful person that I can with my abilities.~~ One of my first

     receive
career goals is to ~~go through the steps of receiving~~ a degree in either elementary or secondary
     `[Added in final draft.]`
education. *If I choose secondary education, my area of emphasis will be science—where I'll*

     palette
introduce students to the intricate ~~palate~~ *of colors and textures of the known and unknown*

which are interwoven into a world of discovery. I also plan to pursue a master's degree in

~~E~~*e*ducation that will ~~help me to~~ further my career, possibly in ~~A~~*a*dministration. I ~~have~~ *'ve* always enjoyed working with children and I hope to inspire ~~their lives~~ *them* as other teachers have ~~done for~~ *inspired* me. ~~The~~ *I want to be a part of the timeless pattern of teachers helping children to learn, doing* ~~pattern of a teacher helping children want to learn can continue for all times and I hope to be~~ *my* part to enrich the tapestry of tomorrow's education. ~~interwoven into that pattern. *to enrich the weave of* tomorrow's educational tapestry.~~

Essay 30: Write a brief essay (100 to 200 words) on your goals as they relate to your education, career, and future plans. (Tylenol)

As a high school senior and honor student, approaching college and the real world, I have begun to set new goals for myself that include my education, career and future. I have many aspirations, one being attending a four-year public university, preferably in my home state of Texas. I plan on majoring in Psychology and ultimately receiving a Ph.D. in the field. Having always taken a vast interest in how the brain words and why people react the way they do, what better opportunity to broaden my horizons and help people in need. As a baton twirler since the age of 8, I hope to utilize my talent and receive a scholarship by twirling with the band program at my selected university. I also intend to use my skill and offer classes as a means of supporting myself through college. Looking forward to a wonderful future, I have expectations of becoming a successful psychiatrist and a well known twirling coach and judge.

Essay 30—Makeover: This student shouldn't include the last part of the last sentence. Right now she may think she will become a twirling coach and judge, but by the time she's a practicing psychologist she may not have time for twirling. A person who wants to become a psychiatrist must attend medical school. When a Ph.D. is earned, a person becomes a psychologist. This essay also tends to be wordy. The student obviously has many aspirations. Anyone reading this essay will discern this. The student states, ". . . preferably in my home state of Texas." All she has to say is "in-state" and she'll reduce the word count.

As a high school senior and honor student, ~~approaching~~ *with* college and the real world*, fast approaching, I've* ~~I have~~ begun

[It's understood that they're your goals.]
to set new goals ~~for myself~~ that include ~~my~~ education, career and future*,* ~~I have many aspirations,~~

I plan to attend   *in-state*

~~one being attending~~ a four-year public university, ~~preferably in my home state of Texas.~~ I plan on

    p   *doctorate,*   *h*   *an*

majoring in Psychology and ultimately receiving a ~~Ph.D. in the field.~~ Having always taken ~~a vast~~

                   k   *. Being a psychology major will*

interest in how the brain words and why people react the way they do, ~~what better opportunity to~~

           show me how to   *eight*

broaden my horizons and help people in need. As a baton twirler since the age of 8, I hope to

utilize my talent and receive a scholarship by twirling with the band program at my selected

I plan to help offset my educational costs by offering private twirling classes. I'm looking forward

university. ~~I also intend to use my skill and offer classes as a means of supporting myself through~~

to the future and all its challenges. Always keeping my eyes on my goals, I will become

~~college. Looking forward to a wonderful future, I have expectations of becoming~~ a successful

       ologist and hope to make a difference in the lives of individuals and families.

psychiatrist ~~and a well known twirling coach and judge.~~

Essay 31: Briefly elaborate on one of your extracurricular, community, or work activities, or other interests (for example, hobby) from which you have gained a sense of personal achievement and/or satisfaction.

I swam at the varsity level for three years, and played water polo all throughout my high school career. The whol experience of a state level waterpolo competition is awe inspiring. I enjoyed playing teams from all over the state, traveling to different pools, and playing under extreme pressure. Under these conditions, one really gets to see what they're made of. Even if you don't return victorious, it is really a learning experience.

Essay 31—Makeover: Water polo competitions are awesome (perhaps), but it seems an overstatement to say they are awe-inspiring. Also, "throughout" means "all," so to say "all throughout" is redundant.

I swam at the varsity level for three years, and played water polo ~~all~~ throughout

[Attending high school is not a career,
unless you never leave.]

                                                  -    *water polo*

my high school ~~career.~~ The ~~whol~~ experience of a state level ~~waterpolo~~ competition is

  awesome

~~awe inspiring.~~ I enjoyed playing teams from all over the state, traveling to different pools, and playing under extreme pressure. Under these conditions, ~~one~~ really gets to see ~~what they're made~~ *a person* ^ *whether he or she*

~~of.~~ Even if you don't return victorious, ~~it is really~~ a learning experience. *can meet a challenge.* *it's* *great*

Essay 32: Pretend you are being interviewed by a member of the Admission Committee who is critiquing your academic record. What conclusions about your academic preparedness, motivation, and aptitude might he or she draw from your admission materials? Are there additional insights or responses you would like to share with the committee member?

I feel that I have matured during my high school years, becoming increasingly mature as my life has gone on. I have had trouble in physics. I have been told that one who enjoys chemistry, hates physics, and vice versa. I feel that is true. I did enjoy it, but I had trouble comprehending the lessons, myself, I enjoy the more abstract thinking that chemistry has to offer. Other than that, I am quite plesed with my academic record and I am proud of my grades.

Essay 32—Makeover: This essay doesn't showcase the student. The student claims to have matured, yet this essay doesn't provide a convincing explanation. With just a few changes, the essay becomes more specific, positive, and convincing.

During my high school years, I've matured to the point of thoroughly enjoying the learning
~~I feel that I have matured during my high school years,~~ ~~becoming increasingly mature as my life~~
process. *Though I've* *, I always scheduled time with my teacher and*
~~has gone on.~~ I have had trouble in physics / ~~I have been told that one who enjoys chemistry, hates~~
peer-tutors, to ensure that I understood the topics.
~~physics, and vice versa. I feel that is true. I did enjoy it, but I had trouble comprehending the~~
I found .
~~lessons, myself,~~ I enjoy the more abstract thinking ~~that chemistry has to offer. Other than that, I am~~
M *academic achievements truly reflect my academic preparedness,*
~~quite plesed with my academic record and I am proud of my grades.~~

motivation, and aptitude.

Essay 33: Write an essay on a challenge you've faced.

One can never forget her loving smile and her warm touch. Through her wisdom and her motherly instinct, she always knew what to say when times were tough. She was one of the strongest and most admirable people I knew: she was my granny. Many think it odd to have a close relationship with your grandmother, but not I. We had that kind of bond that is supported by love.

Over the years, granny had gotten older and weaker. She was frequently in and out of hospitals fighting illness. There were many times when we were told she only had days to live. Not my granny; she always proved the doctors wrong and came out on top. Granny was admitted into the hospital in January of '98 for heart and lung problems. We visited her frequently and she seemed as if she was going to conquer this illness as well. Granny stayed in the hospital and everyone went on their normal daily lives. I had just returned to school from Christmas vacation. It was fourth period and I was sitting in band class. With the sound of the trumpets and horns blazing around me, all noise in my head suddenly came to a halt. The door opened and the office handed the message to the director. The note was for me instructing me to go to the office to be checked out. On my way to the office I ran into my cousins, this was my trigger point. I completely broke down nearly falling to the floor. My cousins ran to help me up, assuring me that everything was okay. The minute I saw my aunt, her eyes bloodshot, I knew something was terribly wrong. I pleaded with my aunt to tell me what had happened, but in my heart I knew my granny was no longer with us. I began to scream, "No, no! This can't be happening!" I became oblivious to the world around me.

As I laid my granny to rest, I realized that my life was about to change forever. I refused to part with my granny. My family struggled to pry me away from the coffin. Letting go of my granny was going to be a great challenge to overcome.

Between my mom and myself, I'm the stronger one. My mom was also very close to my grandmother and she had a hard time dealing with her death. Not knowing how to deal with the situation, my mom fell into a depression. I started talking with my mom about the whole situation, reassuring her that her heart would heal in time. I reminded her of the good times we spent with granny and encouraged her to focus on those memories. Through support and encouragement, I helped bring my mom out of her depression. At that point in time, I realized how strong I really was. Having to support my mom emotionally helped me better deal with the death of my granny.

When she died, my mind was set on the thought of never getting over the situation. When it came down to what I had to do, I did the right thing by taking care of my mother. I learned I was more mature and obliging than I thought. For a fifteen year old, I handled the situation rather well.

The step up from junior high to high school was not all that bad because I was still surrounded by the people I'd grown up with. In college, I'll be surrounded by complete strangers from all over the place. This aspect of college somewhat scares me, but I'm a friendly person and I know I'll adjust and make friends quickly. I also fear my problem with procrastination will give me some trouble with college. I've proved myself strong and I know with some work I can overcome this problem.

Despite how hard my granny's death was on me, it truly made me a stronger person. I recognized qualities I never knew I had. Although I will never forget the day I lost my granny, I will keep her memory in my heart.

Essay 33—Makeover: This essay was rewritten so the student could show us who her grandmother was, instead of just telling us about her. Some creative license is allowable. Remember, you must make your essay come alive to a stranger who doesn't know you.

"What's wrong? You can't fool me, Melanie. Tell your granny what's bothering you." Her frail arms *surrounded me in an embrace that was stronger than steel,* ~~squeezed me tightly.~~ because it was forged in love.

It didn't matter what it was, my granny had a way of helping me through a problem so I could solve it myself. Relying on her wisdom and motherly instinct, she always knew what to say when times were tough. I cried on her shoulder when a boy didn't ask me to a dance or when ~~I had~~ I'd argued with a friend. Her loving smile and her warm touch always eased my worries.

Over the years, Granny had gotten older and weaker. She was frequently in and out of hospitals fighting illness. There were many times when we were told she only had days to live. She always proved the doctors wrong and came out on top. Granny was admitted ~~into~~ the hospital in January of '98 for heart and lung problems. We visited her frequently and ~~she~~ *it* seemed as if she was going to conquer this illness as well. Granny stayed in the hospital and everyone went on with their ~~normal~~ daily lives.

Christmas vacation had just ended. It was fourth period and I was sitting in band class. The sound of the trumpets and horns blared around me. I was barely aware ~~when~~ *that* the door had opened and a note ~~was~~ *had been* delivered to the band director. I was to go to the office. I was needed at home. On my way to the office I ran into my cousins; my thoughts raced ~~ahead.~~ Something was wrong with *G*~~g~~ranny. I completely broke down, nearly falling to the floor. My cousins ran to help me up, assuring me that everything was okay. The minute I saw my aunt's bloodshot eyes I knew something was *, though,* terribly wrong. I pleaded with her to tell me what had happened, but when she answered, I began to scream, "No, no! This can't be happening!" I became oblivious to the world around me.

As I laid my granny to rest, I realized that my life was about to change forever. I refused to part with my granny. My family struggled to pry me away from the coffin. Letting go of my granny was going to be a challenge like no other I'd ever faced. I was so focused on my loss, I wasn't aware that my mother faced the same loss.

Not knowing how to deal with the situation, my mom fell into a depression. I started talking with my mom. We relived all the wonderful times we'd spent with *G*~~g~~ranny. We spent hours talking about her childhood and mine. Focusing on those memories, we both began the healing process. Through support and encouragement, I helped bring my mom out of her depression and I came to a startling realization. My grandmother had helped make me a strong person. For a fifteen-year-old, I handled the situation rather well.

There will be a variety of challenges in college. I'll be surrounded by complete strangers, ~~and~~ *but* ~~though a challenge,~~ making friends ha~~d~~*s* never been difficult for me because I'm a friendly person. I'll need to concentrate on time-management, but my determination to succeed will help me meet every challenge I face.

Despite how difficult my granny's death was, it truly made me a stronger person. Through her loss, I recognized qualities I never knew I had. ~~Although~~ I'll never forget my granny; she'll be in my heart and mind forever.

Essay 34: Write a statement describing yourself and why you would like to be considered for a scholarship.

Silence was in the air and darkness filled the room. I could feel myself breathe heavily with anticipation. Suddenly a stream of light brushed across my face. The ray of light grew gradually encompassing my body with warmth. Dust particles danced around me as I stared into the light. Slowly I placed my hands upon the cool, ivory keys of the 12-foot grand piano that lay before me. That day, I shared my talent in front of five hundred people. It was an experience I would treasure for the rest of my life. It's a dream for musicians to someday present their talent and ideas to the music world through performance, composition, or teaching. However, I believe this dream exists for any profession or life in general. We all strive to achieve the impossible, but first we must learn how to get there.

My passion for playing the piano also spawned a new interest with another instrument with keys as well. This instrument is the computer. Like the piano, I am able to compose creative and unique interactive presentations, web sites, graphic designs, and computer innovative developments. As I press the cubic keys of the computer, ideas flow from my mind into my fingertips and appear on the screen as it does with the notes of music from the piano that soak the air with my thoughts and creativity. Although these are different in nature, the commonality between them exists in their ability to compose. Each are instruments designed to assist humans beings with their talents, dreams, and imagination towards the goal of communicating to the world. My personal endeavor is to become apart of this goal through music and technology. These goals can be met by defining my skills in these areas through a higher education and a scholarship. Through a scholarship my strengths and talents can someday attribute to the evolution of the arts in these two different fields

making them life a better a note and key for us all.

Essay 34—Makeover: This essay was strong, but needed some minor changes.

Silence was in the air and darkness filled the room. ~~I could feel myself breathe heavily~~ *Each labored breath was heavy* with

anticipation. Suddenly a stream of light brush~~ed~~ *seemed to* across my face. The ray of light grew gradually *,*

encompassing my body with warmth. Dust particles danced around me as I stared into the light.

Slowly I placed my ~~hands upon~~ *fingers on* the cool, ivory keys of the ~~12-foot~~ grand piano ~~that lay before me~~ *.*

~~That day, I shared my talent in front of~~ *As the first note rang out, I forgot about the* five hundred people *in the audience.* It was an experience I would treasure

for the rest of my life. ~~It's a dream for~~ *Many* musicians ~~to someday present~~ *dream of presenting* their talent and ideas to the

~~music~~ world through performance, composition, or teaching. However, ~~I believe~~ *for me,* this dream exists

for ~~any~~ *my future* profession ~~or~~ *and* life in general. ~~We all~~ *Though we may* strive to achieve ~~the~~ *what seems* impossible, ~~but first~~ *first* we must learn

how to get there.

My passion for playing the piano also spawned a new interest ~~with~~ *in* another instrument with keys

as well ~~.~~ *;* ~~This instrument is~~ the computer. ~~Like~~ *As with* the piano, ~~I am~~ *I'm* able to compose creative and unique

interactive presentations, web sites, graphic designs, and ~~computer~~ *including* innovative developments. As I

press the cubic keys of the computer, ideas flow from my mind into my fingertips and appear on

the screen as ~~it does with the~~ *just* notes of music from the piano ~~that soak~~ *fill* the air ~~with my thoughts and~~ *.*

~~creativity.~~ Although these are different in nature, the commonality ~~between them exists in their~~ *is composition.*

~~ability to compose.~~ ~~Each~~ *Both* are instruments designed to assist humans ~~beings with~~ *in communicating* their talents*,*

dreams*,* ~~and imagination towards the goal of communicating~~ *and* to the world.

part   aspiration

My personal endeavor is to become ~~apart~~ of this ~~goal~~ through music and technology. These goals

will be   ed   which will help alleviate financial stress for my family.

~~can be met by~~ defining ~~my skills in these areas~~ through a higher education and a scholarship/

A scholarship will fine-tune my strengths and talents to enable me one day to synthesize

~~Through a scholarship my strengths and talents can someday attribute to the evolution of the arts~~

these two vastly different fields into a melody that will be a better note and key for all of us.

~~in these two different fields making them life a better a note and key for us all.~~

Essay 35: Write an essay of no more than 1,200 words about an experience from which you learned something.

It was the summer before my sophomore year. It was August and school was going to start in a couple of weeks. I was in my room listening to the radio when my mom came into my room and said she had some bad news. Goose bumps appeared on my arms. The hair on the back of my neck felt as if it was standing on end. She told me that Mark had been in a car accident and was in a coma at the hospital. I asked "What happened?" She told me that it was raining heavily and he was driving on the access road. He went into a dip and when he came up, a semi-truck pulling a mobile home was taking up both lanes. I asked if he was going to be all right and she said "I don't know." I spent the rest of the day in my room thinking about all the good times Mark and I had. I had just gone to see him in the beginning of the summer. I couldn't believe this had happened.

We went to see him at the hospital the next day. The hospital was cold and lonely. People were rushing to and from patients. His family and friends were crying, but trying not to, trying to stay calm. I moved to his side. There were tubes everywhere, one out of his head and one out of each lung. It scared me to see him like this. He was only sixteen and had his whole life ahead of him.

He passed away a week later. The reality of his death didn't hit me until I was walking away from his grave. It hit me hard and all at once. I was never going to see him again. I broke down and cried for the first time since I was younger. From then on I knew life could end at any moment and I had to live my life to the fullest. Do the best I could at everything I do. Mark's death made me realize several things. Life is special. Life should never be taken it for granted. Mark made me a stronger person.

Since that experience in my life I have set several educational goals. As I accomplish each of these goals, I'll think of Mark. I know I'll be able to face challenges and obstacles and overcome them because nothing in the world can prove that I can't, except myself. This is what Mark's death taught me.

Essay 35—Makeover: The first version of this essay is only 420 words in length, though the upper limit was 1,200 words. Though students don't have to write up to the maximum word count, an essay must provide essential information. Where does this essay need to be expanded and enhanced? More detail is needed in the final paragraph. The student didn't necessarily need to discuss his goals because the assigned topic is to discuss how he's strong as a result of his experience. The revised essay is 748 words in length.

It was the summer before my sophomore year. It was August and school was going to start in a couple of weeks. I was ~~in my room~~ listening to the radio when my mom came into my room and said she had some bad news. Goose bumps appeared on my arms. The hair on the back of my neck felt as if it *were* ~~was~~ standing on end. *"* ~~She told me that~~ Mark *was* ~~had been~~ in a car accident *. He's* ~~and was~~ in a coma at the hospital. *"* ~~I asked~~

"What happened?" I asked.

~~She told me that it was raining heavily and he was~~ *He'd been* driving on the access road *during a rainstorm.* ~~He went into a dip~~ *The access road dipped, then had a sharp incline. As he came to the top of the incline, an 18-wheel truck pulling* ~~and when he came up, a semi-truck pulling a mobile home was taking up both lanes.~~ *a mobile home was taking up both lanes.* I asked if he was going to be all right and she said simply, "I don't know."

I'd [More information about Mark was inserted here.]
~~I had~~ known Mark since the first grade. We met on the first day of school. Since we only lived a couple of blocks from each other, we pretty much spent all day together. During one sleep-over, we'd become blood brothers and vowed our friendship would last a lifetime. Just before ninth grade, Mark's family moved to a community about an hour away. Now we went to different high schools and had new friends. Though we weren't able to spend as much time together, we did plan special days and times together.

[Memories about Mark were inserted here.]

I spent the rest of the day in my room thinking about all the good times ~~Mark and I had.~~ we'd / ~~I had~~ I'd

just ~~gone to see him in~~ seen at *the beginning of* ~~the~~ *summer.* ~~We had~~ We'd *spent a day tubing on the*

Guadalupe River and camped out in his backyard. We stretched out on our sleeping bags under

the stars, with crickets and cicadas playing background music, and talked for hours about our

plans for the future. It seemed we had as many hopes and dreams as there were stars in our

Texas sky. He wanted to be a dentist and I wanted to be a doctor. We planned on having our

offices next door to each other. Though we didn't even have steady girlfriends, we figured when

we got married our wives would be friends and any future kids we had would be friends. Now

this. I couldn't believe this had happened.

As I walked down the hallway, t

We went to see him at the hospital the next day. The hospital ~~was~~ seemed cold and lonely. People were

rushing to and from patients. ~~His~~ Mark's family and friends were crying, but trying not to, trying to stay

calm. I moved to his side. There were tubes everywhere, one out of his head and one out of each

[The original end of this sentence was a bit cliché, so the student changed it.]

was just beginning to travel the road leading to his future.

lung. It scared me to see him like this. He was only sixteen and ~~had his whole life ahead of him.~~

He never regained consciousness and

~~He~~ passed away a week later. The reality of his death didn't hit me until I was walking away from

his grave. It hit me hard and all at once. I was never going to see him again. I broke down and cried

that   that

for the first time since I was younger. From then on I knew life could end at any moment and ~~I had~~

, doing   undertook and experiencing

to live my life to the fullest. ~~Do~~ the best I could at everything I ~~do.~~ ~~Experience~~ everything in life.

[Moved two sentences down.]

[~~Mark's death made me realize several things.~~] Life is special. Life should never be taken ~~it~~ for

granted. Mark's death made me realize these things. Mark made me a stronger person.

,   I've

Since that experience ~~in my life I have~~ set some goals for myself. I want to be in the top ten in

my class. I want to sit on the stage that I will walk across to get my high school diploma. I want to

get the highest scores I can on my calculus and biology II advanced placement tests. I would love

to go ~~into~~ college with seventeen hours of credit under my belt.

In college at Texas A&M, I want to have at least a 3.5 grade point average all the way through
school. College will ~~be~~ *take* about eight years, but I know I can do it and be successful. After ~~college~~ *completing my education* I
want to ~~find~~ *establish* a ~~stable job~~ *steady practice* and settle down with a family. I want to be financially secure. I don't want
my kids or wife to have to worry about money.

I believe I can do all this because nothing in the world can prove that I can't except myself. That
is what Mark's death taught me.

Essay 36: In 500 words or less, write about the greatest challenge you have ever faced.

In all of my seventeen years of existence, I would say my greatest challenge was my first job. I
had babysitting jobs before and mowed my neighbor's lawn, this time was different. Thunder
America's favorite drive-in was the first to respond to my application. I was on my way to having
my first real job. Harry, the manager called me in for an interview and I was hired on the spot. That
first night I worked as a carhop and as to be expected I was nervous. It was my school's prom night
and that in itself made me anxious. All the while I knew I could work well with people, but I never
had given change out before or run out orders. Part of my training was having my manager watch
me every step of the way. There were some embarrassing moments like when I dropped drinks and
orders. One thing I could not drop was my smile. I use to think Pre-Calculus was a challenge.
Working at Thunder was ranking first on my greatest list of challenges.

By the end of the second week my manager decided to move me to work in the fountain area,
where we make our famous Cherry-Limeades and shakes. This shift up the corporate ladder made
was exciting. I was happy that I could contribute more, at the same time I was feeling
apprehensive. Making drinks started out slow, and it didn't take long before I looked up at my
screen and found I had six more orders to make. I had never worked so hard to squeeze the juice
from a line and blend strawberries and other fruits together for shakes. The hardest part wasn't the
quantity of drinks I had to make it was learning all the different combinations of drinks to make.

What size cup you need; how many squirts to put into each cup; how high to fill the cups up with ice cream; you name it I was making them. It was an overwhelming and I practiced my breathing techniques. The reward was soon to come: I received a raise it was an accomplishment for me.

From this experience I learned I can do anything I set my mind to. I know what I've learned will carry over with me throughout my years in college and life. The fields of study I choose will be a challenge, although with dedication and a positive attitude I can face whatever challenges come my way.

Essay 36—Makeover: The original essay was scrapped and the essay was rewritten in a shorter, more interesting form.

"You're hired," Harry, the Thunder Drive-In manager told me.

"Really? I've got the job?" I asked, surprised that my first interview led to my first job. I'd babysat and mowed lawns before; this was different.

On my first night, I was going to be a carhop. I was nervous. It was also my school's prom night. The only thing I kept thinking was "Don't forget to smile." There were some embarrassing moments when I dropped drinks and orders, but I never dropped my smile. I used to think pre-calculus was a challenge. Working at Thunder was ranking first on my greatest list of challenges.

At the end of my second week, Floyd moved me to the fountain area. I couldn't help thinking I was moving up the corporate ladder. I was happy I could contribute, but I was apprehensive. My job was now to make our famous Cherry-Limeades and shakes. I started out slow and it wasn't long before I looked up at the screen and found I had six more orders to make. I'd never worked so hard to squeeze the juice from a lime and blend strawberries and other fruits for shakes.

The hardest part wasn't the quantity of drinks I had to make; it was learning all the different combinations of drinks to make, what size cup I needed to use, how many squirts to put in each cup, and how high to fill the cups with ice cream. You name it, I was making it. During the most overwhelming moments, I practiced breathing techniques. The reward was soon to come: I received a raise.

It doesn't matter what my intended goal is, I can accomplish anything I set my mind to. Everything I've learned I'll carry with me throughout college and life. Pursuing a double major in business and public relations will be a challenge, but with my dedication and positive attitude, I can face whatever challenges come my way.

Essay 37: Write an essay about a person who has had an important influence on your life. What qualities in that person do you admire, and how have you grown from knowing that person? (The text below isn't the entire essay, but we wanted to share this as an excellent example of giving a committee member a view into the student's world and personality.)

"Latrine Duty"—two words that send shivers throughout any self-respecting Boy Scout's body. The first reaction is the wrinkling of the nose followed by an outcry of "YUCK"! It s a disgusting job, but somebody has to do it. Without alienating any one person with the worst job, without being antagonistic, how does one deal with this problem? As the senior patrol leader for this year's Boy Scout troop at camp, I was going to have to choose somebody for this job. I knew what was involved and also knew that it is considered torture for a younger scout. . . almost thought of as a punishment, never as a character builder. I had observed many ways that people had tried to make latrine duty more of an enjoyable assignment rather than an agonizing tribulation. From bribes of candy to promises of merit, it was still a formidable job. It was my goal to get somebody to clean the latrine without begging and without promising him compensation. I began to wonder . . . What would Mr. Adams do in a situation such as this?

Essay 37—Makeover:

"Latrine Duty"—two words that send shivers throughout any self-respecting Boy Scout's body. The first reaction is the wrinkling of the nose followed by an outcry of "YUCK!" It's a disgusting job, but somebody has to do it. ~~Without alienating any one person with the worst job, without being antagonistic,~~ How does one deal with this problem?

[Delete—unclear.]

As the senior patrol leader for this year's Boy Scout troop at camp, I was going to have to choose somebody for this job. I knew what was involved and also knew that ~~it is~~ *it's* considered torture for a younger scout /|/ almost thought of as a punishment, never as a character builder. ~~I had~~ *I'd* observed many ways ~~that~~ people had tried to make latrine duty *a* more ~~of an~~ enjoyable assignment rather than an agonizing tribulation. From bribes of candy/ to promises of merit, it was still a formidable job. It was my goal to get somebody to clean the latrine without begging and without promising ~~him~~ compensation. I began to wonder . . . What would Mr. Adams do in a situation such as this?

Essay 38: On one page only, write an essay about a person, event, or experience that influenced your life.

Approaching Kennedy High School, my nervousness took control of me. I grew cold and was overcome with a numbness that surged through my body. I'd never experienced this type of pressure. I'd been to countless competitions, and didn't understand why I was losing my concentration. I've always been a positive competitor, and had grown accustomed to winning. With my reputation growing for being consistent and powerful, I never doubted myself. I always expected to perform perfectly, and it seemed others expected this perfection as well.

Essay 38—Makeover: Though you want to portray confidence, you don't want to sound arrogant. The tone of this essay had to be softened.

Approaching Kennedy High School, my nervousness took control of me. I grew cold and was *by* overcome ~~with~~ a numbness that surged through my body. I'd never experienced this type of

[What kind of competitions?]

pressure. I'd been to countless competitions, and didn't understand why I was losing my

["accustomed" makes you sound arrogant]

I enjoy

concentration. I've always been a positive competitor, and ~~had grown accustomed to~~ winning.

With my reputation growing for being consistent and powerful, I never doubted myself. I always

to the best of my ability   [No one is perfect.]

expected to perform ~~perfectly~~, and it seemed others expected this ~~perfection~~ as well.

Essay 39:

The volunteer work, which has been the most significant experience I have participated in is the Elf Louise Program which has benefited numerous families. The Elf Louise Program is an organization that lends a helping hand to those who are less fortunate during the Christmas Holidays. People from our society joins in to wrap and deliver gifts. The people who unite together weeks before Christmas Day, are my family and friends. From the clusters of family names that are received, you are to select about six to ten families and choose from over a thousand donations and wrap their presents. Prior to Christmas Day, my family and I return to the Elf Louise Program and are banded over a list of addresses and gifts to deliver throughout the city. Imagine arriving at the residence were children who are in need of comfort, food, and something just to brighten up their Christmas. The boys and girls express happiness in their faces, when their name is on the gifts especially for them. It could be a football, to a doll, or even a jump rope. Looking into their eyes seeing a sparkling look of contentment reflexes how fortunate I am to be able to help people in need. It creates immense personal satisfaction for me when I saw their eyes light up at my approach. In just a few minutes while visiting with the families and listening to their stories some very touching, sad, or even some funny ones makes me wonder how their life's are day to day. I felt they knew that I was someone who cared to listen to their stories and enjoyed talking to them. It's special to know that I have made their Christmas a more pleasant one. I wonder how such little gifts with time and effort can bring smiles and enthusiasm to the many needy families which is brought together by my family and myself. I value the experience I have learned from this and the memories I will always treasure.

Essay 39—Makeover #1: Though the original essay provides information about the Elf Louise Program, it just doesn't capture the reader's attention. It also contains some major grammatical problems, and it's one long paragraph. We instructed the student to start over, focusing on one family and taking some creative license with the events to capture the drama of them. Also, few people remember dialogue exactly. We suggested that the student start with being in the warehouse, selecting gifts for the family. Background information on the Elf Louise Program can be woven into the story. The following makeover provides more information, but it still misses the mark. The student is still telling, not showing. It also needs to include more than just one paragraph. The primary goal here is to present the essay as a story, sharing a part of the student's life in an interesting and memorable way.

~~The~~ *My* volunteer work, which has been the most significant experience I have participated in is the

[This statement leads the reader

Elf Louise Program which has benefited numerous families. The Elf Louise Program is an

to think that they are only less fortunate during the Christmas season.]
organization that lends a helping hand to those who are less fortunate during the Christmas

Volunteers   *that are kept* *a*   *containing*
Holidays. ~~People from our society joins in to~~ wrap and deliver gifts in ~~this~~ huge warehouse, ~~with~~

children
thousands of donated gifts. ~~from different stores.~~ The toys are for ~~all~~ ages one through fifteen. ~~Most~~

[Delete—irrelevant.]   [This statement implies that
~~of the time, the Elf Louise Program is located in a huge warehouse or a vacant store in a mall~~ ~~The~~
only your family and friends are involved in this program.] *M*
~~people who unite together weeks before Christmas Day,~~ are ~~my~~ family and friends/ we usually pick

s.
out a week to wrap and a couple of days to deliver gift/ ~~My family makes it out to be fun and to me~~

Doing it together as a family is fun.
~~it also turns out to be such great family time for us.~~ When we arrive we sign in and ~~from the clusters~~

the names of   *We gather at*
~~of family names that are received, we get to~~ select about six to ten families. ~~Next, we pick out~~ a big

where   *we're wrapping gifts for*   *, we check the*
table ~~so~~ we can spread out and wrap gifts. When ~~we are~~ done ~~with that~~ one family ~~we always make~~

list and then check it twice, so
~~sure someone comes around and checks out the names against a list~~ we don't ~~want to~~ leave anyone

A   *for*
out. ~~Once someone checks out the name against a list that person~~ bags ~~all~~ the gifts ~~that belong to~~

are placed   *, to make sure each family received the right gifts.*
that one family in a huge bag/ ~~You see that is how they get delivered to the same family at the~~

[Already said above—delete.]
~~same time and no one gets left out.~~ ~~And we get to start the process all over again and again how~~
[Delete—irrelevant. This fact has nothing to do with you.]
~~wonderful it is to help.~~ ~~At the same time there are many other families, friends, different~~

into   *adventure filled with*
~~organizations, groups of schools helping out to.~~ It turns ~~out to be~~ one great big family ~~warehouse~~

and   *,*
~~full of~~ toys, tables, wrapping paper, happy music with everyone having an exciting ~~fun~~ time

wrapping away. [New Paragraph.]

,   *wrapped .*
A few days before Christmas families sign up to deliver the gifts ~~that are wrapped~~

When   *, we're*
~~up and ready to be delivered. Prior to Christmas Day,~~ my family and I return ~~to the Elf Louis~~

~~Program and are~~ handed a list of addresses and gifts to deliver throughout the city. ~~Before we~~

M *d* *dresses* *, complete*
~~deliver the gifts guess what m~~y wonderful *D*ad ~~gets to dress~~ up as Santa Claus with a huge white

. The *After loading* *d* *, we* *drive*
beard/ the rest of us are dressed as Santa's Helpers. ~~We load up my D~~ad's truck ~~and imagine driving~~

[How do you stare with excitement? You don't know what they're thinking.] *Look,*
down the highway with people staring ~~with excitement and thinking~~ and saying, "~~look~~ it's Santa."

others *and wave, while others laugh* *we're*
Some people ~~would~~ point, honk their horns/ ~~waved, and some even laughed~~ at us. By this time ~~we~~

. It feels *know*
~~were~~ having a blast/ ~~it felted~~ a little strange being dressed in these outfits but we ~~knew~~ what

a difference we'll make. *When we* *e* *,*
~~we were about to encounter.~~ Upon arriving at the residence of our ~~very~~ first family they invite

into *home. We're greeted by* *seem* *, and*
us ~~in their living room these are~~ children who ~~are~~ in need of comfort, food just a little something to

The rooms are sparsely furnished. *It's*
brighten up their Christmas. ~~It was sad to see the family had very little furniture it was also~~ hard to

it's *, because there's*
believe ~~because with it being~~ Christmas Eve ~~there was~~ no Christmas tree in their home, ~~not to~~

much less any
~~mention there were no~~ gifts to be opened on Christmas Day. ~~As we handed or placed the~~

[Delete—you repeat this later.] *The children's eyes*
~~gifts for the children on the floor with their very own names on them, the children expressed such~~

and faces reflect the excitement and wonder of Christmas.
~~excitement and cheerfulness in their faces. By this time, I could not just placed their gifts on the~~

I place each gift into waiting, eager
~~floor I felt like I needed to hand their own gifts in their~~ little hands. I wanted each one of them to

. S
spend a few extra minutes with Santa ~~s~~ome of the children ~~would~~ pull on Santa's beard. ~~So in order~~

~~for this to happen I would take extra time in their home.~~ *[New paragraph.]*

. I'll
This was the greatest satisfaction anyone can have ~~I will~~ always remember the look on their

They may have just received *just* *it didn't matter. All that*
faces. ~~It could be~~ a football, ~~to~~ a doll, or ~~even~~ a simple jump rope, but ~~just looking into their eyes~~

mattered was that Santa remembered. I realized just *. Being*
~~seeing a sparkling look of contentment reflects~~ how fortunate I am ~~to be~~ able to help people in

provided me with
need/ ~~It creates~~ immense personal satisfaction ~~for me~~ when I saw their eyes light up and their

soar *our* *Within* *,*
spirits ~~were lifted immediately~~ at ~~my~~ approach. ~~In~~ just a few minutes ~~while visiting with the~~

~~families and listening to their stories some very touching, some were sad, even some funny stories,~~

~~that makes me wonder how their life's are day to day.~~ I felt they knew ~~that~~ I was someone who cared to listen to their stories and enjoyed talking to them. As we ~~leave~~ *left* the home the parents ~~of the children~~ *hugged* hug each and every one of ~~my family members~~ *us,* saying thanks over and over ~~of how grateful they are from joy they saw in their children.~~ It's special to know ~~that I have made~~ their [*It was fulfilling*] [*I was able to make*] Christmas a more pleasant one. ~~I wonder how such little gifts with~~ *Our gift of* time and effort ~~can bring~~ *brought* smiles and ~~enthusiasm to the many needy families which are brought together by my family and myself. I~~ *joy.* *I will always treasure* ~~value~~ the experience ~~I have learned from this~~ and the memories ~~I will always treasure.~~

Essay 39—Makeover #2: Despite the changes we suggested in the first draft, this version still doesn't hit the mark. The student includes the right information, but presents it awkwardly, still telling, not showing. An essay should contain more than one paragraph.

The volunteer work ~~which~~ *that* has been the most significant experience in my life is the Elf Louise Program. The Elf Louise Program is an organization that lends a helping hand to those who are less fortunate during the Christmas Holidays. People from our ~~society~~ *community* join in to wrap and deliver gifts in ~~this~~ *a* huge warehouse / ~~with~~ *containing* thousands of donated gifts from ~~different~~ *many* stores. ~~The people who unite together~~ *W*weeks before Christmas Day, ~~are my family and friends~~ / ~~We usually pick out a week~~ *gather* to wrap and ~~a couple of days to~~ deliver gift*s*. When we arrive at this huge warehouse, first we sign in, then ~~we~~ select six to ten families from ~~this list~~ *a* / ~~It includes a list of all children~~ *containing children's names* and their ages. Then we select appropriate gifts and wrap them. Before the gifts are set aside for ~~delivering~~ *delivery*, someone ~~has~~ to ~~check~~ *checks* and ~~double check~~ *double-checks* the gifts against the list. Prior to Christmas Day, my family and I return to deliver gifts throughout the city. Before we deliver the gifts, my father gets dressed up as Santa Claus*.* ~~he~~ *He* even ~~wore~~ *wears* a thick white beard. The rest of us ~~were~~ *are* dressed as Santa's Helpers or elves. Our first stop ~~was~~ *is* a small framed run*-*down house. The family ~~invited~~ *invites* us into their living room where ~~it was~~ *it's* plain to see that the children ~~were~~ *are* in need of comfort, food, and just a little something to brighten up their Christmas. As we entered*,* the children crowded together on a bare sofa. ~~It was~~ *It's*

~~sad to see the~~ *, that* family ~~had very~~ *has* little furniture, but ~~what was~~ *what's* most touching ~~was~~ *is* the lack of a

Christmas tree and presents. As we handed the gifts to the children*,* their eyes ~~lit~~ *light* up like sparklers.

Their gift
~~It~~ could be a football, ~~to~~ a doll, or even a ~~simple~~ jump rope. Christmas had come to their house.

They hadn't been forgotten. ~~A sparkling look of~~ *Their obvious* contentment ~~reflects~~ *helps me realize* how fortunate I am to be able

doesn't *spends*
to help people in need. It ~~didn't~~ take long for the children to crowd around Santa. Santa ~~spent~~ a

yanks *I felt*
few minutes with each child, even the one who ~~yanked~~ on his beard. ~~It created~~ immense personal

satisfaction ~~for me~~ when I saw their eyes light up and their spirits ~~were~~ lifted immediately at my

approach. ~~In just a few minutes, while visiting with the families and listening to their stories some~~

~~were touching, some were sad even some funny stories, that makes me wonder how their life's are~~

~~day today.~~ I felt they knew I was someone who cared to listen to their ~~stores~~ *stories* and enjoyed talking to

their *us,*
them. As we start to leave the home*,* the parents ~~of the children~~ hugged each one of ~~my family~~

to *for bringing*
~~members~~ saying thanks over and over again. It showed how grateful they were ~~for us~~ ~~to bring~~

children's lives *when* *children's joy.*
happiness into their ~~children's life.~~ The parents even shed a tear ~~from joy~~ they saw ~~in their children.~~

I've *at*
It's special to know that ~~I have~~ made their Christmas a more pleasant one. I wonder how such little

so *.*
gifts of time and effort can bring smiles and enthusiasm to ~~the~~ many needy families ~~which are~~

what *experience*
~~brought together by the family and myself.~~ I value ~~the experience~~ I ~~have~~ learned from this and the

I'll
memories ~~I will~~ always treasure.

Essay 39—Makeover #3: This is the finished essay.

As my family and I walked
~~Walking~~ into the huge warehouse, the air was filled with the sounds of people chatting and

laughing, items being selected, paper being cut, gifts being wrapped, and above it all familiar

Christmas carols floated through the air, warming the room better than any heater could have done. A woman approached us with our assignment. Sign in. Select six to ten families from ~~this~~ a list of all the children and their ages. Then select appropriate gifts and wrap them. Before the bundle of gifts ~~are~~ is set aside for delivering, ~~someone has to~~ check and double-check the list. And most of all, have fun. We all walked ~~through~~ down aisle after aisle of gifts, wanting to select just the right gifts for our assigned families.

Christmas. The word brings wonderfully warm memories to mind because of the incredible experiences I've had working with the Elf Louise Program. Louise started by helping a child or two. Today literally thousands of families, who ~~through~~ for a variety of reasons were facing difficult times, have been helped.

It was three days until Christmas and delivery day had arrived. My father, better known as Santa Claus, was dressed in red and ~~had~~ wore a thick white beard. The rest of us were "Santa's Helpers" and dressed as elves. Driving down the highway, we ~~hear,~~ heard, " Look, it's Santa!" People wave, point, honk their horns, and yes, some laughed, but it was great. We were having a blast.

Our first stop was a small, run-down house in a depressed part of town. As we entered, the children were crowded together on a ~~thread-bare~~ threadbare sofa. The room was sparsely furnished, but what was ~~the~~ most touching was the lack of a Christmas tree and presents.

It didn't take long for the kids to crowd around Santa. Santa spent a few minutes with each child, even the one who yanked on his beard. The faces of the urchins seemed to radiate ~~and sparkle.~~ Their eyes lit up like sparklers on the Fourth of July. Their joy bubbled over into giggles and squirming. The presents ranged from footballs to dolls, and even a simple jump rope. The gift itself didn't matter. Christmas had come to their house. They hadn't been forgotten.

"Thank you so much," ~~the~~ their mother said, wiping a tear from the corner of her eye.

"You don't know what this means to our children and us," the father seconded. The couple stood next to each other, grinning from ear to ear as their children gave shouts of glee as they opened their presents. Moment*s* later, as we went out the door, everyone kept saying thanks.

As I sit in my room and remember those children, I realize that with little effort on my part, I made the world a better place for those families whose lives we touched. Christmas at our house was wonderful because we all had more than the usual thanks *to give* for gifts received. I also gave thanks for being able to touch the lives of others. Most importantly, I was grateful for the little things I'd always taken for granted until I put on my pointy elf shoes and ridiculous costume and realized just how much I truly had.

Essay 40:

Knowing exactly what it was that I would need to do, I began school at Manor High School. On this road to higher learning, I have prepared myself for the future by taking three courses of Spanish, four years of History, English, and Science, and three years of Math. I also took the opportunity to take the TEAMS class, which is a class structured around leadership and community service. Other classes that I have taken include two computer courses, two health classes, two years in Drama, Dance and Band. Currently I am a member of the Thespian Society, Interact Club, and I'm the president of the Future Business Leaders of America (FBLA). Outside of school I have been volunteering for a local music teacher for the past six years ,and also formed and instructed my own jazz band, consisting of students between the ages of ten and eighteen. My other volunteer roles include that of a Big Brother in the Big Brother/Big Sister program, assistant in the Senior Olympics and a volunteer worker at the American Heart Association for the past five years.

Essay 40—Makeover: This essay was too detailed. There was no need to include information from other parts of the application. The essay consisted of only one paragraph. With deletions and corrections, the essay is stronger.

[Everyone goes to high school. You didn't have to prepare or plan for it.]

~~Knowing exactly what it was that I would need to do, I began school at Manor High School.~~

Wanting to provide myself with options on the   *I've taken*   *years*

On this road to higher learning, ~~I have prepared myself for the future by taking~~ three ~~courses~~ of

instead of two.   [The rest of these classes are generally required.]   *advantage of*

Spanish, ~~four years of History, English, and Science, and three years of Math.~~ I also took the

opportunity to take the TEAMS class, which is a class structured around leadership and community

[It's unnecessary to repeat information that's included on your transcript.]

service. ~~Other classes that I have taken include two computer courses, two health classes, two~~

~~years in Drama, Dance and Band.~~ [New paragraph.]

     I'm   *am*

Currently ~~I am~~ a member of the Thespian Society, Interact Club, and ~~I'm~~ the president

, which has provided me with direction toward achieving my career goals.   *I've*   *ed*

of the Future Business Leaders of America (FBLA)/ ~~Outside of school I have~~ volunteering for

         even   *directed*

a local music teacher for the past six years, and ~~also~~ formed and ~~instructed~~ my own jazz band,

               This year, I've participated as

consisting of students between the ages of ten and eighteen. ~~My other volunteer roles include that~~

            been an   *,*

~~of~~ a Big Brother in the Big Brother/Big Sister program, assistant in the Senior Olympics and

for the past five years have been

a volunteer worker at the American Heart Association ~~for the past five years.~~

Essay 41:

Years ago when I was younger and dreaming of my future, I set goals for myself. Since that period

of my life, the goals have changed from time to time. As I have matured, I have managed to

accomplish many of them, but there have also been many disappointments. I feel every time I have

hit a barricade, I have had to learn to detour. Determination has been my ultimate goal and has

helped me to develop the tenacity to attain others. I have always worked to the highest of my

ability. I was tested for the gifted and talented program in elementary school because of my

willingness to learn. In my elementary and secondary education, I never made anything lower than

a B, with mostly A's. As I approached high school, it has become harder for me to maintain this goal.

I have enrolled in honors classes in which I have struggled, but have continued until I completed

them. I will be accomplishing one of my ambitions by receiving the advanced seal on my diploma upon completion of my graduation. Though this may not seem large to many, it will to me. I have

been surrounded by my peers who have been extremely successful academically. I have worked

beside them and worked just as hard as they have. Most of the time I have come to aid them in

their studies due to my ability to take accurate and complete notes. I pride myself in my ability to

turn in all assignments and earn extra credit when possible. I have participated in every extra

curricular program that time permits and have a resume of accomplishments. I come from a family

of two very ambitious parents that devote their life to working unselfishly to help others.

Essay 41—Makeover: The final sentence was moved to the end of the first paragraph where it makes a bit more sense.

[Insert your age here. Everyone is younger in the past.]

Years ago when I was ~~younger~~ and dreaming of my future, I set goals for myself. ~~Since that period~~

These *I've*
~~of my life, the~~ goals have changed from time to time. ~~As I have matured, I have~~ managed to

some *When I've*
accomplish many of them, but there have ~~also~~ been ~~many~~ disappointments. ~~I feel every time I have~~

learned
hit a barricade, I ~~have had to learn~~ to detour. Determination ~~has been my ultimate goal and has~~

meet goals [Moved from end of essay.]
helped me to develop the tenacity to ~~attain~~ others. I come from a family of two ambitious people

who devote their life to working unselfishly to help others. [New paragraph.]

best [Delete—irrelevent.]
I ~~have~~ always worked to the ~~highest~~ of my ability. ~~I was tested for the gifted and talented~~

school
~~program in elementary school because of my willingness to learn.~~ In my elementary ~~and secondary~~

a grade .
~~education,~~ I never made a~~nything~~ lower than a B/ ~~with mostly A's.~~ [New paragraph.]

It's *my GPA in high school.*
~~As I approached high school, it has~~ become harder ~~for me~~ to maintain ~~this goal. I have enrolled in~~

with honors classes, *successfully*
~~honors classes in which~~ I ~~have~~ struggled/ but ~~have~~ continued until I completed them. ~~I will be~~

0 *was to graduate with an* *, which I've accomplished.*
~~accomplishing~~ one of my ambitions ~~by receiving the~~ advanced seal on my diploma ~~upon~~

[Irrelevant.] *I've*
~~completion of my graduation. Though this may not seem large to many, it will to me.~~ I have been

who've
surrounded by ~~my~~ peers ~~who have~~ been extremely successful academically. ~~I have worked beside~~

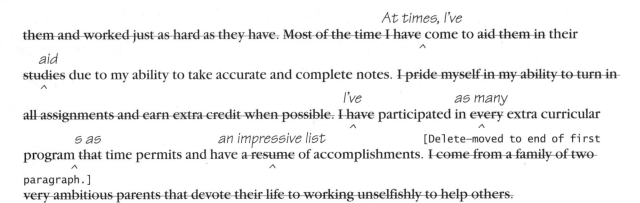

At times, I've

~~them and worked just as hard as they have.~~ ~~Most of the time I have~~ come to ~~aid them in~~ their

aid

~~studies~~ due to my ability to take accurate and complete notes. ~~I pride myself in my ability to turn in~~

I've   *as many*

~~all assignments and earn extra credit when possible.~~ ~~I have~~ participated in ~~every~~ extra curricular

s as   *an impressive list*   [Delete—moved to end of first

program ~~that~~ time permits and have ~~a resume~~ of accomplishments. ~~I come from a family of two~~

paragraph.]

~~very ambitious parents that devote their life to working unselfishly to help others.~~

Essay 42: On one page only, write an essay about a person, event, or experience that influenced your life.

Boarding that plane to Chicago to spend seven days with two hundred other students from

across the nation that I had never met, proved to be the beginning of an experience that I will

never forget. Preparations for this trip began months before and although I had anticipated this

week, I felt apprehensive. I had met the criteria set forth for acceptance to the week-long

conference, but any confidence seemed undermined as I thought to myself, "What if I have trouble

making friends or what if I have to eat alone"? I settled myself as best I could forgetting that the

venue of the conference, The University of Chicago, would have no air-conditioning and unaware

that there would be one bathroom for five girls or that a full night sleep would have to wait until I

returned home! These would be the least of my challenges of the week.

Essay 42—Makeover: This essay needed a few changes. Always avoid the use of exclamation points unless the situation is dramatic or unless you're screaming in your story. Don't use quotation marks around internal conversations. Punctuation is generally inside quotation marks.

Boarding that plane to Chicago to spend seven days with two hundred other students from

who I'd   *I'll*

across the nation ~~that I had~~ never met, proved to be the beginning of an experience that ~~I will~~

had begun   ,   *I'd*   *it,*

never forget. Preparations for this trip ~~began~~ months before and although ~~I had~~ anticipated ~~this~~

~~week,~~ I felt apprehensive. ~~I had~~ *I'd* met the criteria set forth for acceptance to the week-long conference, but ~~any~~ *my* confidence seemed undermined as I thought to myself, ~~W~~What if I have trouble [Delete quotation marks—none needed.] making friends or what if I have to eat alone? ~~I settled myself as best I could forgetting that the~~ *I would soon find out that* ~~venue of the conference,~~ ~~T~~the University of Chicago *dormitories* ~~would~~ have no air-conditioning ~~and unaware~~, that there would be one bathroom for five girls ~~or~~ *, and* that a full night*'s* sleep would have to wait until I returned home. These would be the least of my challenges *that* ~~of the~~ week.

Essay 43: Write an essay about an experience that influenced your life.

The knots in my stomach were pulsating as I sat in the San Antonio airport. My parents were talking about walking the dogs, and taking out the trash, and a cool draft made me feel even more isolated. I was contemplating how I was going to handle the seven day Lorenzo de Zavala Youth Legislative Session in Chicago, Illinois, which I was accepted into my junior year. When I heard my plane had arrived I wanted to cry and hold on to my mom because it was something I had been anticipating the hole year and suddenly felt apprehensive. I felt like I was three years old, not wanting my mommy to leave, but instead I was the one leaving. I said a short goodbye without cracking and walked through that tunnel to face my future. The time I spent waiting while the attendants checked boarding passes were the scariest moments of my life. My mind was blocking out all the noise, so I was left alone with just my thoughts and fears. "I'm not gonna make any friends! What if I have to eat by myself?" It almost felt like the first day of school, but a school thousands of miles away. The plane ride, alone, was even worse because then I knew there was no turning back.

[This is the concluding paragraph to the previous essay.]

As I sat in that enormous airport waiting for my flight to take me home, there were no knots in my stomach or feelings of apprehension because when I look back I know I can be proud and even better when I look forward I am prepared for whatever comes my way.

Essay 43—Makeover: This was a good essay, but it needed to be tightened.

The knots in my stomach were pulsating as I sat in the San Antonio airport. My parents were talking about walking the dogs/ and taking out the trash/ ~~and a~~ *A* cool draft made me feel even more isolated. I was contemplating how I was going to handle the seven day Lorenzo de Zavala Youth Legislative Session in Chicago, Illinois, which I was accepted int~~o~~ *to* my junior year. ~~When~~ I heard my

flight announced. Suddenly, I felt apprehensive, and held onto [Delete-meaning unclear.]
plane ~~had arrived I wanted to cry and hold on to~~ my mom ~~because it was something I had been anticipating the hole year and suddenly felt apprehensive.~~ I felt ~~like~~ *as if* I ~~was~~ *were* three years old, not

in this case
wanting my mommy to leave, but ~~instead~~ I was the one leaving. I said a short goodbye without my voice cracking and walked through that tunnel to face my future.

The time I spent waiting while the attendants checked boarding passes were the scariest moments of my life. My mind was blocking out all the noise, so I was left alone with just my
[Delete quotation marks–unnecessary.]
going to
thoughts and fears/ "I'm not ~~gonna~~ make any friends/ What if I have to eat by myself?" It almost felt
at
like the first day of school, but a school thousands of miles away. ~~The plane ride, alone, was even~~
Once I boarded that plane,
~~worse because then~~ I knew there was no turning back.

[This is the concluding paragraph to the previous essay.]
As I sat in that enormous airport waiting for my flight to take me home, there were no knots in
W   on what I accomplished,
my stomach or feelings of apprehension ~~because~~ when I look back ~~I know~~ I can be proud ~~and even~~
As   , I'm
~~better when~~ I look forward ~~I am~~ prepared for whatever comes my way.

Essay 44: Choose one volunteer experience and briefly describe how the experience benefited others. Describe what happened in your life or in the life of your family as a result of your volunteer service experience. The essay may be up to, but not more than, one typewritten, double-spaced page.

The Flood of '98 had a monumental impact on myself on a personal level as well as on a community level. My family and I were already in a dismayed state of mind when we received news of the floods. Having attended my cousin's funeral in East Texas, we came home to a devastated community. My grandmother's house had been filled with four feet of water. Fortunately, my grandfather was able to salvage some of their belongings. It was rumored that a dam was to be opened and once again our small community would be swept by roaring waters. Not was person was seen sitting: everyone worked to do their part. Men lifted furniture to higher ground while women drove to restore any item not filled with mud. Ironically, many of the people helping out were strangers. I helped clean and gather many belongings that were unruined. Although the dam was never opened and the "second flood" never came, we were prepared. The clean up did not come over night. Neighbors, friends, and family worked together to rebuild the community. Many families were left homeless without even the basic necessities of food and water. Donations came pouring in. Hundreds of gallons of sanitized water, canned foods, and items of clothing were available to the victims of the flood. Hot meals as well as shelters were also serviceable to the victims. As well as cleaning up my grandparent's house, I also helped in cleaning the mess that was left. I assisted in picking up trash left close to roads or all along the banks of the rivers.

A year later and the damages are still making a difference in our lives. My grandparents are currently living in my home due to the flood. We are having to rebuild starting from the basic framework. We frequently go out to their house and help pain, clean up, what ever needs to be done. I am very proud to have participated in this battle to reestablish the lives' of the people affected by the flood. Despite the devastating and unforgettable destruction caused by the Flood of '98, it caused the community and the whole area of Central Texas to unite and help others in need.

Essay 44—Makeover: Read your essay aloud to check for redundancies. This student states: ". . . on myself on a personal level . . ." There can't be any other kind of level. It's much the same as stating, "personal friend" or "unexpected accident."

The Flood of '98 had a monumental ~~impact~~ *effect* on ~~myself on a personal level~~ *my life,* as well as on a *my* community ~~level~~. [Moved from later in paragraph.] Having just attended my cousin's funeral in East Texas, *M*y family and I were already in a dismayed state of mind when we received news of the floods/ *that devastated our community.* ~~Having attended my~~

~~cousin's funeral in East Texas, we came home to a devastated community.~~ My grandmother's house
[Delete—not absolutely necessary.]
~~had been~~ filled with four feet of water. ~~Fortunately, my grandfather was able to salvage some of~~

~~their belongings.~~ It was rumored that a dam was to be opened and once again our small community
one
would be swept by roaring waters. Not ~~was~~ person was seen sitting: everyone worked to do their
tried *save*
part. Men lifted furniture to higher ground while women ~~drove~~ to ~~restore~~ any item not filled with

mud. Ironically, many of the people helping out were strangers. I helped clean and gather many
weren't ruined.
belongings that ~~were unruined.~~ Although the dam was never opened and the "second flood" never

came, we were prepared. [New paragraph.]
didn't happen
The cleanup ~~did not come~~ overnight. Neighbors, friends, and family worked together to rebuild

the community. Many families were left homeless ~~without even the basic necessities of food and~~

~~water.~~ Donations came pouring in. Hundreds of gallons of sanitized water, canned foods, and items
flood *,* *,*
of clothing were available to the victims ~~of the flood.~~ Hot meals as well as shelters were also
available. *grandparents'*
~~serviceable to the victims.~~ As well as cleaning up my ~~grandparent's~~ house, ~~I also helped in cleaning~~
and
~~the mess that was left.~~ I assisted in picking up trash left close to roads ~~or all~~ along the banks of the

rivers.
, the flood and its
A year later ~~and the~~ damages are still making a difference in our lives. My grandparents are
our *We're* *their home*
currently living in ~~my~~ home ~~due to the flood.~~ ~~We are~~ having to rebuild starting from the basic
paint, *or do* *else*
framework. We frequently go ~~out~~ to their house and help ~~pain,~~ clean up, whatever needs to be
I'm
done. ~~I am very~~ proud to have participated in this battle to reestablish the lives/ of the people

affected by the flood. Despite the devastating and unforgettable destruction caused by the Flood of

'98, it caused the community and the whole area of Central Texas to unite and help others in need.

Essay 45: *Seventeen/Cover Girl* are looking for leadership, initiative, and caring for the greater good in a way that has made a significant impact on your community or the world at large. In 200 words or less, share your specific contribution in the fields of volunteerism and public services which enhance your community and the world.

The majority of my volunteer service is centered on children. I find working with children gives me the most satisfaction because I know that I am really contributing to their life and hopefully I can influence them in a positive way. Young children really are open-minded and love to learn new things, so I try to be the best role model by my actions and behavior.

Several children-related volunteer services include working in Day Cares, Elf Louise, Parent-Teacher Network Programs, Inner City Games, Kid-Care Program and several other organizations. However, my most recent service project was working with children between the ages of four and twelve at a local church with their Vacation Bible School Program, which lasted two weeks.

Working at this local church with these children from all walks of life has been my most enjoyable volunteer activity. Not only did we have to wake up extremely early in the middle of the summer, but we had to go with a wonderful attitude every morning waiting to face a group of energetic children. Each day was a new adventure because we never knew what was going to happen next with these children.

I believe working as a volunteer throughout your community has wonderful benefits for yourself as well as your community. The children learned to become our friends as well as somewhat of a teacher. They gave us the respect, which we were entitled and in return knew they could approach us in a comfortable way. I believe we taught them to respect themselves as well as authority. We provided a good example of what it is like growing up and being in high school and almost in the real world.

Working with children has definitely made me a better person. It's taught me a lot of patience, which in the beginning I can admit I didn't have a lot of. I believe patience is good and is definitely needed in every day life. It also taught me to communicate and work better with children, which will benefit me throughout my life. This experience also helped me to appreciate children and to realize that being a parent is a difficult job. After working with these children for two weeks I really started to admire the parents of these children because they provided so much for their children.

Every experience I have encountered through volunteer work has taught me something new about myself as well as others. All of these lessons will be put to good use as I continue on through life. The general fact that you do not get paid for doing community service is a big reason why people do not want to get involved. They fell that you have to get something back for working hard. Despite this fact, I feel that you are getting something more valuable than money back after you donate your time to better somebody's life. You take home valuable lessons and experiences in which money could never teach you.

I have really enjoyed being involved in my community and plan to continue my service throughout college. I believe that everybody has something different to offer the world, so share it and let your talents and hard work better the community around you.

Essay 45—Makeover: At 542 words, this essay is too long and lacks focus. Since this competition is based solely on the essay, it needs to be focused on the applicant's volunteer achievements. The deleted areas are those that weaken the essay.

[Delete the first two sentences. They ramble and state the obvious.]
The majority of my volunteer service is centered on children. I find working with children gives me the most satisfaction because I know that I am really contributing to their life and hopefully I
[Move this sentence to the end of the next paragraph.]
can influence them in a positive way. Young children really are open-minded and love to learn new things, so I try to be the best role model by my actions and behavior.

My most rewarding volunteer work was working with
Several children-related volunteer services include working in Day Cares, Elf Louise, Parent-Teacher Network Programs, Inner City Games, Kid-Care Program and several other organizations.

However, my most recent service project was working with children between the ages of four and
[Moved from next paragraph.]
's   . Each day was an adventure
twelve at a local church with their Vacation Bible School Program, which lasted two weeks.
because we never knew what was going [Moved from first paragraph.]   Through my actions,
to happen next. The children were open-minded and loved to learn new things. I tried to be the

best example, role model, and mentor ~~I could be through my actions and behavior~~

```
[Delete-already said.]
```
~~Working at this local church with these children from all walks of life has been my most~~
Though I had   *during*
~~enjoyable volunteer activity.~~ Not only did we have to wake up ~~extremely~~ early ~~in the middle of the~~
time, it wasn't difficult
summer, but we had to go with a wonderful attitude every morning ~~waiting~~ to face a group of

```
[Moved to previous paragraph.]
```
energetic children. ~~Each day was a new adventure because we never knew what was going to happen next with these children.~~

```
[Delete-understood.]
```
~~I believe working as a volunteer throughout your community has wonderful benefits for yourself~~
These   *became*   *and, in some ways, our teachers.*
~~as well as your community.~~ The children ~~learned to become~~ our friends ~~as well as somewhat of a~~
and
~~teacher.~~ They gave us the respect, ~~which we were entitled and in return knew they could approach us in a comfortable way.~~ I believe we taught them to respect themselves ~~as well as authority. We provided a good example of what it is like growing up and being in high school and almost in the real world.~~

```
[Impact should not be used as a verb.]
```
          we were trying to have a positive effect   the   *w*
Though the ~~point to volunteering was to impact~~ on ~~that group of energetic~~ children, ~~W~~orking
   them
with ~~children has definitely~~ made me a better person. It's taught me ~~a lot of patience, which in the beginning I can admit I didn't have a lot of.~~ I believe patience ~~is good and is definitely needed in~~
communication skills,
~~every day life.~~ It also taught me to communicate and work better with children, ~~which will benefit me throughout my life.~~ This experience also ~~helped me~~ to appreciate children and to realize that being a parent is a difficult job. ~~After working with these children for two weeks I really started to admire the parents of these children because they provided so much for their children.~~

~~Every experience I have encountered through volunteer work has taught me something new~~
          I've put a   .
~~about myself as well as others.~~ All of these lessons ~~will be put~~ to good use ~~as I continue on through life. The general fact that you do not get paid for doing community service is a big reason why~~

~~people do not want to get involved. They fell that you have to get something back for working hard.~~

Volunteering gives rewards

~~Despite this fact, I feel that you are getting something~~ more valuable than money ~~back after you~~

~~donate your time to better somebody's life. You take home valuable lessons and experiences in~~

~~which money could never teach you.~~

I

I ~~have really enjoyed being involved in my community and~~ plan to continue my service

Everyone   *unique*

throughout college. ~~I believe that everybody~~ has something ~~different~~ to offer the world, so share it

and let your talents and hard work better the community around you.

Essay 46: Make a statement of your plans as they relate to your educational and career objectives and future goals. Describe your creative talents and special skills. There's no word limit.

When I was about six years old I designed a collection of clothes based on the circus. I did four dresses based on a lion, cotton candy, a hot dog, and a box of popcorn. They were supposed to be made of large masses of dyed ostrich feathers and embroidered silk. I have been designing clothes since then. I tried my hand at sewing when I was younger, but it wasn't until a few years ago that I really started to make clothes. This year, I am putting on my own ten piece collection for a class in which he student studies a career field of their choice. I make all my own patterns and I create my own way of putting them together. For many years all I would do is take clothes apart, so I use that as a basis of clothes construction.

My mother used to draw and paint all the time. She taught me most of what I know in terms of two-dimensional art. But, to be honest, I've never had much formal training. I took two art classes in high school. The teacher in my high school had us draw from magazine pictures and other's drawings. Because I've always been able to draw very well, I did not feel that I was learning very much, or that this was letting me try new things. For the past few months I've been visiting an art teacher at another high school, and I am learning much more from him. I gives me ideas for projects and we discuss other's works. I can try new things and I have more freedom for creativity.

My ultimate goal is to house my own fashion design company. Even though I've been designing since I was very young, I know I need training to be able to direct my creativity. From what I've read and seen about the Art Institute of Chicago, I feel that it is an excellent place for students to submerge themselves from an artistic atmosphere and see things from all new perspectives. I love the idea of so many different ways to approach things and of approaching fashion design from a creative aspect and not so much cut and dry mass market practicality. I am extremely focused and goal oriented. The intensive study of art and design that the Institute offers is perfect for me as a student to be able to wander creatively the way I want and need to so badly.

Essay 46—Makeover:

When I was about six years old*,* I designed a collection of clothes ~~based on the~~ circus*, with a theme. designed* I ~~did~~ four *to look like* dresses ~~based on~~ a lion, cotton candy, a hot dog, and a box of popcorn. ~~They were supposed to be~~ *[Delete-unclear.]* ~~made of large masses of dyed ostrich feathers and embroidered silk.~~ I *'ve* ~~have~~ *ever* been designing clothes since ~~then.~~ I tried my hand at sewing when I was younger, but it wasn't until a few years ago that I really started to make clothes. This year, ~~I am~~ *I'm* putting on ~~my own~~ *a show of a* ten piece collection ~~for a class in~~ *an Independent Student/Mentor Class where I was paired with a professional. I made all the* ~~which he student studies a career field of their choice. I make all my own patterns and I create my~~ *patterns and designed how to put* ~~own way of putting~~ them together. For ~~many~~ years ~~all I would do is take~~ *I took* clothes apart, ~~so~~ *and now* I use that *the for understanding* as a basis ~~of~~ clothes construction.

My mother used to draw and paint all the time. She taught me most of what I know in terms of *[There isn't any reason to emphasize this.]* two-dimensional art. ~~But, to be honest, I've never had much formal training.~~ *I've taken* ~~I took~~ two art classes in high school. ~~The teacher in my high school had us draw from magazine pictures and other's drawings. Because I've always been able to draw very well, I did not feel that I was learning very much, or that this was letting me try new things.~~ For the past few months I've been visiting an art teacher at another high school, and ~~I am~~ *I'm* learning much ~~more~~ *so* from him. ~~I~~ *These classes* gives me ideas for projects ~~and we discuss other's works.~~ I can try new things and I have more freedom for creativity, and we discuss others' works.

My ultimate goal is to ~~house~~ *establish* my own fashion design company. Even though I've been designing since I was ~~very~~ young, ~~I know~~ I need training to be able to direct my creativity. From what I've read and seen about the Art Institute of Chicago, ~~I feel that it is an excellent place for~~ students ~~to submerge themselves~~ *are immersed* in an artistic atmosphere ~~and see things from all~~ *that presents and nurtures* new perspectives. ~~I love the idea of so many different ways to approach things and of~~ *The Institute provides a variety of ways to* approaching fashion design from a creative aspect ~~and not so much cut and dry mass market practicality.~~ *rather than a commercial* . ~~I am~~ *I'm* extremely focused and goal oriented. The intensive ~~study~~ *program* of art and design that the Institute ~~offers is perfect~~ *will provide* ~~for me as a student to be able to wander creatively the way I want and need to so badly.~~ *an environment where I'll be able to study and grow creatively.*

Essay 47: Please describe your creative talents and special talents. Your essay may be no longer than one double-spaced page.

It comes in poems that flow from my pen and music from the touch of my fingers on ivory keys. Ever since I can remember, I've been bubbling with creativity. When I was nine, I painted nature scenes. In elementary school, I started piano lessons and continued them up into my freshman year in high school. For my last recital in May of 1995, I arranged a medley of songs from Andrew Lloyd Weber's *The Phantom of the Opera*. I've been writing since I was in middle school. I was published in my high school's literary magazine my freshman and junior year. This talent has blossomed and recently awarded me with the position of Poetry Editor.

This intense interest in anything creative has taught me some interesting things and put me in some enjoyable places. I've found myself at the annual jazz festival, learning to swing to the sounds of Manhattan Transfer. I also learned how to do various Irish dances. Being involved in the Cultural Exchange Club exposes me to many different ethnic traditions, such as learning how to use castanets. Also, sometimes while at nursing homes for the enjoyment of the residents, I will play the piano.

Although I have a wide base of interests and creative talents, most of my creativity goes into my writing. I have always enjoyed writing and reading the writings of others. This is my second year on the literary magazine staff and my first on the executive staff. I was entrusted with the job of Poetry Editor because of the lyrical quality of my work and my knowledge of the styles and works of other poets. I'm constantly working to improve my writing and expand my style.

I also have many unique skills. One skill I possess is the ease and enjoyment I derive from learning. I have always been quick at understanding things. If I don't naturally understand a principal or idea, my inquisitive nature rolls into action, prodding me to research it as much as I can to comprehend it. Another skill I have is my manner with people. I enjoy people and they tend to enjoy me. I work at having good relationships with everyone I know, and being comfortable with them.

Being a very creative person will help me in my choice of studies as well. Looking creatively at life and biology, I will be able to come up with explanations of phenomenons that the strictly scientific mind may overlook. My skills will aid me in dealing with people and being a success in college and in life.

Essay 47—Makeover: Though well-written, this essay is too long and needs to be cut by approximately 125 words. It tends to be repetitive. The second paragraph needs to be cut because it has nothing to do with the topic. The resulting essay is stronger and to the point.

My creativity · · · *words in the form of* · · · [Moved from third sentence.] · · · ,
It comes in poems that flow from my pen, pictures from the feathery touch of my paintbrush and

in · · · [Delete-irrelevant.]
music from the touch of my fingers on ivory keys. ~~Ever since I can remember, I've been bubbling~~

[Moved from first sentence.]
~~with creativity.~~ ~~When I was nine, I painted nature scenes.~~ In elementary school, I started piano

through
lessons and continued them ~~up into~~ my freshman year in high school. For my last recital in May of

Webber's
1995, I arranged a medley of songs from Andrew Lloyd ~~Weber's~~ The Phantom of the Opera. ~~I've~~

during

~~been writing since I was in middle school.~~ I was published in my high school's literary magazine

, and currently hold

my freshman and junior year/ ~~This talent has blossomed and recently awarded me with~~ the position

of Poetry Editor.

~~This intense interest in anything creative has taught me some interesting things and put me in~~

~~some enjoyable places. I've found myself at the annual jazz festival, learning to swing to the sounds~~

~~of Manhattan Transfer. I also learned how to do various Irish dances. Being involved in the Cultural~~

~~Exchange Club exposes me to many different ethnic traditions, such as learning how to use~~

~~castanets. Also, sometimes while at nursing homes for the enjoyment of the residents, I will play the~~

~~piano.~~

range

Although I have a wide ~~base~~ of interests and creative talents, most of my creativity goes into my

I've   [Redundant—delete.]

writing. ~~I have~~ always enjoyed writing and reading the writings of others. ~~This is my second year~~

[Delete—irrelevant.]

~~on the literary magazine staff and my first on the executive staff. I was entrusted with the job of~~

~~Poetry Editor because of the lyrical quality of my work and my knowledge of the styles and works~~

~~of other poets.~~ I'm constantly working to improve my writing and expand my style.

[Delete—everyone does.]

~~I also have many unique skills.~~ One skill I possess is the ease and enjoyment I derive from

learning. ~~I have always been quick at understanding things.~~ If I don't naturally understand a

principle or idea, my inquisitive nature rolls into action, prodding me to research it as much as I can

I'm a people person.

to comprehend it. ~~Another skill I have is my manner with people. I enjoy people and they tend to~~

~~enjoy me.~~ I work at having good relationships ~~with everyone I know~~ and being comfortable with

everyone I know.

~~them.~~

Being a ~~very~~ creative person will help me in my choice of studies ~~as well.~~ Looking creatively at

I'll   *a*

life and biology, ~~I will~~ be able to come up with explanations of phenomen~~ons~~ that the strictly

learning and people   *in*   *ful*

scientific mind may overlook. My skills will aid me in dealing with people and being ~~a~~ success in

college and in life.

Essay 48: Goals and Aspirations. Make a statement of your plans as they relate to your educational and career objectives and future goals. Your essay may be no more than one double-spaced page.

There are many things I hope to accomplish and achieve in my lifetime. Some of these plans are short-termed and will be obtained within the next few years. A goal I have for the remainder of my senior year is to benefit as much as I can from my current classes. Doing all the required work, talking with my teachers, and getting help when necessary are a few of the things I'll do to help me obtain my goal. Another thing I have planned for high school is to help produce an award-winning literary magazine with my school and peers by dedicating myself to the magazine and devoting my time as Poetry Editor. After I've obtained these goals, I have college to look forward to.

In college, a whole other world will offer itself to me. I plan to take a wide variety of life science courses while in college. This will help me narrow my career choice to a specific field in biology, such as microbiology, biophysics, or genetics, that I can continue studying in graduate school. I also plan to get involved in more activities than I am currently involved in. Living in a single-parent home, transportation to and from school is often restricted to a time schedule. In college this hindrance will be removed and I will be able to get involved in many activities, like Habitat for Humanity, volunteer work at nursing homes and the Animal Defense League, and intercollegiate sailing. By doing these things I will gain valuable and become a well-rounded person who is able to handle any situation.

My plans after college and graduate school are more nebulous but will become clearer as I approach my college graduation date. I want to be content with the life I make for myself. To do this, I plan to influence people by what I do professionally. Whether I'm counseling a woman about genetic testing or researching protein synthesis in the cell, I want my work to help people. This is why I'm interested in biology, literally the study of life. The more I know about the way life works, the more I can change it for the better. I also hope to keep learning. The mystery of life intrigues me and I want to understand as much as I can. By gathering knowledge I will expand and augment my impact on the lives of others. I also will continue my volunteer work, helping those in need.

Every stage of my life is filled with goals and the plans to achieve them. All of my plans build on each other. By understanding my present studies, I will be able to enter into college with a more comprehensive idea of how they affect my chosen field of biology. By narrowing my choice of careers in college, I'll be able to enter into graduate school with ease and then be satisfied with my choice of professions. Everything I hope to accomplish will work to make me a better individual.

Essay 48—Makeover: We condensed this essay by removing redundancy and digression. The resulting essay is 305 words in length and fits on one double-spaced page.

[Delete—redundant.]
There are many things I hope to ~~accomplish and~~ achieve in my lifetime. ~~Some of these plans are short-termed and will be obtained within the next few years. A goal I have for the remainder of my~~

My immediate goals include getting the most [Rambling—delete.]
~~senior year is to benefit as much as I can from my~~ ~~current~~ classes. ~~Doing all the required work,~~ ~~talking with my teachers, and getting help when necessary are a few of the things I'll do to help me~~

I also want
~~obtain my goal. Another thing I have planned for high school is~~ to help produce an award-winning

for *. I'm committing*
literary magazine ~~with~~ my school and peers ~~by~~ ~~dedicating~~ myself to the magazine and devoting my

[Understood—delete.]
time as Poetry Editor. ~~After I've obtained these goals, I have college to look forward to.~~

C *will open* *new* *for*
~~In~~ ¢ollege / a whole ~~other~~ world ~~will offer itself to me~~ I plan to take a wide variety of life science

. Those courses and experiences
courses ~~while in college.~~ ~~This~~ will help me narrow my career choice to a specific field in biology, such as microbiology, biophysics, or genetics, that I can continue studying in graduate school.

[Unnecessary—delete.]
~~I also plan to get involved in more activities than I am currently involved in.~~ [New paragraph.]

by
Living in a single-parent home, transportation to and from school is often restricted ~~to~~ a time

I'll
schedule. In college this hindrance will be removed and ~~I will~~ be able to get involved in many

ing *,*
activities, like Habitat for Humanity, volunteer ~~work~~ at nursing homes ~~and~~ the Animal Defense

, I'll *experience*
League, and intercollegiate sailing. By doing these things ~~I will~~ gain valuable and become a well-rounded person who is able to handle any situation.

professional goals
My ~~plans after college and graduate school~~ are more nebulous but will become clearer as I

the end of my education
approach ~~my college graduation date.~~ I want to be content with the life I make for myself. To do

this, I plan to influence people by what I do professionally. Whether I'm counseling a woman about

genetic testing or researching protein synthesis in the cell, I want my work to help people. This is

why I'm interested in biology, literally the study of life. The more I know about the way life works,

[Move this next sentence to beginning of next paragraph.]
the more I can change it for the better. ~~I also hope to keep learning. The mystery of life intrigues~~

~~me and I want to understand as much as I can. By gathering knowledge I will expand and augment~~

~~my impact on the lives of others. I also will continue my volunteer work, helping those in need.~~

[Moved from previous paragraph.]   *for*   *ing*
I also want to keep learning. Every stage of my life is filled with goals and ~~the~~ plans ~~to~~ achieve

[Delete—already stated.]
them. All of my plans build on each other. ~~By understanding my present studies, I will be able to~~

~~enter into college with a more comprehensive idea of how they affect my chosen field of biology.~~

~~By narrowing my choice of careers in college, I'll be able to enter into graduate school with ease~~

~~and then be satisfied with my choice of professions.~~ Everything I hope to accomplish will work to

make me a better individual.

Essay 49: In 500 words or less, describe and evaluate one experience that significantly influenced your academic interests. Be sure to explain how this experience led to your setting the goals you now have for yourself, and why you think the academic program for which you are applying will help you to reach those goals.

Ever since fifth grade I've known what I wanted to do once I "grew up." What I remember most as

a kid is making airplanes. It didn't matter what I made them out of. I used whatever I could get my

little hands on. My creations had to be more than regular folded airplanes. It was more challenging

and fun that way. Not all of the designs flew, but my determination led to more and more flying

models.

One particular day I can remember, I made a model of NASA's space shuttle. I even made the

solid fuel booster rockets and the storage tank in the middle. After spending an hour or so on the whole thing, I felt really proud. It basically looked like the real thing. It didn't have the right colors and was a bit flimsy because I made it out of notebook paper. Then came the moment of truth. I stood up and threw it toward the other side of my room. It was a dismal failure. As soon as it left my hand air resistance got the better of it. It appeared to hit a wall and fell. It was too light, especially in the front, not to mention the fact that the wings almost came off when I threw it. As I looked at it in its mangled state on the floor, I thought about what happened when I let it go. I I immediately formulated changes to fix the problems, or at least most of them.

Persistent, I picked it up and went back to work. After working on it for several hours, it looked as good as new and not as flimsy. I added some weight to the nose so it would fly better. Undaunted, I stood up again and threw it across the room. This time instead of falling, it flew the great distance of three whole feet, but that didn't matter. The plane had flown.

As I sat and made more improvements, I realized it would be great to do this every day. From that moment on I knew I wanted to design and test airplanes and vehicles that would push the limits of conventional travel. It was as simple as that. There was no long trying time of indecision to figure out what I wanted to do when I "grew up." Only later did I learn that there are actually words for what I wanted to be: aerospace engineer.

I want to major in aerospace engineering, with a concentration on atmospheric flight. My dream is to create vehicles that will change the way society travels. In the future I see families traveling in flying cars that I designed. When they travel between cities, they won't be restricted to any highway or have to deal with the inconveniences of rush hour.

These dreams have been a part of my life since I was eleven. This scholarship is an important part of the necessary funds that will allow me to further my education. With my ability to think creatively and divergently, work well with others, and produce new ideas, I can achieve my goals and revolutionize the way the human race travels.

Essay 49—Makeover: Though this essay is well written, it's too long. With a few minor changes, this is a strong essay. The resulting essay is 480 words in length.

Since fifth grade I've known what I want to do, where I want to go to college, and even whom I want to work for. What I remember most as a kid is making airplanes. It didn't matter what I made them out of, I used whatever I could get my little hands on. ~~Mine had to be more than regular folded airplanes. It was more challenging and fun that way.~~ Not all of the designs flew, but my determination led to more and more flying models.

One particular day ~~I can remember,~~ I made a model of NASA's space shuttle. I even made the solid fuel booster rockets and the storage tank in the middle. After spending an hour or so on the whole thing, I felt really proud of myself. It looked basically like the real thing. Sure, it didn't have the right colors and it was kind of flimsy, but hey, I had made it out of notebook paper. Then came the moment of truth. I stood up and threw it toward the other side of my room. It was a dismal failure. As soon as it left my hand, air resistance got the better of it. It hit a wall and fell. It was too light, especially in the front. Not to mention the fact that the wings almost came off when I threw it. As I looked at ~~its~~ the mangled ~~state~~ mess on the floor, I thought about what happened when I let it go. I immediately formulated changes to fix the problems, or at least most of them. Persistent, I picked it up and went back to work. After working on it for several hours, it looked as good as new and not as flimsy. I added some weight to the nose so it would fly better. Undaunted, I stood up again and threw it across the room. This time, instead of falling, it flew the great distance of three whole feet. But that didn't matter, I knew I'd gotten somewhere.

As I sat and tried to ~~fix it some more~~ improve the design, I thought to myself, wouldn't it be great to do this every day? From that moment on, I knew I wanted to design and build flying things, whether they would fly be in space or in the air. It was as simple as that. ~~There was no long trying time of indecision as I figured out what I wanted to do.~~ Only later did I learn there ~~was~~ were actually words for what I wanted to be: an aerospace engineer.

When I discovered the "official" title for my future career, I asked around to find out ~~where~~ *which college* would

be a good place to ~~go to college~~ *attend* for an aerospace engineering degree. I was told by many people

that Texas A&M University was a good school for that degree.

I'm looking forward to successfully completing my degree, one of the biggest challenges I'll

probably ever encounter. When I graduate, my degree will help me get my "Dream Job." I aspire to

share the same dream ~~with~~ *as* Neil Armstrong and Alan Shepard as an employee of NASA.

Essay 50: The same student who wrote Essay 49 also had the following assignment: "In your own words, please describe in 75 words or less why you want to be a recipient of the Sam Walton Community Scholarship. Please include the course of study or major field of interest you plan to follow, your proposed occupation or profession, and other abilities you have that were not previously mentioned in this form." The student's task in this case was to cut his previous essay from 480 words to 75 words. We've reprinted the corrected long version of the essay so you can try your hand at cutting this essay.

Since fifth grade I've known what I want to do, where I want to go to college, and even whom I

want to work for. What I remember most as a kid is making airplanes. It didn't matter what I made

them out of, I used whatever I could get my little hands on. Not all of the designs flew, but my

determination led to more and more flying models.

One particular day, I made a model of NASA's space shuttle, I even made the solid fuel booster

rockets and the storage tank in the middle. After spending an hour or so on the whole thing, I felt

really proud of myself. It looked basically like the real thing. Sure, it didn't have the right colors and

it was kind of flimsy, but hey, I had made it out of notebook paper. Then came the moment of truth.

I stood up and threw it toward the other side of my room. It was a dismal failure. As soon as it left

my hand air resistance got the better of it. It hit a wall and fell. It was too light, especially in the

front. Not to mention the fact that the wings almost came off when I threw it. As I looked at its

mangled state on the floor, I thought about what happened when I let it go. I immediately

formulated changes to fix the problems, or at least most of them. Persistent, I picked it up and went back to work. After working on it for several hours, it looked as good as new and not as flimsy. I added some weight to the nose so it would fly better. Undaunted, I stood up again and threw it across the room. This time instead of falling, it flew the great distance of three whole feet. But that didn't matter, I knew I'd gotten somewhere.

As I sat and tried to fix it some more, I thought to myself, wouldn't it be great to do this every day. From that moment on I knew I wanted to design and build flying things, whether they would be in space or in the air. It was as simple as that. There was no long trying time of indecision as I figured out what I wanted to do. Only later did I learn there was actually words for what I wanted to be: an aerospace engineer.

When I discovered the "official" title for my future career, I asked around to find out where would be a good place to go to college for an aerospace engineering degree. I was told by many people that Texas A&M University was a good school for that degree.

I'm looking forward to successfully completing my degree, one of the biggest challenges I'll probably ever encounter. When I graduate, my degree will help me get my "Dream Job." I aspire to share the same dream with Neil Armstrong and Alan Shepard as an employee of NASA.

Essay 50—Makeover: This is the essay cut down to 75 words. It contains only the essential information, yet it's still interesting to read.

Since making paper airplanes in fifth grade, I've wanted to major in aerospace engineering, concentrating in atmospheric flight. My dream is to create vehicles that will revolutionize the way humans travel. In the future I see families traveling in flying cars that I've designed. As I have in Odyssey of the Mind, thinking creatively and divergently, working well with others, and producing new ideas, I can achieve my goals and change the way people travel. [Odyssey of the Mind is a program in which students of all ages and levels are challenged to find creative answers to several tough problems. Teams compete at the local, regional, national, and world levels.]

Essay 51: Write an essay of no more than 1,000 words on your goals.

My work in life has varied over the years, but my goal has never faltered. I have always known that I wanted to work in the medical profession. The problem I suppose as my father once said to me is that I had to grow up. Some people it may take days, or months, but for me it took years. It wasn't until I was in my early thirties that I had made up my mind, and my life, that I was going to follow my ideals of being a physician.

It's unfortunate that fate does not have the same ideals as the individual. When I had finished High school my grades were not up to the standards needed for the medical schools. This led me to the problem of what to do. I finally decided that I would follow the crows, and I went to the College of Aeronautics. This being a wonderful school in its own right I soon discovered that it was not for me. However, my ideals of never say die keep me going. I did graduate with a not so great GPA, and an associate's in applied science (design).

In 1982 when I graduated, the job market for aerospace engineers technicians was not the best in the New York area, so I applied for a position as a mechanical drafter. Although at the time I felt that this was to be only a temporary position I remained with that job for six (6) years. I left that job for a new and better one, which unfortunately closed after two (2) years. After this time as a mechanical drafter I decided to re-enter school. I went to the community college to further my career as an engineer. It was there that I had realized that I was after the wrong goal. I decided to rethink my concept of my career goal this is when I tried my hand at an acting career.

I was in need of a new life and some friends of mine, actually challenged me to go out for an audition, that was going on in the neighborhood. I did and that started me off on what I thought was going to be a full-time career for me. Acting, singing and dancing were not the best things that I could do. At each musical audition that I would go to I would get a spot on the show for my singing but, never because I could act. This I found a little discouraging, I knew that I could offer more. I stayed with the acting career for three (3) years never getting above the community theater status.

Then it came during one of the road shows, I was talking to the other actors, all of whom were part-time actors and full-time other. They all told me that I could do both professions that I like to do, one being acting and the other being in the medical profession, this is when I finally decided that I would go for my first dream.

Since I started studying for the Physician's Assistant's degree I have never regretted it. I have the belief that all of my past experiences that I have in life were all geared for this goals. My work as a mechanical engineer allows me to see the internals of the human body in my mind. This is a skill that I have been told and discovered is very useful. The three (3) years that I spent as an actor I have also found to be very helpful to me. I found that I can relate to the other students and the professors in a more friendly and assured fashion. I know that this will help me in my treatment of patients, because now I feel that I can relate to them better. Even to say that because it took me longer to grow up and make adult decisions, this too will be helpful to me. I wish to study to be a Physician Assistant to a Pediatric Doctor so being a kid awhile will be very helpful in allowing me to understand and be able to talk to the children.

After some twelve (12) years after college of floating about with no real place or goal to go to. I now know that this is what I am supposed to be doing. The classes are more interesting to me and the studies come to me as though I already have some knowledge of them. I enjoy this time in college more so than before and this to me shows that I am doing the right thing, I know that I can proceed to be a Physician's Assistant.

Essay 51—Makeover: This shorter 412 word version is tighter and smoother. During editing, information that wasn't vital to the story was deleted.

[Where else could it be? In death?]

My work ~~in life~~ has varied over the years, but my goal has never faltered. ~~I have~~ I've always known

[Delete the next two sentences. Never emphasize a negative.]

that I wanted to work in the medical profession. ~~The problem I suppose as my father once said to me is that I had to grow up. Some people it may take days, or months, but for me it took years.~~ It wasn't until I was in my early thirties that I ~~had~~ made up my mind/ ~~and my life, that I was going~~ to

dream

follow my ~~ideals~~ of being a physician.

[Delete—implies grades were left up to fate.]

~~It's unfortunate that fate does not have the same ideals as the individual.~~ When I had finished

h   *,*   *weren't*   *a pre-med major.*

~~H~~igh school my grades ~~were not~~ up to the standards needed for ~~the medical schools. This led me to~~

~~the problem of what to do.~~ I ~~finally~~ decided ~~that~~ I would follow the crowd, and ~~I~~ went to the

Though it was a

College of Aeronautics. ~~This being a~~ wonderful school, ~~in its own right~~ I ~~soon~~ discovered ~~that it~~

wasn't   *kept*   *d*

~~was not~~ for me. However, my ideals of never say die ~~keep~~ me going. I ~~did~~ graduate with

[Never emphasize a negative.]   *degree*

~~a not so great GPA, and~~ an associate's in applied science (design).

engineering   *wasn't strong*

In 1982 ~~when I graduated,~~ the job market for aerospace ~~engineers~~ technicians ~~was not the best~~

in the Los Angeles area, so I applied for a position as a mechanical drafter. Although at the time I felt

,   *in that profession for eight*   [Delete—a bit

this was to be only a temporary position I remained ~~with that job for six (6)~~ years. ~~I left that job for~~

too much information.]

~~a new and better one, which unfortunately closed after two (2) years. After this time as a~~

return to school and enrolled in a local   *.*

~~mechanical drafter~~ I decided to ~~re-enter school. I went to the~~ community college ~~to further my~~

[Delete these sentences. It makes you sound wishy-washy about your goals.]

~~career as an engineer. It was there that I had realized that I was after the wrong goal. I decided to~~

~~rethink my concept of my career goal this is when I tried my hand at an acting career.~~

During that time,   *attend a neigborhood*

~~I was in need of a new life and~~ some friends ~~of mine, actually~~ challenged me to ~~go out for an~~

theater audition.   *T*

~~audition, that was going on in the neighborhood.~~ I did and ~~t~~hat started me ~~off~~ on what I thought

.   [Delete—negative.]

was going to be a full-time career ~~for me. Acting, singing and dancing were not the best things that I~~

,   *I'd*   *.*   [Negative—

~~could do.~~ At each musical audition ~~that I would go to~~ I would get a spot on the show ~~for my singing~~

delete.]

~~but, never because I could act. This I found a little discouraging, I knew that I could offer more.~~ I

[Three years is hardly a career.]

community theater

stayed with ~~the acting career~~ for three ~~(3)~~ years ~~never getting above the community theater status.~~

D

~~Then it came~~ ~~d~~uring one of the road shows, I was talking to the other actors, all of whom were part-

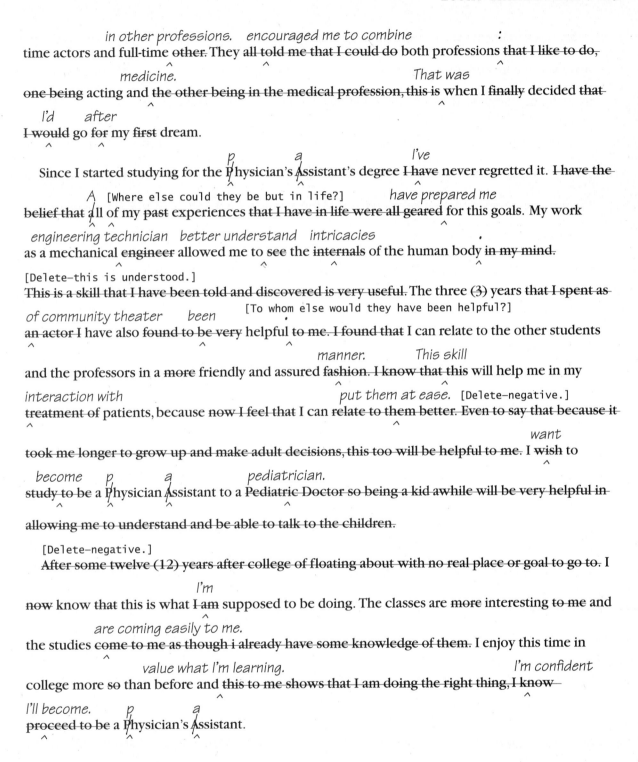

in other professions.   *encouraged me to combine*   :
time actors and full-time ~~other~~. They ~~all told me that I could do~~ both professions ~~that I like to do,~~

            medicine.   *That was*
~~one being~~ acting and ~~the other being in the medical profession, this is~~ when I ~~finally~~ decided ~~that~~

     I'd   *after*
~~I would~~ go ~~for~~ my ~~first~~ dream.

                                            p   *a*   *I've*
    Since I started studying for the ~~P~~hysician's ~~A~~ssistant's degree ~~I have~~ never regretted it. ~~I have the~~

         A [Where else could they be but in life?]   *have prepared me*
~~belief that~~ ~~a~~ll of my ~~past~~ experiences ~~that I have in life were all geared~~ for this ~~goals~~. My work

       engineering technician   *better understand*   *intricacies*
as a mechanical ~~engineer~~ allowed me to ~~see~~ the ~~internals~~ of the human body ~~in my mind~~.

[Delete-this is understood.]
~~This is a skill that I have been told and discovered is very useful.~~ The three ~~(3)~~ years ~~that I spent as~~

     of community theater   *been*   [To whom else would they have been helpful?]
~~an actor~~ I have also ~~found to be very~~ helpful ~~to me. I found that~~ I can relate to the other students

                                               manner.   *This skill*
and the professors in a ~~more~~ friendly and assured ~~fashion. I know that this~~ will help me in my

interaction with   *put them at ease.* [Delete-negative.]
~~treatment of~~ patients, because ~~now I feel that I can~~ ~~relate to them better. Even to say that because it~~

                                                                    want
~~took me longer to grow up and make adult decisions, this too will be helpful to me.~~ I ~~wish~~ to

      become *p*   *a*   *pediatrician.*
~~study to be a~~ ~~P~~hysician ~~A~~ssistant ~~to a Pediatric Doctor so being a kid awhile will be very helpful in~~

~~allowing me to understand and be able to talk to the children.~~

    [Delete-negative.]
    ~~After some twelve (12) years after college of floating about with no real place or goal to go to.~~ I

                             I'm
~~now~~ know ~~that~~ this is what ~~I am~~ supposed to be doing. The classes are ~~more~~ interesting ~~to me~~ and

              are coming easily to me.
the studies ~~come to me as though i already have some knowledge of them~~. I enjoy this time in

               value what I'm learning.   *I'm confident*
college more ~~so~~ than before and ~~this to me shows that I am doing the right thing, I know~~

I'll become.   *p*   *a*
~~proceed to be a~~ ~~P~~hysician's ~~A~~ssistant.

Essay 52: The same student wanted to adapt the previous essay for a shorter essay on goals. The student made some changes to the previously edited version. This 441-word essay must be cut down to 200 words.

My work in life has varied over the years, but my goal has never faltered. I have always known that I wanted to work in the medical profession. It wasn't until I was in my early thirties that I had made up my mind that I was going to follow my dream of being a physician.

Unfortunately, fate doesn't always have the same plans as an individual. When I finished high school my grades were not up to the rigorous standards needed for a pre-med major. This led me to the problem of what to do. I decided I would follow the crowd, and went to the College of Aeronautics. Though it was a wonderful school, I discovered it wasn't for me. However, my ideals of never say die kept me going. I graduated with an associate's degree in applied science (design).

In 1982, the job market for aerospace engineering technicians wasn't strong in the Los Angeles area, so I applied for a position as a mechanical drafter. Although at the time I felt that this was to be only a temporary position I remained in that profession for eight years. I decided to return to school and enrolled in a local community college.

I was in need of a new life. Some friends challenged me to go out for a neighborhood audition. I started off on what I thought might become a full-time career. At each musical audition I would get a spot on the show. I stayed with community theater acting for three years. During one of the road shows, I met several actors who were part-time actors and worked full-time at other careers. They encouraged me to combine both professions, acting and medicine. This when I decided I would go after my dream.

Since I started studying for the physician's assistant's degree I've never regretted it. All of my experiences have preparing me for this goal. My work as a mechanical engineering technician allows me to better understand the intricacies of the human body. The three years of community have been helpful. I can relate to the other students and the professors in a friendly and assured fashion. I know this will help me in my interaction with patients, because I'm able to put them at ease.

I want to become a physician assistant to a pediatrician. This is truly what I'm supposed to be doing. The classes are interesting and the studies are coming easily to me. I enjoy this time in college more so than before and value what I'm learning. With financial assistance, I'll be able to reach my goal and become a physician assistant.

Essay 52—Makeover: The edited essay is based on the previous edited essay (51) and is 187 words in length.

My work ~~in life~~ has varied over the years, but my goal has never faltered. ~~I have~~ *I've* always ~~known that~~ wanted to work in the medical profession. ~~It wasn't until I was in my early thirties that I had~~ [No new paragraph.] ~~made up my mind that I was going to follow my dream of being a physician. Unfortunately, fate doesn't always have the same plans as an individual.~~ When I finished high school*,* my grades were not up to the ~~rigorous~~ standards needed for a pre-med major. ~~This led me to the problem of what to do.~~ I decided *to pursue* ~~I would follow the crowd, and went to the College of Aeronautics. Though it was a wonderful school, I discovered it wasn't for me. However, my ideals of never say die kept me going. I graduated with~~ an associate's degree in applied science (design).

In 1982, the job market for aerospace engineering technicians wasn't *the best,* ~~strong in the Los Angeles area,~~ so I applied for a position as a mechanical drafter. ~~Although at the time I felt that this was to be only a temporary position I remained in that profession for~~ *After* eight years*,* I decided to ~~return to school and~~ enrolled in a ~~local~~ community college.

~~I was in need of a new life.~~ Some friends challenged me to *attend* ~~go out for~~ a neighborhood *theater* audition. ~~I started off on what I thought might become a full-time career.~~ At each musical audition *I'd* ~~I would~~ get a spot on the show. ~~I stayed with community theater acting for three years.~~ During one of the road shows, I met several actors who were part-time actors and *had* ~~worked~~ full-time ~~at other~~ careers. ~~They encouraged me to combine both professions, acting and medicine.~~ *That was* ~~This~~ when I decided *I'd* ~~I would~~ go after my dream.

~~Since I started studying for the physician's assistant's degree I've never regretted it. All~~

~~of my experiences have preparing me for this goal.~~ My ~~work as a mechanical~~ engineering
background helps *Community*
technician allows me to better understand how the intricacies of the human body. ~~The three years~~
theater helped me gain confidence, which means I'll be able to put patients at ease.
~~of community have been helpful. I can relate to the other students and the professors in a friendly~~

~~and assured fashion. I know this will help me in my interaction with patients, because I'm able to~~

[No new paragraph.] *'s* *and work with*
~~put them at ease.~~ I want to become a physician assistant ~~to~~ a pediatrician. ~~This is truly what I'm~~

~~supposed to be doing. The classes are interesting and the studies are coming easily to me. I enjoy~~

this time in college more than before.
~~this time in college more so than before and value what I'm learning.~~ With financial assistance,
I can do it.
~~I'll be able to reach my goal and become a physician assistant.~~

Essay 53: Write an essay of approximately 1,000 words about your goals. Students might want to touch on an experience that affected their lives. (University of Texas, Austin)

How much happier could I get? I was on my way to a concert of the band I loved. Their best songs were playing selectively in my head. My sister began to ask me a question, as we exited the freeway. She never finished.

It was as if I was in one of the action movies where the audience watches a car wreck from the inside of the driver's car. The wreck did not seem real to me as it happened or after it had happened. Once I had regained consciousness, I was repulsed by the smell, like a damp cave. I could not remember what had happened. I saw a red hash then I blacked out. Now I was scared. The car was filled with smoke. Instinct told me the car was going to explode, yet there was an eerie tranquillity. Using action hero strength, I ripped my brother out of the car seat and at the same time managed to get my sister out of the car. I had stepped out of the gray car, into the pandemonium of the outside. The clear sunny sky was reflected on all the tiny strands of glass that littered the road. My shoes stepped on the glass making the strands pop under my weight. I sat on the sidewalk and waited. As I waited for the car to explode. like I had seen so many times in the movies, the car just stood there crippled. Apparently my car wasn't aware of this fact. EMS came leading fire trucks and the police. The scene must have seemed like a nightmare for some traffic reporter on a radio some where. I imagined the reporter on the local radio station, "I-90 is backed for miles where a head on collision has occurred. EMS and rescue crews are on the scene." The crews worked like ants, going from one destroyed car to the next, pulling, pushing pieces of the cars. The EMS workers came over to me and asked how I felt. "Stupid" was the only word I could muster. The lady that kept asking me questions talked slowly and used big gestures as if she was telling me a camp fire story. She looked at my brother and sister real fast and realized they were off playing in greenest grass I had ever seen on the bank behind me. The lady came back with a big guy. Both wore rubber gloves and looked at me as if they were about to experiment on some unknown substance. They broke their huddle for a moment, and asked me if I was sure I was okay. "Yes, of course" the words slowly ran out. Then they left me alone with an ice pack and a bandaged gash on my forehead as the only souvenir of their visit. I had some sudden crazy impulse to still go to the concert. I called my friend's parents from the bank to come pick up my group. They took me to the concert. I went to the concert. What I heard was great. However, I spent the rest of the night recounting the story of the wreck to all the giggly girls who surrounded me.

A few days later my mom made me relive the accident. After I had related the entire incident, she asked me how I felt. As I explained my headaches and "grogginess" she shriveled up and I could see the fear in her face. She began to ask all kinds of specific questions, and I watched her apprehension grow. My mom was not worried that I had in some way injured myself to the extent that any average teenager could not bounce back from. Instead she was worried that I had injured myself to the extent that some one who was hydrocephalic couldn't bounce back.

When I was 6 months old I was diagnosed as being hydrocephalic. The doctor place a shunt in my brain to drain the excess fluids. They told my mom that she would need to be careful about what I did and not to he surprised if I was not as fast as the other kids or as smart. My mom never thought for a second that her son was going to live a different life then any other kid, so she enrolled me in every sport and class imaginable. At the age of seven, the doctors told me I was no longer chunt dependent. however I needed to he careful what I did. The doctors at Mayo clinic explained that at any moment I could go back to being chunt-dependent. With one incident I could go from normal to abnormal. I refused to believe that would ever happen so I did not let that advise effect me. Up until the day of the accident I had forgotten about the chunt and my hydrocephalic background. However, not the past was affecting the future. I went to the emergency center and explained my symptoms to the neurologist, Dr. Mary Ramirez. She told me they would have to run some tests. I was horrified as they fitted me with a purple dinosaur gown. That's what I get for going to a Children's Hospital. The doctor ordered some tests to be done. Once she got the results I began to hear an argument happening outside my curtain prison. It was my mom and Dr. Ramirez and they were talking loud enough for me to hear. I was not worried that they were arguing so I began to dream about what would it be like to take black paint and paint over the wall paper, which showed happy letters playing on a playground. covered the two walls. Then I heard it, the argument escalated, and a nurse came in with a smile that seemed permanently frozen on her face, and in no way was that smile genuine. She began to talk to me about school but she could not stop me from hearing the argument. The neurologist was telling my mom I need a new chunt placed in me, because the old one was broken and I would surely die if I did not have this operation immediately. At this point I began to cry, for the first time I felt different from everyone else I felt handicapped. Nothing now mattered, I realized, my awards, my grades, who I knew, if someone thought I was handicapped then there would be no way to persuade them no matter how hard I tried. I gave up and thus cried harder, maybe it was because the nurse with the plastic smile was wondering if I wanted to watch a Disney movie. I wanted to hit her so badly at that point but restrained myself, couldn't she see my life was being determined, and all she cared about is whether the seven dwarfs would keep me happy instead of Aladdin. I heard the argument get louder then suddenly the argument stopped. The neurologist came through the curtain and nodded at the nurse to leave. The doctor stared at me, with eyes of sympathy, "Well, we are going to have to put another chunt in to you, sorry about this." Immediately the statistics that my mother told me ran through my head, I would have a fifty percent chance on getting an infection, and then another twenty percent chance on becoming mentally handicapped. I was never one to play my luck, so I did what any teenager would do, I wined. I tried explaining to the doctor about all my awards, my academic success, and the sports I played. The doctor put a smirk on her face and just kept looking beyond me. After I had finished giving her my resume, she explained to me that if I was under her care since the beginning, I would of been properly taken care of. I was then to into the conversation to back down from this statement, so I asked what "properly taken care of" entailed? The neurologist told me that all her patients got a new chunt every seven years, and none of her patients were allowed to play any sports, especially not some sport like soccer. I became irate and started to hate her and the dinosaurs that I wore. This doctor who stood in front of me did not care whether or not a kid would be a kid, but whether or not they would come in for a check up of some sought. This type of person was the same type of people I had been fighting against my whole life. Those people that told me I could not because they saw me as some sort of crippled.

I fended off the doctor for about an hour, she wanted to start the anastesha, however I pulled a tantrum and told them to wait for my mother who was somewhere. To tell the truth I was scared, I was scared that I would become something that I had never considered myself, different. I was half way through Beauty and the Beast when my mom burst through the door with the doctor at her side. My mom quickly explained the situation, either my mom found a way to charter a private medical plane by midnight or the neurosurgeon would take custody of me and complete her surgery. It was funny, all this time I had not once felt any symptoms that I had registered with, thus I felt it time to leave this place of madness. However, I now had a security guard posted at my door. The guard, an elderly man, reminded me of Collin Powell in many ways, and for that reason only did I capitulate to his insistence on escorting me to the bathroom, and making sure I did not escape. I tried my best to make the situation fun, a habit I have anytime I am in a situation that is extremely trying on my sanity. Thus, I tried to think how easily I could turn this situation into a made-for-television movie entitled, "For the Love of All My Children" starring some out of work actors. While I was having fun, my mom was able to charter the plane we needed to get, to take me to Mayo Clinic. She charted the plane just in time too, considering the Child Protective Service agents were at my door waiting to help the neurologist undo numerous years of work and achievements. However, no one was going to hurt me today, no one was going to keep me in dinosaur gowns making me watch Disney movies (I knew all of them by heart).

I learned many things from this experience and from what I learned I can now better face any problem life gives me.

Essay 53—Makeover: The original essay doesn't have a concluding paragraph, goes into too much detail, and is much too long: 1,793 words. This edited version offers suggestions on making the essay more interesting, deleting information unnecessary to the story line, and cutting it down to approximately 940 words. Though the essay still rambles, the student shows his story, so the length serves a purpose.

How much happier could I get? I was on my way to a concert ~~of the band I loved. Their best~~ *band*.

~~songs were playing selectively in my head.~~ *As we exited the freeway, my* My sister began to ask me a question~~,~~ ~~as we exited the~~ ~~freeway.~~ She never finished.

There was an accident, though I don't remember what happened.
~~It was as if I was in one of the action movies where the audience watches a car wreck from the~~ ~~inside of the driver's car. The wreck did not seem real to me as it happened or after it had~~ ~~happened. Once I had regained consciousness, I was repulsed by the smell, like a damp cave. I~~ ~~could not remember what had happened. I saw a red hash then I blacked out. Now I was scared.~~ The car was filled with smoke. There were glass shards everywhere.

[Delete—unnecessary.]
~~Instinct told me the car was going to explode, yet there was an eerie tranquillity. Using action~~ ~~hero strength, I ripped my brother out of the car seat and at the same time managed to get my sister~~ ~~out of the car. I had stepped out of the gray car, into the pandemonium of the outside. The clear~~ ~~sunny sky was reflected on all the tiny strands of glass that littered the road. My shoes stepped on~~ ~~the glass making the strands pop under my weight. I sat on the sidewalk and waited. As I waited for~~ ~~the car to explode. like I had seen so many times in the movies, the car just stood there crippled.~~

arrived, followed by fire trucks

~~Apparently my car wasn't aware of this fact.~~ EMS came ~~leading firetrucks~~ and the police. ~~The scene~~

~~must have seemed like a nightmare for some traffic reporter on a radio some where. I imagined the~~

~~reporter on the local radio station, "I-90 is backed for miles where a head on collision has occurred.~~

~~EMS and rescue crews are on the scene." The crews worked like ants, going from one destroyed car~~

~~to the next, pulling, pushing pieces of the cars. The EMS workers came over to me and asked how I~~

~~felt. "Stupid" was the only word I could muster. The lady that kept asking me questions talked~~

~~slowly and used big gestures as if she was telling me a camp fire story. She looked at my brother~~

~~and sister real fast and realized they were off playing in greenest grass I had ever seen on the bank~~

Two paramedics wearing

~~behind me. The lady came back with a big guy. Both wore~~ rubber gloves and looked at me as if they

were about to experiment on some unknown substance. ~~They broke their huddle for a moment,~~

~~and asked me if I was sure I was okay. "Yes, of course" the words slowly ran out. Then they left me~~

After being examined, I sat   *if the bandage was a badge of honor.*

~~alone~~ with an ice pack and a bandaged gash on my forehead as ~~the only souvenir of their visit.~~

Despite all that happened and after my family went home, I decided to attend

~~I had some sudden crazy impulse to still go to~~ the concert. ~~I called my friend's parents from the~~

Why should this unexpected event change my plans? Aside from the cut, I was fine. I called a friend and we went

~~bank to come pick up my group. They took me~~ to the concert. ~~I went to the concert. What I heard~~

~~was great. However, I spent the rest of the night recounting the story of the wreck to all the giggly~~

~~girls who surrounded me.~~

the next day, I realized I wasn't fine.   *to admit to my mother I'd*

After school, ~~my mom made me relive the accident. After~~ I had ~~related the entire incident, she~~

experienced   *, disorientation, and*   *all day long*

~~asked me how I felt. As I explained my~~ headaches and "grogginess" ~~she shriveled up and I could see~~

~~the fear in her face. She began to ask all kinds of specific questions, and I watched her~~

A   *crossed her face, much like a cloud moving in front of the sun to cast a long shadow.*

~~Apprehension grow. My mom was not worried that I had in some way injured myself to the extent~~

~~that any average teenager could not bounce back from. Instead she was worried that I had injured~~

Though any parent would have worried, my mother knew I   *like the average teenager.*

~~myself to the extent that some one who was hydrocephalic~~ couldn't bounce back.

At six months of age,   *Doctors at the Mayo Clinic*   d
~~When I was 6 months old~~ I was diagnosed as ~~being~~ hydrocephalic. ~~The doctor~~ place a shunt in

     M   *had to*   *carefully monitor*
my brain to drain the excess fluids. ~~They told~~ my mom ~~that she would need to be careful about~~

    was advised   *wasn't*   *or smart as*   .
what I did and not to be surprised if I ~~was not~~ as fast as the other kids ~~or as smart.~~ [New paragraph.]

     I'd be   *from*
My mom never thought ~~for a second that her son was going to live a~~ different ~~life then any~~ other

kid.   *S*   *When I was*   *my*   *announced*
kid~~, so~~ she enrolled me in every sport and class imaginable. ~~At the age of~~ seven~~, the doctors~~ ~~told me~~

    shunt-   *, but*
I was no longer ~~shunt~~ dependent/ ~~However I needed to be careful what I did. The doctors at Mayo~~

    they were quick to point out   *shunt-*
~~clinic explained that at any moment~~ I could go back to being ~~shunt~~ dependent. With one incident I

could go from normal to abnormal. [New paragraph.]

didn't let their advice dominate my life.   *U*
I ~~refused to believe that would ever happen so I did not let that advise effect me. Up~~ until the

    , I'd   *s*   *medical history.*
day of the accident ~~I had~~ forgotten about the shunt and my ~~hydrocephalic background.~~ However,

now
~~not~~ the past was affecting the future.

My mother rushed me   *, Dr. Mary*
I ~~went~~ to the emergency center and explained my symptoms to the neurologist/ ~~She told me~~

Ramirez, who ordered a series of
~~they would have to run some~~ tests. ~~I was horrified as they fitted me with a purple dinosaur gown.~~

~~That's what I get for going to a Children's Hospital. The doctor ordered some tests to be done. Once~~

When the results arrived, my mother and Dr. Ramirez talked
~~she got the results I began to hear an argument happening~~ outside my curtain prison. ~~It was my~~

~~mom and the neurologist and they were talking loud enough for me to hear. I was not worried that~~

~~they were arguing so I began to dream about what would it be like to take black paint and paint~~

~~over the wall paper, which showed happy letters playing on a playground covered the two walls.~~

~~Then I heard it, the argument escalated, and a nurse came in with a smile that seemed permanently~~

~~frozen on her face, and in no way was that smile genuine. She began to talk to me about school but~~

~~she could not stop me from hearing the argument.~~ [New paragraph.]

    felt   *needed*   *shunt,*
Dr. Ramirez ~~was telling my mom~~ I ~~need~~ a new ~~shunt~~ placed in me~~,~~ because the old one was

    [This sentence was added.]
    . Though I was no longer shunt-dependent, the recent injury could cause fluid buildup.
broken ~~and I would surely die if I did not have this operation immediately. At this point I began to~~

Without the new shunt, I could die. For the first time,   .   , disabled, and inadequate. What would
~~cry,~~ for the first time I felt different from everyone else I felt handicapped/ ~~Nothing now mattered, I~~

my life be like? I felt empty. Tears flowed down my cheeks. My future was being determined,
~~realized, my awards, my grades, who I knew, if someone thought I was handicapped then there~~

yet I had no voice in the decision.
~~would be no way to persuade them no matter how hard I tried. I gave up and thus cried harder,~~

~~maybe it was because the nurse with the plastic smile was wondering if I wanted to watch a Disney~~

~~movie. I wanted to hit her so badly at that point but restrained myself, couldn't she see my life was~~

~~being determined, and all she cared about is whether the seven dwarfs would keep me happy~~

~~instead of Aladdin.~~ [New paragraph.]

The discussion got   and
~~I heard the argument~~ get louder then suddenly ~~the argument~~ stopped. Dr. Ramirez came

sympathetically.
through the curtain and ~~nodded at the nurse to leave.~~ The doctor stared at me/ ~~with eyes of~~

"We're   in   s   , in case the injury causes fluid
~~sympathy,~~ "Well, we are going to have to put another ¢hunt ~~in to you, sorry about this." Immediately~~

buildup. Unfortunately, you'll have an increased susceptibility to infection, and the shunt could
~~the statistics that my mother told me ran through my head, I would have a fifty percent chance on~~

alter mental function." There was only one viable option.
~~getting an infection, and then another twenty percent chance on becoming mentally handicapped.~~

. argued
~~I was never one to play my luck, so~~ I did what any teenager would do/ I ~~wined.~~

I tried explaining to Dr. Ramirez about all my awards, my academic success, and the sports I

With   , Dr. Ramirez just looked   I'd
played. ~~The doctor put~~ a smirk on her face ~~and just kept looking~~ beyond me. After ~~I had~~ finished

reciting   I'd been   from   I'd have
~~giving her~~ my resume, she explained ~~to me~~ that if ~~I was~~ under her care ~~since~~ the beginning, ~~I would~~

*   "   "*
~~of~~ been properly taken care of. ~~I was then to into the conversation to back down from this~~

A
~~statement, so I asked what "properly taken care of" entailed?~~ The neurologist told me that ~~a~~ll her

s   .   N
patients got a new ¢hunt every seven years/ and ηone of her patients were allowed to play any

sports, especially ~~not some sport like~~ soccer. ~~I became irate and started to hate her and the~~

didn't
~~dinosaurs that I wore.~~ This doctor ~~who stood in front of me did not~~ care whether or not a kid

c   came   -   sort.
~~w~~ould be a kid, but whether or not they ~~would come~~ in for a check up of some ~~sought.~~ ~~This type of~~

person I'd · *I've known people who*
person was the same type of ~~people I had~~ been fighting ~~against~~ my whole life. ~~Those people that~~

decided I couldn't accomplish anything   only my limitations.
~~told me I could not~~ because they saw ~~me as some sort of crippled.~~

.S · *anesthesia. I refused.*
I fended off the doctor for ~~about~~ an hour/ ~~s~~he wanted to start the ~~anastesha, however I pulled a~~

~~tantrum and told them to wait for my mother who was somewhere.~~ To tell the truth I was scared/

My future seemed hopeless.
~~I was scared that I would become something that I had never considered myself, different. I was~~

[New paragraph.] *Suddenly,* · *Dr. Ramirez*
~~half way through Beauty and the Beast when~~ my mom burst through the door with ~~the doctor~~ at

: she had to take action
her side. My mom quickly explained the situation/ ~~either my mom found a way to charter a private~~

perform the
~~medical plane~~ by midnight or Dr. Ramirez would take custody of me and ~~complete her~~ surgery.

What   really strange was that during all the commotion, I hadn't felt any of the symptoms I'd experienced earlier.
~~It was funny, all this time I had not once felt any symptoms that I had registered with,~~ [New paragraph.]

It was
~~thus I felt it~~ time to leave this place of madness. However, I now had a security guard posted at

Colin   ,
my door. The guard/ ~~an elderly man,~~ reminded me of ~~Collin~~ Powell ~~in many ways,~~ and for that

reason only did I capitulate to his insistence on escorting me to the bathroom/ ~~and making sure I~~

~~did not escape. I tried my best to make the situation fun, a habit I have anytime I am in a situation~~

~~that is extremely~~ trying on my sanity. Thus, I tried to think how easily I could turn this situation into

~~a made-for-television movie entitled, "For the Love of All My Children" starring some out of work~~

As always, my mother triumphed. She chartered a plane
~~actors. While I was having fun, my mom was able to charter the plane we needed to get,~~ to take

us to the   for a second opinion, and not a moment too soon. T
me to Mayo Clinic/ ~~She charted the plane just in time too, considering~~ the Child Protective Service

Dr. Ramirez.
agents were at my door waiting to help ~~the neurologist undo numerous years of work and~~

that night.
~~achievements.~~ However, no one was going to hurt me ~~today, no one was going to keep me in~~

~~dinosaur gowns making me watch Disney movies (I knew all of them by heart).~~

[After making cuts in earlier paragraphs, the student could now add an effective conclusion and remain within the requisite word count.]

I learned many things from ~~this experience and from what I learned I can now better face any~~ *that nightmarish experience.*

~~problem life gives me.~~ *I learned* to question any "authority who ~~had my~~ *may not* have *my* best interests in mind." No one can arbitrarily mandate what I can achieve or dream of achieving. There might be things I can't do, but what person doesn't have limitations of some sort?

My mother always taught me to depend on myself when the chips are down and others say I can't. That night I had to face limitations to which I'd always turned a blind eye, but I could meet those limitation*s* head-on and still achieve. Whether I'm having to face limitations, my future, or an untried task, I know I'm up to the challenge. Look out world*.* *H*ere I come.

Essay 54: Here's the edited version of Essay 53, cut down to 940 words. Now cut it down to approximately 500 words.

How much happier could I get? I was on my way to a band concert. As we exited the freeway, my sister began to ask me a question. She never finished.

There was an accident, though I don't remember what happened. The car filled with smoke. There were glass shards everywhere. EMS arrived, followed by fire trucks and the police.

Two paramedics wearing rubber gloves looked at me as if they were about to experiment on some unknown substance. After being examined I sat with an ice pack and a bandaged gash on my forehead as if the bandage was a badge of honor.

Despite all that happened and my family went home, I decided to attend the concert. Why should this unexpected event change my plans? Aside from the cut, I was fine. I called a friend and we went to the concert.

After school, the next day, I realized I wasn't fine. I had to admit to my mother I'd experienced headaches, disorientation, and "grogginess" all day long. Apprehension crossed her face, much like a cloud moving in front of the sun to cast a long shadow. Though any parent would have worried, my mother knew I couldn't bounce back like the average teenager.

At six months of age, I was diagnosed as hydrocephalic. Doctors at the Mayo Clinic placed a shunt in my brain to drain excess fluids. My mom had to carefully monitor what I did and was advised not to be surprised if I wasn't as fast or as smart as other kids.

My mom never thought I'd be different from other kids. She enrolled me in every sport and class imaginable. When I was seven, my doctors announced I was no longer shunt-dependent, but they were quick to point out I could go back to being shunt-dependent. With one incident I could go from normal to abnormal.

I didn't let their advice dominate my life. Until the day of the accident, I'd forgotten about the shunt and my medical history. However, now the past was affecting the future.

My mother rushed me to the emergency center and explained my symptoms to the neurologist, Dr. Mary Ramirez, who ordered a series of tests. When the results arrived, my mother and Dr. Ramirez talked outside my curtain prison.

Dr. Ramirez felt I needed a new shunt, because the old one was broken. Though I was no longer shunt-dependent, the recent injury could cause fluid buildup. Without the new shunt, I could die. For the first time, I felt different from everyone else. I felt handicapped, disabled, and inadequate. What would my life be like? I felt empty. Tears flowed down my cheeks. My future was being determined, yet I had no voice in the decision.

The discussion got louder and then suddenly stopped. Dr. Ramirez came through the curtain and stared at me sympathetically. "We're going to have to put in another shunt, in case the injury causes fluid build-up. Unfortunately, you'll have an increased susceptibility to infection, and the shunt could alter mental function." There was only one viable option. I did what any teenager would do. I argued.

I tried explaining to Dr. Ramirez about all my awards, my academic success, and the sports I played. With a smirk on her face, Dr. Ramirez just looked beyond me. After I'd finished reciting my resume, she explained that if I'd been under her care from the beginning, I'd have been "properly taken care of." All her patients got a new shunt every seven years. None of her patients were allowed to play any sports, especially soccer. This doctor didn't care whether or not a kid could be a kid, but whether or not they came in for a check-up of some sort. This was the type of person I'd been fighting my whole life. I've known people who decided I couldn't accomplish anything because they saw only my limitations.

I fended off the doctor for an hour. She wanted to start the anesthesia. I refused. I was scared. My future seemed hopeless.

Suddenly, my mom burst through the door with Dr. Ramirez at her side. My mom quickly explained the situation: she had to take action by midnight or Dr. Ramirez would take custody of me and perform the surgery. What was really strange was that during all the commotion, I hadn't felt any of the symptoms I'd had experienced earlier.

It was time to leave this place of madness. However, I now had a security guard posted at my door. The guard reminded me of Colin Powell, and for that reason only did I capitulate to his insistence on escorting me to the bathroom. As always, my mother triumphed. She chartered a plane to take us to the Mayo Clinic for a second opinion, and not a moment too soon. The Child Protective Service agents were at my door waiting to help Dr. Ramirez. However, no one was going to hurt me that night.

I learned many things from that nightmarish experience. I learned to question any "authority" who may not have my best interests in mind. No one can arbitrarily mandate what I can achieve or dream of achieving. There might be things I can't do, but what person doesn't have limitations of some sort?

My mother always taught me to depend on myself when the chips are down and others say I can't. That night I had to face limitations to which I'd always turned a blind eye, but I could meet those limitations head-on and still achieve. Whether I'm having to face limitations, my future, or an untried task, I know I'm up to the challenge. Look out world. Here I come.

Essay 54—Makeover: Here's how to cut this version down to approximately 500 words.

How much happier could I get? I was on my way to a band concert. ~~As we exited the freeway,~~ [No paragraph break.] *Suddenly, t*~~my sister began to ask me a question. She never finished. T~~here was an accident, ~~though~~ I don't *much about* remember what happened. The car filled with smoke. There were glass shards everywhere. *It wasn't long before the* EMS *ambulance* arrived, followed by fire trucks and the police.

~~Two paramedics wearing rubber gloves looked at me as if they were about to experiment on some unknown substance.~~ After being examined, I sat with an ice pack and a bandaged gash on my forehead ~~as if the bandage was a badge of honor.~~ Despite all that happened *after* and my family went home, I decided to attend the concert. Why should this unexpected event change my plans? Aside from the cut, I was fine. I called a friend and we went to the concert.

After school, the next day, I realized I wasn't fine. I had to admit to my mother I'd experienced headaches, ~~and~~ disorientation, *and* "grogginess" all day long. ~~Apprehension crossed her face, much like a cloud moving in front of the sun to cast a long shadow.~~ Though any parent would have worried, my *had an added dimension to her worries.* mother ~~knew I couldn't bounce back like the average teenager.~~

At six months of age, I was diagnosed as hydrocephalic. Doctors at the Mayo Clinic placed a shunt in my brain to drain excess fluids. My mom had to carefully monitor what I did ~~and was advised not to be surprised if I wasn't as fast or as smart as other kids.~~

Though concerned about the doctors' advice, my mom never treated me as if I had limitations. ~~My mom never thought I'd be different from other kids. She enrolled me in every sport and class imaginable.~~ When I was seven, my doctors announced I was no longer shunt-dependent, *though* ~~but they were quick to point out~~ I could ~~go back to being~~ *become* shunt-dependent ~~With one incident I could go from normal to abnormal.~~ *again.* [New paragraph.]

~~I didn't let their advice dominate my life.~~ Until the day of the accident, I'd forgotten about the shunt and my medical history. However, now the past was affecting the future.

My mother rushed me to the emergency center and explained my symptoms to the neurologist, Dr. Mary Ramirez *. After* ~~who ordered~~ a series of tests ~~When the results arrived, my mother and Dr. Ramirez talked outside my curtain prison.~~ Dr. Ramirez ~~felt~~ *announced* I needed a new shunt, because the old one was broken *and* ~~Though I was no longer shunt-dependent, the recent injury could cause fluid buildup.~~ *W*ithout ~~the~~ *a* new shunt, I could die. For the first time, I felt different from everyone else I felt handicapped, disabled, and inadequate. What would my life be like *from now on?* ~~I felt empty. Tears flowed down my cheeks. My future was being determined, yet I had no voice in the decision.~~

~~The discussion got louder and then suddenly stopped. Dr. Ramirez came through the curtain and stared at me sympathetically. "We're going to have to put in another shunt, in case the injury causes fluid build-up. Unfortunately, you'll have an increased susceptibility to infection, and the shunt could alter mental function." There was only one viable option. I did what any teenager would do. I argued.~~

~~I tried explaining to Dr. Ramirez about all my awards, my academic success, and the sports I played. With a smirk on her face, Dr. Ramirez just looked beyond me. After I'd finished reciting my resume,~~ she explained that ~~if I'd been under her care from the beginning, I'd have been "properly taken care of."~~ *a*ll her patients got a new shunt every seven years. None of her patients were allowed to play any sports, especially soccer.

~~This doctor didn't care whether or not a kid could be a kid, but whether or not they came in for a check-up of some sort. This was the type of person I'd been fighting my whole life. I've known people who decided I couldn't accomplish anything because they saw only my limitations.~~

          about

I fended off the doctor for an hour. She wanted to start the anesthesia. I refused. ~~I was scared.~~

My future seemed hopeless. I could become something I'd never considered myself to be: different.

    Suddenly, my mom burst through the door ~~with Dr. Ramirez at her side. My mom quickly~~

~~explained the situation: she had to take action by midnight or Dr. Ramirez would take custody of~~

~~me and perform the surgery. What was really strange was that during all the commotion, I hadn't~~

~~felt any of the symptoms I'd had experienced earlier.~~

    ~~It was time to leave this place of madness. However, I now had a security guard posted at my~~

~~door. The guard reminded me of Colin Powell, and for that reason only did I capitulate to his~~

~~insistence on escorting me to the bathroom.~~

[No new paragraph.]   *'d*   *for a second*

    ~~As always, my mother triumphed.~~ She chartered a plane to take us to the Mayo Clinic ~~and not a~~

opinion.

~~moment too soon. The Child Protective Service agents were at my door waiting to help Dr.~~

~~Ramirez. However, no one was going to hurt me that night.~~

    I learned many things from that nightmarish experience. I learned to question any "authority "

       my

who may not have best interests in mind. No one can arbitrarily mandate what I can achieve or

                 will   *might not be able to*

dream of achieving. There ~~might~~ be things I ~~can't~~ do, but what person doesn't have limitations of

some sort?

    ~~My mother always taught me to depend on myself when the chips are down and others say I~~

                                      I learned

~~can't. That night I had to face limitations to which I'd always turned a blind eye,~~ but I could meet

       s

those limitation head-on and still achieve. Whether I'm having to face limitations, my future, or an

untried task, ~~I know~~ I'm up to the challenge. Look out world. Here I come.

Essay 55: Here's the edited essay, cut down to 478 words. Now cut it down to approximately 200 words.

    How much happier could I get? I was on my way to a band concert. Suddenly, there was an

accident. I don't remember much about what happened. The car filled with smoke. There were glass shards everywhere. It wasn't long before the EMS ambulance arrived, followed by fire trucks and the police.

Afterward, I sat with an ice pack and a bandaged gash on my forehead. Despite all that happened and after my family went home, I decided to attend the concert. Why should this unexpected event change my plans? Aside from the cut, I was fine. I called a friend and we went to the concert.

After school the next day, I realized I wasn't fine. I had to admit to my mother I'd experienced headaches, disorientation, and "grogginess" all day long. Though any parent would have worried, my mother had an added dimension to her worries.

At six months of age, I was diagnosed as hydrocephalic. Doctors at the Mayo Clinic placed a shunt in my brain to drain excess fluids. My mom had to carefully monitor what I did.

Though concerned about the doctors' advice, my mom never treated me as if I had limitations. When I was seven, my doctors announced I was no longer shunt-dependent, though I could become shunt-dependent again.

Until the day of the accident, I'd forgotten about the shunt and my medical history. However, now the past was affecting the future.

My mother rushed me to the emergency center and explained my symptoms to the neurologist, Dr. Mary Ramirez. After a series of tests, Dr. Ramirez announced I needed a new shunt, because the old one was broken and without a new shunt, I could die. For the first time, I felt different from everyone else. I felt handicapped, disabled, and inadequate. What would my life be like from now on? Dr. Ramirez explained that all her patients got a new shunt every seven years. None of her patients were allowed to play any sports, especially soccer.

I fended off the doctor for about an hour. She wanted to start the anesthesia. I refused. My future seemed hopeless. I could become something I'd never considered myself to be: different.

Suddenly, my mom burst through the door. She'd chartered a plane to take us to the Mayo Clinic for a second opinion.

I learned many things from that nightmarish experience. I learned to question any "authority" who may not have my best interests in mind. No one can arbitrarily mandate what I can achieve or dream of achieving. There will be things I might not be able to do, but what person doesn't have limitations of some sort?

I learned I could meet those limitation head-on and still achieve. Whether I'm having to face limitations, my future, or an untried task, I'm up to the challenge. Look out world. Here I come.

Essay 55—Makeover: The revised version is 200 words in length. Though not as descriptive as the longest version, it still contains the story—it's just more concise.

How much happier could I get? I was on my way to a band concert. ~~Suddenly, there was an~~ *One event changed that.* *We had a car accident.* ~~accident. I don't remember much about what happened. The car filled with smoke. There were glass shards everywhere. It wasn't long before the EMS ambulance arrived, followed by fire trucks and the police.~~

~~Afterward, I sat with an ice pack and a bandaged gash on my forehead. Despite all that happened and my family went home, I decided to attend the concert. Why should this unexpected event change my plans? Aside from the cut, I was fine. I called a friend and we went to the concert.~~

After school the next day, I realized I wasn't fine. ~~I had to admit to my mother I'd experienced~~ *I was complaining about* headaches, ~~and~~ disorientation, and grogginess ~~all day long.~~ Though any parent would have worried, my mother had an added dimension to her worries.

At six months of age, I was diagnosed as hydrocephalic. Doctors at the Mayo Clinic placed a shunt in my brain to drain excess fluids. ~~My mom had to carefully monitor what I did. Though concerned about the doctors' advice,~~ *M*my mom never treated me as if I had limitations. When I was seven, ~~my doctors announced~~ I was no longer shunt-dependent. ~~though I could become shunt-dependent, again.~~

~~Until the day of the accident, I'd forgotten about the shunt and my medical history. However, now the past was affecting the future.~~

We *an* *, where* *a*
~~My mother~~ rushed me to the emergency center ~~and explained my symptoms to the~~ neurologist,

, ordered
Dr. Mary Ramirez / ~~After~~ a series of tests / Dr. Ramirez announced I needed a new shunt, because the old one was broken and without a new shunt, I could die. For the first time, I felt different from everyone else. I felt handicapped, disabled, and inadequate. ~~What would my life be like from now on? Dr. Ramirez explained that all her patients got a new shunt every seven years. None of her patients were allowed to play any sports, especially soccer.~~

~~I fended off the doctor for about an hour. She wanted to start the anesthesia. I refused. My future seemed hopeless. I could become something I'd never considered myself to be: different.~~

[No new paragraph.]
Fortunately,
~~Suddenly,~~ my mom ~~burst through the door.~~ She'd chartered a plane to take us to the Mayo Clinic for a second opinion.

Through this
~~I learned many things from that~~ nightmarish experience / I learned to question any "authority"

s
who ~~may not have best interests in mind.~~ No one ~~can~~ arbitrarily mandate what I can achieve or

I may have limitations, but who doesn't?
dream of achieving. ~~There will be things I might not be able to do, but what person doesn't have limitations of some sort? I learned I could meet those limitation head-on and still achieve.~~ Whether

the
I'm having to face limitations, my future, or an untried task, I'm up to the challenge. ~~Look out world. Here I come.~~

Essay 56: Write a personal statement of no more than 1,000 words.

Even now, five years later, I can remember the day, time, and place clearly. I had come home from work with the sun igniting the western horizon in fiery shades of burnt orange, glowing yellows, and flaming reds. There had been a late-afternoon thunderstorm that refreshed the desert and a gentle breeze blew the pungent scent of creosote through my open windows. I was debating what to make for dinner and humming along as "Rolling on the River" played on the radio.

When I pulled up to the trailer, I noticed Alby's truck wasn't there, but at the neighbor's. I parked and went inside to change out of my work clothes. I decided to wait on dinner and go see what my husband, Alby, and Susan were up to, then I noticed Alby coming across the gulch. Instead, I went to fill the bird feeders. I can remember hearing a distant canyon wren singing wistfully and thinking to myself how beautiful and uplifting his song was.

By now Alby had reached the trailer and without any preamble, he dropped the megabomb, "I want a divorce." He gave no reason, no excuses, *nada*—just that simple statement. He turned around and walked back to Susan's house. Shortly after that, they left town together.

After my divorce, I stopped thinking about my actions and feelings. I wasn't willing to admit that I was human and that all humans make mistakes. Although I hadn't committed any crimes against my husband, I blamed myself. He, on the other hand, had committed many in our marriage. Due to my inner turmoil, I made some wrong choices during the nine months after the breakup and ended up in prison for eleven months with three years probation. I now have less than six months to complete my probation time. I can also truly say that my divorce and subsequent imprisonment helped me to focus on my goals—to follow my dream of watching birds for a living and to share that with other people.

Recently, I was laid off from my job with a road construction company. Taking a giant leap of faith, I enrolled in the local community college to complete required courses in preparation for the spring semester. I recently attended my ten-year high school class reunion. That experience made me look at where I want to be in ten years. I used to joke that if I could get paid to watch birds, I'd die happy, though poor. Today, due to habitat destruction of the rain forest and other biomes throughout Latin America, many bird species are declining. To understand this trend, many organizations and universities are researching the problem. The results are important, not just to bird watchers and the general public in our country, but to our neighbors south of the border. My aim is to be a part of the solution, not the problem.

I've been bird watching for over twenty years, traveling throughout the United States and northern Mexico. My goal is to major in ornithology and minor in ethnobotany. In the spring, I'll be enrolled full-time and I've also signed up for a summer semester in anthropology conducted in Querotero, Mexico. Next fall, I will transfer to Texas A&M University, Kingsville.

I've always been fascinated by bird migration and bird populations. I've kept daily field logs for the past fifteen years. This interest has led to my involvement with the state chapter of the Audubon Society helping with bird records. Here in Port Aransas, I've been involved with several local bird watchers to help produce a local bird checklist. Eventually, I would like to initiate an Audubon Chapter in Port Aransas. My long-term educational goals are to obtain a doctoral degree and eventually conduct work with a university as the head of a research department.

Looking back to that day five years ago, I can honestly say that my thoughts, emotions, and actions have changed immensely for the better. Before my divorce, I didn't have enough faith in myself to venture into the unknown in pursuit of my dreams. Now I know I can accomplish whatever goals I set. My passion is birds and that passion fuels my desire to finish my education. By pursuing my degree and entering into the world of avian research, I hope to make a difference in our relationship to earth.

Essay 56—Makeover: Several sentences needed to be deleted from this essay because they would confuse the reader. After some changes, it was an honest essay in which the student took responsibility for her actions. The revised essay is approximately 700 words in length.

Even now, five years later, I can remember the day, time, and place clearly. I'd ~~had~~ come home from work with the sun igniting the western horizon in fiery shades of burnt orange, glowing yellows, and flaming reds. There ~~had~~ 'd been a late afternoon thunderstorm that refreshed the desert and a gentle breeze blew the ~~poignant~~ [pungent] scent of creosote through my open windows. I was debating what [Replace, otherwise implies the radio is also humming.]

to make for dinner and humming along "Rolling on the River" ~~with~~ [as / played on] the radio.

When I pulled up to the trailer, I noticed my husband's truck wasn't there, but at the neighbor's. [Alby's,]

~~So~~ I parked and went inside to change out of my work clothes. I decided to wait on dinner and go

see what Alby and Susan were up to. I never got there. I saw Alby coming across the gulch, so I [instead]

went to fill the bird feeders[.] [Since you didn't know it was about to happen, don't foreshadow.] ~~unaware of the immense mental and emotional blow that was about to~~

~~fall.~~ I can remember ~~hear~~ [hearing] a distant canyon wren singing wistfully and thinking to myself how

beautiful and uplifting his song was.

By now Alby had reached the trailer and without any preamble, ~~no "Hi, how was your day?"~~ he

dropped the megabomb[:] "I want a divorce." He gave no reason, no excuses, *nada*—just that simple

statement. ~~Then he~~ [He] turned ~~around~~ and walked back ~~over~~ to Susan's house. Shortly after that, they

left town together.

~~There was a time in my life, for about nine months,~~ [After my divorce,] I stopped ~~being responsible for my~~ [thinking about my] actions

and ~~my~~ feelings. I wasn't willing to admit that I was ~~a~~ human and all humans make mistakes. ~~And~~ [that]

[A]~~lthough~~ I hadn't committed any crimes against my husband, I blamed myself. He, had committed [on the other hand,]

many in our marriage. ~~Because of~~ [Due to] my inner turmoil, I made some wrong choices and ended up in [during the nine months after the breakup]

prison for eleven months with three years probation. ~~Now I~~ [I now] have less than six months to complete

[probation time.]
my ~~sentence.~~ I can also truly say that my divorce and subsequent imprisonment helped me to focus

on my goals[:] ~~—~~ to follow my dream of watching birds for a living and to share that with other

people.

Recently, I was laid off from my job with a road construction company. Taking a giant leap of

faith, I enrolled in the community college ~~for parallel~~ [local] [to complete required] courses in preparation for the spring semester. I ~~had also just returned from~~ *recently attended* my ten year high school class reunion. That experience ~~had also~~ made me look at where I want to be in ten years. I used to joke that if I could get paid to watch birds, I'd die happy, *though* ~~if~~ poor. Today, due to habitat destruction of the rain forest and other biomes throughout Latin America, many bird species are declining. To understand this trend, many organizations and universities are researching the problem ~~at the source.~~ All of the results are important, not just to bird watchers and the general public in our country, but to our neighbors south of the border. My aim is to be a part of the solution, not the problem.

I've ~~I have~~ been bird watching for over twenty years, traveling throughout the United States and northern Mexico. My ~~specific degree program~~ *goal* is to major in ornithology and minor in Ethnobotany.
[Delete—could confuse the reader.]
~~In lieu of this, I am majoring in Wildlife Biology with a minor in Anthropology.~~ In the spring, I'll be enrolled full-time and I've also signed up for a summer semester in anthropology conducted in Querotero, Mexico. Next fall, I will transfer to Texas A&M University, Kingsville ~~for my degree program.~~

I've always been fascinated by bird migration and bird populations. I've kept daily field logs for the past fifteen years. This interest has led to my involvement with the state chapter of the Audubon Society helping with Bird Records. ~~And~~ Here in Port Aransas, I've been involved with several local bird watchers to help produce a local bird checklist. Eventually, I would like to initiate an Audubon Chapter ~~here~~ in Port Aransas. My long-term educational goals are to obtain *a doctoral* ~~my doctorate~~ degree and eventually *conduct studies at* ~~work with~~ a university as the head of a research department.

Looking back to that day five years ago, I can honestly say that my thoughts, emotions, and actions have changed immensely for the better. Before *my divorce.* I didn't have enough faith in myself to venture into the unknown in pursuit of my dreams. Now ~~I know~~ I can accomplish
[Who else would you set goals for?]
whatever goals I set. ~~for myself.~~ My passion is birds and that passion ~~is what~~ fuels my desire to

finish my education. By pursuing ~~my~~ *a* degree and entering into the world of avian research, I hope to make a difference in our relationship to ~~our~~ *E*arth. [This makes it sound as if there's more than one earth: ours and someone else's.]

Essay 57: This essay is now approximately 700 words in length. The student now wanted to use the same story, but in a much shorter essay on a different assigned topic: Write a brief essay (100 to 200 words) on your goals as they relate to your education, career, and future plans. (Tylenol)

Even now, five years later, I can remember the day, time, and place clearly. I had come home from work with the sun igniting the western horizon in fiery shades of burnt orange, glowing yellows, and flaming reds. There had been a late-afternoon thunderstorm that refreshed the desert and a gentle breeze blew the pungent scent of creosote through my open windows. I was debating what to make for dinner and humming along as "Rolling on the River" played on the radio.

When I pulled up to the trailer, I noticed my husband Alby's truck wasn't there, but at the neighbor's. I parked and went inside to change out of my work clothes. I decided to wait on dinner and go see what Alby and Susan were up to. I never got there. I saw Alby coming across the gulch, so instead, I went to fill the bird feeders. I can remember hearing a distant canyon wren singing wistfully and thinking to myself how beautiful and uplifting his song was.

By now Alby had reached the trailer and without any preamble, he dropped the megabomb: "I want a divorce." He gave no reason, no excuses, *nada*—just that simple statement. He turned and walked back to Susan's house. Shortly after that, they left town together.

After my divorce, I stopped thinking about my actions and feelings. I wasn't willing to admit that I was human and that all humans make mistakes. Although I hadn't committed any crimes against my husband, I blamed myself. He, on the other hand, had committed many in our marriage. Due to my inner turmoil, I made some wrong choices during the nine months after the breakup and ended up in prison for eleven months with three years probation. I now have less than six months to complete my probation time. I can also truly say that my divorce and subsequent imprisonment helped me to focus on my goals: to follow my dream of watching birds for a living and to share that with other people.

Recently, I was laid off from my job with a road construction company. Taking a giant leap of faith, I enrolled in the local community college to complete required courses in preparation for the spring semester. I recently attended my ten-year high school class reunion. That experience made me look at where I want to be in ten years. I used to joke that if I could get paid to watch birds, I'd die happy, though poor. Today, due to habitat destruction of the rain forest and other biomes throughout Latin America, many bird species are declining. To understand this trend, many organizations and universities are researching the problem. The results are important, not just to bird watchers and the general public in our country, but to our neighbors south of the border. My aim is to be a part of the solution, not the problem.

I've been bird watching for over twenty years, traveling throughout the United States and northern Mexico. My goal is to major in ornithology and minor in ethnobotany. In the spring, I'll be enrolled full-time and I've also signed up for a summer semester in anthropology conducted in Querotero, Mexico. Next fall, I will transfer to Texas A&M University, Kingsville.

I've always been fascinated by bird migration and bird populations. I've kept daily field logs for the past fifteen years. This interest has led to my involvement with the state chapter of the Audubon Society helping with bird records. Here in Port Aransas, I've been involved with several local bird watchers to help produce a local bird checklist. Eventually, I would like to initiate an Audubon Chapter in Port Aransas. My long-term educational goals are to obtain a doctoral degree and eventually conduct work with a university as the head of a research department.

Looking back to that day five years ago, I can honestly say that my thoughts, emotions, and actions have changed immensely for the better. Before my divorce, I didn't have enough faith in myself to venture into the unknown in pursuit of my dreams. Now I can accomplish whatever goals I set. My passion is birds and that passion fuels my desire to finish my education. By pursuing my degree and entering into the world of avian research, I hope to make a difference in our relationship to Earth.

Essay 57—Makeover: The first major change is to delete the first three paragraphs—though they're colorful, they aren't essential to the shorter essay.

~~Even now, five years later, I can remember the day, time, and place clearly. I had come home from work with the sun igniting the western horizon in fiery shades of burnt orange, glowing yellows, and flaming reds. There had been a late-afternoon thunderstorm that refreshed the desert and a gentle breeze blew the pungent scent of creosote through my open windows. I was debating what to make for dinner and humming along as "Rolling on the River" played on the radio.~~

~~When I pulled up to the trailer, I noticed Alby's truck wasn't there, but at the neighbor's. I parked and went inside to change out of my work clothes. I decided to wait on dinner and go see what my husband, Alby, and Susan were up to, then I noticed Alby coming across the gulch. Instead, I went to fill the bird feeders. I can remember hearing a distant canyon wren singing wistfully and thinking to myself how beautiful and uplifting his song was.~~

~~By now Alby had reached the trailer and without any preamble, he dropped the megabomb: "I want a divorce." He gave no reason, no excuses, *nada*—just that simple statement. He turned and walked back to Susan's house. Shortly after that, they left town together.~~

Five years after an unexpected divorce,

~~After my divorce,~~ I stopped thinking about my actions ~~and feelings. I wasn't willing to admit that I was human and that all humans make mistakes. Although I hadn't committed any crimes against my husband, I blamed myself. He, on the other hand, had committed many in our marriage. Due to my inner turmoil,~~ I made some wrong choices ~~during the nine months after the breakup~~ and ended up in prison for eleven months with three years probation. *In* ~~I now have~~ less than six months ~~to~~ *I'll* complete my probation *ary period.* ~~time. I can also truly say that my divorce and subsequent imprisonment helped me to focus on my goals—to follow my dream of watching birds for a living and to share that with other people.~~

~~Recently, I was laid off from my job with a road construction company. Taking a giant leap of~~ *This semester,* ~~faith,~~ I enrolled in the local community college. ~~to complete required courses in preparation for the spring semester. I recently attended my ten-year high school class reunion. That experience made me look at where I want to be in ten years.~~ I used to joke that if I could get paid to watch birds, I'd die happy, though poor. Today, due to habitat destruction of the rain forest and other biomes throughout Latin America, many bird species are declining. To understand this trend, many organizations and universities are researching the problem. ~~The results are important, not just to bird watchers and the general public in our country, but to our neighbors south of the border.~~ My aim is to be a part of the solution, not the problem.

~~I've been bird watching for over twenty years, traveling throughout the United States and northern Mexico.~~ My goal is to major in ornithology and minor in ethnobotany. ~~In the spring,~~ I'll be enrolled full-time, and ~~I've also signed up for a summer semester in anthropology conducted in Querotero, Mexico.~~ *I'll* [No paragraph break.] Next fall, ~~I will~~ transfer to Texas A&M University, Kingsville. ~~I've always been fascinated by bird migration and bird populations. I've kept daily field logs for the past fifteen years. This interest has led to my involvement with the state chapter of the Audubon Society helping with bird records. Here in Port Aransas, I've been involved with several local bird watchers to help produce a local bird checklist. Eventually, I would like to initiate an Audubon Chapter in Port Aransas.~~ My long-term educational goals are to obtain a doctoral degree and eventually conduct *avian research.* ~~work with a university as the head of a research department.~~

~~Looking back to that day five years ago, I can honestly say that~~ *M*y thoughts, emotions, and actions have changed immensely for the better *in the last five years.* Before my divorce, I didn't have enough faith in myself to venture into the unknown in pursuit of my dreams. Now I can accomplish whatever goals I set. ~~My passion is birds and that passion fuels my desire to finish my education. By pursuing my degree and entering into the world of avian research, I hope to make a difference in our relationship to Earth.~~

Essay 58: Write an essay between 200 and 400 words in length describing a person, event, or activity that has made a significant impact on your life.

I can imagine a picture of a 15 year-old girl walking into a convenience store to buy a cold six pack of beer. Her face painted with anticipation as I waited in line to complete the purchase. The girl holding the cold six pack in one hand and the hidden camera in a large, bulky purse was me.

My freshman year in high school, I went on a minor sting operation for the Texas Alcohol Beverage Commission or TABC. We were taken to the location where we were going to carry out the operation. Another girl and myself were given a hidden camera disguised as a purse and a secret microphone or wire to attach to ourselves. After we were equipped with out secret deviccs, they sent us into the store. We would go into various locations and try to buy an alcoholic beverage. Being a fifteen year old girl, I was surprised how often than not employees at the convenience stores sold me alcohol.

These employees were irresponsible. They were selling alcohol to a teenager who was hardly able to drive a car. Minors aren't mature enough to drink alcohol. Plain and simple, both parties are irresponsible. Who is more irresponsible: the man that "tries to be kind" to young kids and sells them alcohol, or the sixteen year old girl who just got her license and paralyzes herself and kills her bestfriend because she drove drunk?

This volunteer activity was important because I made society better as a whole. Finding the adults that sell alcohol to minors and removing them from their jobs prevents the trafficking of liquor among immature teens. I know I saved at least one teen's life by removing just one employee who broke the rules. It was the one tean that decided to drive drunk, ran the red light to knock the family of four into the guardrail to kill them all. I protected myself from a drunk driver running into me, or one of my parents. I learned a great deal of responsibility from this activity. My family knows I am responsible enough not to try to go out and but alcohol. This activity gives them more assurance that I won't get hurt on the way home from work by someone who is drunk.

I feel that by participating in this activity I have made a better place in society for all the people who shouldn't have to suffer from a teens poorly thought out actions. After all, they don't think of the fact that the some body they hit has a family that loves them. The person they kill or put in a wheel chair could be one of you children, a spouse, or your. This activity prevents illegal activity and helps all people live in a safer city. I am planning on continuing to volunteer for the TABC. I am also planning on continuing to volunteer work for TABC. I'm also planning on getting my other friends to get involved so they can experience the importance I feel by participating in these minor sting operation.

Essay 58—Makeover: This is a good essay; it just needed some changes to make it a strong essay.

~~I can imagine a picture of a 15~~ *A fifteen-* year-old girl ~~walking~~ *walks* into a convenience store to buy a cold six pack of beer. Her face ~~painted~~ *is alight* with anticipation as ~~I waited~~ *she waits* in line to complete the purchase. *She's* ~~The girl~~ holding the cold six pack in one hand and ~~the~~ *a* hidden camera in a large, bulky purse. *Her stomach is filled with butterflies.* ~~was me.~~

During ~~My~~ freshman year in high school, I ~~went on~~ *participated in* a minor sting operation for the Texas Alcohol Beverage Commission ~~or TABC.~~ *(TABC).* We were taken to the location where we were going to carry out the operation. Another girl and ~~myself~~ *I* were given a hidden camera disguised as a purse and a *hidden* ~~secret~~ microphone ~~or wire to attach to ourselves.~~ *.* After we were equipped with ~~out~~ *our* secret devices, ~~they sent us~~ *we went* into ~~the store.~~ *stores at* ~~We would go into~~ various locations and ~~try~~ *tried* to buy an alcoholic beverage. ~~Being a fifteen year old girl,~~ I was surprised how often ~~than not~~ employees ~~at the convenience stores~~ *, a fifteen-year-old,* sold me alcohol.

These employees were irresponsible. They were selling alcohol to a teenager who ~~was hardly~~ *wasn't even* [Move to end of this paragraph.] able to drive a car. Minors aren't mature enough to drink alcohol. ~~Plain and simple, both parties are~~

's   *who*

~~irresponsible.~~ Who is more irresponsible: the man ~~that~~ *who* "tries to be kind" to young kids and sells them

teenager   *his/her*   *who gets into an accident, killing his/her*

alcohol, or the ~~sixteen year old girl~~ *teenager* who just got ~~her~~ *his/her* license ~~and paralyzes herself and~~

best friend, and becoming paralyzed, all because of drinking and driving?   *are*

~~kills her bestfriend because she drove drunk?~~ Plain and simple, both parties ~~were~~ *are* irresponsible.

Participating in this   *for TABC*   *a difference.*

~~This~~ *Participating in this* volunteer activity was important because I made ~~society better as a whole.~~ *for TABC* *a difference.* Finding the

who

adults ~~that~~ *who* sell alcohol to minors and removing them from their jobs prevents the trafficking of

underage   *may have*   *that*

liquor among ~~immature~~ *underage* teens. ~~I know~~ *may have* I saved at least one teen's life by removing ~~just~~ one employee *that*

may have been a   *who would have*   *running a*   *and sending*

who broke the rules. It ~~was the one~~ *may have been a* teen ~~that~~ *who would have* decided to drive drunk, ~~ran the~~ *running a* red light ~~to knock the~~ *and sending*

the car of a   *, killing them all.*   *may have*

family of four into the guardrail ~~to kill them all.~~ I protected myself from a drunk driver running into

me, or one of my parents. I learned a great deal of responsibility from this activity. My family knows

I'm   *buy*   *That knowledge*

~~I am~~ *I'm* responsible enough not to try to ~~go out and but~~ *buy* alcohol. ~~This activity~~ *That knowledge* gives them more

[It's not possible to control other's behavior—only your own.] *drinking and driving.*

assurances that I won't get hurt on the way home from ~~work by someone who is drunk.~~

By   *our community a safer*

~~I feel that by~~ *By* participating in this activity I have made ~~a better~~ *our community a safer* place ~~in society~~ for all the people

teen's   -

who shouldn't have to suffer from a ~~teens~~ *teen's* poorly thought out actions. ~~After all, they don't think of~~

~~the fact that the some body they hit has a family that loves them. The person they kill or put in a~~

My volunteer work helped prevent an   *.*

~~wheel chair could be one of you children, a spouse, or you.~~ ~~This activity prevents~~ *My volunteer work helped prevent an* illegal activity ~~and~~

I'm   *my*   *work*

~~helps all people live in a safer city.~~ ~~I am~~ *I'm* planning on continuing ~~to~~ *my* volunteer *work* for the TABC. I'm also

effect of

planning on getting ~~my~~ other friends ~~to get~~ involved so they can experience the ~~importance I feel~~ *effect of*

operations.

~~by~~ participating in these ~~minor~~ sting ~~operation.~~

Essay 59: In 1,200 words or less write a true, first-person story about an experience that changed you. It need not be highly dramatic or unusual, but it should demonstrate how faith in God has made a difference in your life. (Guideposts Essay Writing Competition)

As I walked up the steps to the portable classroom, my heart was racing. I remembered how I looked in the mirror that morning and wondered what I would look like to everyone else. Being a five-year old kindergartner isn't easy, and when you have your front teeth pulled out it isn't any easier. I walked in the classroom and the little boy who sat next to me asked where I had been the day before. As soon as I opened my mouth he started yelling, "You look like a vampire! Vampire! Vampire!" Well that certainly didn't help matters much. At that moment, I didn't like dentists.

I didn't trust dentists at all. I hated going. I'd make excuses, like pretending I was sick. This lack of dental care led me to become lazy in my dental hygiene. In first grade, my aunt bribe me to brush my teeth everyday. She said that if I brushed every day for forty days, she'd give me a dollar for every day. It worked but I didn't keep up the habit after pocketing forty dollars.

At the end of my fifth grade year, my Dad decided I needed to see an orthodontist. I protested, but dad made me go see the doctor. Petrified by fear, I sat in the dimly lit waiting room aware of everything. I felt I was suffocating since the two slow moving ceiling fans didn't stir up too much of a breeze. I was imprisoned by four gray walls. Grey may be a soothing color, but that day it seemed hostile. I complained about how ugly the office was, I wanted to leave because nothing good was going to come out of it. My father, however, was patient and waited for me calmly. I could smell the cleansing smell of the dentist's office and hear the women's joyful voices behind the closed door. That visit changed my life. I finally got called in to the doctor's chair and a nice woman performed some procedures on me before the doctor came in to visit with me. His name was Dr. Smith. That man gave me the encouragement I needed to not only change my appearance, but change the way I look at myself by giving me the self-esteem to be outgoing, courageous, and enthusiastic about myself. He told me the basic steps and procedures I'd need to go through to get braces. He told me that if I tried and tried, I could have beautiful teeth and a wonderful smile.

The day finally came when Dr. Smith took off the braces and my teeth fit perfectly. I couldn't stop showing people and smiling. I was ecstatic. I want to share that feeling with everyone. From that day on I have had high self-esteem. I came out of my shell and blossomed into a confident young lady. The best way to share what I received from my dentist is to achieve success in college. How hard can it be after six years of braces? I'll work hard to become a dental hygienist.

Essay 59—Makeover: The first version of this essay didn't offer enough personal information. It also didn't touch on how the student's faith in God affected this experience. This second draft contains some additional information.

As I walked up the steps to the portable classroom, my heart was racing, *and my hands were sweating.* [Moved to middle of paragraph.] ~~I remembered how I looked in the mirror that morning and wondered what I would look like to everyone else.~~ Being a *Though the sun was shining, my day didn't feel too bright.* five-year old kindergartner isn't easy, *but* ~~and~~ when ~~you have~~ *you've just had* your front teeth pulled ~~out it isn't any easier.~~ *it's even worse.* I remembered how I looked in the mirror that morning and wondered what I would look like to everyone else. I walked ~~in~~ *into* the classroom and ~~the~~ little boy who sat next to me asked where *sat down hoping no one would notice. The immediately* I had been the day ~~before. As soon~~ *previous.* as I opened my mouth he started yelling, "You look like a *I'd A to answer,* vampire! Vampire! Vampire!" [Moved to beginning of next paragraph.]

Well that certainly didn't help matters much. At that moment, I didn't like dentists. I didn't trust dentists at all. I hated going. I'd make excuses, *to get out of seeing the dentist,* like pretending I was sick. This lack of dental care led me to become lazy in my dental hygiene. In first grade, my aunt ~~bribe~~ *bribed* me ~~to brush my teeth~~ *by promising to give me a dollar for every day I brushed my teeth. It worked for forty days, but after pocketing the money, I'm embarrassed to say,* ~~everyday. She said that if I brushed every day for forty days, she'd give me a dollar for every day. It~~ ~~worked but~~ I didn't keep up the habit ~~after pocketing forty dollars.~~

At the end of my fifth grade year, my *d*~~D~~ad decided I needed to see an orthodontist. I protested, but *D*~~d~~ad made me go see the ~~doctor.~~ *specialist* Petrified by fear, I sat in the dimly lit waiting room aware of everything. ~~I felt I was suffocating since~~ *T*he two slow moving ceiling fans didn't stir up too much *and I felt as if I were suffocating. I felt as trapped as the dead moths in the frosted light fixture. Four gray walls imprisoned me.*

of a breeze / ~~I was imprisoned by four gray walls.~~ Gray may be a soothing color, but that day it

[This sentence was moved.]

seemed hostile. ~~I complained about how ugly the office was, I wanted to leave because nothing~~

~~good was going to come out of it. My father, however, was patient and waited for me calmly.~~ I could

antiseptic *cheerful*
smell the ~~cleansing~~ smell of the dentist's office and hear the women's ~~joyful~~ voices behind the

to my father
closed door. I complained about how ugly the office was, I wanted to leave because nothing good

calmly *with* *.*
was going to come ~~out~~ of it. My father / ~~however,~~ was patient and waited ~~for~~ me ~~calmly.~~ That visit

Once I sat *,*
changed my life. ~~I finally got called~~ in ~~to~~ the doctor's chair ~~and~~ a nice woman performed some

.
procedures on me before the doctor came in ~~to visit with me.~~ His name was Dr. Smith. That man

to *to*
gave me the encouragement I needed ~~to~~ not only change my appearance, but change the way I look

, *.*
at myself ~~by~~ giving me the self-esteem to be outgoing, courageous, and enthusiastic ~~about myself.~~

outlined
He ~~told me~~ the basic steps and procedures I'd need to go through to get braces. He told me that if I

tried ~~and tried,~~ I could have beautiful teeth and a wonderful smile.

aligned
The day finally came when Dr. Smith took off the braces and my teeth ~~fit~~ perfectly. I couldn't

smiling at everyone.
stop ~~showing people and smiling.~~ I was ecstatic. I want to share that feeling with everyone.

[These sentences were added.]
I've
God worked through my dentist to make me a better, stronger person. From that day on ~~I have~~

and the self-confidence not just to set goals,
had high self-esteem / *but to work hard to achieve each and every one of them.* I came out of my

an assertive, determined, hard-working young lady.
shell and blossomed into ~~a confident young lady. The best way to share what I received from my~~

~~dentist is to achieve success in college. How hard can it be after six years of braces? I'll work hard~~

~~to become a dental hygienist.~~

God continued to lead me toward the dental field. Since that memorable fifth-grade visit, I've
be *spent*
been interested in dentistry. How could I not? I ~~was a child and teenager for~~ six years with

enough wire in my mouth to encircle the Ponderosa. My next guiding light was my Health

Science Technology Cooperative Education class teacher who suggested I work at a dentist's

This

on

office. ~~My current~~ job is giving me a head-start ~~toward~~ my future career.

One day, I hope to help a shy little girl discover herself and her God-given talents by teaching her all I know about dental hygiene. I want to make a difference in children's lives, as well as in the lives of their families. God gives each of us many talents and gifts, but only one set of adult teeth. I take it as my personal challenge to help others make the most of their talents and teeth.

I firmly believe in God and know that He's worked through others to show me my personal road to the future. The best way to share what I received through my experiences is to continue to follow God's guiding hand as I achieve success in college. How hard can it be to become a dental hygienist after enduring six years of braces?

Essay 60: Write a 250-word essay on "The Importance of Dental Health." Note: For this assignment, the student wanted to use the essay she'd written for the Guidepost Youth Writing Contest (Entry 59).

As I walked up the steps to the portable classroom, my heart was racing and my hands were sweating. Though the sun was shining, my day didn't feel too bright. Being a five-year-old kindergartner isn't easy, but when you've just had your front teeth pulled it's even worse. I remembered how I looked in the mirror that morning and wondered what I would look like to everyone else. I walked into class room and sat down hoping no one would notice. The little boy who sat next to me immediately asked where I'd been the previous day. I opened my mouth to answer he started yelling, "You look like a vampire! Vampire! Vampire!

Well, that certainly didn't help matters much. At that moment, I didn't like dentists. I didn't trust dentists at all. I hated going. I'd make excuses, to get out of seeing a dentist like pretending I was sick. This lack of dental care led me to become lazy in my dental hygiene. In first grade, my aunt bribe me to brush my teeth everyday. She said that if I brushed every teeth. It worked for forty days, but after pocketing the money, I'm embarrassed to say, day for forty days, she'd give me a dollar for every day. It worked but I didn't keep up the habit after pocketing forty dollars.

At the end of my fifth grade year, my Dad decided I needed to see an orthodontist. I protested, but dad made me go see the ~~doctor~~. Petrified by fear, I sat in the dimly lit waiting room aware of everything. The two slow moving ceiling fans didn't stir up too much of a breeze and I felt as if I were suffocating. I felt as trapped as the dead moths in the frosted light fixture. Four gray walls imprisoned me. Gray may be a soothing color, but that day it seemed hostile. I could smell the antiseptic smell of the dentist's office and hear the women's cheerful voices behind the closed door. I complained to my father about how ugly the office was, I wanted to leave because nothing good was going to come out of it. My father was patient and waited for me calmly.

That visit changed my life. Once in to the doctor's chair, a nice woman performed some procedures on me before the doctor came in. His name was Dr. Smith. That man gave me the encouragement I needed not only to change my appearance, but to change the way I look at myself, giving me the self-esteem to be outgoing, courageous, and enthusiastic. He outlined the basic steps and procedures I'd need to go through to get braces. He told me that if I tried, I could have beautiful teeth and a wonderful smile.

The day finally came when Dr. Smith took off the braces and my teeth fit perfectly. I couldn't stop smiling at everyone. I was ecstatic. I want to share that feeling with everyone. God worked through my dentist to make me a better, stronger person. From that day on I've had the self-confidence not just to set goals, but to work hard to achieve each and every one of them. I came out of my shell and blossomed into an assertive, determined, hard-working young lady.

God continued to lead me toward the dental field. Since that memorable fifth-grade visit, I've been interested in dentistry. How could I not? I spent six years with enough wire in my mouth to encircle the Ponderosa. My next guiding light was my Health Science Technology Cooperative Education class teacher, who suggested I work at a dentist's office. This job is giving me a head-start on my future career.

One day, I hope to help a shy little girl discover herself and her God-given talents by teaching her all I know about dental hygiene. I want to make a difference in children's lives, as well as in the lives of their families. God gives each of us many talents and gifts, but only one set of adult teeth. I take it as my personal challenge to help others make the most of their talents and teeth.

I firmly believe in God and know that He's worked through others to show me my personal road to the future. The best way to share what I received through my experiences is to continue to follow God's guiding hand as I achieve success in college. How hard can it be to become a dental hygienist after enduring six years of braces?

Essay 60—Makeover: The essay the student wanted to use is three times too long and needed to be refocused. All references to God also needed to be removed. This was the version she started with and needed to cut down. The resulting essay is 249 words in length.

~~As I walked up the steps to the portable classroom,~~ **M**y heart was racing and my hands were sweating. ~~Though the sun was shining, my day didn't feel too bright.~~ Being a five-year-old kindergartner isn't easy, but ~~when you've just had~~ *I'd just had my* ~~just had your~~ front teeth pulled ~~it's even worse~~. I remembered how I looked in the mirror that morning ~~and wondered what I would look like to everyone else. I walked into the classroom and sat down hoping no one would notice~~. *Would anyone notice?* The little boy who sat next to me ~~immediately~~ asked where I'd been the previous day. *As* I opened my mouth ~~to answer~~ he started yelling, "You look like a vampire! Vampire! Vampire!"

~~Well, that certainly didn't help matters much. At that moment,~~ I didn't like dentists~~,~~ *, and I* ~~I didn't trust dentists at all. I hated going. I'd make excuses, to get out of seeing a dentist like pretending I was sick. This lack of dental care led me to~~ bec**a**me lazy in my dental hygiene. In first grade, my aunt ~~bribed me by promising to~~ g**a**ve me a dollar for every day I brushed my teeth. It worked for forty days, but after pocketing the money, ~~I'm embarrassed to say,~~ I didn't keep up the habit.

When I was eleven, ~~At the end of my fifth grade year,~~ my **D**ad decided I needed to see an orthodontist. ~~I protested, but Dad made me go see the specialist. Petrified by fear, I sat in the dimly lit waiting room, aware of~~

~~everything.~~ The two slow moving ceiling fans didn't stir up too much of a breeze. ~~and I felt as if I were suffocating.~~ I felt as trapped as the dead moths in the frosted light fixture. ~~Four gray walls imprisoned me. Gray may be a soothing color, but that day it seemed hostile. I could smell the antiseptic smell of the dentist's office and hear the women's cheerful voices behind the closed.~~

, but went and never regretted it.

~~door.~~ I complained to my father about how ugly the office was, ^ ~~I wanted to leave because nothing good was going to come of it. My father was patient, and waited for me calmly.~~

~~That visit changed my life. Once in to the doctor's chair, a nice woman performed some procedures on me before the doctor came in. His name was Dr. Smith. That man gave me the encouragement I needed not only to change my appearance, but to change the way I look at myself, giving me the self-esteem to be outgoing, courageous, and enthusiastic.~~ *The dentist* He outlined the basic steps ^

, and

~~and~~ procedures I'd need to go through to get braces/ ^ He ~~told me that if I tried, I could have~~ beautiful teeth and a wonderful smile.

When my   came off,

~~The day finally came when Dr. Smith took off the~~ braces ^ and my teeth aligned perfectly. ^ I couldn't stop smiling at everyone. ~~I was ecstatic. I want to share that feeling with everyone. God worked through my dentist to make me a better, stronger person. From that day on I've had the self-confidence not just to set goals, but to work hard to achieve each and every one of them. I came out of my shell and blossomed into an assertive, determined, hard-working young lady.~~

~~God continued to lead me toward the dental field. Since that memorable fifth-grade visit,~~

I became   For   I had

~~I've been~~ interested in dentistry. How could I not be? ~~I~~ spent six years with enough wire in my ^ mouth to encircle the Ponderosa. ~~My next guiding light was my Health Science Technology Cooperative Education class teacher, who suggested I work at a dentist's office. This job is giving me a head-start on my future career.~~

One day, I hope to help a shy little girl discover herself and her ~~God-given~~ talents by teaching her all I know about dental hygiene. I want to make a difference in ~~children's lives, as well as in the~~ ^

~~lives of their families.~~ God gives ~~each~~ of us many talents and gifts, but only one set of adult teeth. ~~I~~

~~take it as my~~ personal challenge to help others make the most of their talents and teeth.

E / *has*

M / *is*

~~I firmly believe in God and know that He's worked through others to show me my personal road to the future. The best way to share what I received through my experiences is to continue to follow God's guiding hand as I achieve success in college. How hard can it be to become a dental hygienist after enduring six years of braces?~~

Essay 61: This essay was actually the cover letter that accompanied this student's application packet, requesting her congressman's nomination to the Naval Academy. The letter could be no more than 250 words in length.

For many years I have been looking forward to my college years and beyond. This year I am extremely excited and determined to gain entrance into the Naval Academy.

For the past four years in high school I have been active in many clubs, athletics, and community service. I believe that I am one of the top candidates you can nominate for the academy. I am strong and aggressive in many areas. The other day I heard this quote and I thought wow, this is me! "Some succeed because they're destined to, but most succeed because they're determined to." I know that I have the qualifications and the determination to make it in the academy.

I realize that no other college offers the moral, mental, and physical challenge that the academy does. I have taken it upon myself to face all three challenges. The major factor in my desire for a nomination is for my future career. I am determined to become a naval aviator, and your nomination is a stepping stone towards my goal.

I ask that you consider me for a nomination, I realize that you as a Senator must make a very hard decision choosing the right people to represent Texas. I believe that you would choose a person who is committed, determined, and has the courage to face the challenges of the academy. I ask that you remember me, Jane Garcia. One who is willing to step up to the plate and face all three

challenges, as well as representing your good judgement from the state of Texas.

Essay 61—Makeover: The original essay won't convince a committee and, at 263 words, this essay was too long. It also didn't showcase the student's achievements. There was no reason to describe what the school offers. The committee already knows that. Instead, a brief explanation of a challenge the student took on would be appropriate—a challenge which many might have thought insurmountable, but which this student undertook and conquered, revealing that she can achieve when she tackles a challenge. This is an instance where one quotation is acceptable, because it reflects the point the student is making about herself. The new essay is within the word count. Upon reading the first draft, we discussed the problems with the student. In the second draft, the student made changes to the sequence of the text and some was added.

"Some succeed because they are destined to but most succeed because they are determined to."

When I read this quotation, I thought, "Wow, this is me!"   [Delete. You must "show" not
~~I remember the day I read this quote and I thought Wow, that's me. I'm strong, aggressive,~~

"tell" the committee member who you are. Why should they believe you? How do you know you're
~~determined and I know I have the qualifications to make it in Academy. I'm one of the top~~
one of the top candidates?]
~~candidates you can nominate for the Academy.~~

[Delete. Never state the obvious.]
~~The Academy is noted for excellence. It makes students into strong leaders, and prepares them~~

~~for life. The Academy is the first step towards a career in the military. Though the classes are tough, I~~

~~know I can meet the challenge. I have tried really hard in school. Though, I am in the top quarter of~~

               [How do you know this?]
~~my class, I know I will do better in college.~~

When I was fourteen years old, I was introduced to the Law Enforcement Explorer Program. At
          Explorer   *dis*
that time, the Post was ~~un~~organized and on the verge of collapse. In order for the program to
                                                                    people
continue, we had to maintain six people at every meeting and there were only five in the program.

Under my direction, the Explorers appealed to churches, the community, and local schools for
                            ,   *began to*
support. Shortly thereafter ~~we began to see~~ our program grow. Within two months, I earned the

rank of lieutenant. From that point on, our Explorer Post grew past my expectations.

This nomination would be the first step toward a challenging college curriculum, a commission

as an ensign in the Navy, and ~~for~~ my future career. I want to earn a bachelor's degree in aerospace

engineering, in order to become a naval aviator.

[Though your scores needed to be explained, this explanation isn't sufficient.]
~~I realize that my SAT and ACT scores appear low. However, I have not received my other test~~
                                                    [Why?]
~~scores. I have been intensely studying to try and improve my scores. I feel that the standardized test~~

~~does not reflect my ability to perform well in the Academy.~~

[This paragraph regarding test scores was added in the next draft.]
I realize my SAT and ACT scores may not be considered competitive for admission to the
                                                    with the goal of   *ing*
Academy. I took an intensive study course ~~and, hopefully,~~ improved my scores on the October test.
                                           ^   ^
Knowing that I will do whatever it takes to accomplish a task, I don't feel these standardized tests

reflect my potential for success. Just as I was able to take a troubled Explorers Post and turn it

around, ~~I know~~ I can achieve my goals.

I respectfully request your consideration concerning my nomination.

Essay 62: Define how your system of values would help you succeed as a student and throughout your lifetime. (Baylor University)

I have always been brought up with the ideology that all people want to be treated with the same

amount of respect that I would want from them. This idea is the basis for my system of values. With

this idea in place I feel I could succeed in your school because I feel the same basis for my values if

what your school basis its own set of values upon. I've encountered many situations that simply

invoking the "golden rule" from the beginning could of stopped the situation from getting out of

hand. Everyone I meet during my years at this school as well as those who encounter on the road of

life, will want to be treated with the dignity they have always been taught they deserve. Because I'm

willing to give them this respect and dignity I feel that I will be able to better succeed because

people will be more willing to help and support me through any situation I may encounter.

Essay 62—Makeover: Never tell a school what it is or what it wants. This essay generalizes too much and makes too many assumptions. Various grammatical changes also had to be made to improve this essay.

                 I've   *believed*
I ~~have~~ always ~~been brought up with the ideology~~ that all people want to be treated with the
         ^   ^
                                        to receive   *belief*
same amount of respect ~~that~~ I would want from them. This ~~idea~~ is the basis for my system of values.
                       ^   ^

I can   *at*   *we share the same*

~~With this idea in place I feel I could~~ succeed in^ your school because^ ~~I feel the same basis for my~~^

[Such as?]   *where*

~~values if what your school basis its own set of values upon.~~ I've encountered many situations that^

have

simply invoking the "golden rule" from the beginning could ~~of~~^ stopped the situation from getting

I will treat everyone I meet in life with the same dignity with which I want others to treat me.

out of hand. ~~Everyone I meet during my years at this school, as well as those who encounter on the~~^

[Cliché.]   [How do you know this?]   [Not everyone has been taught this.]

~~road of life, will want to be treated with the dignity they have always been taught they deserve.~~

[Why?]

~~Because I'm willing to give them this respect and dignity I feel that I will be able to better succeed~~

[You don't know this.]

~~because people will be more willing to help and support me through any situation I may~~

[The student added this sentence in the final draft.]

~~encounter.~~ *By surrounding myself with individuals who have the same values as I do, I will*

succeed in all my endeavors.

Essay 63: Here's a second essay on the same topic written by a different student. (Baylor University)

Throughout my life I have always been a firm believer in moral values. Maintaining an honest character has allowed me to accomplish many goals when participating in a team, group, or even working in a one on one situation. In my high school career I have been active in baseball every year.

My sophomore year on the Junior Varsity team I was playing center field and having a good season. At the same time another player, Mike, who happens to be a freshman was a center fielder, too, but was moved to right field and didn't get to play much because he didn't get noticed enough. I know he was real good and capable of playing just is good and better than the other outfielders, but who was I to tell coach who should be playing and who should not. It was one particular game when Mike got to play in right field after the starting right fielder was injured that helped me to grow stronger in honesty and as a team player. It was our rival school and we had just retaken the lead in our last at bat. Now it was there turn to bat and they ended up with one out and a runner on third. I knew Mike had a strong arm and could throw the man out tagging up from third in a sac fly situation, but then so could I. If this happened then we would win the game in a double play to end the game. Sure enough a fly ball was hit to the outfield, but it wasn't going into right field and it wasn't coming to me in center field instead it was going into right center field. As I ran over to set up to catch it and throw to home plate out of the corner of my eye I saw Mike moving in next to me and since I was the center fielder it was my call to who catches it. In that one moment I decided to give the glory to Mike who not only needed it to prove himself in the outfield but to show the same team unity I believed in my heart and in my mind. As the ball reached its apex and we came to a stop I heeled, "You got it Mike!" So he took it and threw the runner out trying to score. That day I will always remember because Mike was the hero he deserved to be, my team won, and I had won too. I won the respect of my teammates as well as my coach.

Life is a journey not a destination. Next year I will face many challenges, from social, cultural, and economic diversity, to academic pressures and time management. In college and especially through life my integrity and hard work will show as it has in the past. I know that this value will lead me through any challenges in college and in life.

Essay 63—Makeover: This student discusses only one value and needs to explain how the Golden Rule will help him or her face the challenges listed. It also ends rather abruptly.

Throughout my life ~~I have always~~ *I've* been a firm believer in ~~moral values.~~ [Redundant.] *M*aintaining an honest

character ~~has~~ *, which* allowed me to accomplish many goals. ~~when participating in a team, group, or even~~

~~working in a one on one situation. In my high school career I have been active in baseball every~~ [High school is not a career unless you plan to stay there for a long time.] [No new paragraph.]

~~year.~~

An example of this occurred during my   softball .

~~My~~ sophomore year on the Junior Varsity team I was playing center field. ~~and having a good~~

~~season. At the same time another player,~~ Mike, ~~who happens to be a freshman was~~ *also* a center fielder,

~~too, but was moved to right field and~~ didn't get to play much, ~~because he didn't get noticed~~ *didn't get noticed because he   yet he was*

~~enough.~~ ~~I know he was real good and capable of playing just~~ *as* is good ~~and~~ *or* better than the other

outfielders. ~~but who was I to tell coach who should be playing and who should not.~~

During a close game, ~~It was one particular game when~~ Mike ~~got to play in~~ *was playing* right field. ~~after the starting right fielder~~

~~was injured that helped me to grow stronger in honesty and as a team player. It was our rival school~~

We'd ~~and we had~~ just retaken the lead in our last at bat. ~~Now it was there turn to bat and they ended up~~

The other team had ~~with~~ one out and a runner on third. ~~I knew Mike had a strong arm and could throw the man out~~

~~tagging up from third in a sac fly situation, but then so could I. If this happened then we would win~~

~~the game in a double play to end the game.~~ Sure enough *A* ~~a~~ fly ball was hit ~~to the outfield, but it~~

~~wasn't going into right field and it wasn't coming to me in center field instead it was going~~ into

right center field. As I ran *to catch it,* ~~over to set up to catch it and throw to home plate out of the corner of my~~

eye I saw Mike moving in next to me. ~~and since I was the center fielder it was my call to who~~

~~catches it.~~ In that ~~one~~ moment I *realized Mike* ~~decided to give the glory to mike who not only~~ needed it to prove *to make the play*

himself, *and I decided to demonstrate* ~~in the outfield but to show~~ the same team unity I believed in *firmly* ~~my heart and in my mind~~. As

the ball reached its apex, ~~and we came to a stop~~ I *yelled* ~~heeled~~, "You got it Mike!" *He caught the ball* So he took ~~it~~ and threw

the runner out. ~~trying to score.~~ *I'll* ~~That day I will~~ always remember *that day* because Mike was the hero he

deserved to be, my team won, and I ~~had~~ won *also*/ ~~too.~~ I won the respect of my teammates, as well as *of* my

coach.

[No clear meaning in this context.]
~~Life is a journey, not a destination.~~ Next year *I'll* ~~I will~~ face many challenges/ *:* from social, cultural, and

economic diversity/ to academic ~~pressures~~ and time management/ *pressures.* ~~In college and especially through~~

~~life~~ *My values* my integrity and hard work will *help* ~~show as it has in the past. I know that this value~~ will lead me

conquer ~~through~~ any challenges in college and in life.

Essay 64: Write an essay of no more than 500 words on any subject that interests you. You may choose to write on an issue about which you feel strongly, an experience that has greatly influenced your life, or other circumstances that you would like the admissions staff to consider in reviewing your application. These are only suggestions, however; the choice is yours. (Boston University)

There are many turning points in our lives, today was one for me. I always knew something would happen in my life that would have an impact, but I never knew when, where, or how.

It's a week until our choir Christmas concert and our director suffered a severe heart attack. He had been on vacation with his spouse when this occurred. His son called to inform me of what took place. I guess he thought I should be one of the first to know, being the president of the top choir. I immediately called an officer meeting to discuss the upcoming concert. We proceeded with the concert and all went smoothly. When it was all over, I looked back on the entire situation and could not believe what we accomplished. It was a very good feeling, knowing that we as officers could pull together and use everything our director taught us to finish the work he had already started. Wow, maybe you do really learn from your teachers. Maybe they were all right when they said "If you are not careful you might just learn something."

A few days later our director canceled our annual musical for that year. The decision impacted my life greatly. It shocked many students and hurt most. I felt angry and upset. Instead of fighting a lost cause, I felt I had to take what I had learned from my director and find something new. I did not depend on someone else to have a show waiting there for me, but instead I created my own. I am directing my own show for a theater project. I am using what I have learned. I guess being your own person and making choices really is not as scary as I thought it would be. I am aware there will be future challenges. I will win some and lose some, but only I can make the choices to determine the outcome.

Essay 64—Makeover: The revised essay is only 263 words in length. If the student wants to make the essay longer, he might want to answer these questions: How did you arrive at the decision to do your own show? Did you choose the theme, students, costumes, set, etc.? How much assistance was provided by your teacher and the school? How many students were involved? How did you promote it? The student could add a few sentences at the end to discuss how he'll be using this experience in college, in his major, and in life. Or the student can leave this essay as it is. Never "pad" a strong essay to fill out a maximum word count. Based on our experience as committee members, the questions above would have occurred to us in reading this essay.

There are many turning point[s] in our lives[.] ~~today was one for me.~~ I always knew something would happen in my life that would have an [such effect] ~~impact~~, but I never knew when, where, or how.

[A] ~~It's~~ a week ~~until~~ [before] our ~~choir~~ [Choir] Christmas concert ~~and~~ [,] our director suffered a severe heart attack. ~~He had~~ [He'd] been on vacation with his ~~spouse when this occurred.~~ [wife.] His son called to inform me ~~of what took place. I guess he~~ [He] thought I should be one of the first to know, ~~being~~ [since I was] the president of the top choir.

[What is "top choir?" Add a brief definition.]

[The student should have described how it was possible to still hold the concert without the director.]

choir. I immediately called an officer['s] meeting to discuss the upcoming concert. We proceeded with the concert and all went smoothly. When it was all over, I ~~looked back on the entire situation and could not~~ [couldn't] believe what ~~we~~ [we'd] accomplished. It was a ~~very~~ good feeling, knowing ~~that we as officers~~ could pull together and use everything our director taught us to finish the work ~~he had already~~ [he'd] started. Wow, maybe ~~you~~ [we] do really learn from ~~your~~ [our] teachers. Maybe ~~they were all~~ right ~~when they said~~ [the saying is]: "If ~~you are~~ [you're] not careful[,] you might just learn something."

A few days later our director canceled our annual musical ~~for that year. The decision impacted my life greatly.~~ It shocked many students ~~and hurt most.~~ [This] and hurt[.] I felt angry and upset[.] ~~Instead of fighting a lost cause,~~ [Though initially] I ~~felt I had to take~~ [took] what ~~I had~~ [I'd] learned from my director and ~~find something new.~~ [found a solution.] I ~~did not~~ [didn't] depend on someone else to ~~have a show~~ [make the show.] ~~waiting there for me, but~~ [I] instead I created my own. ~~I am~~ [I'm] directing my own show for a theater project. ~~I am~~ [I'm] using what ~~I have~~ [I've] learned. ~~I guess~~ [B]eing your own person and making choices really ~~is not~~ [isn't] as scary as I thought it would be. ~~I am aware there will be~~ [There will be] future challenges. ~~I will~~ [I'll] win some and lose some, but only I can make the choices to determine the outcome.

[Feeling angry seems harsh. The man had just had a heart attack.]

Essay 65: Write an essay on any topic you find interesting. (Boston University)

To some mathematics is an ugly swirl of computations, arcane symbols, and toilsome formulas. Mathematics is not merely about computations and formulas to me, to me it is about grasping the essential, solving challenging problems and finding absolute truth.

There is a great deal of beauty to be found in mathematics, and although to perceive it one must put forth more effort than is necessary to enjoy a symphony or a painting, the rewards are well worth the exertion. The beauty of mathematics lies in the joining of a number of ideas into one abstraction, and in the absolute surety one can find in mathematics that exists nowhere else. If one proceeds from a few given definitions and axioms and takes each step in a proof with careful logic one can be completely assured that the result obtained is true, however fantastic it might seem, and thus mathematics does not have to rewrite itself as the other sciences have repeatedly been obliged to when unexpected results came in. Euclid is still an authority, Ptolemy belongs only to history. All branches of mathematics are intertwined; one might find that to prove a result involving Cantor sets in two dimensional space one will have to refer to linear algebra, eigenvectors, and linear transformations, as I did in the course of my summer research in mathematics. The ubiquitous interweaving of ideas, and the often unexpected ways in which ideas come together constitute another facet of the beauty of mathematics.

Another aspect of mathematics that I love is the challenge. There are various challenges in mathematics, but the two chief forms these challenges take are modeling in applied and proof in pure mathematics. Modeling can be very difficult, since one must imagine all sorts of factors that might influence how a system behaves and yet one must not become lost in the tangle of trivial factors that don't affect the essential aspects of the system. However, the joy of constructing a model and then testing it successfully is well worth the toil. Proofs tend to look simpler than they are. In my research this summer I investigated the cardinality of a two dimensional cantor set by looking at how it intersected a one dimensional Cantor set on a line that passed through a domain of the two dimensional Cantor set. The proofs constructed were not exceedingly long, but to be able to produce and understand them I had to understand topology, set theory, and linear algebra. It was difficult to bring so many ideas together and to create a proof, and the amount of effort I exerted is belied by the succinct nature of the result. Once again, the very difficulty to the task made the end result all the more rewarding.

To conclude, I love mathematics because it is a difficult discipline, and an art. With mathematics one can both solve difficult problems and create proofs and possess great beauty in their absolute truth.

Essay 65—Makeover: The first thing to do to make this essay more approachable, friendlier, and memorable would be to use contractions. Though the topic of this essay is unusual, the fact that the student could explain the concept of Cantor Sets clearly to the layperson is what provides the unseen committee member with an understanding of who the student is.

To some, mathematics is an ugly swirl of computations, arcane symbols, and ~~toilsome~~ formulas.

[Delete–repetitive.]
~~Mathematics is not merely about computations and formulas to me,~~ To me it's about grasping the essential, solving challenging problems, and finding absolute truth.

Although there is a beauty in mathematics, to
~~There is a great deal of beauty to be found in mathematics, and although to~~ perceive it one must put forth more effort than is necessary to enjoy a symphony or a painting. The rewards are well worth the exertion. The beauty ~~of mathematics~~ lies in the joining of a number of ideas into one abstraction, and in the absolute surety one can find ~~in mathematics that exists~~ nowhere else. If one proceeds from a few given definitions and axioms, and takes each step in a proof with careful logic, one can be completely assured that the result obtained is true.

[Delete–unnecessary.]
~~however fantastic it might seem, and thus mathematics does not have to rewrite itself as the other sciences have repeatedly been obliged to when unexpected results came in. Euclid is still an authority, Ptolemy belongs only to history.~~ All branches of mathematics are intertwined; one might find that to prove a result involving Cantor Sets in two-dimensional space, one will have to refer to linear algebra, eigenvectors, and linear

transformations, as I did in the course of my summer research in mathematics. The ubiquitous interweaving of ideas, and the often unexpected ways in which ideas come together, constitute another facet of the beauty of mathematics.

I enjoy the
~~Another aspect of mathematics that I love is the challenge.~~ There are various challenges in mathematics; ~~but~~ the ~~two~~ chief forms these challenges take are modeling in applied and proof in mathematics pure mathematics. Modeling can be ~~very~~ difficult, since one must imagine how a system behaves, all sorts of factors that might influence ~~and~~ yet one must not become lost in the tangle of trivial factors that don't affect the essential aspects of the system. However, the joy of constructing a model and then testing it successfully is well worth the toil.

[The student inserted these sentences into the final version to explain where he did the research.]

This semester I was able to gain some modeling experience in my Differential Equations class, where I modeled the Lorentz equation, from which the Chaos Theory was born; the wave equation, where only through differential equations can one arrive at a formula that makes physical sense; and many others. I enjoyed applying mathematics to physical problems as much as I enjoyed the mathematics itself. Differential Equations spurred my interest in applied mathematics, which I wish to pursue further. [New paragraph.]

Proofs tend to look simpler than they are. In my research this summer, I investigated the cardinality of a two dimensional Cantor Set by looking at how it intersected a one dimensional Cantor Set on a line that passed through a domain of the two dimensional Cantor Set. The proofs weren't constructed ~~were not~~ exceedingly long, but to be able to produce and understand them I had to understand topology, set theory, and linear algebra. My summer research made it clear to me that ~~It was difficult to bring so many ideas together~~ I wanted to study mathematics, since I enjoyed learning the material and especially the idea ~~and to create a proof, and the amount of effort I exerted is belied by the succinct nature of the~~ that I might discover something unknown. ~~result. Once again, the very difficulty to the task made the end result all the more rewarding.~~

I'm drawn to   *it's*

To conclude, ~~I love~~ mathematics because ~~it is~~ a difficult discipline / and an art. With mathematics

that

one can both solve difficult problems and create proofs ~~and~~ possess great beauty in their absolute

truth.

Essay 66: We're interested in knowing about you as a person. To this end, write an essay on an event or events that have shaped your life. (California Institute of Technology)

Ever since I have had access to electronics and computers, I have been fascinated with them. I started by playing Atari at age four. I was content with playing video games and using electronics only in that way for a long time. In fact, I played them so much that I won a citywide video game championship when I was 8 years old. My computer game phase quickly followed. I admit I still haven't completely grown out of that one, but I have progressed beyond it. I felt limited by using computer programs designed by someone else that didn't necessarily meet my specifications. I wanted to tell that big hunk of processing power what to do.

This desire logically led me to my next phase, programming. This started simply with qBASIC and eventually to high school courses in various flavors of C++. This year, I am designing graphics software for Dr. Thomas Smith, a Southwest Research Institute scientist. I'm developing a computer visualization of ballistic penetration as calculated by the Walker-Anderson model for long rod penetration, used to predict the interactions of weapon rounds and various materials, such as fabrics and ceramics. I'm creating the program using cutting-edge graphics software called the Visualization Toolkit that is used in many other scientific applications. This is undoubtedly the greatest academic challenge I have faced in high school but also the most stimulating.

Through this project, I'm beginning to see how math and science can be applied to solve real world problems. My project has solidified my decision to seek an Electrical Engineering degree. I want to design the machines that are running the software.

The fact that Electrical Engineers are making the horsepower that runs the Information Age is captivating to me. I have a passion for math and physics, areas I know are involved in designing the circuitry in computers and electronics. I plan to major in Mathematics in addition to Electrical Engineering.

Beyond college, I am currently considering two career paths. I want to use my skills in math and electronics for the benefit of others. Through my senior year Independent Study Mentorship program, I am experiencing life at Southwest Research Institute and have observed the importance of the research that is done in that facility. Being a research scientist at Southwest Research is a likely career for me. I would love to be a part of the cutting edge research in things like quantum computers.

Another possibility is working for an organization like the National Security Agency to serve and protect my country. I have always felt a duty towards America and would enjoy using my talents to protect the freedom of the nation. I can hardly imagine the amazing technologies that are used for encryption and signal analysis.

To be content, I need to learn and be challenged. I continually seek out new opportunities and experiences in order to use my talents to help others. I am thrilled to be able to study Electrical Engineering in college.

Essay 66—Makeover: This essay needed a friendlier tone and a vividness to make it memorable. We suggested the student start over, writing it as if he were watching his life in a video. We also suggested he insert a few more views into his childhood. This is the finished version with a few minor changes.

The lights have been dimmed, the smell of buttered popcorn wafts through the air. The family is in their regular places on the couch.

My life, written, produced, and conducted by Devlin O'Connor and his parents. I fast-forward through the credits. I hate wasting time. I already know who we are.

"Five. Seven. Ten. Three," Mom says ~~out loud~~ in her clear*,* commanding voice. ~~I am~~ *I'm* sitting snuggled up against her as she sits in a yoga position. I'm not going anywhere. At six months of age, I can't walk yet. ~~I am~~ *I'm* bombarded with dot flashcards from the "Better Baby Institute" intended to increase my mathematical aptitude.

Where's that remote control? Here it is. Fast-forward again.

There, I am at four~~-years-old~~ *age*. I'm completely enthralled by my Atari and have to be reminded to go outside.

Fast forward. At six~~-years~~ *age* I'm spending my Saturdays building rockets and studying sea urchins instead of watching cartoons.

Move ahead three more years. A crowd is awed when I complete one row of Tetris after another to win the *C*itywide *V*ideo *G*ame *C*hampionship.

Jump ahead to the seventh grade. I do my algebra homework and compete in Regional Science Fair for one reason: I like it.

Freshman year I'm sitting at my desk mapping out and organizing a charity walk-a-thon for my Eagle Scout project.

Finally, senior year. I'm writing graphics software and using Saturdays to take competitive academic tests.

As the musical score is play~~ed~~*ing* in the background, the video goes to a blue screen. The rest of the movie has yet to be recorded. What will it show? Where will I go from here? Only time will tell.

My life may seem to many like a strange existence, but I wouldn't have it any other way. I need to learn and be challenged to be content. I enjoy learning about everything, not just the areas in which I have natural aptitude. I continually seek out new challenges and experiences. While I'm gifted in mathematics and scientific fields and have a great passion for these subjects, I also pursue learning about the humanities.

I've
~~I have~~ worked hard to be well-rounded. I've always been captivated by the idea of the
^

I've
"Renaissance man." ~~I have~~ strived in all that I do to have varied interests. I've led a ten-man crew for
^

two weeks at Philmont Scout Ranch in Cimarron, New Mexico, and served others by repairing roofs

in Memphis, Tennessee. I gain great satisfaction from doing a trig integral and from playing Chopin's

Prelude #15. I often play Ultimate Frisbee and basketball with my friends and have played clarinet

areas
in the school marching band. My goal has been to be a "jack of all trades" and a master of as many as
^

I can.

In all that I do, I try my hardest to be fair and honorable in my actions. My extensive involvement

with Boy Scouts, besides teaching me how to tie a knot for anything and everything, has instilled in

me a strong sense of self-reliance, cooperation, and justice that causes me to be strongly attracted to

Caltech's Honor Code. Growing up going to church has also made a strong impression on me about

treating others fairly. I frequently think of the quote, "Man is tallest when he's on his knees."

I see Caltech as the educational means to my ends: improving life and ultimately serving God.

The events of my life have shaped me into someone who has a fascination with discovery,

knowledge, and a desire to help others.

I can already see the rest of my video coming to life in front of my eyes.

Essay 67: Write an essay (minimum 500 words) describing the leadership skills you believe are necessary to achieve your personal goals in the food service and hospitality industry and how you think completion of the bachelor's degree will help you acquire those skills. (Culinary Institute of America)

As most students and parents learn, the burden of financing a college education today can be

astronomical. The estimated cost of a four-year education in 1997 is $44,188 at a public institution

and $92,323 at a private one. The cost of an education at the Culinary Institute of America is

$32,000 for an associate's degree plus $10,000 expenses; and $31,000 for a bachelor's degree plus

$10,000 for expenses.

The total cost of my education will be approximately $80,805. The government could possibly provide $10,000 through Pell Grants and Supplimental Educational Opportunity grants. I can provide $6,408 from work and savings. The majority of my education funding will come from loans at the cost of $66,605. This amount amounts to the price of a new luxury car or a medium size house in middle-class neighborhood in San Antonio.

Since financing an education is so expensive, receiving the scholarship offered by the American Culinary Federation would help relieve some of the pressure related to the expense associated with obtaining a degree. This money would allow me to devote my full attention to my studies at school. Receiving this scholarship will also allow me to fulfill my life-long dreams of receiving a degree and starting my own business by paying off my school loans sooner.

Essay 67—Makeover: At 212 words, this essay is not just too short, it doesn't provide the information requested. It's also not interesting or memorable. We suggested the student open the essay with a more personalized touch. The second draft of the essay is 755 words in length. After editing, the essay is 682 words in length and addresses the topic appropriately.

One day I want to own and operate my own business. ~~I am~~ *I'm* up to the challenge because during

[Delete—"tells," doesn't "show."]

my lifetime I have learned three lessons. ~~The first lesson was learned by example.~~ My father started his printing business out of my parents' home in San Antonio's *S*outhside. The first ~~five to~~ ten years were a struggle. Our family was solely supported by my mother's teaching salary. Texas Lithographers has now been in business for over ~~25~~ *twenty-five* years. Lesson one: you ~~must~~ work hard to reach your goals.

[Delete—"tells," doesn't "show."]

~~The second lesson I learned from my mother.~~ My mother retired after twenty-seven years of teaching. Lesson two: if you choose a profession you love, you can do it all your life. Today she teases me that she, my grandmother, and great grandmother worked hard to get out of the kitchen and ~~here I am~~ *I'm eagerly* going back in.

[Negative—delete.]

Due to bad planning ~~and choices~~, when I graduated from high school I had few options. Though

I was frightened and suffered from low self-esteem, I undertook a full load of courses at Texas

Women's University. At the end of the first year, I earned a 3.8 GPA, something I'd ~~I had~~ never done in

high school. Lesson three: I could be as bright as my peers if I applied ~~apply~~ myself.

Armed with the encouragement of my family and the lessons I've ~~I have~~ learned, I've ~~I have~~ set becoming

a chef as one of my long-term goals. I chose culinary arts as a career because I experience pleasure

while eating food, enjoy cooking it, and like the challenge of food preparation ~~is a challenge~~.

Changing careers after fifteen years in retail and a divorce provided the opportunity to enter the

food service industry. Unfortunately, the Culinary Institute of America (CIA) requires students to

have experience in a professional kitchen and I had none. A local restaurant hired me as a food

server. After two weeks, I was offered pastry training. Within a year, I gained the respect of

management and became the pastry chef.

Armed with this new experience and the lessons I learned, I applied to and was accepted to ~~decided to apply to~~ the Culinary

Institute of America ~~(CIA). I was accepted and went on to~~, where I'd receive an associate's degree. Now I

want to obtain a bachelor's degree in culinary management from the Institute ~~CIA~~.

As most students and parents learn, the burden of financing a college education today can be

[Delete—irrelevant.]

astronomical. ~~The estimated cost of a four-year education in 1997 is $44,188 at a public institution~~

~~and $92,323 at a private one.~~ The cost of an education at the Culinary Institute of America will be ~~is~~

~~$32,000 for an associate's degree plus $10,000 expenses; and~~ approximately $31,000 for a bachelor's degree plus

[No new paragraph.]   [Delete—already covered.]

$10,000 for expenses. ~~The total cost of my education will be approximately $80,805.~~ The

government could possibly provide $10,000 through Pell Grants and Supplemental ~~Supplimental~~ Educational

Opportunity Grants. I can provide $6,408 from work and savings. The majority of my education

[Delete—cost can vary.] The total indebtedness could be enough to
funding will come from loans. ~~at the cost of $66,605. This amount amounts to the price of a new~~
cover the cost of
~~luxury car or~~ a medium size house in a middle-class neighborhood in San Antonio.

Since financing an education is so expensive, receiving the scholarship offered by the American

Culinary Federation would help relieve some of the pressure ~~related to the expense associated with~~
and
~~obtaining a degree. This money would~~ allow me to devote my full attention to my studies ~~at school.~~
help me to pay off my school loans sooner, and enable
Receiving this scholarship will ~~also allow~~ me to fulfill my life-long dreams of receiving a degree and
[Moved to earlier in sentence.]
starting my own business ~~by paying off my school loans sooner.~~

I've
~~I have~~ always wanted to own and operate my own business, just like my father and grandfather.

To be taken seriously in this industry, you have to be extremely good at what you're doing,

especially if you're a woman. To be successful in business and achieve my goals, I'll need a good
Culinary Institute of America
education. The ~~CIA~~ offers the best hands-on training with the most certified master chefs in the

industry. While pursuing my associate's degree, I maintained a strong academic record (consistently
scored percent -
above a 3.0 GPA), received recognition for perfect attendance, 96% on the fifth term Cooking

Practical, and received two scholarships for academic excellence.

After establishing a successful restaurant, I want to mentor other individuals, especially women,
who're
~~who are~~ interested in cooking. I want to give them the opportunity to reach their dreams. One day,
R
I hope to remarry and have a family. ~~I can assure you that~~ retirement is out of the question.
In time, I'd like to
~~I plan on~~ opening a bed and breakfast in the King William district in San Antonio.

Essay 68: What do you think is the most important thing for us to know about you? Your response
must be no more than 300 words in length. (Marquette University)

There is one thing that I have come to value above all others in dealing with myself and with

others. I expect it from others, and I expect that they expect it and so I practice it. Because of my belief in honesty, I have often been referred to as blunt and tactless. I have always told people what

I think, and I have hoped that they would do the same for me.

It is my belief that without honesty, we could not know where we stand on anything. If you like

an idea or a person, say so. If you don't, then don't say, "I don't like you" and don't pretend that

you're their best friend when you can't stand them. I get irritated at the people around me who

refuse to let a person know how they feel, and then talk about them behind their backs. With me,

you always know where you stand. I don't like being led on, and so I don't lead people on. I'm not

afraid to disagree with someone just because I think they will get mad either. I do not do all of this

to the point of being rude or mean, but I let it known how I feel.

I think that, as cliched as it is, "Honesty is the best policy." Honesty in everything, if you screw up

or do something wrong, you get more respect for being honest and admitting your mistake than

you do if you try to hide it or lie about it. The truth is, I value my belief in honesty above almost

everything else and that is what I think you should know about me.

Essay 68—Makeover: At 280 words, this essay just needed to be tightened up. We made some deletions and changes. Precious word count was wasted on unnecessary phrases: "I think . . ." "It's my belief . . ." and "The truth is . . ." The topic selected is a good one. Focusing on honesty is always appropriate, since all schools have honor codes.

~~There is~~ one thing that ~~I have~~ come to value above all others ~~in dealing with myself and with~~ _There's_ _I've_ _:_ _honesty._

~~others.~~ I expect it from others, and I ~~expect that they expect it and so I practice it. Because of my~~ _extend it to others._

~~belief in honesty, I have often been referred to as blunt and~~ tactless. ~~I have~~ always told people what _Some may think I'm blunt, but I always try not to be_ _I've_

I think, and ~~I have~~ hoped ~~that they would~~ do the same for me. _I've_ _they'd_

~~It is my belief that~~ ~~w~~ithout honesty, we ~~could not~~ know where we stand ~~on anything.~~ If you like _W_ _wouldn't_ _._

an idea or a person, say so. If you don't, then don't say, "I don't like you~~,~~ ~~and~~ ~~d~~on't pretend ~~that~~ _."_ _D_

you're their best friend when you can't stand them. I get irritated at the people ~~around me~~ who

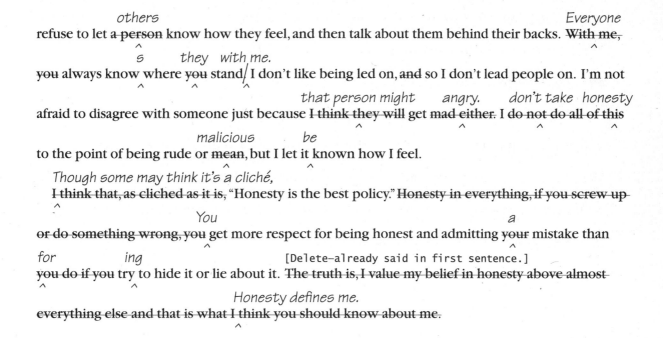

others   *Everyone*

refuse to let ~~a person~~ know how they feel, and then talk about them behind their backs. ~~With me,~~

s   *they with me.*

~~you~~ always know where ~~you~~ stand/ I don't like being led on, ~~and~~ so I don't lead people on. I'm not

                             that person might   *angry.*   *don't take honesty*

afraid to disagree with someone just because ~~I think they will~~ get ~~mad either.~~ ~~I do not do all of this~~

                  malicious   *be*

to the point of being rude or ~~mean,~~ but I let it known how I feel.

    Though some may think it's a cliché,

~~I think that, as cliched as it is,~~ "Honesty is the best policy." ~~Honesty in everything, if you screw up~~

                 You   *a*

~~or do something wrong, you~~ get more respect for being honest and admitting ~~your~~ mistake than

for   *ing*   [Delete—already said in first sentence.]

~~you do if~~ you try to hide it or lie about it. ~~The truth is, I value my belief in honesty above almost~~

                         Honesty defines me.

~~everything else and that is what I think you should know about me.~~

Essay 69: Make up your own question and answer it. Your essay should not be more than 500 words in length. (Massachusetts Institute of Technology)

If you could be any substance, what and why?

If I were to think of myself as some substance, either natural or artificial, it would have to be Non-dairy creamer. While I do not dissolve in liquids, I do share many of the characteristics of this unusual substance, if only in analogy.

In non-dairy creamer, modern technology has taken something naturally occurring and improved it. Through artificial chemicals and processes, all of the negatives of the natural sweetener like fats and calories have been eliminated in its surrogate. In the same way, modern technology has improved me beyond my natural state. I have been able to pursue independent learning through the Internet and the experimenting power in my school's educational resources and through the availability of information, like all this interesting facts about non-dairy creamer. I have been able to visualize concepts and phenomena more clearly thanks to computers. Technology has definitely accelerated my understanding and increased my enthusiasm for science while allowing me more time for exploration and play, also important in true scientific reasoning.

Non-dairy creamer is given what may seem to some a meager task of sweetening someone's beverage. However, this role as a servant to me is one of the most important and noble tasks anything or anyone can fulfill. I enjoy helping and collaborating with people in anyway I can. I often tutor people because I like to see other succeed and aid them in reaching their goal in whatever way possible. An example is the 6 hour Physics study group I held for anyone in the class since I had already completed the course. I like to think that, like coffee and non-Dairy Creamer, both parties gain from the experience and are better off than they were alone. I like serving others in other, non-academic ways like spending a week in Memphis repairing houses needy families. In all that I do, I try to put service over self.

Finally, given the correct conditions, non-dairy creamer can reach it's full potential: a spectacular flame when it is suspended in air over an open flame (don't try this, it's dangerous!). I, too, flourish under the correct conditions. A place that supplies a strong source of creative and intellectual energy beneath me in the form of vast educational and personal resources helps me to improve my problem-solving skills and learn more material better. The combination of this Shangri-La of learning with the synergy from being immersed with peers that are as passionate as I am about science and knowledge is explosive.

Overall, while we may not taste the same, non-dairy creamer and I are pretty close to each other, which I think is a good thing to be. I just hope I'm not as likely to spontaneously combust.

Essay 69—Makeover: Though the assignment was conventional, the student's approach was uniquely his. This was a great approach to what could have been a stodgy litany on a dry topic. Though this was a strong essay, it did need a few changes to tighten the language.

would you be,
If you could be any substance, what and why?

If I were to think of myself as some substance, either natural or artificial, it would have to be

[Sentences added here.]

Non-dairy creamer. *Surprisingly, non-dairy creamer isn't just for coffee. It's been living a double life. By day, it's a mild-mannered servant of sleepy adults, but by night, a dynamic figure,*

manifesting itself in striking displays of power.

[New paragraph.]

While I ~~do not~~ don't dissolve in liquids, I do share many of the characteristics of this unusual

substance, if only in analogy.

~~In non-dairy creamer,~~ Modern technology has taken something naturally occurring and

improved it. ~~/~~ Through artificial chemicals and processes, all of the negatives of sugar (fats and calories) ~~of the natural sweetener like fats and calories~~ have been eliminated in its surrogate *while maintaining the*

sweetening property. Likewise, ~~In the same way,~~ modern technology has ~~improved~~ allowed me to improve myself by ~~beyond my natural~~

~~state.~~ ~~I have been able to~~ pursuing independent learning through the Internet and ~~the~~ experimenting

with ~~power in~~ my school's educational resources, ~~and through the availability of information, like all this~~

~~interesting facts about non-dairy creamer. I have been able to visualize concepts and phenomena~~

~~more clearly thanks to computers. Technology has definitely~~ accelerating my understanding and

increasing my enthusiasm for science while allowing me more time for exploration and play. ~~also~~

~~important in true scientific reasoning.~~ *I use all this extra knowledge to serve humanity.*

[Sentence added.]

Just as non-dairy creamer is given ~~what may seem to some~~ the meager task of sweetening someone's

beverage, ~~However, this role as a servant to me is one of the most important and noble tasks~~

~~anything or anyone can fulfill.~~ I enjoy helping and collaborating with people in any way ~~anyway~~ I can.

[Sentence added.]

I always put service over self, whether it's free tutoring outside of school, service for an

organization, or spending a week in Memphis repairing houses for needy families. ~~I often tutor~~

~~people because I like to see other succeed and aid them in reaching their goal in whatever way~~

~~possible. An example is the 6 hour Physics study group I held for anyone in the class since I had~~

~~already completed the course. I like to think that,~~ Like coffee and non-Dairy Creamer, both parties

gain from the experience and are better off than they were alone. ~~I like serving others in other,~~

[Moved to earlier in paragraph.]

~~non-academic ways like [spending a week in Memphis repairing houses needy families. In all that I~~

~~do, I try to put service over self.]~~

One of the unique things about non-dairy creamer is its extreme flammability. However, you

can't just throw a match in a container and run. There's not enough air and space to provide

the oxygen for the combustion. ~~*Likewise,*~~ *If you aerate non-dairy creamer without a flame, all*

that happens is a sneeze. However, given both conditions, ~~Finally, given the correct conditions,~~

becomes

non-dairy creamer ~~can reach it's full potential~~: a spectacular flame when ~~it is~~ *it's* suspended in air over

;

an open flame (don't try this / *it's dangerous!*). *Just be sure to drop the creamer when the*

combustion starts or your hand will get pretty warm.

I need a

I, too, flourish under the correct conditions. ~~A~~ place that supplies a strong source of creative and

. *The faculty and a school's resources are the main components of the blaze*

intellectual energy ~~beneath me in the form of vast educational and personal resources helps me to~~

beneath me as a student, providing me with new, mind-expanding experiences and knowledge.

~~improve my problem-solving skills and learn more material better. The combination of this Shangri-~~

However, all this motivation and opportunity are in vain if I fizzle, losing my passion and resolve.

~~La of learning with the synergy from being immersed with peers that are as passionate as I am~~

I've got to be surrounded with peers who are as passionate as I am about science and knowledge.

~~about science and knowledge is explosive.~~

Once these factors are combined, boom! You've got a potent and volatile learning experience.

Luckily, I've been presented with these necessary conditions to prosper through challenging

programs and peers who are also fired up about learning and succeeding. MIT is the most

the

productive environment with the largest flame and biggest cloud of non-dairy creamer students.

I want to be a part of this inferno of research and understanding.

similar. I look

Overall, while we may not taste the same, non-dairy creamer and I are pretty ~~close to each other,~~

forward to combusting in the near future.

~~which I think is a good thing to be. I just hope I'm not as likely to spontaneously combust.~~

Essay 70: Describe the contributions of an adult whom you know. How has this person's experiences inspired you or affected you? The essay must be 300 words or less. (Massachusetts Institute of Technology, MITE^{2}S Summer Program)

My grandmother inspires me. She has an insatiable need to learn. She graduated from the Incarnate Word in Mexico. When she was seventeen she moved to the United States to continue her education. She learned English and attended the University of the Incarnate Word in San Antonio. She does a lot of traveling, and, in fact, works as a travel agent. In her thirties, she went back to college and studied at both San Antonio College and the University of Texas at San Antonio.

She taught me experimentation. There were no easy answers in her house. "Grandma, is it heavy?" "You tell me. Try to lift it." "But what if it breaks?" "Well, then you'll know it's fragile." She didn't teach me knowledge. Nobody can give me knowledge. She gave me something more. She gave me a process of acquiring knowledge. In the greater scheme of things, that contribution may seem small. But to me this intangible something is huge. My grandmother gave me the world, and that is no small feat.

Essay 70—Makeover: The student has a great story to tell about her grandmother. She just needed to restructure the essay. Had the student wanted, she could have inserted more information about her grandmother, but due to deadline limitations, she chose to use this version.

maternal
My grandmother inspires me. She has an insatiable need to learn. ~~*She was born and educated*~~

At the age of ,
~~*in Mexico.*~~ She graduated from the Incarnate Word in Mexico. ~~When she was~~ seventeen

without knowing a word of English,
she moved to the United States to continue her education. She learned English and attended the

[Delete—irrelevant.]
University of the Incarnate Word in San Antonio. ~~She does a lot of traveling, and, in fact, works as a travel agent.~~ In her thirties, she went back to college and studied at both San Antonio College and the University of Texas at San Antonio.

are
She taught me experimentation. There ~~were~~ no easy answers in her house.

"Grandma, is it heavy?"

"You tell me. Try to lift it."

"But what if it breaks?"

it's also
"Well, then you'll know ~~it's~~ fragile."

"give"

She didn't ~~teach~~ me knowledge. ~~Nobody can give you knowledge.~~ *She taught me that nobody*
                    ^   ^

                                                                      for

can "give you knowledge." She gave me something more. She gave me a process ~~of~~ acquiring
                                                                                    ^

                                                        may seem   *it's*

knowledge. In the greater scheme of things, ~~I suppose~~ that contribution ~~is~~ small. But to me ~~this~~
                                                                            ^   ^

                                                          that's

~~intangible something is~~ huge. My grandmother gave me the world, and ~~that is~~ no small feat.
                                                                       ^

Essay 71: Which one of your extracurricular or volunteer activities is most important to you and why? The essay must be 300 words or less. (Massachusetts Institute of Technology, MITE[2] Summer Program)

The work I do for the March of Dimes is by far the most rewarding work that I've ever done. The March of Dimes is an organization that educates the public on proper child care. The goal of the March of Dimes is to prevent birth defects. I began volunteering at the March of Dimes during the summer after my freshman year of high school. The next summer they began a youth program called Chain Reaction. It is a national organization but this would be the first time that the program would be implemented in the San Antonio area. When they asked me to join, I was very enthusiastic. That year I was elected Vice-Chair of Fundraising for Chain Reaction and was given the opportunity to travel to Washington, D.C. To attend the March of Dimes' Chair Reaction National Convention.

This convention was truly inspiring. Never had I seen so many of my peers united and determined to achieve a common goal. It is a very selfless thing to work for the health of someone you will never know. That is what the March of Dimes and Chain Reaction do every day. Chain Reaction works hard to educate future parents about the best way to care for their children before they are even born. Chain Reaction raises money for research that could develop vaccines or cures that could save thousands of babies. It is very important that every child has the opportunity for a healthy life. I feel so strongly about this that I have gone to the Texas Capitol at Austin to lobby for better children's health insurance. I wrote an editorial for the San Antonio Express-News on the importance of children's health coverage. I have fundraised, educated, recruited volunteers, and

developed petitions. The purpose of this organization goes beyond the present. The purpose

reaches the future.

Essay 71—Makeover: The essay was strong, but a bit jumbled. The essay needed to start with her lobbying experience because it's truly a unique endeavor that most students won't have done.

[Student added this sentence in the second draft.]   *on*
Walking up the stairs to the Texas Capital Building, I reflected ~~back to~~ *how this adventure*

[Moved to first sentence of fifth paragraph.]
started. [~~The work I do for the March of Dimes is by far the most rewarding work that I've ever~~

~~done. The March of Dimes is an organization that educates the public on proper child care. The~~

~~goal of the March of Dimes is to prevent birth defects.~~] I began volunteering at the March of Dimes
                                                    following   *, the local affiliate*
during the summer after my freshman year of high school. The ~~next~~ summer ~~they~~ began a youth

              Though it's   *program,*   *it*
program called Chain Reaction. ~~It is~~ a national ~~organization but~~ this would be the first time ~~that the~~
                                                          and I couldn't wait to start.
~~program~~ would be implemented in the San Antonio area / ~~When they asked me to join, I was very~~

[Moved to first sentence of third paragraph.]
~~enthusiastic.~~ [~~That year I was elected Vice-Chair of Fundraising for Chain Reaction and was given~~

~~the opportunity to travel to Washington, D.C. To attend the March of Dimes' Chain Reaction~~

~~National Convention.~~]

[Moved to new fourth paragraph.]
[~~This convention was truly inspiring. Never had I seen so many of my peers united and~~

~~determined to achieve a common goal. It is a very selfless thing to work for the health of someone~~

~~you will never know. That is what the March of Dimes and Chain Reaction do every day.~~] Chain
                    s
Reaction ~~works hard to~~ educate future parents about the best way to care for their children before
              and   *research*   *to*
they are even born / ~~Chain Reaction~~ raises money ~~for research that could~~ develop vaccines or cures
                                            [Delete—obvious.]
that could save thousands of babies. ~~It is very important that every child has the opportunity for a~~
        My fervor is   *was in*
~~healthy life. I feel~~ so strongly ~~about this~~ that I ~~have gone to the Texas Capitol at~~ Austin to lobby for
                                        [Moved to second sentence of new third paragraph.]
better children's health insurance. [~~I wrote an editorial for the San Antonio Express-News on the~~

[importance of children's health coverage. I have fundraised, educated, recruited volunteers, and developed petitions. The purpose of this organization goes beyond the present. The purpose reaches the future.]

Fundraising

I was elected Vice-Chair of ~~Fund Raising~~ for Chain Reaction. I wrote an editorial for the *San Antonio Express-News* on the importance of children's health coverage. ~~I have~~ *I've* fund raised, educated, recruited volunteers, and developed petitions. The purpose of this organization goes beyond the present. It reaches to the future.

Last summer, I was given the opportunity to attend the March of Dimes' Chain Reaction National Convention in Washington, D.C. *, which* ~~It~~ was truly inspiring. Never had I seen so many of my peers united *with such determination* ~~and determined~~ to achieve a common goal. *It's truly* ~~It is a very~~ selfless thing to work for the health of someone you will never *meet, yet it's* ~~know. That is~~ what the March of Dimes and Chain Reaction do every day.

The work I do for the March of Dimes is by far the most rewarding work I've ever done. The March of Dimes is an organization that educates the public on proper child care and helps fund research to prevent birth defects. I want to always be a part of that mission.

Essay 72: What do you think people who know you would be surprised to learn about you? Limit your response to one double-spaced page. (Rice University)

I find it quite ironic that this is one of the essay questions I am required to answer for Rice's Admission Process. It was just last week that one of my coaches, whom I have known for three years, expressed a state of surprise when she realized that I was in the top 10% of my graduating senior class. Actually, I rank in the top 6.5% of my class, but I did not make this known to her at the time. Many of my friends, neighbors, and relatives would not suspect this of me either, but I do have certain expectations of my own. Though I sometimes feel overwhelmed by all the work that is expected of me as an athlete and a student. I can truly say that my dedication and persistence has paid off.

Throughout life, I have had many friends of all types of backgrounds and by this I mean of different social statuses. I grew up in a neighborhood where I knew I just did not belong (well it wasn't until I was older that I reached this conclusion), and many of the kids I associated with came from broken families. Because of my parent's middle to average income, I found myself befriending kids whose parents did not have the same aspirations for their children as mind had for me. It would literally be an overstatement to say that someone from my neighborhood graduated in the top 10% of his/her class. I, however, am proud of remaining focused these past twelve years of my life and accomplishing all that I have. It is without a doubt that if I was reunited with any of my friends that I grew up with in grade school or in middle school, they would be amazed by the fact that I rank 38 in a class of 582.

As for my relatives, well about the highest level of education any of them received was a high school diploma. Some were fortunate enough to go back to college but few took an education seriously. I can rest assured that they do not view me as not taking my education seriously, but they would be shocked to hear that I have excelled as well in school.

I have always been told by my parents that hard work and determination pay off in the long run, and I have seen evidence of this throughout my life. It is because of this that I continue to strive to be the best I can be. My fellow peers in my honors classes could be quick to confirm this, but there will always be those friends of mine who never thought this possible.

Essay 72—Makeover: Though students shouldn't be hesitant to relate their successes and talents, students shouldn't sound pompous or as if they're comparing their achievements to those of other students. With a few deletions and changes, this essay is much more reader-friendly.

~~I find it quite ironic that this is one of the essay questions I am required to answer for Rice's Admission Process. It was~~ ~J~ust last week ~~that~~ one of my coaches, whom ~~I have~~ *I've* known for three years, expressed ~~a state of~~ surprise when she realized ~~that~~ I was in the top 10% *percent* of my graduating senior class. Actually, I rank in the top 6.5% *percent* of my class, but I ~~did not~~ *didn't* make this known to her ~~at the~~

~~time.~~ Many of my friends, neighbors, and relatives ~~would not~~ *wouldn't* suspect ~~this of me~~ *it* either, but I do have certain expectations of my own. Though I sometimes feel overwhelmed by all the work ~~that is~~ *that's* expected of me as an athlete and a student*,* I can truly say that my dedication and persistence ~~has~~ *have* paid off.

~~Throughout life, I have~~ *I've* had many friends ~~of all types of~~ *from various* backgrounds ~~and by this I mean of different social statuses.~~ *being a focused, goal-setting student wasn't the norm.* I grew up in a neighborhood where ~~I knew I just did not belong (well it wasn't until I was older that I reached this conclusion), and~~ *M*any of the kids ~~I associated with~~ came from broken families. Because of my ~~parents~~ *[parents']* ~~middle to~~ average income, I found myself befriending kids whose parents ~~did not~~ *didn't* have the same aspirations for their children as min~~d~~*e* had for me.

[Delete—makes reader think you feel you're superior to them.]
~~It would literally be an overstatement to say that someone from my neighborhood graduated in the top 10% of his/her class.~~ ~~I,~~ *H*owever, ~~am~~ *I'm* proud of remaining focused these past twelve years ~~of my~~ *over* life and accomplishing all that I have. ~~It is without a doubt that~~ *if* I ~~was~~ *were* reunited with any of my ~~friends that I grew up with in grade school or in middle school~~ *grade school and middle school friends*, they would be amazed ~~by the fact~~ that I rank 38 in a class of 582.

Most of ~~As for~~ my relatives*,* ~~well about the highest level of education any of them~~ received ~~was~~ *only* a high school diploma. Some were fortunate enough to go ~~back~~ to college*,* but few took ~~an~~ *their* education seriously. *Though they know I take* ~~I can rest assured that they do not view me as not taking~~ my education seriously, ~~but they~~ would be shocked to hear ~~that I have~~ *I've* excelled ~~as well~~ in school.

My parents always encouraged me, saying ~~I have always been told by my parents~~ that hard work and determination pay off in the long run, and ~~I have~~ *I've* seen evidence of this ~~throughout my life.~~*.* ~~It is because of this that I~~ *I'll always* continue to strive to be the best I can be. ~~My fellow peers in my honors classes could be quick to confirm this, but there will always be those friends of mine who never thought this possible.~~

Essay 73: The quality of Rice's academic life and the residential college system is heavily influenced by the unique life experiences and cultural traditions each student brings. What perspective do you feel that you will be able to share with others as a result of your own life experiences and background? Cite a personal experience to illustrate this.

It was 5:03 a.m., and my eyes were heavy with insomnia. The cold air of the early dawn seeped through my skin as I clung to my silver Bach trumpet. The cool metal of the trumpet numbed my hand. The stars dull glow gave us little light to see in the darkness. I began to circulate warm air through the pipes of my trumpet. I was ready to play and perform. The trumpets of the band started the music while the other instruments joined in. The music filled the black, starry morning as the people in the house that we were serenading came out into the moonlight. The music filled their hearts with joy as we played into the night air. As soon as the final notes were played of our songs, we quickly loaded our equipment into our transportation and rode off into the night. One house down, nineteen more to go. As we drove to the next house, I would have never guessed that this would be the longest and one of the most meaningful experiences in my life. From this day forward this day, Mother's Day, would strike me with new meaning and appreciation. Through the music of my ancestors, I would learn a lesson of a lifetime that only first hand experience can reveal.

When I first joined our newly founded high school *mariachi* band, I did not know what I might discover in the education of my culture's music. Living in Central Texas, I've heard many *mariachi* groups play at weddings, festivals, and *quinceñeras*. However, I had never been apart of one. As a young Hispanic female, I became interested in *mariachi* music that is a trademark in Mexican culture. My journey towards the meaning of my heritage had begun as a sophomore and I knew that there was more to come through out my high school career.

Soon, the sun began to rise caressing each musician's body with warmth. We had just finished serenading our fifth household and were walking to the next one in the same neighbor hood. The time was 8:25 am and began to fill the surroundings with our music. The graceful notes of these traditional love songs danced in the trees. When the doors of the home were opened, the notes would float into their living rooms bringing the mothers outside to hear our dedications to them.

In this one particular house when the doors opened the mother appeared in her bathrobe. She stepped out on to her porch and listened as we played. Her daughter came out also and wrapped her arms around her mother. Tears of joy streamed down the mother's delicate face. I did not realize or understand until that moment the meaning behind the music. This music has been passed down from generation to generation serenading loved ones for hundreds of years. These traditional songs were being played by a young generation of students that will start their lives in adulthood in the new millennium to an older generation that lived through the depression. On this day a bridge was connected from one generation to another.

We as a *mariachi* band broke through the silence with our music to give love and joy back to our mothers in the community. As a high school *mariachi* band, we had a diverse group of students. Through the same learning experience, two ethnic groups came upon an understanding of Mexican together which brought us closer together.

This one event has been a major impact in my life. If I could reach these mothers through my music, imagine what I as an individual can present to a new social surrounding. Whether it be with my music, classes, or having a conversation, I am confident and believe that I can contribute important cultural characteristics and experiences.

Essay 73—Makeover: This is a good essay and with just a few minor changes, the result is a strong essay which "shows" the reader who she is.

[Insomnia means you can't sleep, and thus your eyes wouldn't be heavy.] *sleep*

It was 5:03 a.m., and my eyes were heavy with ~~insomnia~~. The cold air of the early dawn seeped

my clothes to

through my skin as I clung to my silver Bach trumpet. The cool metal of the trumpet numbed my

, *.* *puffing into the mouth piece*

hand. The stars dull glow gave us little light ~~to see in the darkness.~~ I began ~~to circulate warm air~~

~~through the pipes~~ of my trumpet. I was ready to play and perform. The trumpets ~~of the band~~

in the band *M*

started the music while the other instruments joined in. ~~The~~ music filled the black, starry morning

[How could you know this?]

who *drifted of the house and* *From the looks*

as the people ~~in the house that~~ we were serenading ~~came~~ out into the moonlight. ~~The music filled~~

on their faces and in their eyes, our music must have filled their hearts with joy.   ,

~~their hearts with joy as we played into the night air.~~ As soon as the final notes were played ~~of our~~

and ourselves

~~songs,~~ we quickly loaded our equipment into our transportation and rode off into the night. One

[The rest of this paragraph needs to be moved to later in the

house down, nineteen more to go. ~~As we drove to the next house, I would have never guessed that~~

essay. You didn't know it at the time, so you can't relate it to the reader at this point in

~~this would be the longest and one of the most meaningful experiences in my life. From this day~~

your essay.]

~~forward this day, Mother's Day, would strike me with new meaning and appreciation. Through the~~

~~music of my ancestors, I would learn a lesson of a lifetime that only first hand experience can~~

~~reveal.~~

wanted to learn a new aspect

When I first joined our newly founded high school *mariachi* band, I ~~did not know what I might~~

of my culture: its music.

~~discover in the education of my culture's music.~~ Living in Central Texas, I've heard many *mariachi*

I'd   *a part*

groups play at weddings, festivals, and *quinceñeras.* However, ~~I had~~ never been ~~apart~~ of one. As a

,

young Hispanic female, I became interested in *mariachi* music ~~that is~~ a trademark in Mexican

[In the U.S., we use "toward," the United Kingdom uses "towards."] [Try to avoid using: I know,

culture. My journey towards ~~the meaning of~~ my heritage had begun as a sophomore and ~~I knew~~

[High school is not a career, unless you never leave.]

I think, I feel, etc.]   *throughout*   *time in*   ,

~~that~~ there was more to come ~~through out~~ my high school ~~career.~~

,   *We'd*

Soon, the sun began to rise caressing each musician's body with warmth. ~~We had~~ just finished

neighborhood. It

serenading our fifth household and were walking to the next one in the same ~~neighbor hood. The~~

a.m. as we   *air*

~~time~~ was 8:25 ~~am and~~ began to fill the ~~surroundings~~ with our music. The graceful notes of these

As

traditional love songs danced in the trees. ~~When the~~ doors ~~of the home were~~ opened, the notes

residents'   ,

would float into ~~their~~ living rooms bringing the mothers outside to hear our dedications to them.

,   *was*   *, as she*

In ~~this~~ one particular house ~~when the doors opened~~ the mother ~~appeared~~ in her bathrobe/ She

onto   *-also*

stepped ~~out on to~~ her porch and listened as we played. Her daughter came out ~~also~~ and wrapped

didn't

her arms around her mother. Tears of joy streamed down the mother's delicate face. I ~~did not~~

~~realize or~~ understand until that moment the meaning behind the music. This music has been passed

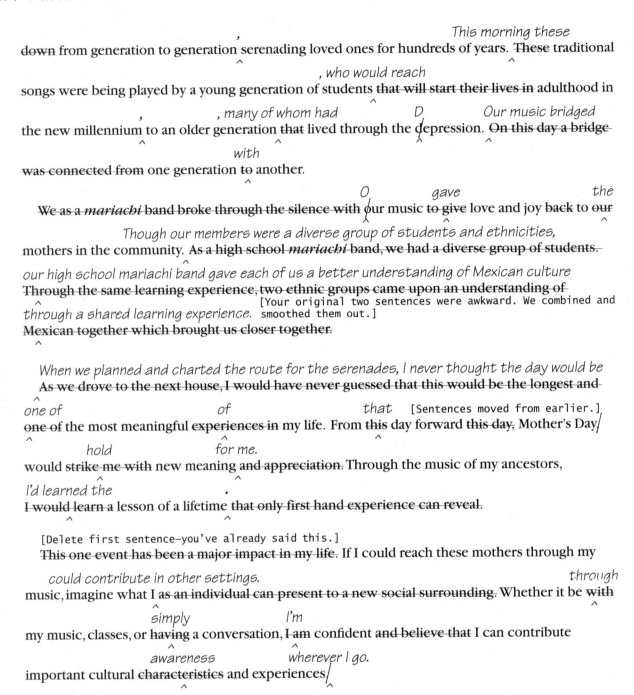

~~down~~ from generation to generation, serenading loved ones for hundreds of years. ~~These~~ traditional *This morning these*

songs were being played by a young generation of students ~~that will start their lives in~~ adulthood in *, who would reach*

the new millennium to an older generation ~~that~~ lived through the ~~d~~epression. ~~On this day a bridge~~ *, many of whom had* *D* *Our music bridged*

~~was connected from~~ one generation ~~to~~ another. *with*

~~We as a mariachi band broke through the silence with~~ ~~o~~ur music ~~to give~~ love and joy ~~back to~~ ~~our~~ *O* *gave* *the*

mothers in the community. ~~As a high school mariachi band, we had a diverse group of students.~~ *Though our members were a diverse group of students and ethnicities,*

~~Through the same learning experience, two ethnic groups came upon an understanding of~~ *our high school mariachi band gave each of us a better understanding of Mexican culture*

~~Mexican together which brought us closer together.~~ *through a shared learning experience.* [Your original two sentences were awkward. We combined and smoothed them out.]

~~As we drove to the next house, I would have never guessed that this would be the longest and~~ *When we planned and charted the route for the serenades, I never thought the day would be*

~~one of~~ the most meaningful ~~experiences in~~ my life. From ~~this~~ day forward ~~this day,~~ Mother's Day *one of* *of* *that* [Sentences moved from earlier.]

would ~~strike me with~~ new meaning ~~and appreciation.~~ Through the music of my ancestors, *hold* *for me.*

~~I would learn a~~ lesson of a lifetime ~~that only first hand experience can reveal.~~ *I'd learned the* *.*

[Delete first sentence—you've already said this.]
~~This one event has been a major impact in my life.~~ If I could reach these mothers through my

music, imagine what I ~~as an individual can present to a new social surrounding.~~ Whether it be ~~with~~ *could contribute in other settings.* *through*

my music, classes, or ~~having~~ a conversation, ~~I am~~ confident ~~and believe that~~ I can contribute *simply* *I'm*

important cultural ~~characteristics~~ and experiences. *awareness* *wherever I go.*

Essay 74: Describe one experience in which you were involved in a leadership role. What were your goals and how, specifically, did you go about accomplishing them? The essay can be a maximum of four double-spaced pages. (Southern Methodist University)

Imagine sleeping under the stars on top of a mountain in New Mexico when heavy breathing

and thumping footsteps suddenly awaken you. I had been warned about the black bears whose habitat we were invading. My mind raced to identify the proximity of the unwanted guest and what could be attracting him. Perhaps, he was attracted by the residual meaty smell from our dinner. The food was hoisted into the trees and every crewmember had been advised on the handling of "smellables" such as toothpaste, chapstick, medication, and Gatorade. As crew leader, I was responsible for the lives of nine others. How will I warn my sleeping comrades without becoming a target for the bear? The crewmembers know how to react in this situation but could some of them still be sleeping after our seven-hour hike yesterday? If there is something in our campsite that the bear wants, I want him to have it as long as I can assure the safety of my crew. This is just one of my experiences at Philmont Scout Ranch in the summer of 1998. My ten-year involvement with Scouting's many physically and mentally challenging experiences, including my Eagle project of organizing and executing the Juvenile Diabetes Foundation's "Walk for the Cure" charity run, have shaped me into who I am today. Undoubtedly, the pinnacle was my Philmont hiking trek. Words cannot completely convey the magnitude of this leadership experience.

I was elected crew leader to direct my group of scouts and adults through two weeks and 73 miles of hiking in the mountains and valleys of this Boy Scout reservation near Cimarron, New Mexico. My crew trained for months before setting off for Philmont. We carried everything that we needed in our backpacks, weighing 50-60 pounds each. We purified our own water and forgot about how good a shower feels. We attempted to "leave no trace" along the trail, known as zero-impact hiking. My goal was simple: to guide my crew through the woods safely and to allow all crewmembers to have a once-in-a-lifetime experience. Like many things in life, my goal was not easily accomplished.

This journey required my sustained focus, total commitment to the best interests of others, and constant exercise of leadership and judgment. Experiences along the way taught me flexibility, caution, and respect for nature and others. My leadership and fortitude were tested under extreme physical and mental fatigue.

The first day was spent in base camp, but this was not the first time the crew had spent preparing. For many previous months, I helped the group to train for this trek with hikes and "shakedowns" to make sure everyone had the necessary items for the trip and only the necessary ones. I also had to decide which route to take. I was given a few different itineraries and weighed different variables like distances between activities offered at camps, availability of water, and other changing aspects of the trail. The next morning we started out on the trail. After a harrowing ride on arguably one of the bumpiest roads in existence, my crew got off the bus and started the short initial hike to the first campsite. The first two days of our trek, we were accompanied by an experienced Philmont ranger and an Air Force Academy Cadet, Ryan, who would help us adapt to our new environment. Ryan insisted that he would be only a resource to us and that I still had to make all decisions with and for my crew. Since it was our first night in the woods, I came up with a schedule for all of the cooking and cleaning chores for each campsite, aiding the workers wherever I could. I found that leading by example increased the integrity of the group and made other scouts work faster. I had to make the ten individuals into a cohesive crew.

After the initial two days of instruction by the ranger, my crew was on their own. We had proven to the ranger that we were physically and mentally capable of completing the trek. With the help of the other scouts, I successfully got us to our next campsite, called Miner's Park, where we participated in rock climbing and environmental awareness training. Some members of the group preferred to stay at the campsite to rest. I took notice of who wanted to do what and made sure that everyone had a buddy and an adult advisor.

The next morning's hike to Clark's Fork was the longest so far. I made sure that everyone had plenty of water to last them until we got there. Throughout the hike, I reminded everyone to stay hydrated and take frequent water breaks. After a long but safe hike, we arrived at Clark's Fork. After supervising camp set up, we were all able to rest for a little while since we didn't have to make dinner that evening. We soon learned that we were not alone in this part of the woods. The workers at Clark's Fork told us of the eager black bear neighbors. After dinner, I checked to see that all odious items were stored in bear bags hung from trees for out protection.

That night, we had some visitors to our campsite. A large black bear, estimated to be around 600 pounds, walked through camp. Nothing in our campsite was disturbed. However, our sister crew wasn't as lucky. Someone had left an empty bottle that he had used for Gatorade sitting on top of his pack. The bear quickly crunched through the hard plastic container to get to the inside, even though there was no Gatorade in it. Thankfully, there were no other damages or injuries. After this incident, no one had to be convinced that precautions were necessary.

The next morning, we headed to Ute Springs. We had two different routes we could take, one more scenic and longer than the other. By this point in the trip, people were starting to get a little worn out. I talked with all the crew and decided that it would be worth it to take the more scenic route. There was some initial grumbling, but after we got up to the top of the valley walls, the grumbling had ceased. The view was magnificent. Even those crewmembers who had initially been against taking this route were thankful we had. I was satisfied that I had pleased the crew with my decision. After a night at an unmanned trail camp at Cimarron River, we headed for Head of Dean. This was an especially long hike so I decided the crew should wake up early to hit the trail. Midmorning, one member of my crew, Carlos, stood up too quickly after a rest break and lost his balance, striking his head on a pack frame as he fell. Because Carlos had suffered a concussion, he was unable to continue. I sent some scouts for a search and rescue crew while other crewmembers and I stayed and applied first aid to Carlos. After several hours, a search and rescue team arrived to take Carlos to the infirmary. We now had a dilemma involving daylight and water, two things that we take for granted in civilization. Could we to get to the next camp with the little water that we had left? I decided that we should press on instead of backtracking to get water even though we had a long hike ahead. I estimated that we still had 6 hours of daylight and camp was at least another 10 hours away. Before we reached camp, my crew and I had to encourage each other that we could make it. I later responded when an adult crewmember became delirious from exhaustion and dehydration on the trail by keeping the morale of the group up. Thankfully, we made camp just before midnight. This was the most trying day both physically and as a leader. I was pleased that the crew had pulled together through a difficult time. Everyone was glad that Carlos was able to rejoin our group the next day.

After a deep sleep at Head of Dean, we traveled to Miranda. We were to stay here two nights because we were going to climb Mount Baldy, the highest point in the camp. The first day we were required to participate in a conservation project. It was tough to convince the crewmembers to do the project, but, after some persuasion, I was able to get them to follow me to the project. We were assigned the exciting task of cutting down trees with axes and picks. I resisted the temptation to whine about the task at hand and instead lead by being cheerful and ignoring negative comments about the service. With everyone actively and positively contributing, the time went by quickly.

The next morning, I went around to every tent to make doubly sure that all of my crew had gotten up for this important day. After breakfast, I made pack assignments for the trek to Baldy and back. After a long ascent, we reached a beautiful meadow near the top that looked like something out of "The Sound of Music." We stopped for a quick lunch before heading up the loose shale path to the top. As we approached, I noticed that there were rain clouds gathering. The top of Baldy is above the timberline, so anyone standing on top is an excellent target for lightning. Everyone, including me, wanted to reach the top. Am I willing to gamble with the lives of my crew? Seeing the danger, I instructed everyone to stay below the timberline until the storm passed. Just after everyone had gotten to a safe place on the mountain, the hail and lightning started. Thankfully, we were protected and were able to wait out the strongest part of storm. When we couldn't wait any longer for the entire storm to blow over to safely ascend Baldy, I decided that we had to start our descent if we were to make it before nightfall. On our way down, we saw the danger that missed us: lightning had struck a tree right next to the trail. After arriving at camp, we got much needed rest before going home.

While I don't think I'll be forced to climb any physical mountains at SMU, I will be required to overcome obstacles and to draw upon my inner strength. Like Philmont, college life is demanding, stressful, and requires mature decision-making. My experiences in Scouting taught me self-reliance and gave me confidence that I will be able to face whatever challenges and responsibilities await me.

Essay 74—Makeover: This essay was interesting, but it was too long. There are many places where too much information was provided. Though students should provide detail, something must be cut when space or word count is limited, and it's usually excess detail.

My crew of nine and I were blissfully
~~Imagine~~ sleeping under the stars on top of a mountain in New Mexico when heavy breathing
woke me. I'd
and thumping footsteps suddenly ~~awaken you. I had~~ been warned about the black bears whose habitat we were invading. My mind raced to identify the proximity of the unwanted guest and
H   probably
what could be attracting him. ~~Perhaps,~~ he was attracted by the residual meaty smell from our
crew member
dinner. The food was hoisted into the trees and every ~~crewmember~~ had been advised on the
C
handling of "smellables" such as toothpaste, chapstick, medication, and Gatorade. As crew leader, I
could
was responsible for the lives of nine others. How ~~will~~ I warn my sleeping comrades without
crew members   ,
becoming a target for the bear? The ~~crewmembers~~ know how to react in this situation but ~~could~~
might groggy with   .   *there's*
some of them still be ~~sleeping~~ after our seven-hour hike yesterday? If ~~there is~~ something in our
he can have it—just leave my crew alone.
campsite that the bear wants, ~~I want him to have it as long as I can assure the safety of~~
~~my crew.~~ [New paragraph.]

~~This is just one of my experiences at Philmont Scout Ranch in the summer of 1998. My ten-year involvement with Scouting's many physically and mentally challenging experiences, including my Eagle project of organizing and executing the Juvenile Diabetes Foundation's "Walk for the Cure" charity run, have shaped me into who I am today. Undoubtedly, the pinnacle was my Philmont hiking trek. Words cannot completely convey the magnitude of this leadership experience.~~

[Moved from paragraph ten.]
We estimated the large black bear weighed approximately 600 pounds. He walked through the camp, but nothing was disturbed. After this incident, no one had to be convinced that precautions were necessary.

I'd been
~~I was~~ elected crew leader to direct my group of scouts and adults through two weeks and 73 miles of hiking in the mountains and valleys of this Boy Scout reservation near Cimarron, New Mexico. My crew trained for months before setting off for Philmont. We carried everything that we needed in our backpacks, weighing 50–60 pounds each. ~~We purified our own water and forgot about how good a shower feels.~~ We attempted to "leave no trace" along the trail, known as zero-impact hiking. My goal was simple: to guide my crew through the woods safely and to allow all
crew members   *wasn't*
~~crewmembers~~ to have a once-in-a-lifetime experience. Like many things in life, my goal ~~was not~~ easily accomplished.

This journey required my sustained focus, total commitment to the best interests of others, and constant exercise of leadership and judgment. Experiences along the way taught me flexibility,
                                   for   *in conditions of*
caution, and respect for nature and others. My leadership and fortitude were tested ~~under~~ extreme physical and mental fatigue.

The first day was spent in base camp, but this was not the first time the crew had spent preparing/ ~~For many previous months, I helped the group to train for this trek with hikes and "shakedowns" to make sure everyone had the necessary items~~ for the trip ~~and only the necessary~~
            It was my decision
~~ones. I also had to decide~~ which route to take. I was given a few different itineraries and weighed
                                                    different
different variables like ~~distances between~~ activities offered at camps, availability of water, and other changing aspects of the trail. [New paragraph. Four paragraphs start with "The next morning." The essay needs variety.]

We started out on the trail first thing in the morning.
~~The next morning we started out on the trail.~~ After a harrowing ride on arguably one of the bumpiest roads in existence, my crew got off the bus and started the short initial hike to the first
                                                    Ryan,
campsite. The first two days of our trek, we were accompanied by an experienced Philmont ranger

and an Air Force Academy Cadet, ~~Ryan,~~ who would help us adapt to our new environment. Ryan insisted that he would be only a resource to us and that I still had to make all decisions with and for my crew. Since it was our first night in the woods, I came up with a schedule for all of the cooking and cleaning chores for each campsite, aiding the workers wherever I could. ~~I found that~~ Leading by example increased the integrity of the group and made other scouts work faster. I had to make ~~the~~ ten individuals into a cohesive crew.

After the initial two days of instruction by the ranger, my crew was on their own. ~~We had~~ We'd proven to the ranger that we were physically and mentally capable of completing the trek. With the help of the other scouts, I successfully got us to our next campsite, called Miner's Park, where we participated in rock climbing and environmental awareness training. ~~Some members of the group preferred to stay at the campsite to rest. I took notice of who wanted to do what and made sure that everyone had a buddy and an adult advisor.~~

The ~~next morning's~~ hike to Clark's Fork was the longest so far. ~~I made sure that everyone had plenty of water to last them until we got there. Throughout the hike, I reminded everyone to stay hydrated and take frequent water breaks.~~ After a long but safe hike, we arrived at Clark's Fork. After supervising camp setup, we were all able to rest for a little while, since we didn't have to make dinner that evening. We soon learned that we were not alone in this part of the woods. ~~The workers at Clark's Fork told us of the eager black bear neighbors. After dinner, I checked to see that all odious items were stored in bear bags hung from trees for out protection.~~

[Moved to second paragraph.]
~~That night, we had some visitors to our campsite. A large black bear, estimated to be around 600 pounds, walked through camp. Nothing in our campsite was disturbed. However, our sister crew wasn't as lucky. Someone had left an empty bottle that he had used for Gatorade sitting on top of his pack. The bear quickly crunched through the hard plastic container to get to the inside, even though there was no Gatorade in it. Thankfully, there were no other damages or injuries. After this incident, no one had to be convinced that precautions were necessary.~~

We headed to Ute Springs the next morning. There were
~~The next morning, we headed to Ute Springs. We had~~ two different routes we could take, one more scenic and longer than the other. By this point in the trip, people were starting to get a little worn out. I talked with ~~all~~ the crew and decided that it would be worth it to take the more scenic route. ~~There was some initial grumbling, but after we got up to the top of the valley walls, the grumbling had ceased.~~ The view was magnificent. ~~Even those crewmembers who had initially been against taking this route were thankful we had. I was satisfied that I had pleased the crew with my decision. After a night at an unmanned trail camp at Cimarron River, we headed for Head of Dean. This was an especially long hike so I decided the crew should wake up early to hit the trail. Midmorning, one member of my crew, Carlos, stood up too quickly after a rest break and lost his balance, striking his head on a pack frame as he fell. Because Carlos had suffered a concussion, he was unable to continue. I sent some scouts for a search and rescue crew while other crewmembers and I stayed and applied first aid to Carlos. After several hours, a search and rescue team arrived to take Carlos to the infirmary. We now had a dilemma involving daylight and water, two things that we take for granted in civilization. Could we to get to the next camp with the little water that we had left? I decided that we should press on instead of backtracking to get water even though we had a long hike ahead. I estimated that we still had 6 hours of daylight and camp was at least another 10 hours away. Before we reached camp, my crew and I had to encourage each other that we could make it. I later responded when an adult crewmember became delirious from exhaustion and dehydration on the trail by keeping the morale of the group up. Thankfully, we made camp just before midnight. This was the most trying day both physically and as a leader. I was pleased that the crew had pulled together through a difficult time. Everyone was glad that Carlos was able to rejoin our group the next day.~~

After a deep sleep ~~at Head of Dean,~~ we traveled to Miranda. We were to stay here two nights because we were going to climb Mount Baldy, the highest point in the camp. ~~The first day we were required to participate in a conservation project. It was tough to convince the crewmembers to do the project, but, after some persuasion, I was able to get them to follow me to the project. We were~~

~~assigned the exciting task of cutting down trees with axes and picks. I resisted the temptation to whine about the task at hand and instead lead by being cheerful and ignoring negative comments about the service. With everyone actively and positively contributing, the time went by quickly.~~

The next morning, I went around to every tent to make doubly sure that all of my crew had gotten up for this important day. After breakfast, I made pack assignments for the trek to Baldy and back. After a long ascent, we reached a beautiful meadow near the top that looked like something out of "The Sound of Music." We stopped for a quick lunch before heading up the loose shale path to the top. As we approached, I noticed that ~~there~~ *were* rain clouds gathering. ~~Unfortunately,~~ ~~The top of~~ Baldy is above the timberline, ~~so~~ *which meant that* anyone standing on top is an excellent target for lightning. Everyone/ ~~including me,~~ wanted to reach the top. ~~Am~~ *Was* I willing to gamble with the lives of my crew *just to reach the top?* Seeing the danger, I instructed everyone to stay below the timberline until the storm passed. Just after everyone had gotten to a safe place on the mountain, the hail and lightning started. Thankfully, we were protected and were able to wait out the strongest part of storm. ~~When~~ *W*e couldn't wait ~~any longer~~ for the entire storm to blow over to safely ascend Baldy, ~~I decided that we had to start our descent~~ if we were to make it before nightfall. On our way down, we saw the danger that missed us: lightning had struck a tree right next to the trail. After arriving at camp, we got much needed rest before going home.

While I don't think I'll be forced to climb any ~~physical~~ *actual* mountains at SMU, I will be required to overcome obstacles and to draw upon my inner strength. Like Philmont, college life is demanding, stressful, and requires mature decisionmaking. My experiences in Scouting taught me self-reliance and gave me confidence that ~~I will~~ *I'll* be able to face whatever challenges and responsibilities await me.

Essay 75: How has the place in which you live influenced the person you are? Define "place" any way that you like . . . as a context, a country, a city, a community, a house, a point in time. (Stanford University)

My place in the scheme of things in this small present threshold of time didn't appear from a vacuum. I'm standing at a vantage point atop a tower built from the blocks of past experiences and knowledge and the mortar of future expectations and preparations. From this point, I can better appreciate the past and see what's to come. To this end, the place in which I live has provided me with the material needed to build this point of vision so I'm prepared to understand and tackle the future.

San Antonio, my hometown, is a rare place. It's a mixture of people, ideas, cultures, heritage, and mindsets that aren't easily found anywhere else. To begin with, Texas itself is a diverse place demographically, geographically, and otherwise. San Antonio is a conglomeration of history, culture, business, and innovation in this state's distinct setting. The city is the home of Spanish missions, cultural celebrations such as Fiesta, huge companies like Southwestern Bell and USAA, and places of invention like Southwest Research Institute.

The city's diversity has opened doors and exposed me to experiences I'd have never learned about otherwise. I grew up embracing other cultures through celebrations like Fiesta, Dia De Los Muertos, the Texas Folklife Festival, and Wurstfest as well as education in the history and language of different cultures. Being culturally aware enables me to empathize with fellow San Antonians, thus erasing any stigmas or preconceived ideas about others.

I've also gained from San Antonio's status as a premier research area through the Young Engineers and Scientists (YES) Program at Southwest Research Institute (SwRI) over this past summer. The YES program changed me by solidifying my desire to become a scientist/engineer, particularly in computers and electronics, and by giving me a taste of the exciting work in various fields of study that researchers are exploring. My independent study is a predecessor for a career in research, giving me insight into the work so I can decide whether this career path is the most fulfilling for me. With these experiences from the place and time in which I have lived, I can go on to climb to greater heights and explore unknown territory.

Essay 75—Makeover: Though this essay is strong, it didn't reveal much about Texas. The student enlarged on his essay and improved it substantially.

~~My place in the scheme of things in this small present threshold of time didn't appear from a~~ *I'm*
~~vacuum.~~ ~~I am~~ standing a*t* a vantage point atop a tower built from the blocks of past experiences

and knowledge and the mortar of future expectations and preparations. From this point, I can
and learn from
better appreciate the past and prepare myself for the future. ~~To this end,~~ *T*he place in which I live

has provided me with the material I needed to build this point of vision so I'm prepared to

understand and tackle the future.

There is something special about being a Texan. Texans are known for their state loyalty. I'm a

native and have spent most of my life in San Antonio. San Antonio was once voted "one of the

nation's four unique cities" along with New Orleans, New York, and San Francisco. I feel fortunate

to have grown up here. My parents moved back to my mother's hometown after I was born. They

both started their professional careers in Washington, D.C., but came home to Texas to raise a family.

Such are Texans. Texans want their children to have big backyards, frequent visits with

grandparents, and an appreciation for the Longhorn-Aggie rivalry.

[Delete this paragraph. The committee might think your mother could convince you not to go west,
~~"Let them go east and they will come home. But if they go west, they will never return." You may~~
if you're accepted to Stanford.]
~~not be aware that this is the battle cry of Texas mothers. Princeton, Harvard, Yale, no problem.~~

~~However, nothing strikes more fear in the heart of a Texas mother than an application to Stanford.~~

~~Living in~~ Texas , ~~and~~ especially in San Antonio , is a mixture of people, ideas, cultures, heritages, and
not
mind sets easily found elsewhere. ~~To begin with,~~ Texas ~~itself~~ is a diverse demographically,

geographically, politically, and economically. Texas is big. From San Antonio, you can drive for 8

hours and still be within the state. Texas varies significantly from region to region. San Antonio is

the first big city north of the Rio Grande and ~~therefore~~ is heavily influenced by its proximity to

Mexico. The city's Hispanic population is now in the majority. Spanish is spoken everywhere; I said

"luna" before I said "moon." *Piñatas* and *cascarones* are part of my family's celebrations.

~~When you visit San Antonio~~ *is a* ~~you are impressed by its~~ contrasts of old and new. ~~San Antonio is~~ *It's* a conglomeration of history, culture, business, and innovation in this state's distinct setting. ~~It is~~ *It's* the home of the Alamo and Spanish missions, *and* traditional cultural celebrations such as Fiesta. This city is also the headquarters for huge companies like Southwestern Bell and ~~USAA.~~ *United Services Automobile Association (USAA).* Many professionals are employed in places of invention like Southwest Research Institute and Southwest Center for Biomedical Research. San Antonio is home to four community colleges, five universities, a medical school, *a* dental school, *an* allied health school, a nursing school, and a law school. San Antonio has come a long way since my mother was growing up*,* when the city's only manufactur~~ing~~*ed* products were tortillas and cement.

San Antonio is both cosmopolitan and cowboy. During one week, I ~~could~~ *might* choose to go to a George Strait concert, attend the Nutcracker performed by our own ballet company and symphony, go to a Spurs basketball game, meet with leading *aerospace* researchers ~~in aerospace~~ for a symposium, build a barbed wire fence at my grandfather's ranch, and read in the newspaper about groundbreaking cancer research being performed here. I know how to do the Cotton-eyed Joe and *how* to play a Chopin Prelude.

The diversity of this city has opened doors and exposed me to varied experiences. I grew up embracing other cultures through celebrations like Fiesta, *Dia De Los Muertos,* the Texas Folklife Festival, and Wurstfest as well as *through* education in the history and language of different cultures. Being culturally aware enables me to empathize with fellow San Antonians, thus erasing any ~~stigmas or~~ preconceived ideas about others.

I've ~~I have~~ also benefited from San Antonio's status as a premiere research area from the Young Engineers and Scientists (YES) Program at Southwest Research Institute (SwRI) this past summer. The YES program changed me by solidifying my desire to become a scientist/engineer, particularly in computers and electronics, and by giving me glimpses of the exciting work in various fields of study. My independent study project is an activity ~~that is~~ *that's* a predecessor ~~for~~ *to* a career in research, giving me a taste of the work so I can see ~~if~~ *whether* this career path ~~is the most~~ *will be* fulfilling ~~for~~ *to* me.

The firm foundation of the rich and diverse past of San Antonio, held together by the spirit of discovery and enhancement of the industry and science of the city, have given me a lofty outlook. With these experiences from the place and the time in which ~~I have~~ *I've* lived, ~~I am~~ *I'm* ready to explore unknown territory.

Essay 76: What additional personal information do you wish to be considered in our decision? For example: exceptional hardship, personal responsibilities, exceptional achievements, educational goals and choice of majors, or ways you have associated with Texas A&M University.

The 12th man is who I am. In my heart and in my mind, I have always been a Texas Aggie. As long as I can remember, I have wanted to attend the university of my father, my grandfather, and my uncle. Texas A&M has been a part of my conscious thoughts as long as I can remember. I have always seen myself as "Maroon and White."

The 'Spirit of Aggieland' and the stories about A&M's traditions have been interesting to me. Tales of the Corps life in my grandfather's day (Class of '47), academic achievements of my father in Vet school (Class of '74), and my uncle's success in Premed (Class of '73) have been the subject at numerous family gatherings. These stories have always been an inspiration to me and I know them by heart. I am anxious to start some of my own. I know I have what it takes to contribute to the spirit of Aggieland. I am waiting to come onto the field, into arena of college and campus life.

I'm eager to associate myself with the commitment of excellence A&M is famous for. The thought of achieving a degree in engineering, from a notable university such as A&M, and applying it towards a career is my dream. I know I can fulfill this goal at the collegiate level, by demonstrating some of the same qualities I have regimented myself to follow in high school.

I have positioned myself to better reach this goal by placing an influence on succeeding scholastically as well as in leadership skills. I intend to continue the same leadership qualities in college as I have demonstrated in high school. Through involvement in varsity basketball, Winner's Circle Advisory Council, National Honor Society, and working a part-time job for three years, I've gained valuable skills in commitment, loyalty, and leadership. I intend to continue the same leadership qualities in college as I have demonstrated in high school.

As a Winner's Circle Advisory Council Representative I am one of twelve persons out of 750 seniors who commit ourselves to promoting and leading chemical-free lifestyles for high school students. As a drug and alcohol free individual, I set an example to my classmates by being moral, ethical and conservative. Yes, I do go out with my buddies occasionally to attend school dances, participate in the school "social scene," but it is satisfying for me to know that negative peer pressure cannot change my views and beliefs that I hold for myself and others to follow.

Competing and achieving a position on the basketball team for four years at a 5A high school, keeping a 94 GPA at a school of 3500, and laboring on my parent's ranch as a ranch hand and a veterinarian's assistant, I have learned to physically work hard under stressful conditions. I have learned to manage the responsibilities, to follow schedules, to set goals and work toward those goals daily. I knew that instant gratification isn't as rewarding as using hard work, and perseverance to reach long term goals. These are the worth ethic values I will use to achieve an engineering degree from Texas A&M.

Between the demanding school, sports and family activities that I'm involved with, I've managed to work part-time since I was sixteen. I worked at Bill Miller's Bar B-Q restaurant for a year and a half. I was trusted with the responsibilities of the drive-through food orders (memorizing all the different food costs) and managing the cash register with hundreds of dollars in it. I've also worked at a high volume car wash. I was trusted with operating heavy machinery, driving and detailing client's expensive vehicles. Half of the money that I have earned has been used to buy and operate my own vehicle, and the other half I have put into my savings account.

With leadership, loyalty, and commitment I stand in readiness like E. King Gill to be a 'Fighting Texas Aggie.' I am waiting to come on the field into the arena of Texas A&M. The 12th man is who I am!

Essay 76—Makeover: "Twelfth man" is a football term and refers to the fans showing moral support.

The 12th man is who I am. In my heart and in my mind, ~~I have~~ *I've* always been a Texas Aggie. ~~As long~~ *For a* as I can remember, ~~I have~~ *I've* wanted to attend the university ~~of my~~ *Texas A&M,* father, *attended by my* my grandfather, and my uncle. ~~Texas A&M has been a part of my conscious thoughts as long as I can remember.~~ I have always seen myself as "Maroon and White."

~~The~~ *I grew up with the* "Spirit of Aggieland" and the stories about A&M's traditions *with* ~~have been interesting to~~ *, which fascinated* me. Tales of ~~the~~ Corps life in my grandfather's day (Class of '47), academic achievements of my father in *V* ~~Vet~~ school (Class of '74), and my uncle's success in *P*remed (Class of '73) have been the subject*s* at numerous family gatherings. These stories have always been an inspiration to me and I know them by heart. ~~I am anxious~~ *I'm ready* to start some of my own. [How could you know this?] ~~I know I have what it takes to contribute to the spirit of Aggieland.~~ [The last sentence of this paragraph was moved to the next paragraph.]

~~I am~~ *I'm eagerly* waiting to ~~come onto the field, into~~ *enter the* arena of college and campus life. ~~I'm eager to associate~~ [Delete-schools know what they're noted for.] ~~myself with the commitment of excellence A&M is famous for. The thought of achieving a degree in engineering, from a notable university such as A&M, and applying it towards a career is my dream. I~~

obtain a degree in engineering   Texas A&M University,
~~know~~ I can ~~fulfill this goal~~ at ~~the collegiate level,~~ by demonstrating some of the same qualities
I've shown
~~I have regimented myself to follow~~ in high school.

[Rambling-delete. Move remaining text to previous paragraph.]
~~I have positioned myself to better reach this goal by placing an influence on succeeding scholastically as well as in leadership skills. I intend to continue the same leadership qualities in college as I have demonstrated in high school.~~ Through involvement in varsity basketball, Winner's

Circle Advisory Council, National Honor Society, and ~~working~~ *the past* a part-time job for three years, I've

gained valuable skills in commitment, loyalty, and leadership. ~~I intend to continue the same~~ [Delete—redundant.]

~~leadership qualities in college as I have demonstrated in high school.~~

As a Winner's Circle Advisory Council Representative ~~I am~~ *, I'm* one of twelve ~~persons~~ *students* out of 750

seniors who commit ~~our~~ *them*selves to promoting and leading chemical-free lifestyles for high school

students. As a drug *-* and alcohol *-* free individual, I set an example to my classmates by being moral,

ethical *,* and conservative. Yes, I do go out with my buddies occasionally to attend school dances, *and I*

participate in the school "social scene," but ~~it is~~ *it's* satisfying ~~for me~~ to know that negative peer

pressure ~~cannot~~ *can't* change ~~my~~ *the* views and beliefs that I hold for myself and others *would like* to follow.

While ~~C~~*c*ompeting and achieving a position on the basketball team *for* four years at a 5A high school,

keeping a 94 GPA at a school of 3500, and laboring on my ~~parent's~~ *parents'* ranch as a ranch hand and a

veterinarian's assistant, ~~I have~~ *I've* learned to ~~physically~~ *physically* work hard under stressful conditions. ~~I have~~ *I've*

learned to manage ~~the~~ responsibilities, ~~to~~ follow schedules, ~~to~~ set goals *,* and work toward those

goals daily. ~~I knew that instant~~ *Instant* gratification isn't as rewarding as ~~using~~ hard work / and perseverance

to reach long *-* term goals. These are the ~~worth~~ *work* ethic *and* values ~~I will~~ *I'll* use to achieve an engineering

degree ~~from~~ *at* Texas A&M *University.* /

Between the demanding school, sports *,* and family activities that I'm involved with, I've managed

to work part-time since I was sixteen. I worked at Bill Miller's Bar B-Q restaurant for a year and a

half. I was trusted with the responsibilities of the drive-through food orders (memoriz~~ing~~*en* all the *the prices of*

different food ~~cost~~*s* ~~costs~~) and managing the cash register ~~with~~ *containing* hundreds of dollars ~~in it~~ *.* I've also worked

at a high *-* volume car wash. I was trusted with operat~~ing~~*en* heavy machinery, driving *,* and detailing *as well as*

clients'
~~client's~~ expensive vehicles. Half of the money ~~that I have~~ earned ~~has been~~ *was* used to buy and operate

I've
my own vehicle, and the other half ~~I have~~ put into my savings account.

With leadership, loyalty, and commitment I stand in readiness like E. King Gill to be a "Fighting

I'm
Texas Aggie." ~~I am~~ waiting to come on the field into the arena of Texas A&M. The 12th man is who

University.

I am!

Essay 77: What additional personal information do you wish to be considered in our decision? (Texas A&M University)

I have been fortunate to vacation and travel throughout America and be exposed to other

cultures while visiting England and Scotland. My artistic talents have developed through music

planing the piano and clarinet, dance lessons and crafts. Participating in a bowling league for many

years has increased my bowling average , I have received several average, games, and top series

awards. I have always loved animals; hamsters, rabbits, dogs being a part of my life as well as and

caring for ten day old abandoned kittens.

My goal in obtaining this Scholarship is to enable me to secure a college degree. I have endured

through High School with a grade point average of an A minus, while participating in High School

football, basketball, and track. I would like to participate in college athletics, however I realize that I

must keep a grade point average between a 3.5 to a 4.0, thus being at the top of my class I will have

a better opportunity to secure a top job for my future.

Essay 77—Makeover:

I've   *be exposed to other cultures while vacationing and traveling throughout*
~~I have~~ been fortunate to ~~vacation and travel throughout America and be exposed to other~~
the United States, England, and Scotland.
                                                                                    playing
~~cultures while visiting England and Scotland.~~ My artistic talents have developed through ~~music~~

~~planing~~ the piano and clarinet, dance lessons, and crafts. Participating in a bowling league for many

raised *and I've* [What is this?]

years has ~~increased~~ my bowling average, ~~I have~~ received several average/ games, and top series

Animals have been an important part of my life, from raising hamsters, rabbits, and

awards. ~~I have always loved animals; hamsters, rabbits, dogs being a part of my life as well as and~~

dogs to

caring for ten-day old abandoned kittens.

applying for *s* *receive financial assistance in obtaining* *I've maintained*

My goal in ~~obtaining~~ this $cholarship is to ~~enable me to secure~~ a college degree. ~~I have endured~~

an A- grade point average (GPA) throughout high school,

~~through High School with a grade point average of an A minus,~~ while participating in H*h*igh $chool

I'd

football, basketball, and track. ~~I would~~ like to participate in college athletics, however I realize ~~that~~ I

strive to earn a 3.5 GPA or better to ensure that I graduate near *This will*

must ~~keep a grade point average between a 3.5 to a 4.0, thus being at~~ the top of my class. ~~I will~~

assure me of *as I prepare myself for the*

~~have~~ a better opportunity to secure a top job ~~for my~~ future.

Essay 78: What additional personal information do you wish to be considered in our decision? (Texas A&M University)

There are many reasons why I would like to attend Texas A&M University. I love the tradition of the school and the people at Texas A&M. Everyone there is down to earth, and I want to surround myself with this type of atmosphere.

I earned my Eagle Scout Award and only 1% of Boy Scouts in America d so. I feel that with my experience in Boy Scouts, the way I had to be flexible and rotate my busy schedule around to meet all of the requirements for Eagle, that I can overcome any challenge in college, and I am actually looking forward to it.

I would like to pursue a major in either Finance and Accounting or Nutritional Sciences. I am very open-minded, though, and I want to major in something that I will be happy doing for a career. I am interested in Finance and accounting because I have always loved the stockmarket and economics. I am always fascinated at how easily money can be earned or lost, and how the little things can effect our economy so greatly.

My grandfather, Marcus Warren was in the class of '35, and my father, Marcus Carter Warren graduated from Texas A&M in 1962. They both dearly loved A&M and have instilled that love in me. My uncle, Charles Parker graduated from A&M in 1963, and his brother Dr. Martin Preston Parker graduated in 1967, and his father Martin Parker graduated in 1940 and became a well respected professor who taught in the College of Agriculture. at Texas A&M. Also, my great uncle, Winston Warren graduated from A&m IN 1941. He earned the Congressional Medal of Honor for his action in World War II, and I am very proud of him as are all of the Warrens. There is a park and a dorm on campus named after him. His picture hangs in MSC. I attended his funeral at Texas A&M in December 1986, and walked with my father behind the riderless horse and caisson. I have a rich heritage with Texas A&M University.

I am very interested in sports and have followed Texas A&M football ever since I can remember. I attend all of the home games with my parents and many of the away games too, including Cotton Bowls, the Alamo Bowl, two Colorado games, LSU games and this year's Sugar Bowl. I have attended R.C. Slocum's Football Camp every summer since I was in 8th grade. I have never considered going to any college except Texas A&M. I hope that I can follow in my father's and uncle's footsteps and go to the University of Texas A&M. It is the only college to which I am applying. I know it is the school for me!

Essay 78—Makeover: This student needs to use contractions in this essay. People use contractions in conversations. An essay should be read like a written interview. Contractions bridge the gap between writer and reader. Though family legacy will be a major factor in this student's application, discussion of it isn't a dramatic way to begin the essay. The essay should open with the vivid description of the funeral. We've made a few changes throughout the new draft, and one strong suggestion for the last paragraph: Do not under any circumstances say, "This is the only college to which I am applying." You want to let the committee know that this college is your number one choice, but not the only one.

I'll never forget that somber day in December of 1986. My father and I walked behind the riderless horse and caisson at Texas A&M, to say a final goodbye to my great uncle, Winston Warren, Texas A&M Class of 1941. The day was sunny, but cold. The wind ~~flapped~~ *slapped* at my coat and ~~on~~ *at* the flag draping the coffin. There was much to honor about Uncle Winston. He received the Congressional

Medal of Honor for his heroic actions in World War II. His picture hangs in the Memorial Student

Center (MSC).

Whenever there was a family gathering, Texas A&M was not only a topic of discussion, but a rich *part of our*

family heritage. I knew in elementary school that my grandfather, Marcus Warren, was in the Class of

1935. My father, Marcus Carter Warren, was in the Class of '62. My uncles, Charles Parker was Class

of '63, Martin Preston Parker was in the Class of '67, *and my uncle* and their father, Dr. Martin Charles Parker was

~~not only~~ in the Class of '40, ~~but~~ *and* became a well-respected Texas A&M professor who taught in the

College of Agriculture.

All of my family has a deep, abiding love for A&M and they instilled that love in me. That

connection was further strengthened because of my interest in sports. I've followed Texas A&M

football ever since I can remember. I attend all of the home games with my parents and many of the

away games, too, including the Cotton Bowls, the Alamo Bowl, two Colorado games, LSU games, and

this year's Sugar Bowl. I've attended R.C. Slocum's Football Camp every summer since ~~I was in~~

eighth grade.

All of these reasons guided my decision to ~~want to~~ *apply* ~~attend~~ Texas A&M University. The Texas A&M

traditions have always been a part of my life. ~~The individuals who make up Texas A&M~~ *Aggies* are down-to-

earth. I want to ~~surround~~ *immerse* myself ~~with~~ *in* this type of atmosphere.

Having always had Texas A&M as part of my family life isn't ~~the~~ *my* only reason for wanting to attend

Texas A&M. I am in the 1percent of all Boy Scouts of America who earned the Eagle Scout Award. I

learned a great deal from ~~my~~ *this* experience. I had to be flexible and rotate my busy academic and

social schedule to meet all of the requirements for Eagle. ~~Obtaining the award meant~~ I had to utilize

all of my determination and focus to work on my project and keep all my other obligations going at

the same time. I'll use what I learned from that experience to meet and overcome any challenge that comes my way in college. I'm actually looking forward to it.

I want to ~~pursue a~~ major in either finance and accounting/ or nutritional sciences. I'm open-minded, though and realize I want to major in something I'll be happy doing for a career. I'm interested in finance and accounting because I've always been interested in the stock market and

[Delete-repetitious.]

economics. I'm ~~always~~ fascinated at *how* easily money can be earned or lost, and little things can

a

~~e~~ffect our economy so greatly.

but

I've never considered going to any other college ~~except~~ Texas A&M University. I hope I can

attend

follow in my father's, uncles', and grandfather's footsteps and ~~go to~~ Texas A&M University. A&M is

and in my mind and heart;

number one on my list of colleges/ it always has been and always will be.

Essay 79: What additional personal information do you wish to be considered in our admission/scholarship decision? (Texas A&M University)

My experiences as a hospital volunteer has widened my understanding of human frailties. I enjoyed assisting the friendly nurses who cared for the patients in the out-patient surgical unit. I value the opportunity to have experienced nursing. I assisted with room preparation, supply care, patient forms, and escorting patients. Patients enjoyed the attention from young volunteers. I am grateful that I was able to make patients feel more comfortable and see them leave with a smile to return home. The nurses welcomed all volunteers, making it a family atmosphere.

I was privileged to observe an appendectomy operation on camera. The Doctor explained each procedural step of surgery, it was fascinating to see inside the human body.

Lack of health resulted in the loss of three grandparents, expiring all within one week. I value the quality time spent with my grandparents as I see death as a "moving away" of a loved one. The loss of a friend and classmate was a devastating experience when he tragically died. Life is precious and priceless.

Volunteering was a part of my upbringing. I participated in Church events, school activities, neighborhood projects and holiday packaging.

I developed self-confidence while performing to an audience at music and dance recitals. Each year performance at a retirement home was a holiday feast for the Seniors. Performance with the high school clarinet ensemble for UIL competition resulted in superior rating for our performances.

As a Band Drum Major I participated in training at A&M Kingsville and as President, Secretary and Treasurer in school organizations. I am in a leadership role where my actions must be thoughtfully executed in a positive manner as I am being observed by others.

Animals are a part of the world. Hamsters, rabbits, dogs, and 10 day old abandoned kittens were a part of my life. Caring for the kittens was similar to caring for a helpless baby, as I was responsible for the nightly feedings. I love animals and always want to care for those who are helpless or homeless.

Learning about another culture through travels throughout the United States, Scotland, and England enabled me to appreciate the uniqueness of that area's tradition and history.

I view education as a valuable commodity and a necessity in today's society. I enjoy learning and I have been raised in a family that places a positive emphasis on education. I want to be a part of the Aggie family and participate in A&M's excellent academic programs. I want to have the chance to develop my leadership skills, professional awareness and talents whether it be in the field of veterinary medicine, research mathematics or communications. The Aggie world is open to many challenging opportunities.

Essay 79—Makeover: Paragraph four was moved to become the essay's opening sentence. Several changes and deletions were also made. The student needed to learn to use words appropriately.

Volunteering has been a part of my upbringing. I have always participated in church events, school activities, neighborhood projects, and holiday programs. My experiences

have

as a hospital volunteer ~~has~~ widened my understanding of human frailties. I enjoyed

assisting the friendly nurses who cared for the patients in the out-patient surgical unit.

[You weren't a nurse. You were a volunteer.]
~~I value the opportunity to have experienced nursing.~~ I assisted with room preparation, supply

care, patient forms, and escorting patients. Patients enjoyed the attention from young

I'm

volunteers. ~~I am~~ grateful that I was able to make patients feel more comfortable and see them

the hospital smiling.

leave ~~with a smile to return home.~~ The nurses welcomed all volunteers, making it a family

atmosphere.
[Combine this paragraph with previous one.]

lucky enough   *d*

I was ~~privileged~~ to observe an appendectomy ~~operation on camera.~~ The Doctor

during the . I

explained each ~~procedural~~ step ~~of surgery~~ it was fascinating to see inside the human body.

Due to poor ,   *of my   died,*

the ~~Lack of~~ health ~~resulted in the loss of~~ three grandparents ~~expiring~~ all within one week. I value

Recently, the sudden tragic death

quality time spent with my grandparents as I see death as a "moving away" of a loved one. ~~The loss~~

fellow   *helped me realize that*   *life*

of a ~~friend and~~ classmate ~~was a devastating experience when he tragically died. Life~~ is precious and

priceless.
[This sentence was moved to the opening paragraph.]

has been   *have always*   *c*

[Volunteering ~~was~~ a part of my upbringing. I participated in Church events, school activities,

,   *programs.*

neighborhood projects and holiday ~~packaging.~~]

before   *s*

I developed self-confidence while performing ~~to an~~ audience at music and dance recitals.

I've always taken the time to   s, providing a special treat   s citizens.

~~Each year~~ performance at a retirement home ~~was a holiday feast~~ for the Seniors Performance

University Interscholastic League (UIL)

with the high school clarinet ensemble for ~~UIL~~ competition resulted in superior rating for our

performances.

Presently b d m , I'm in a leadership role. My thoughts and actions are on display

As a Band Drum Major ~~I participated in training at A&M Kingsville and as President, Secretary~~

and are observed and evaluated by others. I've also participated in leadership training at Texas

~~and Treasurer in school organizations. I am in a leadership role where my actions must be~~

A&M University, Kingsville. Currently, I'm president, secretary, and treasurer in various school
~~thoughtfully executed in a positive manner as I am being observed by others.~~
organizations.
[Animals are a part of everyone's world. Be specific.]
an important   my
Animals are ~~a part of the~~ world. Hamsters, rabbits, dogs, and 10 day old abandoned kittens
at various times have been placed in my care. Being responsible for the   . My job was
~~were a part of my life. Caring for the~~ kittens was similar to caring for a helpless baby/ ~~as I was~~
to give them their
~~responsible for the~~ nightly feedings. I love animals and always want to care for those who are

helpless or homeless.

I have had the opportunity to learn about other people and cultures while traveling
~~Learning about another culture through travels~~ throughout the United States, Scotland, and
. My experiences made me appreciate my heritage and other people's traditions and history.
England ~~enabled me to appreciate the uniqueness of that area's tradition and history.~~

I view education as a valuable commodity and a necessity in today's society. I enjoy learning and
I've   who
~~I have~~ been raised in a family ~~that~~ places a positive emphasis on education. I want to be a part of
where I'll
the Aggie family and participate in A&M's excellent ~~academic~~ programs/ ~~I want to~~ have the chance

to develop my leadership skills, professional awareness and talents whether it be in the field of
won't just provide challenges, but
veterinary medicine, research mathematics or communications. The Aggie world ~~is open to many~~
will prepare me to confidently meet those challenges head-on and will open the door to a
~~challenging opportunities.~~

veritable cornucopia of opportunities.

Essay 80: Write a brief essay on your goals. (Texas Tech University)

Under the guidance of wonderful teachers and the support of family and friends I have applied

and hope to gain acceptance to Texas Tech University. The accomplishments that I have made in

high school have helped me to expand my horizons. I am an active member of my church youth

council which entails visiting the homebound of the community and raising food in the parish food

drives. In addition to my church service I volunteer every summer with the Police Summer Youth

Activities League. There I am a chaperone and friend to many kids in my home town and

surrounding areas. Along with my community work I am improving my grade point average and expanding my extracurricular activities. I am a three year recipient of the Who's Who Among

American High School Students and a two year member of National Honor Society.

Essay 80—Makeover: This student needed to pay attention to his choice of words. He also needed to provide more information on how he was expanding his extracurricular activities. Students must find ways to include essential information even in short essays.

Under the ~~guidance~~ *supervision* of wonderful teachers and the support of family and friends, ~~I have~~ *I've* applied

and hope to gain ~~acceptance~~ *admission* to Texas Tech University. ~~The accomplishments~~ *My high school* ~~that I have made in~~

~~high school~~ have helped me ~~to expand~~ *broaden* [How?] my horizons. ~~I am~~ *I'm* an active member of my church youth

council, which entails visiting ~~the~~ homebound *individuals in* of the community and ~~raising food in the~~ *working on* parish

food drives. ~~In addition to my church service~~ I volunteer every summer with the Police Summer *also*

Youth Activities League, ~~There I am~~ *where I'm* a chaperone and friend to many kids in my hometown and

surrounding areas. Along with my community work, ~~I am~~ *I'm* improving my grade point average and [How?]

~~expanding my~~ *participating in several other* [Such as?] extracurricular activities. ~~I am a three year recipient of the~~ *I've been listed in* Who's Who Among

American High School Students ~~and~~ *for the past three years and am* a two year member of National Honor Society.

Essay 81: What is the most influential movie or book you've seen recently and why? (University of Notre Dame)

The most influential film that I have ever seen was the movie *Rudy*. Rudy did not listen to what

people had to say about him going to college. He set his mind on going to college and did

everything possible to get to his favorite college. From Rudy, I learned not to sit around as my

chances for opportunity come, but to get up, take charge of my life, and try my best at everything so

that I would know that there was nothing that there was nothing that stopped me from reaching

my goal. Everything that Rudy did, he made sure to do it at full speed, and took all the punishment that anyone could put out, and come back for more. When I take on a challenge, whether it is physical or mental, I try to think that if I do not try to do all that there is to do that I might fail and not be able to redeem myself. I know that in this beautiful cruel world that we live in there are not many second chances to correct mistakes done in the past. So make your first try your best and if you do fail, but get a second chance to raise the level of expectations so that you pass with flying colors. Rudy took the level of going all out and raised it another 2 - 3 notches and even though I have been known to slack I always, every time seem to come through with the big punch right when I need it. One last think that I know I have in common with Rudy, is the desire to go to the finest college in the land—Notre Dame University.

Essay 81—Makeover: This essay needs to focus on the student, not on the unseen reader or others. Never draw attention to a negative, such as in: "I've been known to slack . . ."

The most influential film ~~that I have~~ *I've* ever seen was the movie *Rudy*. Rudy ~~did not~~ *didn't* listen to what people had to say about him going to college. He set his mind on ~~going to~~ *attending* college and did everything possible to get ~~to~~ *into* his favorite college. ~~From Rudy, I learned not to sit around as my~~ *Just like* Rudy, I *don't wait for opportunities to come* ~~chances for opportunity come, but to get up,~~ *along. I* take charge of my life, and try my best at everything *I do.* ~~so that I would know that there was nothing that there was~~ *N*othing *will* stopped me from reaching my goal*s*. [New paragraph.]

Everything ~~that~~ Rudy did, he made sure to do ~~it~~ at full speed, and took ~~all the punishment that~~ *responsibility for his actions. There aren't too many second chances in this beautiful but cruel* ~~anyone could put out, and come back for more. When I take on a challenge, whether it is physical~~ *world, so I take advantage of each and every one. For example, I didn't want to just join the golf* ~~or mental, I try to think that if I do not try to do all that there is to do that I might fail and not be~~ *team; I practiced enough to be selected captain. When the Key Club needed to raise money for* ~~able to redeem myself. I know that in this beautiful cruel world that we live in there are not many~~ *a service project to give our school a face lift, I encouraged everyone to sell enough candy to* ~~second chances to correct mistakes done in the past. So make your first try your best and if you do~~ *repaint a concrete embankment fence and plant flowers throughout the campus.* ~~fail, but get a second chance to raise the level of expectations so that you pass with flying colors.~~

always   *his expectations two to three*   .

Rudy ~~took the level of going all out and raised~~ it ~~another 2 - 3~~ notches ~~and even though I have been~~ ~~known to slack I always, every time seem to come through with the big punch right when I need~~

                                            Just like   *I want*   *school*

~~it. One last think that I know I have in common with~~ Rudy, ~~is the desire~~ to go to the finest ~~college~~ in

               : University of Notre Dame.

the land ~~Notre Dame University.~~

Essay 82: In what field of engineering are you most interested, and why? (University of Texas)

Ever since I have had access to electronics and computers, I have been fascinated with them. I started by playing Atari at age four. I was content with playing video games and using electronics only in that way for a long time. In fact, I played them so much that I won a citywide video game championship when I was 8 years old. My computer game phase quickly followed. I admit I still haven't completely grown out of that one, but I have progressed beyond it. I felt limited by using computer programs designed by someone else that didn't necessarily meet my specifications. I wanted to tell that big hunk of processing power what to do.

This desire logically led me to my next phase, programming. This started simply with qBASIC and eventually to high school courses in various flavors of C++. This year, I am designing graphics software for Dr. Thomas Smith, a Southwest Research Institute scientist. I'm developing a computer visualization of ballistic penetration as calculated by the Walker-Anderson model for long rod penetration, used to predict the interactions of weapon rounds and various materials, such as fabrics and ceramics. I'm creating the program using cutting-edge graphics software called the Visualization Toolkit that is used in many other scientific applications. This is undoubtedly the greatest academic challenge I have faced in high school but also the most stimulating.

Through this project, I'm beginning to see how math and science can be applied to solve real world problems. My project has solidified my decision to seek an Electrical Engineering degree at UT. I want to design the machines that are running the software.

The fact that Electrical Engineers are making the horsepower that runs the Information Age is captivating to me. I have a passion for math and physics, areas I know are involved in designing the circuitry in computers and electronics. I plan to major in Mathematics in addition to Electrical Engineering.

Beyond college, I am currently considering two career paths. I want to use my skills in math and electronics for the benefit of others. Through my senior year Independent Study Mentorship program, I am experiencing life at Southwest Research Institute and have observed the importance of the research that is done in that facility. Being a research scientist at Southwest Research is a likely career for me. I would love to be a part of the cutting edge research in things like quantum computers.

Another possibility is working for an organization like the National Security Agency to serve and protect my country. I have always felt a duty towards America and would enjoy using my talents to protect the freedom of the nation. I can hardly imagine the amazing technologies that are used for encryption and signal analysis.

To be content, I need to learn and be challenged. I continually seek out new opportunities and experiences in order to use my talents to help others. I am thrilled to be able to study Electrical Engineering in college.

Essay 82—Makeover: This essay isn't bad, but it doesn't get the reader's attention. The student needed to start this essay announcing his winning the video game championship. The student took a bit of creative license in his revision, since he didn't remember the exact wording of the announcement. This essay provides the same information as the previous draft but is much more entertaining and memorable.

"The winner in the 1990 Citywide Video Game Championship is eight year old Devlin O'Connor."

The word excitement doesn't do justice to the euphoric bubbling I felt inside. My face had to have been beaming enough to light up Christmas tree lights. ~~Ever since I have had access to~~

To: Editor

From: Devlin O'Connor

Re: New Book Idea

In the wake of the forthcoming film adaptation of J. R. R. Tolkien's The Lord of the Rings, there has been a renewed interest in this great writer's life and works. He is definitely my favorite author and is considered by many to be the best writer of the 20th century. He has single-handedly crafted a mythology for England by creating the intricate universe of Middle-earth, a feat unsurpassed by any fantasy writer since. His most famous works, *The Hobbit* and *The Lord of the Rings* trilogy, focus on only a small point in the history of Middle-earth. Indeed, these books are as comprehensive of the legend of Middle-earth as a history of the Renaissance is of the history of earth. What I would like to see Tolkien write is a set of stories, this time focusing on the Elves of Middle-earth, my favorite race from the books.

The entire history of Middle-earth can be found in *The Silmarillion,* a book he started in 1917 that underwent many changes, additions, and transformations throughout Tolkien's life. This book was the essence of Tolkien's creative drive and imagination. It was published posthumously in 1977 with much help and finishing work from Christopher Tolkien, editor and son of J. R. R. Tolkien. While I wouldn't expect Tolkien to finish the mythology of Middle-earth because of his perfectionistic tendencies, I would like him to write a new book focusing on the story of the Silmarils, powerful gems that Elves tried to protect from despots and sorcerers that would abuse them.

First of all, I think he would write this especially well because the epic nature of *The Silmarillion.* It resembles earlier epics, kindred to stories like *Beowulf* and Norse mythology. Tolkien fans who have read *The Silmarillion* are impressed with the broad scope of the book and the grand tales that are contained within. Tolkien once said "But once upon a time I had a mind to make a body of more or less legend, ranging from the large and cosmogonic to the level of romantic fairy-story—the larger founded on the lesser in contact with the earth, the lesser drawing splendor from the vast backcloths—which I could dedicate simply: to England; to my country." He was most gifted at inventing new civilizations, especially their languages, starting at very young age. The subject matter of *The Silmarillion* showcases this prowess and, by focusing a smaller portion of the legend, like the story of the Elves during a certain time period of Middle-earth, Tolkien would appeal to a large audience and create a worthwhile piece of literature in the process.

Another reason I think Tolkien would write this well is because a story about the Elves has great potential for symbolism. Tolkien used this technique to great effect in many of his other previous works. The Elves of Middle-earth are immortal creatures but ~~very~~ much like humans in most other respects. Tolkien, a devout Catholic, would be sure to weave in subtle references to Original Sin and Godliness to show the Elves as what humanity could have been like without flaws. These references are found throughout his books but are not obviously Christian; the themes are universal themes of humanity, not just one religion. One of the stories, the tale of Beren and Luthien, is a love story between a mortal man and immortal woman, the obstacles Beren overcomes for her, and Luthien's decision to surrender her immortality for their love. This narrative has the potential to be one of the most touching and beautiful passages Tolkien has every written.

Essay 83—Makeover: For this unusual essay topic, the student chose to write about an author who has enchanted readers with his fantasy world rich with characters, plot, and description. We suggested just a few minor changes.

To: Editor

From: Devlin O'Connor

Re: New Book Idea

In the wake of the forthcoming film adaptation of J. R. R. Tolkien's *The Lord of the Rings,*
there's ~~there has~~ been a renewed interest in this great writer's life and works. ~~He is~~ *He's* definitely my favorite author and ~~is~~ considered by many to be the best writer of the twentieth century. He ~~has single-handedly~~ crafted a mythology for England by creating the intricate universe of Middle-earth, a feat

unsurpassed by any fantasy writer since. His most famous works, *The Hobbit* and *The Lord of the Rings* trilogy, focus on only a small point in the history of Middle-earth. Indeed, these books are as comprehensive of the legend of Middle-earth as a history of the Renaissance is ~~of~~ *to* the history of earth. ~~What I would like to see~~ *I propose that* Tolkien write ~~is~~ a set of stories, this time focusing on the Elves of Middle-earth, ~~my favorite race from the books.~~ *[Delete—irrelevant.]*

   The entire history of Middle-earth can be found in *The Silmarillion,* a book he ~~started~~ *began* in 1917 that underwent many changes, additions, and transformations throughout Tolkien's life. This book ~~was~~ *held* the essence of Tolkien's creative drive and imagination. It was published posthumously in 1977 with much help and finishing work from Christopher Tolkien, editor and son of J. R. R. Tolkien.

While I wouldn't expect Tolkien to finish the mythology of Middle-earth because of his perfectionistic tendencies, ~~I would~~ *I'd* like him to write a new book focusing on the story of the Silmarils, powerful gems that Elves tried to protect from despots and sorcerers ~~that~~ *who* would abuse them.

   ~~First of all, I think he would~~ *He'd* write this especially well because the epic nature ~~of~~ *of* *The Silmarillion.* It resembles earlier epics, kindred to stories like *Beowulf* and Norse mythology *those contained in*. Tolkien fans ~~who have~~ *who've* read *The Silmarillion* are impressed with the broad scope of the book and the grand tales ~~that are~~ contained within. Tolkien once said, "But once upon a time I had a mind to make a body of more or less legend, ranging from the large and cosmogonic to the level of romantic fairy-story—the larger founded on the lesser in contact with the earth, the lesser drawing splendor from the vast backcloths—which I could dedicate simply: to England; to my country." He was most gifted at inventing new civilizations, especially their languages, ~~starting at very young age.~~ The subject matter of *The Silmarillion* showcases this prowess and, by focusing *on* a smaller portion of the legend, like the story of the Elves during a certain time period ~~of~~ *in* Middle-earth, Tolkien would appeal to a large audience and create a worthwhile piece of literature in the process.

should
Another reason I think Tolkien ~~would~~ write this ~~well~~ is because a story about the Elves has great

potential for symbolism. Tolkien used this technique to great effect in many of his other previous

are
works. The Elves of Middle-earth are immortal creatures but ~~very~~ much like humans in most other

d   *o*   *s*
respects. Tolkien, a devout Catholic, ~~would be sure to~~ weave in subtle references to Ø̸riginal S̸in

g   *examples of*
and G̸odliness to show the Elves as what humanity could have been like without flaws. These

aren't
references are found throughout his books but ~~are not~~ obviously Christian; the themes are universal

of
themes of humanity, not just one religion. One of the stories, the tale of Beren and Luthien, is a love

an
story between a mortal man and immortal woman, the obstacles Beren overcomes for her, and

Luthien's decision to surrender her immortality for their love. This narrative has the potential to be

one of the most touching and beautiful passages Tolkien has ~~every~~ written.

Essay 84: Tell us why you're different from other students in order to help us know why we should select you. (University of Texas, Plan II)

One aspect that sets me apart from other applicants is that I excel in the classroom and in the

school's athletic program. In the classroom, I have an A average throughout high school. I'm also a

National Merit Semifinalist. I also participate and letter in three of the four sports that are offered:

basketball, tennis, and baseball. In basketball, I am a starter and headed towards being named first

team all-district. In tennis, I have been a quarterfinalist, semifinalist, and finalist at the State

tournament in doubles. In baseball, I am also a starter.

Another aspect that sets me apart is that I am a leader. In basketball, I was selected by my

teammates and coach to be a co-captain of the team. This put me in a position to be a leader on and

off of the court. The votes of my teammates showed that I had my pears confidence and respect

and that they trusted me to be a leader of the team. This made me feel good because I would be in a

position to help my teammates, being either in the classroom or serving as a person that would

express their problems or ideas to the coach.

Anther aspect that sets me apart is that I am active in the community. I have volunteered for over 100 hours at a local hospital, and another 25 for charity organizations. Being of Indian heritage, I participate in many Indian youth functions. I also had a summer job.

I might have many things in common with other scholarship applicants, however I believe that these few things set me apart.

Essay 84—Makeover: The original version wasn't bad, it just wasn't going to get the attention of the admission committee. We suggested the student try a more original approach. The following is the revised essay, which got the student admitted to the highly competitive Honors Program at his first-choice school.

How am I different?

Let me count the ways.

One, I not only excel in the classroom, but also in the school's athletic program. In the classroom, ~~I have~~ *I've held* an A average throughout high school. My transcript and resume list my academic achievements, yet I also participate in three of the four sports that are offered: basketball, baseball, and tennis. In tennis, I have been a quarterfinalist, semifinalist, and finalist in doubles at the State Tournament. I've lettered in basketball and baseball for two years, and *in* tennis for four years.

Two, I'm a leader. In basketball, I was selected by my teammates and coach to be a co-captain of the team. This put me in a position to be a leader on and off of the court. My ~~pears~~ *peers'* confidence *in* and respect ~~and~~ *for me reflected* that they trusted me to be a leader and spokesman in the classroom and ~~as~~ a liaison with the coach.

Three, I have volunteered ~~for over~~ *more than* 100 hours at a local hospital, and another 25 for charity organizations.

Four, being of Indian heritage, I participate in many Indian youth functions.

Five, ~~I have~~ *I've* been gainfully employed, which was a valuable experience because it enabled me to interact with the community and with people my age ~~who are~~ from different backgrounds.

Six, my career goal is to pursue medicine and I arrived at that goal from a unique perspective—

~~from~~ being a critically ill patient as a child. When I was in sixth grade, I had an acute asthma attack,

and I was ~~very~~ *gravely* ill. I was in the Intensive Care *Unit* for several days, ~~however I never realized~~ *never realizing* just how

sick I was. ~~I found out later that I only had a 50% chance of surviving, and this made me realize how~~ *When I was later told that my prognosis for recovery had been only 50 percent,*

~~lucky I was.~~ *I realized exactly how lucky I'd been.* In all likelihood, the doctors and nurses in the ICU saved my life. It was at this point

that I knew I wanted to become a doctor. I experienced firsthand the impact that compassionate

doctors could have on a patient's health and morale. By becoming a doctor, ~~I knew that I would~~ *I'll* be

able to help people the way ~~that~~ I was helped. I ~~now~~ know ~~a doctor~~ *, from a patient's perspective, that a doctor* must make decisions which

can and do affect a person's life and death.

These are just a few of the differences which will set me apart from others and allow me to

achieve my goals, while influencing my classmates to strive toward their goals and the common

good of the school.

Essay 85: Please write an essay about an activity or interest that has been particularly meaningful to you. (Yale University)

I looked up for a moment, slightly startled, and in the doorway I saw a young lady with a flute to

her lips standing beside a young man with a cello. Their music swirled around me, soaring through

the mote filled sunbeams that streamed from the windows and i was carried away. Their duet filled

me with a sense of belonging that I had never experienced before. It was one of those rare

moments in life when one finds one's self in the most perfect of environments. I never wanted to

leave. For three weeks I was surrounded by people the likes of which I had never before

encountered. They understood the frustrations, hardships, decisions, and risks that are part of

striving to succeed. They challenged my view of the world with words as articulate as the ones I

put forward to defend it.

For three weeks I lived in an atmosphere that crackled with synergy. The air was electric with

ideas and aspirations. There was not a task in the world that this group of teenagers could not have

accomplished. It seemed as if the entire field of human expertise was embodied in the vibrant gray matter of this group of artists, musicians, philosophers, theologians, physicists, and mathematicians. The potential for greatness was palpable. A critical mass had been reached the product of which was a spontaneous eruption of thoughts, opinions, conclusions, and ambitions. I loved every minute.

My perception of the worth of my ability to think had value only as it applied toward my academic success. Similarly, I perceived my love of music as an asset only when I could use it to perform. In short I suffered from the same myopia that society as whole seems to struggle with most frequently. I was so caught up in making a living that I neglected to realize the importance of making a life. I was not, however, completely without intellectual fulfillment. I loved music and literature, but I did not see them as valuable in a role other than entertainment. There was still a link missing in my journey toward intellectual self-awareness. I found that link in philosophy.

My intellectual journey began in a poorly lit classroom in the oppressive heat of Beaumont, Texas, the summer after my sophomore year. I was sitting in a chair, wondering how in the world I ended up in a class entitled "A Brief History of Philosophy," when the only courses I had requested all involved some form of drama and music. Then a small man with glasses walked to the front of the room and began to tell a story. It was the story of why and how men think. Over the next several weeks I read Socrates, Plato, Aristotle, Thoreau, Locke, Hobbes, Freud, Jung, Frankl, Newton, Galileo, Hawking, the great minds that have collaborated together to define Mankind's perception of reality. I began to notice my view of the world expanding. As I turned pages, I could feel the mind of the universe racing beside my own. I saw for the first time the great thoughts of any species, and I found that I understood the nature of the men to whom those thoughts belonged. I flew, with ever increasing speed, across words that pushed the boundaries of language, and watched the beauty of thought fast approaching. It is a scary thing to read the works of Socrates or Locke, and to know, with absolute certainty, what lay on the next page. Indeed, I found myself, in the words of Stephen Hawking, to be "reading the mind of God."

A transition occurred during my tenure in Beaumont. I emerged from the maelstrom of diversity and talent to discover that my old views of the world and my place in it had been stripped away. It was a molting of the intellect. I have not stagnated since my return to real life. The people I met are still with me. Our discussions still continue over Email and telephone. We have had our first reunion. But the real thrill is in knowing that my class is not the last class to emerge from this experience. I was fortunate enough to be allowed to return as a Junior Counselor this past summer and I got to watch it all again. I consider myself extremely fortunate because I have had the opportunity to see the capability of the best that Texas has to offer. It has also whetted my appetite. I long to be a part of a student body that is a diverse, talented, and capable as the one I met that hot muggy summer. I thirst for that opportunity to grow.

Essay 85—Makeover: Though this is a strong essay, it makes an overly strong statement of the student's intellect and insight, rather than focusing on what he's done for others and how he's helped others in their personal growth. The student also needs to relate an experience he's had that he believes shows the contribution he can make to life at Yale.

I looked up for a moment, slightly startled, and in the doorway I saw a young lady with a flute ~~to~~ *at* her lips standing beside a young man with a cello. Their music swirled around me, soaring through the mote-filled sunbeams that streamed from the windows ~~and~~ . I was carried away. Their duet filled me with a sense of belonging that ~~I had~~ *I'd* never experienced before. It was one of those rare moments ~~in life~~ [When else?] when one finds ~~one's self~~ *oneself* in the most perfect of environments. I never wanted to leave. For three weeks I was surrounded by people the likes of which ~~I had~~ *I'd* never before encountered. They understood the frustrations, hardships, decisions, and risks that are part of striving to succeed. They challenged my view of the world with ~~words as articulate as the once I put forward to defend it.~~ *equally challenging views.* [The original sentence was the wrong attitude to take.]

For three weeks I lived in an atmosphere that crackled with synergy. The air was electric with ideas and aspirations. ~~There was not a task in the world that this group of teenagers could not have accomplished.~~ [Probably untrue, and sounds arrogant-delete.] It seemed as if the entire field of human expertise was embodied in the vibrant gray

aspiring

matter of this group of ^artists, musicians, philosophers, theologians, physicists, and mathematicians.

[Wrong attitude.]

~~The potential for greatness was palpable.~~ A critical mass had been reached, the product of which ^

was a spontaneous eruption of thoughts, opinions, conclusions, and ambitions. I loved every

minute.

[This paragraph needs to be deleted. It has the wrong attitude.]

~~My perception of the worth of my ability to think had value only as it applied toward my~~

~~academic success. Similarly, I perceived my love of music as an asset only when I could use it to~~

~~perform. In short I suffered from the same myopia that society as whole seems to struggle with~~

[You're too young to be making a living. You live and are living, but you're not making a living.]

~~most frequently. I was so caught up in making a living that I neglected to realize the importance of~~

~~making a life. I was not, however, completely without intellectual fulfillment. I loved music and~~

~~literature, but I did not see them as valuable in a role other than entertainment. There was still a link~~

~~missing in my journey toward intellectual self-awareness. I found that link in philosophy.~~

My intellectual journey began in a poorly lit classroom in the oppressive heat of South Texas, the

'd

summary after my sophomore year. I was sitting in a chair, wondering how in the world I ended up ^

I'd

in a class entitled "A Brief History of Philosophy," when the only courses ~~I had~~ requested all involved ^

some form of drama and music. Then a small man with glasses walked to the front of the room and

began to tell a story. It was the story of why and how men think. Over the next several weeks I

read Socrates, Plato, Aristotle, Thoreau, Locke, Hobbes, Freud, Jung, Frankl, Newton, Galileo,

— *who've* [Redundant.] *in an attempt* *m*

Hawking,/ the great minds ~~that have~~ collaborated ~~together~~ to define ^Mankind's perception of reality. ^ ^ ^

I began to notice my view of the world expanding. As I turned pages, I could feel the mind of the

our

universe racing beside my own. I saw for the first time the great thoughts of ~~any~~ species, and ~~I~~ ^

~~found that~~ I understood the nature of the men to whom those thoughts belonged. I flew, with ~~ever~~

increasing speed, across words that pushed the boundaries of language, and watched the beauty of

[Don't under any circumstances include this sentence, or anything like

thought fast approaching. ~~It is a scary thing to read the works of Socrates or Locke, and to know,~~

it, in an essay.]

~~with absolute certainty, what lay on the next page.~~ Indeed, I found myself, in the words of Stephen

Hawking, to be "reading the mind of God."

A transition occurred during my tenure in Beaumont. I emerged from the maelstrom of diversity and talent to discover that my old views of the world and my place in it had been stripped away. It was a molting of the intellect. I ~~have not~~ *haven't* stagnated since my return to real life. The people I met are still with me. Our discussions still continue over ~~Email~~ *e-mail* and telephone. ~~We have~~ *We've even* had our first reunion. ~~But~~ *T*he real thrill is in knowing that my class is not the last class to emerge from this experience. I was fortunate enough to be allowed to return as a Junior Counselor this past summer and I got to watch it all again. I consider myself extremely fortunate because I have had the opportunity to ~~see the capability of~~ *exchange ideas and learn from* the best that Texas has to offer. ~~It has~~ *It's* also whetted my appetite. I long to be a part of a student body ~~that is a~~ *that's as* diverse, talented, and capable as the one I met that hot muggy summer. I thirst for that opportunity to grow.

Essay 86: This essay topic was part of the 1999 Yale application for early admission. The essay had to be single-spaced and fit on one page.

My interest in youth advocacy began one rainy day during my tenth grade year. I arrived at school and parked in the tiny, far-removed, gravel sophomore parking area. I'd remembered an umbrella, but four inches of water covered the footpath to the school. As I sloshed my way across the quarter mile to the classroom building, I noticed several vacant spaces in the main student lot next to the school itself. By the time I reached class, soaking wet, I had passed 32 empty spaces. Only four sophomore parked in our gravel lot. As I went through the rest of the day, I couldn't help but wonder why the administration would force sophomores to park so far away. I came to the conclusion that it was a lack of communication. The people making the rules must have lost touch with the things that we, the students, felt were important. That afternoon I walked into the first student council meeting of the year with a clear purpose in my mind–to contribute my efforts towards increasing the communications between the student body and the administration.

This conviction led to my appointment as the student representative to my high school's Campus Improvement Team (CIT). The CIT is a body of teachers, parents, administrators and an appointed student, who work together to make all policy decisions for the campus. When I arrived at CIT, I was regarded as a novelty because no one had ever stepped forward before to fill the student slot. It was a learning experience for all of us. I soon realized that if I hoped to be effective as a student representative, I would have to gather the opinions of a wide variety of students. The relationships I developed soon became one of the most rewarding aspects of my position. I've made *quesadillas* with the local leader of the notorious Latin Kings street gang. I've played pool with the state bull-riding champion. I've spoken Tex-Mex with the grandparents of the local president of the Mexican-American Engineers and Scientists chapter during is little sister's *quinceñera*. Now I can draw on this diversity of relationships when I am charged with providing information about an aspect of student life that I am not directly involved in. All in all, my time with CIT has taught me that, while we students may not have all the answers, at the very least, we have an opinion that merits being heard.

Last summer I found another environment that held great potential for advancing the views of young people when I arrived in Austin as one of the one thousand delegates to the 1998 Texas Boys State. As I saw the mock political process evolving at Boys State, I began to become frustrated with the lack of meaning that underlay our endeavors. The prevailing attitude was that the process was more important than the product because, in the end, the laws we passed and the decisions we made would have no impact on the larger world. Then I realized that at Boys State we could have the opportunity to make a real statement to our government about the concerns of youth. We already had to make laws, why not show the laws we make to the larger world? I started sharing this idea with the other delegates and was elected Governor. In this position I arranged for the distribution of our recommendations to every Texas State Senator and Representative. Amazingly, these officials responded to our input with great enthusiasm and over thirty of them have requested assistance in drafting legislation to address our concerns. Articles, written by state legislators, have appeared in several newspapers, expressing gratitude for our input and newly found respect for our generation. We spoke and they listened. However, this was only the beginning. A few weeks later in Washington, D.C., I was elected President of Boys Nation. Through this position, I have gained an opportunity to discuss what we did in Texas with the leaders of other youth-in-government programs from across the country. The response to our ideas has been wonderfully positive and several programs are interested in following our example.

I have recently passed my eighteenth birthday and in the eyes of the law I am now an adult. I have a voter registration card, and my voice will now be heard through the ballot box as well as the soapbox. I also have the comfort of knowing that there are other concerned young people following behind. The other day a motion was brought before the CIT to expand the number of student representatives from one to five. It passed unanimously. After the meeting had adjourned, the principal came up to me and said, "Kevin, you showed us and your fellow classmates what students are capable of contributing. You should be proud." It was one of the best compliments I have ever received. And, the next week, after a year and a half of discussion and a detailed, student-made statistical analysis of the parking situation at my high school, the CIT voted to abolish the sophomore parking lot.

Essay 86—Makeover: With the edits we suggested, this essay was within the required length. It just needed a few changes and to be toned down here and there. The amended essay worked, because the student was accepted.

My interest in youth advocacy began one rainy day during ~~my~~ tenth grade ~~year. I arrived at school and parked in the tiny, far-removed, gravel sophomore parking area. I'd remembered an~~ umbrella, but *F*four inches of water covered the footpath to the school. As I sloshed ~~my way across~~ *from the far-removed sophomore parking area,* the quarter-mile to the classroom building, I noticed several vacant spaces in the main student lot ~~next to the school itself.~~ By the time I reached class, soaking wet, ~~I had~~ *I'd* passed ~~32~~ *thirty-two* empty spaces.

Only four sophomore*s* parked in our ~~gravel~~ lot. ~~As I went through the rest of the day,~~ I couldn't help but wonder why the administration would force sophomores to park so far away. I came to the conclusion that it was ~~due to~~ a lack of communication. ~~The people making the rules must have lost touch with the things that we, the students, felt were important.~~ That afternoon I walked into the first student council meeting of the year with a clear purpose : ~~in my mind~~ to contribute my efforts

[In the U.S. we use "toward." In the U.K., "towards" is used.]

towards increasing ~~the~~ communications between the student body and the administration.

This ~~conviction~~ goal led to my appointment as the student representative to my high school's Campus Improvement Team (CIT). The CIT is a body of teachers, parents, administrators, and an appointed student / who work together to make all policy decisions for the campus. When I arrived at CIT, I was regarded as a novelty because no one had ever stepped forward before to fill the student slot. ~~It was a learning experience for all of us. I soon realized that~~ If I hoped to be effective as a student representative, I ~~would have to gather~~ needed to know the opinions of a wide variety of students. The relationships I developed soon became one of the most rewarding aspects of my position. I've made *quesadillas* with the local leader of the notorious Latin Kings street gang. I've played pool with the state bull-riding champion. I've spoken Tex-Mex with the grandparents of the local president of the Mexican-American Engineers and Scientists chapter during ~~is little~~ his sister's *quinceñera*. Now I can draw on this diversity of relationships when ~~I am~~ I'm charged with providing information about an aspect of student life ~~that I am~~ in which I'm not directly involved ~~in.~~ . ~~All in all,~~ My time with CIT ~~has~~ taught me that / while we students may not have all the answers, at the ~~very~~ least, we have ~~an~~ opinions that merits being heard.

Last summer I found another environment that held great potential for advancing the views of young people when I ~~arrived in Austin as~~ was one of the ~~one~~ thousand delegates to the 1998 Texas Boys State. As I saw the mock political process evolving at Boys State, I ~~began to become~~ became. frustrated with the lack of meaning that ~~underlay~~ permeated our endeavors. The prevailing attitude was that the process was more important than the product because, in the end, the laws we passed and the decisions we made would have no impact on the larger world. ~~Then I realized that~~ at Boys State, we could have the opportunity to make a real statement to our government about the concerns of youth. We ~~already~~ had to make laws; why not show the laws we ~~make~~ made to the larger world? I started sharing this idea with the other delegates and was elected Governor. ~~In this position~~ Texas Boys State I arranged for the distribution of our recommendations to every Texas State Senator and Representative. Amazingly, these officials responded to our input with great enthusiasm and over thirty of them have requested assistance in drafting legislation to address our concerns. Articles, written by state legislators, have appeared in several newspapers, expressing gratitude for our input and newly found respect for our generation. We spoke and they listened. However, this was only the beginning. A few weeks later in Washington, D.C., I was elected President of Boys Nation. ~~Through this position, I have gained an opportunity to discuss~~ discussed what we did in Texas with the leaders of other youth-in-government programs from across the country. The response to our ideas has been wonderfully positive and several programs are interested in following our example.

I ~~have~~ recently passed my eighteenth birthday and ~~in the eyes of the law I am~~ I'm now an adult. I have a voter registration card, and my voice will ~~now~~ be heard through the ballot box as well as the soapbox. ~~I also have the~~ It's a comfort ~~of~~ to knowing that there are other concerned young people who will follow my lead. ~~following behind.~~ The other day a motion was brought before the CIT to expand the number of student representatives from one to five. It passed unanimously. [Delete-unnecessary to the essay.] ~~After the meeting had adjourned, the principal came up to me and said, "Kevin, you showed us and your fellow classmates what students are capable of contributing. You should be proud." It was one of the best compliments I have ever received. And, the next week,~~ After a year and a half of discussion and a detailed, student-made statistical analysis of the parking situation at my high school, the CIT voted to abolish the sophomore parking lot.

Essay 87: Write an essay of no more than 500 words on: "I want to have a career at the National Security Agency (NSA) because . . ."

"I want to have a career at the NSA because . . ."

There are many reasons why I want to work for the NSA. The invigorating environment of other intelligent and energized individuals, the access to cutting edge technology, and my desire to serve my country are all motivating factors in aspiring to work for the NSA.

I have been lucky enough to attend a school where challenges abound and gifted students are encouraged to pursue opportunities they desire. I want to continue to be challenged and to use my abilities to the benefit of others. In this way, the Undergraduate Training Program will serve me twice; first, in allowing me to attend a challenging college without worrying about money, and secondly, working with and being inspired by people at the top of their field working for the NSA. Although I work well alone, I work best when surrounded by other intelligent, motivated colleagues in projects and problem solving exercises. I am sure to find both working environments at the NSA.

At the NSA, I will have access to cutting edge technology with which I could do research and development that would be impossible to accomplish anywhere else. Nowhere else are the resources greater or the problems to solve more interesting and relevant. The magnitude and importance of the responsibilities of NSA are second to none. The combination of the importance of the work and the opportunities for independent research are unbeatable.

Finally, even with all the wonderful opportunities that the NSA provides, my underlying motive for joining the NSA is to serve my country. Through Boy Scouting and church activities, I have been instilled with a great love for freedom and my country. As a young boy, one of my most vivid memories is getting a special tour of FBI headquarters. Recently, I had the honor as NHS President to invite Former FBI Director Judge William S. Sessions to speak at the NHS induction ceremony. My affinity and desire to fight crime and improve America has always endured. Working for the NSA would give me the awesome honor of protecting against enemies of freedom and serving my country.

I recently had a discussion about the NSA with Col. David C. Kirk, Deputy Commander of the Joint Command & Control Warfare Center, who works with signals processing. He used told me that the work that he does is like some of the work done by the NSA. After he gave me a general description of signals processing, I was immediately fascinated. I know that if the work at NSA is like any of the areas he described, I am sure to be captivated as well. In conclusion, employment at the NSA would both present me with phenomenal opportunities and allow me to use my skills to serve my country.

Essay 87—Makeover: This was a strong essay, with just a few minor changes and additions.

There are many reasons why I want to work for the NSA. The invigorating environment of other [*created by*] intelligent and energized individuals, the access to cutting edge technology, and my desire to serve my country are all motivating factors in aspiring to work for the NSA. [*my*]

[*I've*] I have been lucky enough to attend a school where challenges abound and gifted students are encouraged to pursue opportunities they desire. I want to continue to be challenged and to use my abilities to the benefit of others. In this way, the Undergraduate Training Program will serve me twice; first, in allowing me to attend a challenging college without worrying about money, and second, working with and being inspired by people at the top of their field working for the NSA. Although I work well alone, I work best when surrounded by other intelligent, motivated colleagues in projects and problem solving exercises. I am sure to find both working environments at the NSA. [*on*] [*I'm*]

At the NSA, I will have access to cutting edge technology with which I could do research and development that would be impossible to accomplish anywhere else. Nowhere else are the [*I'll*] resources greater or the problems to solve more interesting and relevant. The magnitude and importance of the responsibilities of NSA are second to none. The combination of the importance of the work and the opportunities for independent research are unbeatable.

Finally, even with all the wonderful opportunities that the NSA provides, my underlying motive for joining the NSA is to serve my country. ~~Through~~ Boy Scouting*s* and church activities, ~~I have been instilled with~~ *have instilled in me* a great love for freedom and my country. As a young boy, ~~one of my most vivid memories is getting~~ *for* *I got* a special tour of FBI headquarters. Recently, ~~I had the honor as NHS~~ President *as National Honor Society (NHS)*, *I* ~~to~~ invite*d* Former FBI Director Judge William S. Sessions to speak at the NHS induction ceremony. *His speech lit a fire in me about where to direct my talents and future career path.* My affinity and desire to fight crime and improve America has always endured. Working for the NSA would give me the awesome honor of protecting *us* against enemies of freedom ~~and serving~~ *, enabling me to serve* my country.

I recently had a discussion about the NSA with Col. David C. Kirk, Deputy Commander of the Joint Command *and* ~~&~~ Control Warfare Center, who works with signals processing. He ~~used~~ told me that the work that he does is like some of the work done by the NSA. After he gave me a general description of signals processing, I was immediately fascinated. I know that if the work at NSA is like any of the areas he described, ~~I am~~ *I'm* sure to be captivated as well. In conclusion, employment at the NSA would both present me with phenomenal opportunities and allow me to use my skills to serve my country.

Essay 88: Write an essay of up to 300 words. Essay topic: It's the Year 2020. An article appears in *USA Today* profiling your success. Write that article.

After years of research and numerous experiments, the efforts of a team of scientists at Southwest Research Institute in San Antonio, Texas, have finally paid off. The team, lead by Dr. Devlin O'Connor, synthesized some of the newest technologies, including quantum computing and neural nets, to create a machine that is capable of learning and rational decision making. "While we haven't achieved true sentience, we hope this prototype will be the point of origin of many new journeys into AI," O'Connor explained. However, O'Connor's research team did not just stumble onto the discovery. Dr. O'Connor. has proffered some of the newest ideas in cognitive science, although his Ph.D. from the California Institute of Technology is in electrical engineering. His extensive work in developing better and more complex neural networks was a major tool in the discovery as well. Dr. O'Connor has also contributed to computer visualization by developing more powerful software able to visualize a living human brain down to the synapses in real-time. When asked about his software, O'Connor replied, "I've always been fascinated with computer visualization. During my senior year, I worked with a scientist at Southwest Research developing a computer visualization of his work in materials for bulletproof vests and have been intrigued by it since then."

In addition, O'Connor is working on his second piano sonata and is scheduled to perform a set of Rachmaninoff pieces with the San Antonio Symphony later this year. He has enjoyed some popular success with his last composition. Dr. O'Connor hopes to use the computer to aid in other inventions. "I can't wait to give this computer some problems that are still unsolved and see what it will find," O'Connor said.

Essay 88—Makeover: This is a strong essay. We made some minor changes and broke it up into short paragraphs, which is how newspaper articles are written. It's exactly 300 words in length.

After years of research and numerous experiments, the efforts of a team of scientists at Southwest Research Institute in San Antonio, Texas, have finally paid off. The team, led by Dr. Devlin O'Connor, synthesized ~~some of~~ the newest technologies, including quantum computing and neural nets, to create a machine that is capable of learning and rational decision making.

[New paragraph.]
"While we haven't achieved true sentience, we hope this prototype will be the point of origin of
Artificial Intelligence (AI)   *didn't*
many new journeys into ~~AI~~," O'Connor explained. However, O'Connor's research team ~~did not~~ just stumble onto the discovery. Dr. O'Connor has proffered some of the newest ideas in cognitive

doctorate

science, although his ~~Ph.D.~~ from the California Institute of Technology is in electrical engineering. His extensive work in developing better and more complex neural networks was a major tool in the discovery as well.

[New paragraph.]
Dr. O'Connor ~~has~~ also contributed to computer visualization by developing more powerful software able to visualize a living human brain down to the synapses in real-time. When asked about his software, O'Connor replied, "I've always been fascinated with computer visualization.

high school   *scientist*

During my senior year, I worked with a ~~scientist at~~ Southwest Research developing a computer visualization of his work in materials for bulletproof vests and have been intrigued by it since then."

In addition, O'Connor is working on his second piano sonata and is scheduled to perform a set of

He's

Rachmaninoff pieces with the San Antonio Symphony later this year. ~~He has~~ enjoyed some popular success with his last composition. Dr. O'Connor hopes to use the computer to aid in other inventions. "I can't wait to give this computer some problems that are still unsolved and see what it

[Sentence added.]

will find," O'Connor said. *Though not yet forty, Devlin O'Connor has proven himself to be multifaceted and talented in all his endeavors.*

Essay 89: Describe something about yourself that you feel is significant and that you want a committee member to know.

A number of things have had a significant impact on my life. Because of my inter-racial heritage, I have encountered bigoted people from all kinds of backgrounds, i.e. ignorant people from all races consider me an outsider. Because I have done vast amounts of volunteer service work in a number of capacities in the community I have been around people with life experiences very different from mine. Because I have worked very hard deal and been successful in school and in the work place. I have encountered people who are jealous and envious of my successes. Because I have set very challenging goals for myself (e.g. earning as many Boy Scout merit badges as possible), I have learned something about many different things/fields. Because I have been involved with music all my life, I have been able to encourage my intuitive and creative side. Because I have done deep intuitional practices, I have learned a great deal about myself. Because I have worked hard at sales, I have learned a lot about what appeals to people, and what motivates them. I have continued to work hard on my goals in recent years, in spite of rather contrary family circumstances (parents divorcing, death in the family). Because I have worked hard at sports, I have enjoyed some successes in competitive athletics.

How has all of this affected my outlook on life? Ignorant people are a product of what they have learned, so I have to be careful that I do not limit what I think for the same reasons. I am thankful for my situation and will never look down at anyone else less fortunate, because I know my situation can change in an instant. Working hard brings success in all things, but I have to be prepared to ignore the jealously hard won success sometimes triggers in others. Always learning and being prepared to experience new things really makes life a fun and worthwhile journey.

Essay 89—Makeover: Eight sentences in this essay begin with the word "because." The student generalizes about others' thoughts, which sets the wrong tone. It's okay to express pride in one's accomplishments, but this essay needs to be softened. The edits add variety to sentence structure and show the student in a positive light.

A number of things have had a significant impact on my life. ~~Because of~~ *Due to* my ~~inter-racial~~ *interracial* heritage, ~~I have~~ *I've* encountered ~~bigoted people~~ *bigotry* from all kinds of backgrounds. ~~i.e. ignorant people from all races consider me an outsider.~~ *individuals from* ~~Because I have done vast amounts of~~ *My commitment to community* volunteer service ~~work in a number of capacities in the community I have been around~~ *has exposed me to numerous* people with life experiences ~~very~~ *vastly* different from mine ~~Because I have worked very hard and been successful in school and in the work place, I have encountered people who are jealous and envious of my successes.~~ */ from whom I've learned a great deal.* [You have no way of knowing what others think about you and your successes.] ~~Because I have~~ *Setting* ~~set very~~ challenging goals ~~for myself (e.g. earning as many Boy Scout merit badges as possible), I have~~ *, such as earning as many Boy Scout merit badges as possible, has meant I've* learned ~~something~~ about many different ~~things/fields.~~ *subjects. My interest in* ~~Because I have been involved with~~ music

has enabled me to tap into
~~all my life, I have been able to encourage~~ my intuitive and creative side. ~~Because I have done~~

~~deep intuitional practices, I have learned a great deal about myself. Because I have worked hard~~

My aggressive sales techniques have enabled me to learn   . ~~at sales, I have learned a lot~~ about what appeals to people / ~~and what motivates them. I have~~ *Despite difficult family circumstances,*

I've kept focused   .
~~continued to work hard~~ on my goals ~~in recent years, in spite of rather contrary family~~

~~circumstances (parents divorcing, death in the family). Because I have worked hard at sports,~~

Through hard work and practice, I've
~~I have~~ enjoyed ~~some~~ successes in competitive athletics.

[This is excessively judgmental. Delete.]
How has all of this affected my outlook on life? ~~Ignorant people are a product of what they have~~

~~learned, so I have to be careful that I do not limit what I think for the same reasons.~~ ~~I am~~ *I'm* thankful

all I have and   on   than me
for ~~my situation~~ and will never look down ~~at~~ anyone ~~else~~ less fortunate, because ~~I know~~ my

could
situation ~~can~~ change in an instant. Working hard brings success in all things / ~~but I have to be~~

~~prepared to ignore the jealously hard won success sometimes triggers in others.~~ Always learning

and being prepared to experience new things ~~really~~ makes life a fun and worthwhile journey.

Essay 90: Define leadership and give an example of when you demonstrated leadership.

When I want to see something that I can be proud of, I turn the television on VCR settings, put in

a tape, and watch one of my home video "movie" projects. I see myself and other people acting in

them and I am entertained. I praise myself and realized how much work I put into that movie.

My concept of leadership is an action of someone who directs and supervises a sort of company.

In my case, the company with whom I work with are the people in my videos. In school, they call

me the great movie director because I am the only one in my class who achieved a reputation as a

video director. Many have seen my films and know the work I put into it, but if it weren't for the

other people in my video, it would not have the dexterity it does have. It wouldn't be a great video,

though, without a leader. I chose to be that leader.

I can finally understand what it must have been like for my theater director at school because the production never comes out the exact way the director had it envisioned. It takes hard work and determination to get the cast to do what you want and when you want it. Above all things, it takes plenty of patients to work with everybody. I could never be more responsible when it comes to directing videos compared to anything else. I put in as much time and effort that I have for the sake of a video under my direction. I take care of the editing, no matter how primitive my equipment is, and I always keep the videos within the boundaries of my capabilities. This is what makes a leader—hard work, determination, patience, and responsibility.

[We've deleted a few paragraphs, in order to show the concluding paragraph.]

I positively enjoy creating videos and acting. It is a considerable amount of work, but when I'm done I have something that I can truly be proud of. There are many different types of leadership. In fact I have been an officer for the Drama Club at my school for three years. I have exhibited leadership by helping the other officers run the club. Nevertheless, I think the director of a movie or film shows a great deal of leadership.

Essay 90—Makeover: This essay needed some major changes. This essay also needed a big dose of humility.

When I want to see something ~~that I can be~~ [I'm] proud of, I turn the television ~~on~~ [and] VCR settings, put [on] in a tape, and watch one of my home video "movie" projects. I see ~~myself and other people~~ [When other people and myself] acting in them and ~~I am entertained~~ [I'm]/ ~~I praise myself and~~ [, I] realized how much work I put into that movie.

[I define a leader as a peson who works hard, and has determination, patience, and responsibility.] ~~My concept of leadership is an action of someone who directs and supervises a sort of company.~~

~~In my case, the company with whom~~ I work with ~~are the~~ people in my videos[, I produce]. In school, they call me the great movie director because ~~I am~~ [I'm] the only one in my class who achieved a reputation as a video director. ~~Many have~~ [Those who've] seen my films ~~and~~ know the work I put into ~~it~~ [them], but if it weren't for the [these films wouldn't have been possible.] other people in my videos, ~~it would not have the dexterity it does have.~~ [Objects can't have dexterity.] ~~It wouldn't~~ [No video can] be a ~~great~~ [good] video, though, without a leader. I chose to be that leader.

[Remove this sentence. It's difficult to integrate it into the essay.]
~~I can finally understand what it must have been like for my theater director at school because the production never comes out the exact way the director had it envisioned.~~ It takes hard work and determination to get the cast to do what you want ~~and~~ *,* when you want it. Above all ~~things,~~ it takes plenty of ~~patients~~ *patience* to work with everybody. I ~~could never be more responsible when it comes to~~ *take great care with all aspects of my videos.* ~~directing videos compared to anything else.~~ I put in as much time and effort ~~that I have for the sake~~ *give* *as are necessary to ensure quality.* ~~of a video under my direction.~~ I take care of the editing, ~~no matter~~ *regardless of* how ~~primitive my~~ *limited the* equipment ~~is,~~ *might be.* ~~and~~ I always keep the videos within the boundaries of my capabilities. ~~This is what makes a leader—hard work, determination, patience, and responsibility.~~

handle

[We've deleted a few paragraphs, in order to show the concluding paragraph.]
I ~~positively enjoy~~ *thrive on* creating videos and acting / ~~It is~~ *in them. It's* a considerable amount of work, but when I'm done I have something ~~that~~ I can truly be proud of. ~~There are many different types of leadership. In fact I have been an officer for the Drama Club at my school for three years. I have exhibited leadership by helping the other officers run the club. Nevertheless,~~ I think the director of a movie ~~or film shows a great deal of leadership.~~

Leadership is needed to run a country, guide religious followers, teach students, and accomplish many other goals.

exhibits great leadership skills in order to ensure a successful product.

Essay 91: Relate an experience that affected your life.

All my life I have felt a calling, a need to make a difference in people's lives, especially in the area of law. I always hoped I could make that difference, but I was never sure if my dream would be a reality. Several years ago I was compared to a reed, but I was also told, unlike a reed I would never bend with the wind. As I have grown older, I am finally understanding what they meant by that statement.

I spent this summer in a study program in Paris, and although alcohol consumption was not permitted by the programs rules, we were offered wine twice a week in dinner out groups, since wine is such an intricate part of French cuisine. On my fourth dinner out, I was assigned to my law professor's dinner group. He told us we were going to a quaint French cafe overlooking Notre dame. We left our dormitory and trekked six blocks to the commuter train. We got on the train and I was overwhelmed by the heat inside the train, as well as the stench of body odor. We finally arrived at our stop and disembarked from the train. I was immediately overpowered by the beauty of the evening. The sun was delicately setting behind Notre dame and was creating streams of color across the sky, which were reflected on the Seine River. We entered a lovely cafe with a red and white awning and sat down at tables by the windows. We all continued to gaze enchantingly at the beautiful sunset. We begin to order and Mr. Forey asked us what type of wine we wanted, red or white. Most of the students were saying, "Oh well, red will be fine." I looked at Mr. Forey and asked if I could have a coke or something else instead of wine, and with a puzzled look on his face he asked, "What, you don't want any wine?"

I replied, "No, I don't drink."

He responded, "Well sure, not a problem. OK, so we have eleven people who want wine."

After a few moments, three girls at the end of the table asked if it was all right if they got something else to drink besides wine.

"Sure," he said, "So only eight want wine now."

After that, Mr. Forey was bombarded by a deluge of people requesting soft drinks. When they finished, only one girl decided she still wanted wine. Mr. Forey looked at me and said, "Well, Patricia where ever you go, everyone seems to follow."

Mary, who was sitting across from me, said, "Gosh, I can always count on you, huh, Pat."

I was remotely baffled by the statement, because in my mind I hadn't done anything remarkable. When I asked her what she meant, She said, "You always stick up for things that you believe in, and generally the stuff you do either gets me out of a jam, or lets me do the right thing. Pat, I guess I'd have to say you're gutsy, like the CEO of our company, you argued with the Pizza Hut Manager for

30 minutes to get him to fulfill his contract. Anyway, what I'm trying to say is that I never wanted wine, but I was afraid to be the only one. But you weren't afraid."

I was astounded. I never realized that I had had an impact on her life. Mary's monologue made me realize that if I hadn't been there probably everyone at that table would have had alcohol that night. I never realized that one simple action could have an impact on others. What was the difference between myself and the others at the table they were afraid to be different, even if it was something that they did not want to do.

I know the purpose of college essays is to prove to the admissions officer that you are the right person to go to their school, and to do that you must talk about yourself in a way that shows others how great you are, but I'm sorry that's just not my style. I want people to recognize me for what kind of person I am by what I do and not because of my pompous writing style.

For my last year in high school, my two most important goals are continuing to build a strong relations with my parents and to feel like I am ready for college. Since I have been homeschooled since I was in kindergarten, I was uncertain how I would handle going to college and entering a classroom environment. Last year I took French II and III at a local university, and after successfully completing the first semester, my confidence was bolstered. Three weeks ago, I started classes again, but this year I knew I would have an opportunity to prove to myself that I can cope in a college environment. I am being forced to learn time management, and proper study habits, since I am juggling four college courses, in addition to my five regular high school subjects, work, homework, and extracurricular activities. I realize that this year will be a great learning experience for me and enable me to avoid the pitfalls many freshmen experience.

My goals for this year extend further than just what I do in school. I want to fulfill my duties to Youth and Government and help organize an exciting 50th anniversary conference. Beyond that, my goal is to leave my judicial section more organized by establishing a standard operating procedure manual and initiating a new scoring system and best belief awards.

My short term goals are rather simple. I want to become an attorney, specializing in appeals; and, therefore I will focus myself on preparing myself for law school by improving my writing skills, attaining a high GPA, studying political science and business, and involving myself in student government.

My long range goals are much different, and it all leads back to what I believe my calling in my life is. Ever since I was three years old, I have had only one desire for my life. I have always told my parents that I was going to be the President of the United States. As I become older that desire never changed, and for the past ten years I have wanted to be an attorney also. Within the past two years, I have decided that I want to work for a small firm in Washington, DC, or in New York as an appellate attorney. I hope to one day serve as a Justice, and then step away from the judicial profession to enter politics.

This last statement is not an easy one for me to make because it means leaving something I know I love to enter a profession in which I find many aspects unappealing. I have seen the unflattering side of politics, but I feel that I have a calling in my life, a calling to help lead our nation.

Before I conclude, I want to address an issue that I am not really applies. That issue is my standardized test scores. I have difficulty with SAT tests. I think the main problem I have when I take these tests is that I allow myself to believe that the fate of my college career lies in those tests, and I focus so much on the fact that I have to get a certain score that I freeze up.

Essay 91—Makeover: This is a strong essay, but it needed to be softened.

All my life ~~I have~~ *I've* felt a calling, a need to make a difference in people's lives, especially in the area of law. I always hoped I could make that difference, but I was never sure if my dream would be a reality. Several years ago I was compared to a reed, but I was also told*that,* unlike a reed *, I'd* ~~I would~~ never bend with the wind. ~~As I have grown older,~~ I am *I'm* finally understand~~ing what they meant by~~ *beginning to* that statement.

past

I spent this summer in a study program in Paris, and although alcohol consumption was not

when dining *in*

permitted ~~by the programs rules~~, we were offered wine twice a week ~~in dinner~~ out groups, since

integral

wine is such an ~~intricate~~ part of French cuisine. On my fourth dinner out, I was assigned to my law

D

professor's dinner group. He told us we were going to a quaint French cafe overlooking Notre

dame. We left our dormitory and trekked six blocks to the commuter train. We got on the train and

I was overwhelmed by the heat inside the train, as well as the stench of body odor. We finally

arrived at our stop and disembarked ~~from the train.~~ I was immediately overpowered by the beauty

D *delicate*

of the evening. The sun was ~~delicately~~ setting behind Notre dame and was creating streams of color

in *that had*

across the sky, which were reflected ~~on~~ the Seine River. We entered a lovely cafe ~~with~~ a red and

[You can't gaze enchantingly. You gaze at something which is enchanting.]

, enraptured

white awning and sat down at tables by the windows. We all continued to gaze ~~enchantingly~~ at the

beautiful sunset.

[New paragraph.]

When we began *,*

~~We begin~~ to order ~~and~~ Mr. Forey asked us what type of wine we wanted, red or white. Most of

the students were saying, "Oh well, red will be fine." I looked at Mr. Forey and asked if I could have a

C *.* *W* *?Y*

doke or something else instead of wine and with a puzzled look on his face he asked, "What you

don't want any wine."

alcohol." [Everyone drinks. Be specific.]

I replied, "No, I don't drink."

, *Okay*

He responded, "Well sure, not a problem. ~~OK,~~ so we have eleven people who want wine."

, too,

After a few moments, three girls at the end of the table asked if it was all right if they got

something else to drink ~~besides wine.~~

Mr. Forey

"Sure," ~~he~~ said, "So only eight want wine now."

d with *s for*

After that, Mr. Forey was ~~bombarded by a~~ deluge ~~of people~~ requesting soft drinks. When they

finished, only one girl decided she still wanted wine. Mr. Forey looked at me and said, "Well,

, wherever

Patricia ~~where ever~~ you go, everyone seems to follow."

Mary, who was sitting across from me, said, "Gosh, I can always count on you, huh, Pat?"

I was ~~remotely~~ baffled by the statement. ~~because in my mind~~ I hadn't done anything remarkable.

When I asked her what she meant, she said, "You always stick up for things that you believe in, and

generally the stuff you do either gets me out of a jam, or lets me do the right thing. Pat, I guess I'd
have to say you're gutsy, ~~like the CEO of our company,~~ almost as if you were the ~~you argued with the Pizza Hut Manager for~~ [This allusion is abrupt and confusing.]

~~30 minutes to fulfill his contract. Anyway,~~ what I'm trying to say is that I never wanted

wine, but I was afraid to be the only one. But you weren't afraid." to say so.

I was ~~astounded.~~ surprised. I never realized that ~~I had~~ I'd had an impact on her life. Mary's ~~monologue~~ response made

me realize that if I hadn't been there, ~~probably~~ everyone at that table ~~would have~~ probably would've had alcohol that

night. I never realized that one simple action could have an impact on others. What was the

difference between myself and the others at the table? They were afraid to be different, even if it

~~was~~ meant doing something they ~~did not~~ didn't want to do.

~~I know the purpose of college essays is to prove to the admissions officer that you are the right~~ [Delete this entire paragraph. Never tell a committee you "know" what it wants. Committees
~~person to go to their school, and to do that you must talk about yourself in a way that shows others~~ want to know what you think, not what others think about you. If a committee wants input from
~~how great you are, but I'm sorry that's just not my style. I want people to recognize me for what~~ someone else, it requests recommendation letters, not random quotes selected by the student.]

~~kind of person I am by what I do and not because of my pompous writing style.~~

For my last year in high school, my two most important goals are continuing to build a strong
relations with my parents and to ~~feel like I am ready~~ prepare myself for college. Since ~~I have~~ I've been ~~homeschooled~~ home-schooled hip

since ~~I was in~~ kindergarten, I was uncertain how ~~I would~~ I'd handle going to college and entering a

classroom environment. Last year I took French II and III at a local university, and after successfully

completing the first semester, my confidence was bolstered. Three weeks ago, I started classes
again, ~~but this year I knew I would have an opportunity to prove to myself that I can cope in a~~ [You had an opportunity the year before.]

~~college environment. I am being forced to learn~~ time management, and proper study habits, since and am learning

I'm
~~I am~~ juggling four college courses, in addition to my five regular high school subjects, ~~work,~~ *homework,*

~~homework, and~~ extracurricular activities/ ~~I realize that~~ this year will be a great learning experience *, and work.* *T*

will *many*
for me and enable me to avoid ~~the~~ pitfalls ~~many~~ freshmen experience.

My goals for this year extend further than just what I do in school. I want to fulfill my duties to

Youth and Government and help organize an exciting 50th ^*A*nniversary ^*C*onference. ~~Beyond that,~~

I want
~~my goal is~~ to leave my judicial section more organized by establishing a standard operating

procedure manual and initiating a new scoring system and ^*B*est ^*B*elief ^*A*wards.

. I'm focusing
~~My short term goals are rather simple.~~ I want to become an attorney, specializing in appeals/ ~~and,~~

striving to achieve
~~therefore I will focus myself~~ on preparing ~~myself~~ for law school by improving my writing skills,

undergraduate
~~attaining~~ a high GPA, studying political science and business, and involving myself in student

government.

path
My long range goals are much different, and it all leads back to what I believe my ~~calling~~ in ~~my~~

involves. *I've* *I've*
life ~~is.~~ Ever since I was three years old, ~~I have~~ had only one desire for my life. ~~I have~~ always told my

matured
parents ~~that~~ I was going to be ~~the~~ President of the United States. As I ~~become older~~ that desire

I've also *.*
never changed, and for the past ten years ~~I have~~ wanted to be an attorney ~~also.~~ Within the past two

I've *. .*
years, ~~I have~~ decided ~~that~~ I want to work for a small firm in Washington, DC, or in New York as an

appellate attorney. I hope to one day serve as a Justice, and then step away from the judicial

profession to enter politics.

isn't
This last statement ~~is not~~ an easy one for me to make because it means leaving something I know

in many respects. *I've*
I love to enter a profession ~~in which~~ I find ~~many aspects~~ unappealing/ ~~I have~~ seen the unflattering

side of politics, but ~~I feel that~~ I have a calling ~~in my life, a calling~~ to help lead our nation.

Before I conclude, I want to address ~~an~~ issue ~~that I am not really applies. That issue is~~ my
the   *of*

standardized test scores. I have difficulty with ~~SAT~~ tests. ~~I think the main problem I have~~ ~~w~~hen I
standardized   *W*

take these tests ~~is that~~ I allow myself to believe that the fate of my college career lies in those tests,
,

and I focus so much on the fact that I ~~have to~~ get a ~~certain~~ score that I freeze up.
must   *good*

[This last paragraph could be retained, but only if there is no other place to put it. This essay is upbeat and positive. It's best not to end it on a negative note, as that's what the reader will remember. The student could add a sentence or two on how she's working to manage her anxiety in test situations, but is also undertaking many academic and extracurricular challenges as part of her determination to pursue her goals in law and politics.]

Essay 92: We live in a complex and ever-changing society, yet our family heritage and tradition allow certain values to be maintained. How has your background influenced your personal development and outlook? Is there something special about you as a person you would like the committee to know? Support your statement with experiences you have had. (McDonald's HACER Scholarship)

Over the years as I've grown older I have become more aware of who I am and who I wish to become. In time I have experienced numerous situations that have changed me. Of all my experiences there has yet to be one that has had a major impact on my life. This experience allowed me to view the possibilities in life which I can reach, as well as taught me what is needed to succeed in life.

As a child, growing up on the southside of San Antonio was not an easy job. During that time, I overcame many obstacles and learned many different things that made me become the person that I am today. I have two siblings, a younger sister and an older brother. When I was ten years old, my brother was sixteen and he began to get in a lot of trouble. He was involved in gangs, had no source of income, and rarely attended school. He ended up as a tenth grade drop-out.

My parents tried to help my brother and emphasized the importance of education. As time passed, the situation only worsened, and the only possible solution my family found was prayer. Today my brother works as a stock boy at a local grocery warehouse and has improved his lifestyle.

I learned many valuable lessons because of my brother. I know that what he did may have been negative, yet it had a great positive impact on my life and understanding of it.

I am ready to do something with my life which I will enjoy for as long as I life. I intend to pursue a top-notch education that will not end at my college graduation. With a major in criminal justice, I hope one day to work as an agent for the Federal Bureau of Investigation.

Essay 92—Makeover: This is a good essay, but it needs to supply a bit more information, especially about what the student learned from his experiences. The italicized text was added by the student to flesh out the essay.

[Redundant—delete.]   A   , I've
~~Over the years~~ as I've grown older ~~I have~~ become more aware of who I am and who I wish to
                                    I've
become. ~~In time I have~~ experienced numerous situations that have changed me. Of all my
                , there's   effect
experiences ~~there has yet to be~~ one that has had a major ~~impact~~ on my life. This experience
[You can't reach a possibility. You can attain an achievement.]
            achievements   that   attain,
allowed me to view the ~~possibilities~~ in life ~~which~~ I can ~~reach,~~ as well as taught me what is needed
to succeed in life.

            G   S   wasn't   .
~~As a child,~~ growing up on the southside of San Antonio ~~was not an~~ easy ~~job.~~ During that time, I overcame many obstacles and learned many different things that made me become the person ~~that~~

I am today. I have two siblings, a younger sister and an older brother. When I was ten years old, my
sixteen-year-old   joined a
brother ~~was sixteen and he~~ began to get in a lot of trouble. He ~~was involved in~~ gangs, had no source
                                    thought
of income, and rarely attended school. *He never ~~really cared~~ about the possible consequences of his deeds or where his life was headed. He was totally indifferent to the pain and trauma he was causing our family.* He ended up ~~as~~ a tenth grade drop-out *with no promise for the future.*

        strived
My parents ~~tried~~ to help my brother/~~s life~~ and emphasized the importance of education. As time passed, the situation only worsened, and the only possible solution my family found was *to pray every night hoping my brother would wake up to reality.* Today my brother works as a stock boy

at a local grocery warehouse and has improved his lifestyle. *He often tells me not to make the same mistake that he did.*

I learned many valuable lessons because of my brother: *the importance of a loving family, the importance of values and morals, the benefits of being educated and where it can take you, and what it can make of you. I learned at a young age some of the lessons in life that many* ~~have~~ to [may take years]

experience *personally so as* to ~~come into an understanding of how life is meant to be lived.~~ I know [in order] [how to live productively.]

~~that~~ ѱhat he did may have been negative, yet it had a great positive ~~impact~~ on my life ~~and~~ [W] [my brother] [effect] [.]

~~understanding of it.~~

~~The~~ experiences ~~which I~~ encountered enabled me to fully grasp the possibilities that life has to [This and other] [I've]

offer, and most importantly to perceive the ~~necessities~~ for a successful life. ~~I am now~~ ready to do [necessity] [I'm]

something with my life ~~which~~ I will enjoy ~~for as long as I life.~~ I intend to pursue a top-notch [that] [forever.]

education that ~~will not~~ end at my college graduation. With a major in criminal justice, I hope one [won't]

day to work as an agent for the Federal Bureau of Investigation. *Time flies* ~~by fast~~ *and before you* [,]

know it ~~you are~~ *on the verge of being grown up.* ~~I will~~ *always remember to* ~~stop for a minute~~ *and* [you're] [I'll] [take the time to enjoy]

understand ~~what I can learn from life's everlasting experiences.~~ [important lessons.]   [Everlasting doesn't work with experiences.]

Essay 93: We live in a complex and ever-changing society, yet our family heritage and tradition allow certain values to be maintained. How has your background influenced your personal development and outlook? Is there something special about you as a person you would like the committee to know? Support your statement with experiences you have had. (McDonald's HACER Scholarship)

My goals started taking shape as I watched my sister crying as she walked across the stage to receive her diploma. That's when I knew I wanted to be like her. As a twelve-year-old seventh grader, I'd never seen my family so happy and proud of what she'd accomplished. That was the beginning of my goals. Under Marissa's guidance, I started planning for high school, college, and a future career.

As the President of the Spanish Club, I run the club, keep the club members active, make school announcements, keep records of the member's attendance, run a one-person phone committee, and discuss possible activities with the Spanish Club faculty sponsor.

Three Saturdays a month, I attend the Mexican American Physicians Association (MAPA) Med. Prep. Program, where health care professionals and college representatives discuss possible future careers. We also take classes on time management, goal setting, and take hospital visits.

Interested in a medical career, I focused most of volunteer work at Santa Rosa Hospital for the last two summers. I've decided I want to become a physical therapist.

I also work at a veterinarian's clinic twenty hours a week as an Exam Room Technician. During my two years of employment, I've always worked on weekends, thus giving me the time to participate in school activities.

In January 1999, my father was disabled in an accident, and unfortunately, was uninsured. Until October of 1999, my mother had never worked outside the home. Though she now has a job as a cafeteria worker in a local elementary school, I've continued working with the veterinarian's clinic in order to help my family financially.

I hope to attend St. Mary's University. This small campus with a great student-to-faculty ratio and strong biology department, will provide me with a great start on my future.

Essay 93—Makeover: Though this is a good essay, it didn't provide information about the student's Hispanic heritage. We suggested he review Sample Essay 9 (in Chapter Six), to get an idea of what the committee would look for in an essay. Due to the fact that this essay underwent some major restructuring, only the revised edition, with a few minor changes, is provided.

Twenty-seven years ago, my father came from a poor family in Piedras Negras, Mexico to San Antonio to work in construction. By age ten, my mother had to quit fifth grade in Monterrey, Mexico, in order to work cleaning homes to help provide for her five brothers and sisters. Somehow, my parents met in 1973, married, and sought a better life through hard work. Though hopeful, they only expected their children to follow their ~~same~~ path, which they felt was their lot in life and all a Hispanic could hope for. The oldest, my sister, proved them wrong by excelling in everything she put her mind to.

My sister cried joyously as she walked across the stage to receive her diploma. All the family ~~can~~ could talk about were her scholarships and good grades. That's when I knew I wanted to be like my sister, Marissa. As a twelve-year-old seventh grader, ~~I had~~ I'd never seen my parents and relatives so happy and ~~so~~ proud of the goals my sister had accomplished, but that was just the beginning of ~~my~~ the pursuit of my goals.

Under Marissa's guidance and inspiration, I started early on my search for a college and future career. I found out about programs, such as the Mexican-American Physicians Association (MAPA) ~~Med. Prep.~~ Medical Preparation Program where doctors and college admission representatives ~~come and~~ talk about what they look for in prospective students. I also found out about National Honor Society (NHS) and its requirements. Soon enough, I was doing more than was required in class, taking the initiative and, in the community, at my job, and for my family.

Throughout high school I pushed myself to excel academically, not just the basic required in courses, but also classes like chemistry, precalculus, and extra semesters in during science, history, math, spent and other honor classes. I've also participated in leadership roles, such as President of the Spanish Club and the Senior Editor of the Yearbook.

Proud of what I've accomplished, I also enjoy giving my time in service to the community. Knowing I wanted to become a physical therapist, I wanted my community service to be in a medical surrounding. I've focused most of my volunteer work spending seven hours a week at on Santa Rosa ~~, a local hospital,~~ Hospital for two summers. Watching those patients' faces light up as soon as I walked in to talk with them was my way of enjoying the experience at the hospital. I've also volunteered at the Ronald McDonald House, the Jimenez Thanksgiving Dinner, and the Elf Louise Christmas Toy Program, and I worked to give my school's grounds a facelift.

In order to ~~help to~~ assist my family, I work at a veterinarian's clinic twenty hours a week as an *[financially]*

Exam Room Technician, where I hold the animals during exams, prepare for surgeries, fill

prescriptions, answer the phone, and deal with clients. During my two years of employment, ~~I have~~ *[I've]*

always worked on weekends, thus giving me the time to participate in school activities.

In January 1999, my father was disabled in an accident*[.]* ~~and~~ *[U]*nfortunately, *[he]* was uninsured. Until

October of 1999, my mother had never worked outside the home. Though she now has a job as a

cafeteria worker in a local elementary school, ~~I have~~ *[I've]* continued working ~~with~~ *[at]* the veterinarian's

clinic in order to help my family financially.

My goals include wanting to become a physical therapist, but I also want to give back to my

community, which is primarily Hispanic. After accomplishing my goals, I hope to spend some time

visiting with students from elementary and middle schools ~~which~~ *[that]* are on the predominantly low-

income side of town. I want to make them aware that graduating from high school is a challenge*[and college]*

I'll give back to MAPA *[they can accomplish.]* by volunteering to talk about my experiences and be a mentor to any *[by ing]*

students interested in physical therapy. ~~I would~~ *[I'd]* like to visit Las Colonias and border towns in

Mexico to provide free services to individuals who ~~may not~~ *[might not]* otherwise be able to afford to access a

physical therapist. If I can't find an established group, ~~I will~~ *[I'll]* actively recruit other Hispanic health

professionals to do our part to give back to the Hispanic community.

Dedicating myself to reach*[ing]* my goals requires innovation and determination, but actually reaching

them is something ~~of which~~ my family and I will be proud*[of.]* One day, my parents and sister will see

me graduate from college. ~~I will~~ *[I'll]* have reached my goals with my sister's help—not in her shadow.

Essay 94: In 250 words or less, tell us who you are and how you are unique.

My family is a heritage of hard-working peoples who have suffered to provide for their children and I am proud to be a part of this devoted family. I will be the first woman in my family to pursue a higher education. Like all women do, I wish the best for my family. I crave to be a founder of hope in education, for the future generations in my family. My mother and stepfather have guided me and encouraged me to become a successful person in life. With their support I can achieve my goals.

A task that has been my greatest achievement is graduating in three years. Throughout this journey of responsibility I have established my strengths and weaknesses. One of my strength is that I will never give up and one of my weaknesses is that I am stubborn. Being able to graduate in three years has lead me to find out what a hard working person I am. I now know that anything is possible if you set your mind and heart to it.

My environment is a Hispanic Community. I attend a bilingual church, were both English and Spanish are spoken. At my church I am a member of the Youth Group who doesn't only provide clean-up services around the community, but also provides hope to those in the homeless shelters. We bring those in the homeless shelters: songs and fellowship. We lift their spirits up with the word of God. Sharing love, hope, and faith are the best community services, I think that can be given to our community.

Being a Hispanic woman in this day and age is truly a privilege because know I have a chance to be a leader in this world and try to make a change for my future family.

Essay 94—Makeover: This student needs to pay attention to the sense of the essay. For example, in the first paragraph, the student writes, ". . . encouraged me to become a successful person in life." Where else could you be a success?

       comes from a long line

My family ~~is a heritage~~ of hard/working peoples who have suffered to provide for their children   ,

   I'm   *I'll*

and ~~I am~~ proud to be a part of this devoted family. ~~I will~~ be the first woman in my family to pursue a

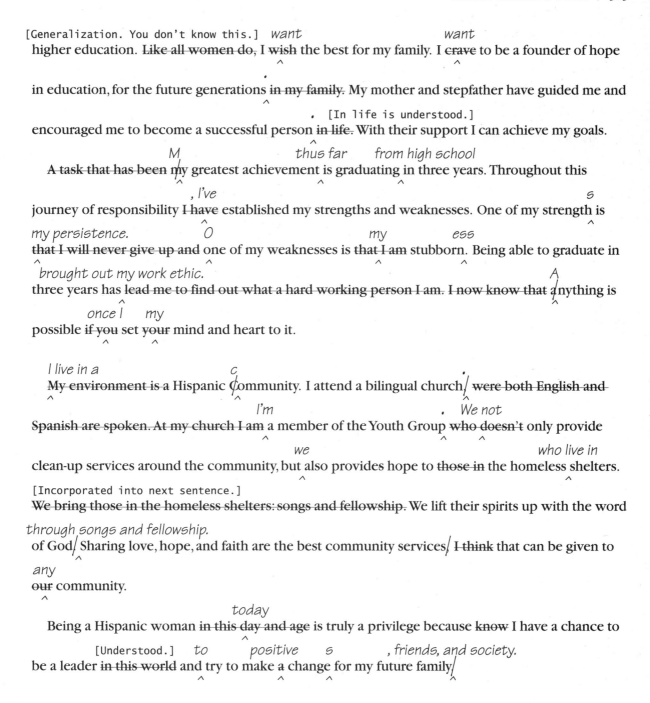

[Generalization. You don't know this.] *want* *want*
higher education. ~~Like all women do,~~ I ~~wish~~ the best for my family. I ~~crave~~ to be a founder of hope

in education, for the future generations ~~in my family.~~ My mother and stepfather have guided me and

[In life is understood.]
encouraged me to become a successful person ~~in life.~~ With their support I can achieve my goals.

M *thus far* *from high school*
~~A task that has been my~~ greatest achievement is graduating in three years. Throughout this

, I've *s*
journey of responsibility ~~I have~~ established my strengths and weaknesses. One of my strength is

my persistence. *O* *my* *ess*
~~that I will never give up and~~ one of my weaknesses is ~~that I am~~ stubborn. Being able to graduate in

brought out my work ethic. *A*
three years has ~~lead me to find out what a hard working person I am. I now know that~~ anything is

once I *my*
possible ~~if you~~ set ~~your~~ mind and heart to it.

I live in a *c*
~~My environment is a~~ Hispanic Community. I attend a bilingual church / ~~were both English and~~

I'm *. We not*
~~Spanish are spoken. At my church I am~~ a member of the Youth Group ~~who doesn't~~ only provide

we *who live in*
clean-up services around the community, but also provides hope to ~~those in~~ the homeless shelters.

[Incorporated into next sentence.]
~~We bring those in the homeless shelters: songs and fellowship.~~ We lift their spirits up with the word

through songs and fellowship.
of God / Sharing love, hope, and faith are the best community services / ~~I think~~ that can be given to

any
~~our~~ community.

today
Being a Hispanic woman ~~in this day and age~~ is truly a privilege because ~~know~~ I have a chance to

[Understood.] *to* *positive* *s* *, friends, and society.*
be a leader ~~in this world~~ and try to make a change for my future family /

Essay 95: Write a brief essay on who you are.

My name is John Smith. I am a seventeen year old senior from Washington High School. I have

lived in Placid City for fourteen and a half years with my mother, stepfather, and my older sister,

Jane. I come from a small town called Sherman Oaks in Kansas. I never knew my 'real' father for we came to this state while I was still a baby.

I am interested and plan to major in Architectural Studies. I think it will be a difficult course, but I also feel that if I prioritize my time and set disciplinary standards in order to reach my goals I can succeed my dream in Architecture. After learning new tactics in studying and enduring a school year with many challenges, I can use and build on the tools I've gained to accomplish whatever I set out to do in college and life.

Essay 95—Makeover: Though students need to share who they are with the reader, students must be selective about what they share. This essay included too much irrelevant information.

[Unnecessary–this information is on the application. Use your word count wisely.] ~~I've~~
~~My name is John Smith. I am a seventeen year old senior from Washington High School.~~ I have

lived in Placid City for fourteen and a half years with my mother, stepfather, and my older sister,
[Unnecessary–delete.]
Jane. ~~I come from a small town called Sherman Oaks in Kansas. I never knew my 'real' father for we came to this state while I was still a baby.~~

architecture.   It'll   career objective
I ~~am interested and~~ plan to major in ~~Architectural Studies. I think it will~~ be a difficult ~~course~~, but
activities   rigorous   reaching
~~I also feel that~~ if I prioritize my ~~time~~ and set ~~disciplinary~~ standards in ~~order to reach~~ my goals, I can
in attaining   of being an architect. Having   ed   study strategies
succeed my dream ~~in Architecture. After~~ learning new ~~tactics in studying~~ and enduring a school
filled   I'll   my goals
year with ~~many~~ challenges, ~~I can~~ use ~~and build on~~ the tools I've gained to accomplish ~~whatever I set~~
in
~~out to do~~ in college and life.

Essay 96: How has participating in sports influenced your development? (Hooked on Sports)

Greetings, I am a First Baptist High School (FBHS) student athlete. My name is Tyrone Washington. Throughout the four years I've spent at FBHS I have participated in the following sports: football, basketball, and baseball. I have also participated in a numerous amount of service hours through my school and church.

I have played varsity football since my sophomore year. In which I hold two state championships metals. Basketball I really didn't get very far because of an injury which occurred when I hyperextended my knee playing in a J.V. basketball game my sophomore year. Which kept me from finishing that basketball season. In baseball I'm proud to say that I have been on the varsity team since my freshmen year.

I believe that through these past four years of participating in sports I've been taught discipline, how to better my game in each particular sport, and how to work with others. The coaches and players of my teams have helped me realize my character. My athletics has molded me to become a motivated student athlete. It has helped me to become devoted to success on and off the field.

In conclusion, I feel as if I would have never played or participated in any types of sports I would not be the aspiring young individual I am today.

Essay 96—Makeover: Don't begin an essay by introducing yourself. Your name is either on the application or it could be that your name shouldn't be on the essay because the committee judges the essays without knowing who wrote them.

[Delete. They already know your name. Redundant.]
Greetings, I am a First Baptist High School (FBHS) student athlete. ~~My name is Tyrone~~

I've
~~Washington.~~ Throughout the four years I've spent at FBHS ~~I have~~ participated in ~~the following~~

I've   contributed
~~sports:~~ football, basketball, and baseball. ~~I have~~ also ~~participated in a~~ numerous ~~amount of~~ service

,   , and community.
hours through my school ~~and~~ church.

I've
~~I have~~ played varsity football since my sophomore year. ~~In which~~ I hold two state championships

medals.   in basketball   that
~~metals. Basketball~~ I ~~really~~ didn't get ~~very~~ far because of an injury ~~which~~ occurred when I

during   The injury
hyperextended my knee playing in a J.V. basketball game ~~my~~ sophomore year. ~~Which~~ kept me from

finishing that basketball season. ~~In baseball~~ I'm proud to say that I have been on the varsity team *(baseball)* since my freshman year.

~~I believe that~~ *T*hrough these past four years of participating in sports I've ~~been taught~~ *learned* discipline, how to ~~better~~ *improve* my game in each ~~particular~~ sport, and how to work with others. The coaches and players ~~of my teams have~~ helped me *fully* realize my character. ~~My~~ *A*thletics has molded me to become a motivated student athlete*.* ~~It has helped me to become~~ devoted to success on and off the field.

~~In conclusion, I feel as if I would have~~ *If I'd* never played or participated in any ~~types of~~ sports I~~,~~ [Student added closing sentence in final draft.] ~~would not~~ *wouldn't* be the aspiring young individual I am today. ~~Being~~ *Because of* ~~an~~ *b*athlete, *I want to one day be a physical therapist specializing in sports injuries.*

Essay 97: This next essay is unique. The essay topic was "What will a college education mean to me or someone I know?" The essay could be no more than 50 words.

A college education to me is an opportunity for me to broaden my education. Enhance my degree of learning. Open doors of opportunity and life up to my full potential. Accomplishing this hopefully someday I will become a recognized attorney. Which due to my college education will bring me lifetime rewards.

Essay 97—Makeover: This essay needed to read more smoothly. The original version was 51 words in length; the edited version, 45 words.

A college education ~~to me is an opportunity for~~ *will allow* me to broaden my education*,* ~~E~~*e*nhance my degree of learning*,* ~~O~~*o*pen doors of opportunity ~~and life~~ *and*, *enabling me to live* up to my full potential. ~~Accomplishing this~~ *A college education will prepare me to be an* ~~hopefully someday I will become a recognized~~ attorney*,* ~~Which due to my college education~~ *w*ill bring me lifetime rewards.

Essay 98: You will graduate from college in the year 2001. How do you think your college education will prepare you for life in the next millennium?

Life in the next millennium will be all about more advanced technology. All aspects of our lives will be run by faster and more efficient computers. When I graduate from college in the year 2001, I will have a head start on those people who did not obtain a higher education. This schooling will only get me started thought. With the technology advancing as quickly as it is, I am sure that I will go back to school a few years after I have finished college and started in my career. I will study further and more often just to keep up with what is going on outside the classroom.

In the last millennium, jobs will be changing more rapidly along with the technology. A 30-year career in the same job, or even in the same field, will be long past. Many of the simple jobs in life will be eliminated, taken over by more efficient computers. The mailing systems on personal computers will become reliable enough to remove the need for the now reliable paper-mail system.

My college education will prepare me for life in the next millennium by guiding me away from linear thinking into becoming more flexible and creative by helping me to learn better oral and written communication skills, by teaching me how to become more analytical, more open in my thinking, more willing and able to accept changes which will come at an ever increasing rate.

By the time I graduate in 2001, telecommunications will be well on its way to converting from narrowband, linear, analog to digital over an almost infinite bandwidth in what George Gilder terms 'The Law of the Telecosm.' Communication in the next millennium will be individual and personal, while at the same time possible with almost every person on earth. Distance won't matter. Language barriers will not matter. Computers and new digital communications techniques will make it all possible. My college education must prepare me to function in such a world.

In college, I must learn to be self-sufficient and independent. Ever more powerful and faster computers will make this not only possible, but necessary. Work will become more independent.

I hope to obtain a degree in aeronautical engineering. One of my greatest goals in life is to be able to make transport aircraft safer. The technological advances on modern airplanes are phenomenal, yet airplane crashes still exist. I would like to help improve the safety and reliability of aircraft. I believe the size of aircraft no longer will continue to increase. People will demand personal point-to-point transportation. Making that possible will require smaller, faster, cheaper aircraft. My vision is to create an aircraft that will be totally controlled by computers and operate in a worldwide air traffic coordination system that precludes conflicts among all air vehicles.

When I graduate in the year 2001, I want to make a noticeable difference in the quality of people's lives. My college education will give me a jumping off point to my career. However, with the ever increasing rate of change, I recognize that I often will have to return to school.

Essay 98—Makeover: This essay didn't flow naturally. We shifted some sentences and deleted several sentences that were repetitive.

Life in the next millennium will be all about ~~more~~ advanced technology. All aspects of our lives

[Moved to second paragraph.]

will be run by faster and more efficient computers. [~~When I graduate from college in the year 2001,~~

[Delete this sentence

~~I'll have a head start on those people who~~ didn't ~~obtain a higher education. This schooling will~~

–understood.]

~~only get me started thought. With the technology advancing as quickly as it is, I am sure that I will~~

~~go back to school a few years after I have finished college and started in my career.~~] I will study

[Delete–understood.]   next

~~further and more often just to keep up with what is going on outside the classroom.~~ In the last

                                                                                   thirty

millennium, jobs will be changing ~~more~~ rapidly along with the technology. A ~~30~~-year career in the

            a thing of the

same job, or even in the same field, will be ~~long~~ past. Many of the simple jobs in life will be

eliminated, taken over by ~~more efficient~~ computers. The mailing systems on personal computers

                                                       current

will become reliable enough to remove the need for the ~~now reliable~~ paper-mail system.

[Moved from first paragraph.]   I'll

When I graduate from college in the year 2001, ~~I will~~ have a head start on those ~~people who~~

~~did not~~ *didn't* obtain a higher education. With ~~the~~ technology advancing as quickly as it is, ~~I am sure~~ *I'm* ~~I will~~ *I'll* go back to school a few years after I've finished college and started ~~in~~ *within* my career. My college

education will prepare me for life in the next millennium by guiding me away from linear thinking into ~~becoming~~ more flexible and creative ~~by helping me to learn~~ *dimensional thinking, thus helping me become* . *It will teach me* better oral and written communication skills, ~~by teaching me how to become~~ more analytical~~,~~ *thinking skills,* ~~more open in my thinking,~~

~~more willing~~ *will make me better* and able to accept changes ~~which~~ *that* will come at an ever increasing rate. I'll learn to be self-sufficient and independent. Ever more powerful and faster computers will make this not only possible, but necessary.

By the time I graduate in 2001, telecommunications will be well on its way to converting from narrowband, linear, analog to digital over an almost infinite bandwidth in what George Gilder terms "The Law of the Telecosm." Communication in the next millennium will be individual and personal, ~~while at the same time possible with almost every person on earth.~~ *continue to* *but on the worldwide scale.* Distance ~~will not~~ *won't* matter. Language ~~differences~~ *barriers* will ~~not matter.~~ *fall.* Computers and new digital communications techniques will make it all possible. My college education must prepare me to function in such a world.

[Moved to second paragraph.]
[~~In college, I must learn to be self-sufficient and independent. Ever more powerful and faster computers will make this not only possible, but necessary.~~] ~~Work will become more independent.~~

I hope to obtain a degree in aeronautical engineering. One of my greatest goals in life is to be able to make transport aircraft safer. The technological advances on modern airplanes are phenomenal, yet airplane crashes still ~~exist.~~ *happen.* I ~~would like~~ *want* to help improve the safety and reliability of aircraft. ~~I believe~~ *The* size of aircraft no longer ~~will continue to~~ *will* increase. People will demand personal point-to-point transportation. ~~Making that possible~~ *Meeting those demands* will require smaller, faster, cheaper aircraft. My vision is to create an aircraft that will be totally controlled by computers and operate in a worldwide air traffic coordination system that precludes conflicts among all air vehicles.

When I graduate in the year 2001, I want to make a noticeable difference in the quality of
be the springboard to a successful   [Delete—already

people's lives. My college education will ~~give me a jumping off point to my~~ career. ~~However, with~~
                                            ^
stated in first paragraph.]
~~the ever increasing rate of change, I recognize that I often will have to return to school.~~

Essay 99: Write an essay of 250 words or less on: The love of wisdom is the guiding principle of life.

What is wisdom? Merrian-Webster states that wisdom is the ability to make use of knowledge,

knowledge being the body of truth, information and principals, acquired by mankind. Marilyn vos

Savant says, "To acquire knowledge, one must study, but to acquire wisdom, one must observe."

Where do we get knowledge? As a man grows from childhood into adulthood, he acquires

knowledge through formal teaching and life experiences. Every culture has a common theme,

religion, a system of beliefs held to with intense faith. Man must have faith, faith in something that is

constant and beyond all change.

Throughout centuries, knowledge was shared from sacred scriptures. From the Christian Bible,

the Jewish Torah or the Muslim Koran, believers follow these principles of truths which provide a

spiritual guide through life. It is written in Psalms 32:8, "I will instruct thee and teach thee in the

way which thou shalt go; I will guide thee with mine eyes." A wise man uses knowledge well.

What do I do with this knowledge? In the Bible, Matthew 7:12 and Luke 6:31, "One should do to

others as he would have others do to him." This Gold Rule is known by some men. Man should

view life experiences as teaching situations. Man sets examples by his words and actions. Be

guided by knowledge and avoid many obstacles along life's road. In Proverbs 8:14, "Counsel is

mine, and sound wisdom; I am understanding, I have strength." These ethics enable man to function

successfully. God guides and counsels, but the decision will be our own.

Today's youth face constant pressure in favor of drugs, premarital sex, alcohol and other

destructive choices. Your faith's standards will be the guiding light in your actions. In Shakespeare's play, *Hamlet,* Polonius says to his son, Laertes, "To thy own self be true." Trust in your intuitive heart to do what is right.

Even before a newborn is thrust into the world he is gaining knowledge about himself and the world around him. Learning becomes a life-long process. Each human being is a complex creature composed of physical, emotional, intellectual, and spiritual attributes. Yet each individual is unique, confronting the world in a specific fashion. Each has talents, abilities, and gifts which should be shared with others.

As man grows through childhood, adolescence into adulthood, he is gaining knowledge and developing his future characteristics through the decisions he makes. Young adults mature through consistency and perseverance in daily relations with another. He develops inner qualities of balance and stability as he endures and overcomes difficulties and trials, which are merely stepping stones to perfection. As a young adult he should seek out and listen to his elders, those with the knowledge, who give sound counsel and love. Grave mistakes can be avoided if good counsel is patiently sought and regarded. Their wisdom can be the guiding lights of our life. We continue to bloom and flourish as we grow older.

Humans gain knowledge through formal teaching and book learning as well as informally through human contact and life experiences. All the book learning in the world means nothing unless it's shared for the benefit of mankind. Never hesitate to help another in need if it's within your power.

Man has a lifetime on earth to work, and apply himself to wisdom. He must be faithful and true to himself to wisdom. He must be faithful and true to himself so others see in his eyes; trust, love, reliability, and perfection.

Essay 99—Makeover: This essay is twice as long as it should be. We had to make some major deletions. The essay also contains too many quotations. Though this essay topic would lead you to think that the essay should be somewhat impersonal and philosophical, an essay must reveal who you are. The student's personality needs to shine through in this essay.

~~What is wisdom? Merrian-Webster states that wisdom is the ability to make use of knowledge;~~

~~knowledge being the body of truth, information, and principals, acquired by mankind. Marilyn vos~~

~~Savant says, "To acquire knowledge, one must study; but to acquire wisdom, one must observe."~~

~~Where do we get knowledge? As a man grows from childhood into adulthood, he acquires~~

~~knowledge through formal teaching and life experiences. Every culture has a common theme,~~

~~religion, a system of beliefs held to with intense faith. Man must have faith, faith in something that is~~

~~constant and beyond all change.~~

~~Throughout centuries, knowledge was shared from sacred scriptures. From the Christian Bible,~~

~~the Jewish Torah or the Muslim Koran, believers follow these principles of truths which provide a~~

~~spiritual guide through life. It is written in Psalms 32:8, "I will instruct thee and teach thee in the~~

~~way which thou shalt go; I will guide thee with mine eyes." A wise man uses knowledge well.~~

~~What do I so with this knowledge? In the Bible, Matthew 7:12 and Luke 6:31 "One should do to~~

~~others as he would have others do to him." This Gold Rule is known by some men. Man should view~~

~~life experiences as teaching situations. Man sets examples by his words and actions. Be guided by~~

~~knowledge and avoid many obstacles along life's road. In Proverbs 8:14, "Counsel is mine, and~~

~~sound wisdom; I am understanding, I have strength." These ethics enable man to function~~

~~successfully. God guides and counsels, but the decision will be our own.~~

~~Today's youth face constant pressure in favor of drugs, premarital sex, alcohol and other~~

~~destructive choices. Your faith's standards will be the guiding light in your actions. In Shakespeare's~~

~~play, *Hamlet,* Polonius says to his son, Laertes, "To thy own self be true." Trust in your intuitive heart~~

~~to do what is right.~~

[New opening sentence.]   *From the moment*

Wisdom is the ability to make use of knowledge. ~~Even before~~ a newborn is thrust into the

        , he's

world ~~he is~~ gaining knowledge about himself and the world around him. Learning becomes a life-

long process. Each human being is a complex creature composed of physical, emotional,

intellectual, and spiritual attributes. Yet each individual is unique, confronting the world in a

                                        that

specific fashion. Each has talents, abilities, and gifts ~~which~~ should be shared with others.

As ~~man~~ *a person* grows ~~through~~ *from* childhood / ~~adolescence~~ into adulthood, he ~~is gaining~~ *s* knowledge and

developing *s* his future characteristics through the decisions he makes. Young adults mature through

consistency and perseverance in daily relations with ~~another. He~~ *others. A young adult* develops inner qualities of

balance and stability as he endures and overcomes difficulties and trials / ~~which are merely stepping~~ [No one can achieve

perfection.]
~~stones to perfection. As a young adult~~ *H*e should seek out and listen to ~~his elders,~~ those ~~with the~~

~~knowledge,~~ who give sound counsel and love. ~~Grave~~ *M*istakes can be avoided if good counsel is

patiently sought and ~~regarded. Their~~ *followed. The* wisdom *of others* can be the guiding lights of our ~~life. We~~ *lives as we* continue to

~~bloom and~~ flourish ~~as we grow older.~~

Humans gain knowledge through formal teaching and book learning as well as informally

through human contact and life experiences. All the book learning in the world means nothing

unless it's shared for the benefit of mankind. Never hesitate to help another in need if it's within

your power.

Man has a lifetime on earth to work, and apply himself to wisdom. He must be faithful and true

to himself so others see ~~in his eyes;~~ trust, love, reliability, *and* ~~and perfection.~~ *in his eyes.* [No one can achieve perfection.]

Essay 100: After working his way through high school, James W. McLamore (co-founder of Burger King) labored for many years in various restaurants, while supporting his wife and four children. In 250 words or less, describe yourself and why you deserve to receive this scholarship.

There are many reasons why I deserve the Burger King Founders Award. My motivation and zest

for life is outstanding. Every experience whether it be good or bad, encourages me in someway. I

always turn a circumstance around for the better no matter how bad the situation is. Even if it's and

extremely horrible thing that happens I still learn form it and keep that lesson I learned in mind if

something similar happens. The motivation in my life makes me a hardworker.

Right now I'm a high school student working my way through school. At school, I'm in advanced placement and honors classes and maintaining and A average. Not only am I working one job, but I have two. One through the Health Science Technology Cooperative Education class at school where i work 16 hours a week Monday through Thursday. The second is a nighttime job where I work a few times a week. Why am I working two jobs you ask? Well, I'm trying to earn money to save for my future. Not only am I going to help pay for my college education, but I'm trying to buy a car, and create a nest egg for myself in the future. Although I maintain my wonderful grades, It is not always easy. It takes a lot of planning and organization to maintain a balance between everything. Working during the week leaves only my weekends for religious activities, service projects, family, and friends. I have found it is easier to incorporate things into one activity instead of trying to separate everything and do activities one at a time. For example, when I volunteer I always ask someone to come with me. It's a good way to share a touching experience with a good friend. I have also encouraged one of my friends to join my religious education class. In our class it helps us get closer not only to each other but others in the community through service projects in the church community. My philosophy is, since there are so many people and only one of me, I always invite someone to join me. Another way I have managed my time is getting my aunt to help me with studying for the SAT, which I plan to do well on with her help. This lets me keep in touch with her and the rest of the family.

In conclusion, I truly deserve the Burger King Founders Award. There's no doubt about the fact I'm a hardworker. The reason I work so hard is because I have set in stone my goals for the future. My parents, encounters with other people, and my service projects are my motivation. Not only do I work hard to please my parents and family, I work hard to accomplish my immediate goals, which are to be a good student in college, graduate in the top of my class, make a difference in my society in many ways, and become a successful dental hygienist. Clearly I'm a person that's very motivated and is a hard worker, and I am the student who deserves the Burger King Founders Award the most.

Essay 100—Makeover: The first paragraph of the original essay was discarded for this shorter version, which catches the reader's attention from the first word. Text in the rest of the essay was changed, deleted, and altered so that the final word count was 249 words. Now it's within the word count and is more memorable.

"Have it your way!" That's what the jingle said. Mr. McLamore firmly believed it and I do, too, because I've always lived that way. I have an unquenchable zest for life. I find the silver lining in every rain cloud and derive encouragement and joy from every experience.

~~There are many reasons why I deserve the Burger King Founders Award. My motivation and zest for life is outstanding. Every experience whether it be good or bad, encourages me in someway. I always turn a circumstance around for the better no matter how bad the situation is. Even if it's and extremely horrible thing that happens I still learn form it and keep that lesson I learned in mind if something similar happens. The motivation in my life makes me a hardworker.~~

I've always challenged myself by taking Advanced Placement and Honors classes, and ~~Right now I'm a high school student working my way through school. At school, I'm in advanced~~ *maintained an A average while working two jobs.* ~~placement and honors classes and maintaining and A average. Not only am I working one job, but I~~

One job is
~~have two.~~ One through the Health Science Technology Cooperative Education class at school ,
sixteen during the ; the second is a nighttime job where I work a few times a week.
where I work ~~16~~ hours a week ~~Monday through Thursday. The second is a nighttime job where I work a few times a week. Why am I working two jobs you ask? Well, I'm trying to earn money to~~

The jobs enable me to save money for which will prepare me
~~save for my future. Not only am I going to help pay for~~ my college education, ~~but I'm trying~~
to be a dental hygienist,
~~to~~ buy a car, and create a nest egg for my~~self in the future. Although I maintain my wonderful grades, It The jobs enable me to save money for my college education to prepare to become a dental hygienist, buy a car, and create a nest egg for my future.~~

It's not easy to strive for academic excellence, but my passion provides the impetus to always do my best. My time-management skills help me maintain a proper balance. Weekends are set aside for religious activities, service projects, friends, and, most importantly, family. It's also easier to incorporate several priorities at one time. For example, when I volunteer I always ask a friend to come with me. This way we ~~get~~ become closer ~~to each other~~ while working on a community service project. My aunt is helping me study for the SAT, allowing me to keep in touch with her and the rest of the family while working to improve my scores.

I'll do it my way, with your help!

Essay 101: Write a brief essay about a hero in your life.

The time is the summer before my fourth grade year. I was having a pretty boring summer until my Aunt Violet stepped in. She invited me to join her at Reagan Tech High School to do a science project. I said alright and I went with her. I thought this was going to be a basic project, but I was wrong. The project I was to do involved subjecting daphnia, a common water flea, to water pollutants. This project sounded exciting and indeed it was. When my aunt handed me a microscope she asked, "Well, what do you see, Danny?" I enthusiastically answered, "Wow! They're swimming around." It was at this moment I knew science and its wonders would become a subject of my fascination. Due to this instance, I consider her my hero for introducing me to the world of science.

What exactly is a Hero? Well, to me a Hero is someone who discovers something special inside of a person and brings this gift out into the world. A hero enables a person to succeed at what he or she is really good at. This hero not only helps other people, but strives to encourage other people who have hidden talents.

Heroes don't have to be famous. They can be your next door neighbor or your teacher. Anyone who takes the time to help someone succeed in life is a hero. Heroes are everywhere waiting to discover the next Einstein, Watson, or Pauling.

[Three paragraphs have been deleted in order to include the concluding paragraph below.]
A hero enables someone to succeed. My aunt Violet has definitely shown he light for many of her students as well as myself. She has discovered those with hidden talent, shown them their options, and lead them down the right paths to success. Many Heros like my aunt have done the same, but everyone of them has their own unique way of bringing out the hidden talent of the children of today.

Essay 101—Makeover: With just some minor changes, this essay was now stronger.

I found my hero , *though I'd known her all my life.*
~~The time is~~ the summer before ~~my~~ fourth grade / ~~year.~~ I was having a ~~pretty~~ boring summer until

my Aunt Violet stepped in. She invited me to join her at Reagan Tech High School to do a science

though *it*
project. ~~I said alright and~~ I went with her, I thought ~~this~~ was going to be a basic project. ~~but I was~~

exposing
~~wrong.~~ The project ~~I was to do~~ involved ~~subjecting~~ *Daphnia*, a common water flea, to water

Pointing toward
pollutants. ~~This project sounded exciting and indeed it was.~~ ~~When my aunt handed me~~ a

microscope, she asked, "Well, what do you see, Danny?" I enthusiastically answered, "Wow! They're
At that *not only*
swimming around." ~~It was at this~~ moment I knew science and its wonders would become a subject

but also my career path. This is why I consider my Aunt Violet my hero.
of ~~my~~ fascination, ~~Due to this instance, I consider her my hero for introducing me to the world of~~

~~science.~~

h *A hero*
What exactly is a ~~H~~ero? ~~Well, to me a Hero~~ is someone who discovers something special inside

others *others*
~~of a person~~ and brings this gift out into the world. A hero enables ~~a person~~ to succeed at what

they do best and makes sure others use their talents to the fullest.
~~he orshe is really good at.~~ ~~This hero not only helps other people, but strives to encourage other~~

~~people who have hidden talents.~~

Heroes don't have to be famous. They can be your next door neighbor or your teacher. Anyone

who takes the time to help someone succeed in life is a hero. Heroes are everywhere, waiting to

discover the next Einstein, Watson, or Pauling.

[Already said—delete.] *A* *the* *to*
~~A hero enables someone to succeed.~~ My ~~a~~unt Violet has definitely shown ~~he~~ light ~~for~~ many of her

to me.
students as well as ~~myself.~~ She has discovered those with hidden talent, shown them their options,

led
and ~~lead~~ them down the ~~right~~ paths to success. ~~Many Heroes like my aunt have done the same, but~~

bring *today's*
~~everyone of them has their own unique way of bringing~~ out the hidden talent of ~~the~~ children. ~~of~~

[The student added this concluding sentence to the final draft.]
~~today.~~ *Aunt Violet isn't only a remarkable person, she's one of those heroes.*

Essay 102: Imagine you are a hero or heroine for one day during any time period and under any circumstances. Write a creative essay describing your experience. Limit the essay to approximately 500 words.

These have got to be the heaviest bags I've ever carried, I thought to myself in sweaty drudgery. My bifocals sneak their way down my nose on this warm day. The sun is causing my face to bead with sweat. The Christmas season has covers the streets with glitter and holly, every street lamp is decorated as a candy canes. Many bags of elaborate dresses needing hemlines and alterations tug on my aching shoulders. They hang from my arms like two dead weights. My arthritic hands dread another night of sewing overtime. My fingers remain cramped from last nights work. They plead for a night of rest. I look down at my shoes. Blisters on ten toes scream at me to stop walking. I take another step.

Finally I reach Cleveland Avenue and wait for the bus to stop Court Square. Moments seem drawn out to hours standing on the busy sidewalk. Finally, I smell the exhaust cloud creeping into my nose. The bus pulls over and I climb aboard taking my first steps toward rest. My weary legs carry me to the first available seat. The tension settles over the bus like a heavy lid as I sit down. I feel the piercing eyes glaring at me. The glaring eyes slowly penetrate my skin.

Creeping to the next stop, the bus brakes squeal and hiss incessantly. My grandmother always said not to follow the crowd. That white man, that just entered the bus, he didn't mind standing. He looked like a good person. I watch one bead of sweat slowly follow a trail down his forehead onto his nostril and picking up speed it fell to the floor. The driver yells, "Niggers to the back." I remember the driver. We met twelve years ago. I remember refusing to walk around the bus to enter through the back. I recognize the same smirk of enjoyment that covered his face. Why should I have to get up and move? The bus driver swerves the bus to the curb. I feel his anger.

My tired body will not leave the forbidden chair. I won't be pushed out of my seat. As I watch the driver approach, I think: What will it be this time? I wonder if he recognizes his old friend. The smell of authority enters my nose. It was nothing more than the coffee and fried onions. I faintly remember the old smell. The driver demands I move to the back. He recognizes me, I am glad he remembers. When I do not move, he storms off the bus. I want to go home.

Time is tweezing me away with tweezers pulling tiny hairs out one by one. I thought he would be back by now. Meanwhile, I thought about what I had done. What am I doing? My hands started to feel nervously cold. Why are people starting to stare?

I sit with sweaty hands, praying to God for protection. I asked God forgiveness for everything. Then I looked over at a white child staring at me. She was innocent. She was scared. Clutching for her mammy so tight with fear. I realize that it is I who spread the fear. In all the ruckus, she starts to cry. The tears I intentionally gave her. I wanted to gather her in my arms, cradling the falling tears into one cup with mine. The cup would overflow with hope, tears of hope.

I'm staring out of the window. The surrounding sights burn permanent pictures in my mind. I'm looking out at the thronging people and a police officer making his way to the bus. I patted the drop of perspiration starting to roll down off my cheekbone. I watched the people disperse.

The blue uniform hat bobs across the parked vehicles. The driver follows like a lost hungry puppy, expecting food and praise. Some relentless something keeps me in my seat. I smile at the officer, as he places the handcuffs around my wrists. My hands are wrinkled. The skin sags around the cold metal. I love my grandmother. Someone says I am a hero. I think I am really tired.

Essay 102—Makeover: This essay is almost 200 words over the limit. The task is to cut the essay, without detracting from the story. This new version is 499 words in length and reads more smoothly.

These have got to be the heaviest bags I've ever carried, ~~I thought to myself in sweaty drudgery.~~
My bifocals ~~sneak their way~~ *slip* down my nose ~~on this warm day.~~ The sun ~~is causing my face to bead~~ *causes beads of sweat to form on my face.*
[Irrelevant—delete.]
~~with sweat. The Christmas season has covers the streets with glitter and holly, every street lamp is~~
~~decorated as a candy canes. Many~~ *The* bags of elaborate dresses *, filled with* needing ~~hemlines~~ *hemming* and *other* alterations tug on
my aching shoulders, ~~They hang from my arms~~ like two dead weights. My arthritic hands dread

another night of sewing overtime. ~~My fingers remain cramped from last nights work.~~ They plead for *wordlessly*

a night of rest. ~~I look down at my shoes.~~ Blisters on ~~ten~~ toes scream at me to stop walking/ I take *The b* *my* *silently* *, yet*

another step.

Finally I reach Cleveland Avenue and wait for the bus ~~to stop Court Square.~~ Moments seem

drawn out to hours ~~standing~~ on the busy sidewalk. ~~Finally, I smell the exhaust cloud creeping into~~ *as I stand*

~~my nose.~~ The bus pulls over and I climb aboard taking my first steps toward rest. My weary legs

carry me to the first available seat. ~~The~~ tension settles over the bus like a heavy lid as I sit down. ~~I~~ *T*

feel the piercing ~~eyes glaring~~ at me. ~~The glaring eyes slowly penetrate my skin.~~ *E* *glare*

~~Creeping to~~ the next stop, the ~~bus~~ brakes squeal and hiss ~~incessantly~~. ~~My grandmother always~~ *At*

~~said not to follow the crowd.~~ That white man/ ~~that just entered the bus, he didn't~~ mind standing. *A* *enters.* *He doesn't seem to*

~~He looked like a good person.~~ I watch ~~one~~ bead of sweat slowly ~~follow a trail~~ down his forehead *A* *trails*

onto his ~~nostril and picking~~ up speed ~~it fell~~ to the floor. [New paragraph.] *nose, then picks* *as it falls*

~~The driver yells,~~ "Niggers to the back/" *, the driver yells.* [New paragraph.]

I remember ~~the~~ driver. ~~We met twelve years ago. I remember refusing~~ to walk around the bus to *this* *Twelve years ago, I refused*

enter through the back. I recognize the same smirk of enjoyment ~~that covered~~ his face. Why should *on*

I have to get up and move? The bus driver swerves the bus to the curb. ~~I feel his anger.~~

My tired body ~~will not leave~~ the forbidden ~~chair. I won't be pushed out of my seat.~~ As I watch the *won't relinquish* *seat.* [You're hardly *foe.* a friend.]

driver ~~approach~~, I think/ What will it be this time? I wonder if he recognizes his old ~~friend. The~~ *approaches* *,*

~~smell of authority enters my nose. It was nothing more than the coffee and fried onions. I faintly~~

~~remember the old smell.~~ The driver demands I move to the back. ~~He recognizes me, I am glad he~~

~~remembers.~~ When I ~~do not~~ move, he storms off the bus. ~~I want to go home.~~ *don't* *A crowd gathers outside the bus.*

Time is ~~tweezing me~~ away ~~with~~ tweezers pulling tiny hairs out one by one. ~~I thought he would~~ *pinching* *at me like*

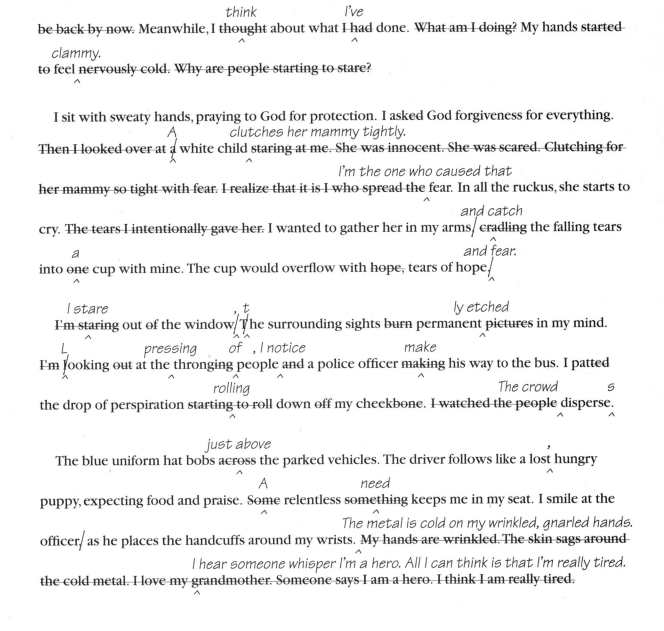

think *I've*
~~be back by now.~~ Meanwhile, I ~~thought~~ about what ~~I had~~ done. ~~What am I doing?~~ My hands ~~started~~
clammy.
~~to feel~~ ~~nervously cold. Why are people starting to stare?~~

I sit with sweaty hands, praying to God for protection. ~~I asked God forgiveness for everything.~~
A *clutches her mammy tightly.*
~~Then I looked over at~~ a white child ~~staring at me. She was innocent. She was scared. Clutching for~~

I'm the one who caused that
~~her mammy so tight with fear. I realize that it is I who spread the fear.~~ In all the ruckus, she starts to

and catch
cry. ~~The tears I intentionally gave her.~~ I wanted to gather her in my arms, ~~cradling~~ the falling tears

a *and fear.*
into ~~one~~ cup with mine. The cup would overflow with ~~hope,~~ tears of hope,

I stare *, t* *ly etched*
~~I'm staring~~ out of the window, ~~The~~ surrounding sights ~~burn~~ permanent ~~pictures~~ in my mind.
L *pressing* *of , I notice* *make*
~~I'm~~ looking ~~out~~ at the ~~thronging~~ people ~~and~~ a police officer ~~making~~ his way to the bus. I ~~patted~~
rolling *The crowd* *s*
the drop of perspiration ~~starting to roll~~ down ~~off~~ my cheekbone. ~~I watched the people~~ disperse.

just above *,*
The blue uniform hat bobs ~~across~~ the parked vehicles. The driver follows like a lost hungry
A *need*
puppy, expecting food and praise. ~~Some~~ relentless ~~something~~ keeps me in my seat. I smile at the
The metal is cold on my wrinkled, gnarled hands.
officer, as he places the handcuffs around my wrists. ~~My hands are wrinkled. The skin sags around~~
I hear someone whisper I'm a hero. All I can think is that I'm really tired.
~~the cold metal. I love my grandmother. Someone says I am a hero. I think I am really tired.~~

Essay 103: Write an essay between 300 and 400 words in length about a topic that is important to you and gives us insight into who you are.

Recently, our local school district made some big changes to their student dress code for middle and high school students. Some of the changes are the banning of visible body piercing jewelry, the banning of specifically "sagging" or "bagging" pants, stating that hair must be neat and clean and not have unconventional multi-colored or spiked hair. Two other changes are that appropriate footwear must be worn, which means no steel toed boots, and the other change being that shorts are now prohibited in grades 6-12. And finally, the big one out of the new changes, is that shirts have to be tucked in regardless of the situation.

Sometimes a dress code will make good changes that will help a student in their daily extremely fun learning experiences, also known as school. I think that the students would agree that they love the new dress code for numerous reasons. For instance, now that students can't wear shorts, they are now able to fully understand geometric equations because their legs don't become frozen and cause the brain to freeze as well. Also, the banning of visible body piercing has now unlocked the door to understanding the great works of literature that had once seemed impossible to comprehend. And now that students may not dye their hair, there has been an emergence of great new scientists. Now that our football team can't wear baggy pants, they have finally found a way to start winning, at least almost winning. And 97.8% of the students polled all agree that the rule on tucking in the shirts is the reason why they all made the straight A Honor Roll.

Who would have ever thought that little dress code changes would finally open the eyes of the students, and make them succeed. One high school staff worker, who has declined to make his name known to the public, has gone on the record by saying, "I always knew these kids were smart, but now with the new dress code, we are finally able to unleash the brain power that baggy pants and untucked shirts has been holding down for many, many years." I guess that he is right, and students all over the campus seem to agree, with no arguments.

Essay 103—Makeover: This student's tongue-in-cheek tone is both funny and insightful. We suggested just a few minor changes.

Recently, our local school district made some ~~big~~ changes to ~~their~~ student dress code for middle and high school students. ~~Some of~~ The changes ~~are the~~ *included* banning ~~of~~ visible body piercing jewelry, ~~the~~ *and a rule* banning ~~of specifically~~ "sagging" or "bagging" pants, stating that hair must be neat and clean and not , ~~have unconventional~~ multicolored or spiked ~~hair.~~ *Another* ~~Two other~~ changes ~~are that~~ *concerns* appropriate footwear :

One change that hits hard in Texas is
~~must be worn, which means~~ no steel toed boots~~/~~ ~~and the other change being~~ that shorts are now

six through twelve. *F* *biggest* *must always*
prohibited in grades ~~6-12.~~ ~~And~~ finally, the ~~big one out of the new~~ changes is that shirts ~~have to~~ be

tucked in ~~regardless of the situation.~~

Sometimes a dress code ~~will make good~~ changes ~~that will~~ help a student in their daily extremely *s* *,*

Some *may enjoy*
fun learning experiences, also known as school. ~~I think that the~~ students ~~would agree that they love~~

a variety of *they're*
the new dress code for ~~numerous~~ reasons. For instance, now that students can't wear shorts, ~~they~~

aren't *, causing*
~~are now~~ able to fully understand geometric equations because their legs ~~don't become~~ frozen ~~and~~

B *jewelry* *flung open*
~~cause the brain to freeze as well.~~ ~~Also, the~~ ~~banning~~ of visible body piercing has now ~~unlocked~~ the

door to understanding the great works of literature that had once seemed impossible to
With hair dyeing banned, there's
comprehend. ~~And now that students may not dye their hair, there has~~ been an emergence of great

they've
new scientists. Now that our football team can't wear baggy pants, ~~they have~~ finally found a way to

—well, *According to a student poll,* *agreed*
start winning~~/~~ at least almost winning. ~~And~~ 97.8% ~~of the students polled all agree~~ that ~~the rule on~~
their *they're on*
tucking in ~~the~~ shirts is the reason ~~why they all made~~ the straight A Honor Roll.

students' eyes and minds
Who would have ~~ever~~ thought that little dress code changes would finally open ~~the eyes of the~~
? *wished to remain anonymous, said,*
~~students,~~ and make them succeed~~/~~ One high school staff worker, who ~~has declined to make his~~

~~name known to the public, has gone on the record by saying,~~ "I always knew these kids were smart~~/~~
W *we're*
~~but now~~ ~~w~~ith the new dress code, ~~we are~~ finally able to unleash the brain power that baggy pants
have *back* *He must be* *because*
and untucked shirts ~~has~~ been holding ~~down~~ for ~~many,~~ many years." ~~I guess that he is~~ right, ~~and~~
agreed.
students all over the campus ~~seem to agree, with no arguments.~~

[This next paragraph was added as a conclusion.]

Our new dress code will surely bring academic accolades to our schools and students. One

the

last advantage of a new dress code is that class reunions will no longer be necessary because my

,   *recipients.*

peers will be able to gather at the next Nobel Prize Award Ceremony where we'll all be ~~receiving~~

~~*awards.*~~

Essay 104: Describe the special, creative, or challenging activities that you have accomplished in your personal, community, or academic life. Unique endeavors are specific activities or efforts completed in the past which demonstrated a special or creative ability. Examples of unique endeavors include: using a special talent to start or expand a program; taking or making an opportunity to visit or live away from your home community; or completing a special course of study. Simply being a member of a club or honor society or achieving a class rank is not considered a unique endeavor. (Discover Card Tribute Award)

I have always found that writing has come easy for me. I have enjoyed writing for as long as I can remember. I would even write poetry back in the third grade. The reason I enjoy writing is because it lets me put all of my feelings on any given subject on paper so that a person can see things through my eyes. When I get assigned an essay in school, my eyes light up because I know that I have the opportunity to showcase my writing abilities. I enjoy writing so much that I have aspirations to enter the field of journalism, both broadcast and print. Through my internship at KENS-TV, I am allowed to write the scripts for some stories that the sportscasters use on-air.

Essay 104—Makeover: This essay tells, it doesn't show. This was the first of four essays the student had to write for this competition. Below is the edited essay. The three subsequent essays were written after the student received and implemented this critique.

I'm an artist. My artwork, however, isn't on the canvas, but on paper. I don't use paintbrushes, but rather a pen or a keyboard. I paint a different kind of picture, a picture of a sea of words that floats together to make my expressions visible as they wash ashore on the printed page. While some artists use chalk, clay, or oils, I use satire, humor, and the facts to highlight, mute, and form a cohesiveness in the stories I tell.

Ever since the first grade, I've been expressing my thoughts through poetry and other writings *that* that often left my teachers saying ~~how~~ I was vastly ahead of my peers in writing. In high school, *I've* ~~I have~~ taken my writing a step further from just writing essays in class to being a *general* ~~main~~ news and sports reporter for my school's newspaper. I also cover the ROTC Unit in the paper because the Naval Science Instructor feels that I know the corps well enough to show others on the campus what we do. This has let me become the Public Affairs Petty Officer of our Unit, and has also helped me to showcase my writing abilities. [Redundant—delete.] ~~On the newspaper, I am a lead reporter who covers all types of stories~~ I enjoy interviewing people for my columns and ~~enjoy~~ helping ~~to~~ put the entire paper together. When my fellow reporters and I are planning *who'll* ~~who will~~ get which stories for the upcoming issue, and the chief editor tells me that *I'm* ~~I am~~ going to have to fill three whole pages, my eyes light up / *with excitement,* ~~and I become excited,~~ and I can't wait to get started on all of my assignments.

At my KENS-TV internship, I often get the *opportunity* ~~chance~~ to help write the stories that *and are posted on the station's web site.* the broadcasters use on the air / *I'm* When ~~I am~~ at the news station *'s* ~~in the~~ control room *sitting with* ~~where~~ the directors *, it's thrilling* ~~are sitting, I feel happy and excited~~ to *hear* ~~see~~ a reporter *speak* ~~say~~ what *I've* ~~I have~~ written.

To me, writing is a way to share the news with everyone. I hope to take my special talent and use it to become a broadcast journalist and ~~also~~ a print journalist in college, and after college.

Essay 105: Describe the special, creative, or challenging activities that you have accomplished in your personal, community, or academic life. Unique endeavors are specific activities or efforts completed in the past which demonstrated a special or creative ability. Examples of unique endeavors include: using a special talent to start or expand a program; taking or making an opportunity to visit or live away from your home community; or completing a special course of study. Simply being a member of a club or honor society or achieving a class rank is not considered a unique endeavor. (Discover Card Tribute Award)

When I was watching the news one night many years ago, I realized that I wanted to be a sports reporter. Flash forward to July 19, 1999. That is the day I first set foot into the newsroom of KENS-

TV to begin my internship. The experience was nerve wracking and surreal. Seeing the way that every person in the newsroom was working together in order to make the show happen, really fired my desires to become a broadcast journalist. When I saw one of my idols of the sports broadcasting world, Dan Cook, it seemed as if I was dreaming. What business does a sixteen year old high school student have working side-by-side with a man who's been a journalist for over half a century? The answer is all of the business in the world because I'm a hard worker who has the motivation and willingness to give whatever it takes to follow in the footsteps of such a gifted and dedicated journalist.

Essay 105—Makeover: This is a good essay, but it doesn't show the reader exactly what the student's experience entailed. The student needed to relate his duties and responsibilities. The student added the final paragraph after the first critique.

When I was watching the news one night many years ago, I realized that I wanted to be a sports reporter. Flash forward to July 19, 1999. ~~That is~~ *That's* the day I first set foot ~~into~~ the newsroom of KENS–TV to begin my internship. The experience was nerve wracking and surreal. Seeing ~~the way that~~ *how* every person in the newsroom ~~was~~ work*ed*ing together in order to make the show happen, ~~really~~ fired my desires to become a broadcast journalist. When I saw one of my idols of the sports broadcasting world, Dan Cook, it seemed as if I was dreaming. What business does a sixteen-year-old high school student have working side-by-side with a man who's been a journalist for over half a century? The answer is all ~~of~~ the business in the world because I'm a hard worker who has the motivation and willingness to give whatever it takes to follow in the footsteps of such a gifted and dedicated journalist.

I've
~~*I have*~~ *worked at KENS-TV since that day*, *spending* ~~*I work*~~ *twenty-five hours every week.* ~~*My duties involve*~~ *checking the wire,* ~~*making sure tapes are cued,*~~ *cuing tapes, writing headers and scripts for the sports-casters, and even helping the producer with his responsibilities. The station's sportscasters have all commented on the fact that they didn't begin participating in internships until they were*

undergraduate juniors. Generally, the station doesn't recruit high school students as interns, but

when I called and made all the required arrangements with my high school counselor and

journalism teacher, all that was left was to get started. At the end of the year, if all goes well, my

internship will turn into a paid internship in which I hope to continue participating as long as

possible.

Essay 106: Describe volunteer work (unpaid) you have done to benefit individuals, groups, non-profit organizations, agencies, schools, or the community at large. Simply attending regular meetings of organizations does NOT qualify as community service. You have two choices in the way you describe community service in your criteria statement: either tell about the activities you have accomplished OR about the hours you have contributed. Do NOT tell us about BOTH activities and hours. Addressing both choices will result in disqualification.

On Saturday mornings, most teenagers are sleeping late after staying up late on Friday night. But for at least one Saturday a month, I am the exception to the rule. I get up early with a good cause in mind, and on the drive over to the Coca-Cola Bottling Company auditorium, I think about how the effort I put in helps those who are less fortunate. I volunteer five hours on Saturday morning, once a month to help collect food for the San Antonio Food Bank, and to date have helped gather more than 7,000 pounds of food for the needy families in San Antonio and surrounding areas.

When I arrive at the Bottling Center, I am ready to work, because I am blessed with being able to always have food on my table. The time I put in is helpful, because if no one were to volunteer than the job wouldn't get done.

Sometimes my friends think I am crazy when I can't stay out late on Friday's with them, but they understand when I tell them that they don't realize how fortunate they are. Even though I do not get monetary payment, I do get paid with the thought that I have helped make it possible for those who are poor to eat a good meal they otherwise would not have had, and that gives me an immense satisfaction.

My helping with the Food Bank isn't just limited to the volunteer time I donate through College Resource Materials, but also through my ROTC Unit. At school, I always donate the most boxes full of food, but I don't do it to show off. I do it to help as many people as possible. My efforts motivate

my fellow cadets, and sometimes a little motivation is all that's needed to get started on a project

that will ultimately be fun, and helpful to many families.

I will never stop helping the Food Bank, because there will always be those who need the food

to survive.

Essay 106—Makeover: This is a good essay that needed just a few minor changes.

At seven o'clock on
~~On~~ Saturday mornings, most teenagers are sleeping late after staying up late on Friday night. But

I'm
for at least one Saturday a month, ~~I am~~ the exception to the rule. I get up early with a good cause in

mind, and on the drive over to the Coca-Cola Bottling Company auditorium, I think about how the

effort I put in helps those who are less fortunate. I volunteer ~~five hours on Saturday morning~~, once
,
a month to help collect food for the San Antonio Food Bank, and to date have helped gather more

than 7,000 pounds of food for the needy families in San Antonio and surrounding areas.

I'm   *I'm*
When I arrive at the Bottling Center, ~~I am~~ ready to work, because ~~I am~~ blessed ~~with being able~~ to

always have food on my table. The time I put in is helpful, because if no one were to volunteer ~~than~~
,
the job wouldn't get done.

I'm
Sometimes my friends think ~~I am~~ crazy when I can't stay out late on Friday/s with them, but they

don't
understand when I tell them that they don't realize how fortunate they are. Even though I ~~do not~~

my reward is knowing I've made
get monetary payment, ~~I do get paid with the thought that I have helped make~~ it possible for those
who're experiencing financial problems   *wouldn't*
~~who are poor~~ to eat a good meal they otherwise ~~would not~~ have had, and that gives me an immense

satisfaction.

My helping with the Food Bank isn't just limited to the volunteer time I donate through College

Resource Materials, but also through my ROTC Unit. At school, I always donate the most boxes full

of food, but I don't do it to show off. I do it to help as many people as possible. My efforts motivate my fellow cadets, and sometimes a little motivation is all that's needed to get started on a project that will ultimately be fun, and helpful to many families.

I'll
~~I will~~ never stop helping the Food Bank, because ~~there will~~ *there'll* always be those who need the food to survive.

Essay 107: Describe your ability to guide, inspire, direct, or set examples for others and demonstrate how you've accomplished these in your personal, community, or academic life. Use examples that show continuing leadership, not just a brief, one-time-only experience. (Discover Card Tribute Award)

In the ROTC Unit at John Marshall High School, I have played an important part since my high school freshman year. I entered the Corps highly motivated, and earned numerous awards and recognitions for my efforts in community service, participation, outstanding conduct, and Cadet of the Six Weeks. I was promoted to Petty Officer Third Class, which is the highest achievement a freshman can earn. During my freshman year, I was selected the first Squad Leader, as one of the best cadets in the entire platoon, and was instilled with and successfully utilized many leadership opportunities. I am still Squad Leader and I have earned the respect of the cadets, regardless of what grade they were in school. I was on the Academic Team during my freshman and sophomore years, winning numerous awards, including several first place medals for winning academic meets.

This year, I decided not to participate in the Academic team, but rather to take on leadership responsibility as the Public Affairs Petty Officer. My job is to "sell" the Corps to other students, show all of the good things the Corps does, and to show how our Unit is always available to help while leading by example.

Next year, I hope to be appointed the Senior Public Affairs Officer, which will enable me to not only write articles about the Corps in the newspaper, but also be instrumental in training students to be future Public Affairs Petty Officer or Officer. I have done a lot of interesting things in NJROTC at Marshall High School and learned a lot about leadership.

Essay 107—Makeover: When using acronyms such as ROTC, students must spell out the organization's full name with the acronym in parenthesis on the first mention, but may then use the acronym alone thereafter.

The Naval Junior Reserve Officer Training Corps (NJROTC) has ~~In the ROTC Unit at John Marshall High School, I have~~ played an important part *in my life, as I have been in NJROTC* ~~since my high school freshman year.~~ *As a freshman,* I entered the Corps highly motivated, and earned numerous awards and recognitions for my efforts in community service, participation, outstanding conduct, and Cadet of the Six Weeks. *also* I was promoted to Petty Officer Third Class, which is the highest achievement a freshman can earn. *Throughout* ~~During~~ my *first* ~~freshman~~ year, I was selected the first Squad Leader, as one of the best cadets in the entire platoon, and was instilled with and successfully utilized many leadership opportunities. *Squad Leader to this day, I've* ~~I am still Squad Leader and I have~~ earned the respect of *other* ~~the~~ cadets, regardless of *their rank or year* ~~what grade they were~~ in school. I *also partook in* ~~was on~~ the Academic Team during my freshman and sophomore years, winning numerous awards, including several first-place medals for winning academic meets.

At the beginning of my junior year, ~~This year,~~ I decided not to participate in the Academic team, but rather to take on leadership responsibility as the Public Affairs Petty Officer. My job is to "sell" the Corps to other students, show*ing* all of the good things the Corps does, and ~~to show~~ how our Unit is always available to help while leading by example.

Next year, I hope to be appointed the Senior Public Affairs Officer, which will enable me to not only write articles about the Corps in the newspaper, but also be instrumental in training students to be future Public Affairs Petty Officer*s* *Public Affairs* or Officers. [Delete–this tells, it doesn't show.] ~~I have done a lot of interesting things in NJROTC~~ [New sentence.] ~~at Marshall High School and learned a lot about~~ leadership. *Since I come* *Coming* from a military family, my maternal grandfather dedicated his life to his *thirty*~~30~~-year Navy career, earning Senior Chief Petty Officer, the *role* leadership aspect came naturally to me. Having always wanted to follow in his footsteps as a leader, I've traveled an interesting journey in NJROTC at Marshall High School, and I'm well on the road to earning my stripes.

Essay 108: This is a unique essay. The student's parents were instructed to write an essay about their student.

As parents of Yvonne Martinez, we are very proud of her accomplishments.

She has self-confidence and is opinionate, with high moral standards. Yvonne from a very young age developed strong disciplinary study habits which have contined through her school years and has shown to be very preseptive beyond her years.

Yvonne is a friendly young lady who is sensitive to those around her. She enjoys challenges which she uses towards her growth.

Yvonne has kept a journal of quotations, sayings, and many other things of interest to her, she loves writing and has written almost a book of poems. In middle school she joined the speech and debate team and has gain so much poise as she presents. In high school she has participated in Poetry and Prose events winning many Honors. Yvonne is a leader and has taken responsibility for the team's support and growth.

In her first year in the State Youth and Government Conference, she was elected the Chief Editor for the year 1995-1996 Conference and was a Representative to the National Youth Government Conference held in Black Mountain, North Carolina this past summer. She felt as we did that it was a great experience and gave her such a good insight of our government.

It is our believe that Yvonne will be a great asset to your university and will achieve her intended goals.

Essay 108—Makeover: We suggested that the parents recall the first moment their daughter came into their lives. This is the revised version, which doesn't show all the editing.

I remember the moment I held Yvonne for the first time. Though my heart was full of love, I didn't realize my tiny bundle of joy would grow into such an accomplished young lady, and in what seemed to be the blink of an eye.

As parents of Yvonne Martinez, we're proud of her accomplishments, from her first hesitant steps to all her high school endeavors. She has self-confidence and remains firm in her convictions, with high moral standards. From a very young age, Yvonne developed strong, disciplined study habits which have continued throughout her school years and *she* has demonstrated perception beyond her years.

Since kindergarten, Yvonne has always been friendly and sensitive to those around her. She faces challenges with courage *and* determination, and always uses what she learns to enhance her growth. Yvonne knows that success comes from trying.

Yvonne went from reading about Jane and Spot to writing almost a complete book of poetry. [Revised and moved from end of paragraph.] She has participated in poetry and prose events in high school and won many honors. She keeps a journal of quotations, her thoughts, and many items of interest to her. In middle school, she joined the Speech and Debate Team and has gained poise and confidence. Due to her natural leadership abilities, she's taken responsibility for the team's support and growth. [Moved to become second sentence in paragraph.] ~~She has participated in poetry and prose events in high school and won many honors. She keeps a journal of quotations, her thoughts, and many items of interest to her.~~

In her first year of participation in the State Youth and Government Conference, she was elected Chief Editor for the 1995–1996 Conference. She was also a representative to the National Youth and Government Conference held in Black Mountain, North Carolina, this past summer. She felt, as we did, that it was a great experience and gave her new insight into our government.

[It's your essay; who else would believe it?] ~~It's our belief that~~ Yvonne will be a great asset to your university. ~~I must be honest and say that in a year~~ *W*hen she leaves for her first day of college, I'll remember her first day of school. Just as *Yvonne succeeded in elementary and secondary school,* ~~on that day many years ago, I know~~ she'll achieve her goals and become a success *postsecondary*.

Essay 109: Write an essay about your student which will enable the committee members to better know your student.

We are writing this letter of recommendation on behalf of our daughter, Mary Smith. Mary is a very determined young lady that has always made us proud. She has made the honor roll for twelve years. She is also an accomplished athlete. Mary has participated in sports since the fourth grade. She has played softball, ran track and excels in her love, volleyball.

Besides her academic skills and athletic ability, she has been able to volunteer over 200 hours of community service.

Mary has received many honors and awards. She is a member of the National Honor Society, All-American Scholars, National Science Merit Award, U.S. Achievement Academy plus many more. Mary has been listed two years in a roll on the "Who's Who Among High School Students."

Mary is a very outgoing, responsible, and lovable young lady.

Mary's goal is to receive her law degree and become an FBI agent.

Essay 109—Makeover: This essay repeated information that was provided elsewhere in the application. The school wanted the parents' perspective. We suggested the parents begin again.

Our daughter, Mary Anne Smith came into this world on February 28, 1982. From that moment *, she's* on ~~she has~~ brought great joy to our lives. As a child she showed great enthusiasm for life and a deep determination to succeed.

we've As Mary Anne's parents, ~~we have~~ tried to instill high morals and self-confidence ~~in her everday life.~~ From an early age Mary Anne has always been able to make friends and develop long lasting relationships.

Always a self-starter, she's ~~Mary Anne has always been a self-starter and has~~ learned to develop ~~very~~ strong study skills. *at* Starting in ~~her~~ sixth grade she challenged herself by taking pre-engineering classes ~~in~~ local universities during ~~her~~ summer months and honor classes throughout her school years.

She faces every
~~Mary Anne has faced many~~ challenges with courage and has utilized her experiences to enhance

undertaken

her growth. One of the most recent challenges she's ~~endeavored~~ is taking fifteen hours of college

credit in her senior year; despite the additional workload and rigorous demand, she's excelling in all

classes   *as well as*   *have*

of them / Her leadership abilities ~~not only~~ in school ~~but~~ in athletics ~~has~~ earned her many honors and

awards.

~~We feel~~ Mary Anne will be a great asset to your university and will one day achieve her goals.

Essay 110: This essay was written for a law school application. After making the appropriate changes were made, the essay was cut down to 1,000 words.

Although I was unable to complete my education as early as I would have wanted, the many

lessons, challenges and accomplishments I have conquered now give me the resourcefulness,

resiliency and traits that will give greater serve me as an attorney. What has led me to this belief is

growing up in a traditional Hispanic family made me rich in culture and values. This richness was

offset by low self-esteem and self-worth.

My mother left school in the eleventh grade to help raise her brothers and sisters, and my father

left school after the fourth grade to help support his family as well. My parent's plan for my future

was that I graduate from high school and find a good man to marry and support me and a family.

My high school counselor confirmed this by advising me that was the appropriate track for

Hispanic females. I was faced with a paramount dilemma: follow my dream to achieve a

professional career and attain self confidence or resign to the destiny that my parents had in mind. I

chose the previous and became committed to attaining a college education. There were many

hurdles to overcome and the most monumental was ignorance of the process that is of where and

how to locate the resources necessary to support and guide me. Through the example of my

mother, who had managed a household and raised six children on my father's meager income of

$500 a month, I learned determination, resiliency and resourcefulness. My senior year in high school I was informed that the family's financial support belonged to my brothers who lacked the interest to attend college. The fact that I was a female did not qualify me for that support. It made me more determined.

I knew that an education was the key to my future when one day my mother told me, "I cannot speak for you to your teachers. They have the education, they must be right." I made a vow never to feel as disenfranchised as my mother probably felt at that moment. I would defy the conventions of my culture and my gender and overcome the adversities faced by a Hispanic female.

At that time the only advice my mother gave me was to assimilate. I felt that was the way out of my situation. I blamed my culture and my heritage for the lack of college opportunities and married someone outside my ethnic group. This union would support my academic goals in that I became geographically and emotionally isolated from the support of my family and friends. I had children and I became a stay-at-home mom and wife. When the children were in grade school, I registered for college and found employment. I had been out of school for fifteen years and I had to learn new skills and make tremendous adjustments in my life. I succeeded by transferring skills, such as problem solving, time management and budgeting which I used to manage a home and family to the classroom. It was challenging and rewarding to find myself with classmates who were young enough to be my children.

At the same time I progressed at work. Within a five year period I advanced from a receptionist to the position of director of the Office of Hispanic Concerns for the Diocese of Austin. I was the voice for the Hispanic population of Central Texas on a local, state and national level. In this position I found myself wrestling with my cultural identity. I met and shared many stories with a diverse group of Hispanics. I listened to the revealing stories of countless newly arrived and undocumented immigrants and native born Hispanics. I discovered a missing component in their/our lives - role models. Furthermore, the need voiced most was for educational opportunities for youth after high school. Parents did not know how to help their children get into college. Having been the first in my family to enter college I empathized with their anxieties. I coordinated college fairs for families to give them the tools to help them make these important decisions. However, I had not achieved my desired goal and my professional activities made me the more anxious to complete my degree. With the parchment I could be the role model I had searched for in my youth and that others were seeking.

I was at a crossroads. In order to make the dream of becoming a lawyer true I had to make the commitment of all my time and energy. I made the decision to leave my job, and to leave my marriage and complete my education. I was an unemployed, student, single mother and homemaker. Unable to find relief for my financial situation I did the unthinkable and I applied for public assistance. In hindsight, the experience gave me a view into a small segment of the world as it is lived by those I had often heard referred to as "freeloaders of the system." I knew that for me the assistance was a temporary necessity because, unlike most of them, I had the skills and education to be independent. However, it made me aware of the need to help empower the disenfranchised.

This year I was granted a divorce, received my undergraduate degree, found employment, and got off public assistance. The determination, resourcefulness and adaptability that brought me to this point will be the motive force that will carry me throughout law school and my legal career.

Essay 110—Makeover: This essay underwent such major revisions that we have only printed the revised edition without showing the editing of the original version. This version dramatizes the effect of what the student faced by putting the reader into the middle of the action, rather than simply telling what happened.

The year was 1968. A timid, slender teenager hesitated outside the door to the ~~kitchen.~~ *kitchen* . What would her mother's reaction be? Her mother *had* left high school in the eleventh grade and her father *had left school* in the fourth grade to help support his family. The teenager desperately wanted to change the pattern of what was expected ~~in~~ *of* her ~~life.~~ *.* Squaring ~~off~~ her shoulders, she tightened her fists and entered.

"*Mamá,* I need your help," she stated simply.

"What do you need, *mija*?" Her mother continued making breakfast.

[Delete-understood from earlier text.]

"*Mamá*, I want to go to college," ~~the teenager bit her lip, unsure what her mother would say.~~

"*Mija*, why do you want to do that? You're a girl. Girls don't go to college." Her mother seemed to be mixing the tortilla dough with a vengeance.

"Girls go to college every day, *Mamá*. You mean Mexican girls don't go to college. You have to help me convince *p*apá to let me go."

"*Mija*, we don't have much money. The money we have must help your brothers go to college. That's the way we do it."

"But *Mamá*, they don't want to go. I do." The young woman blinked furiously, tears stinging her *of anger* ^ eyes ~~from anger.~~

"What do your teachers say about this crazy idea?" Her mother shook her head, deep furrows forming on her forehead from her frown.

[Redundant. Said in next question.]

"*Mamá*, there's no reason I can't go/," ~~the teenager avoided answering the question.~~

"*Mija*, you didn't answer my question. What do your teachers say?" The mother intently watched her daughter.

"My teachers and counselor think I should find a good man to marry and start a family, but . . ." The teenager wasn't allowed to continue.

"*Mija*, how can you expect me to go against your teachers? They have the education. They must be right. They know what they're doing," her mother argued.

"But *Mamá*, they're women and they went to college. They're married and have kids. That's why I want to go. Don't you understand? I can still get married, but I want a chance. That's all I'm asking for, a chance to get more education." The teenager quickly brushed away the tear that had formed in the corner of her eye. She didn't want to cry, not now. She could cry tears of joy once she was in college. Right now she had to convince her mother.

"*Mija,* that's just not what Mexican girls do. Those women are different. Once you're married and have a couple of kids, you'll see. You'll understand then. You have to accept your life for what it is."

"But *Mamá.*" The teenager wanted to continue her argument. Surely she could make her mother understand.

"No more. You need to go and get the sheets off the beds. Today is wash day. This way your father and brothers will have nice clean sheets on their beds. That's what our life is about, *mija.*" Her mother brushed her hands together to get the sticky dough off her fingers and turned her back to her daughter.

The usually shy, obedient teenager seethed with anger, but she couldn't disregard her parents' [Delete—understood.] wishes. Her shoulders sagged ~~from the weight of defeat~~ as she turned and left the room.

That was my life when I was ready to start my college education. I was faced with a paramount dilemma: follow my dream to achieve a professional career and attain self-confidence or resign myself to the destiny that my parents had in mind. I chose to dedicate myself to attaining a college education. The many lessons, challenges, and accomplishments I experienced along my life's road paved the way to resourcefulness and resiliency. I ~~will need not only as~~ won't just be an attorney, but ~~as~~ someone who ~~can~~ 'll make a difference.

My mother's advice those many years ago was the only advice she could have given me. I may have grown up in a traditional Hispanic family which was rich in culture and family values, but females weren't encouraged to attain their full potential. That type of mindset led to my having low self-esteem ~~and self-worth.~~ [Redundant.] I vowed to defy the conventions of my culture and gender and overcome the adversities faced by Hispanic females.

I married, had children, and became a stay-at-home mom and wife. When the children were in grade school, I registered for college and found employment. I succeeded by transferring skills, I used to manage a home and family, such as problem solving, time management, and budgeting, ~~which I used to manage a home and family~~ to the classroom.

Within a five year period, I advanced from a receptionist to Director of the Office of Hispanic Concerns for the Diocese of Austin. I was the voice for the Hispanic population of Central Texas on a local, state, and national level. I discovered a missing component in their/our lives—role models. Parents didn't know how to help their children get into college. Having been the first in my family to enter college, I empathized with their anxieties. I coordinated college fairs for families to give them the tools to help them make these important decisions. With the parchment, I could be the role model I had searched for in my youth and that others were seeking.

I was at a crossroads. In order to make the dream of becoming a lawyer *come* true, I had to make the commitment of all my time and energy. I made the decision to leave my job, leave my marriage, and complete my education. I was an unemployed student, single mother, and homemaker. Unable to find relief for my financial situation, I did the unthinkable and applied for public assistance. Though I knew the assistance was a temporary necessity, it made me aware of the need to help empower the disenfranchised.

This year I was granted a divorce, received my undergraduate degree, found employment, and got off public assistance. The determination, resourcefulness, and adaptability that brought me to this point will be the driving force that will carry me throughout law school and my legal career.

Essay 111: Here's the edited essay, cut down to approximately 1,000 words. Now cut it down to approximately 500 words.

The year was 1968. A timid, slender teenager hesitated outside the kitchen door. What would her mother's reaction be? Her mother had left high school in the eleventh grade and her father had left school in the fourth grade to help support his family. The teenager desperately wanted to change the pattern of what was expected of her. Squaring her shoulders, she tightened her fists and entered.

"*Mamá,* I need your help," she stated simply.

"What do you need, *mija?*" Her mother continued making breakfast.

"*Mamá,* I want to go to college."

"*Mija,* why do you want to do that? You're a girl. Girls don't go to college." Her mother seemed to be mixing the tortilla dough with a vengeance.

"Girls go to college every day, *Mamá.* You mean Mexican girls don't go to college. You have to help me convince *Papá* to let me go."

"*Mija,* we don't have much money. The money we have must help your brothers go to college. That's the way we do it."

"But *Mamá,* they don't want to go. I do." The young woman blinked furiously, tears of anger stinging her eyes.

"What do your teachers say about this crazy idea?" Her mother shook her head, deep furrows forming on her forehead from her frown.

"*Mamá,* there's no reason I can't go."

"*Mija,* you didn't answer my question. What do your teachers say?" The mother intently watched her daughter.

"My teachers and counselor think I should find a good man to marry and start a family, but . . ." The teenager wasn't allowed to continue.

"*Mija,* how can you expect me to go against your teachers? They have the education. They must be right. They know what they're doing," her mother argued.

"But *Mamá*, they're women and they went to college. They're married and have kids. That's why I want to go. Don't you understand? I can still get married, but I want a chance. That's all I'm asking for, a chance to get more education." The teenager quickly brushed away the tear that had formed in the corner of her eye. She didn't want to cry, not now. She could cry tears of joy once she was in college. Right now she had to convince her mother.

"*Mija,* that's just not what Mexican girls do. Those women are different. Once you're married and have a couple of kids, you'll see. You'll understand then. You have to accept your life for what it is."

"But *Mamá.*" The teenager wanted to continue her argument. Surely she could make her mother understand.

"No more. You need to go and get the sheets off the beds. Today is wash day. This way your father and brothers will have nice clean sheets on their beds. That's what our life is about, *mija.*" Her mother brushed her hands together to get the sticky dough off her fingers and turned her back to her daughter.

The usually shy, obedient teenager seethed with anger, but she couldn't disregard her parents' wishes. Her shoulders sagged as she turned and left the room.

That was my life when I was ready to start my college education. I was faced with a paramount dilemma: follow my dream to achieve a professional career and attain self confidence or resign myself to the destiny that my parents had in mind. I chose to dedicate myself to attaining a college education. The many lessons, challenges, and accomplishments I experienced along my life's road paved the way to resourcefulness and resilience. I won't just be an attorney, but someone who'll make a difference.

My mother's advice those many years ago was the only advice she could have given me. I may have grown up in a traditional Hispanic family which was rich in culture and family values, but females weren't encouraged to attain their full potential. That type of mindset led to my having low self-esteem. I vowed to defy the conventions of my culture and gender and overcome the adversities faced by Hispanic females.

I married, had children, and became a stay-at-home mom and wife. When the children were in grade school, I registered for college and found employment. I succeeded by transferring skills I used to manage a home and family, such as problem-solving, time management, and budgeting, to the classroom.

Within a five-year period, I advanced from receptionist to Director of the Office of Hispanic Concerns for the Diocese of Austin. I was the voice for the Hispanic population of Central Texas on a local, state, and national level. I discovered a missing component in their/our lives—role models. Parents didn't know how to help their children get into college. Having been the first in my family to enter college, I empathized with their anxieties. I coordinated college fairs for families to give them the tools to help them make these important decisions. With the parchment, I could be the role model I had searched for in my youth and that others were seeking.

I was at a crossroads. In order to make the dream of becoming a lawyer come true, I had to make the commitment of all my time and energy. I made the decision to leave my job, leave my marriage, and complete my education. I was an unemployed student, single mother and homemaker. Unable to find relief for my financial situation, I did the unthinkable and applied for public assistance. Though I knew the assistance was a temporary necessity, it made me aware of the need to help empower the disenfranchised.

This year I was granted a divorce, received my undergraduate degree, found employment, and got off public assistance. The determination, resourcefulness and adaptability that brought me to this point will be the driving force that will carry me throughout law school and my legal career.

Essay 111—Makeover: This next version shows one way to cut the essay above from approximately 1,000 words to 500 words.

The year was 1968. A timid, slender teenager hesitated outside the kitchen door. What would her mother's reaction be? ~~Her mother had left high school in the eleventh grade and her father had left school in the fourth grade to help support his family.~~ ~~The teenager~~ *She* desperately wanted to change the pattern of what was expected of her. ~~Squaring her shoulders, she tightened her fists and entered.~~

"*Mamá,* I need your help," she stated ~~simply.~~ .

"What do you need, *mija*?" Her mother continued making breakfast.

"*Mamá,* I want to go to college."

"*Mija,* why do you want to do that? You're a girl. Girls don't go to college." ~~Her mother seemed to be mixing the tortilla dough with a vengeance.~~

"Girls go to college every day, *Mamá.* You mean Mexican girls don't go to college." " ~~You have to help me convince papa to let me go.~~"

"*Mija,* ~~we don't have much money.~~ *t*The money we have must help your brothers go to college. " ~~That's the way we do it.~~"

"But *Mamá,* they don't want to go. I do," *she argued.* ~~The young woman blinked furiously, tears of anger stinging her eyes.~~

"What do your teachers say about this crazy idea?" ~~Her mother shook her head, deep furrows forming on her forehead from her frown.~~

~~"*Mama,* there's no reason I can't go."~~

~~"*Mija,* you didn't answer my question. What do your teachers say?" The mother intently watched her daughter.~~

"My teachers and counselor think I should find a good man to marry and start a family, but . . ." ~~The teenager wasn't allowed to continue.~~

"*Mija*, how can you expect me to go against your teachers? They have the education. ~~They must be right.~~ They know what they're doing," her mother argued.

"But *Mamá*, they're women and they went to college. They're married and have kids. That's why I want to go. ~~Don't you understand?~~ I can still get married, ~~but I want a chance.~~ That's all I'm asking for, is a chance to get more education." ~~The teenager quickly brushed away the tear that had formed in the corner of her eye. She didn't want to cry, not now. She could cry tears of joy once she was in college. Right now she had to convince her mother.~~

"*Mija*, that's just not what Mexican girls do. Those women are different. ~~Once you're married and have a couple of kids, you'll see. You'll understand then.~~ You have to accept your life for what it is."

"But *Mamá*," the teenager ~~wanted to continue her argument.~~ *tried to explain.* ~~Surely she could make her mother understand.~~

"No more. You need to go and get the sheets off the beds. Today is wash day. ~~This way your father and brothers will have nice clean sheets on their beds.~~ That's what our life is about, *mija*." ~~Her mother brushed her hands together to get the sticky dough off her fingers and turned her back to her daughter.~~

The usually shy, obedient teenager seethed with anger, but ~~she~~ couldn't disregard her parents' wishes. Her shoulders sagged as she turned and left the room.

~~That was my life when I was ready to start my college education. I was~~ Faced with a paramount dilemma, ~~follow my dream to achieve a professional career and attain self confidence or resign myself to the destiny that my parents had in mind.~~ I chose to dedicate myself to attaining a college education. ~~The many lessons, challenges, and accomplishments I experienced along my life's road paved the way to resourcefulness and resilience. I won't just be an attorney, but someone who'll make a difference.~~

~~My mother's advice those many years ago was the only advice she could have given me. I may~~

have grown up in a traditional Hispanic family which was rich in culture and family values, but females weren't encouraged to attain their full potential. That type of mindset led to my having low self-esteem. I vowed to defy the conventions of my culture and gender and overcome the adversities faced by Hispanic females.

I married, had children, and became a stay-at-home mom and wife. When the children were in grade school, I registered for college and found employment. I succeeded by transferring skills I used to manage a home and family, such as problem solving, time management, and budgeting, to the classroom.

Within a five-year period, I advanced from receptionist to Director of the Office of Hispanic Concerns for the Diocese of Austin. I was the voice for the Hispanic population of Central Texas on a local, state, and national level. I discovered a missing component in their/our lives - role models. *that p*

~~P~~arents didn't know how to help their children get into college. Having been the first in my family to enter college, I empathized with their anxieties. I coordinated college fairs for families to give them the tools to help them make these important decisions. With the parchment, I could be the role model I had searched for in my youth and that others were seeking.

I was at a crossroads. In order to make the dream of becoming a lawyer come true, I had to make the commitment of all my time and energy. I made the decision to leave my job/ leave my marriage, *left* ^ *and* ^

returned to college. Suddenly,

and complete my education. I was an unemployed student, single mother, and homemaker. Unable ^

to find relief for my financial situation, I did the unthinkable and applied for public assistance. Though I knew the assistance was a temporary necessity, it made me aware of the need to help empower the disenfranchised.

This year I was granted a divorce, received my undergraduate degree, found employment, and got off public assistance. The determination, resourcefulness, and adaptability that brought me to this point will be the driving force that will carry me throughout law school and my legal career.

Essay 112: In 500 words or less, describe the setting in which you envision conducting your medical career. Also include how and why you think this setting would help fulfill your interests related to the practice of medicine.

Through hospital volunteer experiences in urology as well as shadowing a radiologist, I realize that in the future I would like to specialize in a particular field of medicine, allowing me to focus on a specific area of medicine rather than on a broader one. Although radiology seems to be an attractive option, I am still unsure which specialty I would like to pursue. However, I do know that I would like to practice medicine in a setting that would enable me to care for the same patients over a long period of time. I would like to conduct my medical career as part of a group practice. This would give me the opportunity to work with similar professionals in a cooperative, team-oriented environment. I believe that being a member of a group practice would only make the practice of medicine that much more enjoyable and fulfilling. Despite my desire to practice medicine in the mentioned forum, I realize that different options may arise in the changing field of medicine. Because of this fact, my future plans are flexible, with the only requirement being that I will be able to practice medicine to the best of my ability, caring for each patient with the same kindness and respect as I was cared for ten years ago.

I envision myself feeling the same way about practicing medicine twenty-five years from now as I do today, the desire to treat and care for patients still burning brightly. I can see advances in medicine enabling me to diagnose and treat patients more effectively, making my job even more fulfilling than even I thought possible. I will love my career more with each passing day, with each smile from a healthy patient or a relieved family member. Lastly, I can see myself waiting for the excitement and satisfaction of my job to fade away, but knowing it never will.

Essay 112—Makeover: We suggested that the student give this essay a slice-of-life feeling and actually describe the setting where he works. The earlier version tells what he wants, while he needs to show what he wants. This vivid new version will be memorable to committee members, drawing the attention and merit this student wants to receive. The new version is 388 words in length.

The morning sun has yet to kiss the dew off the flowers, but I'm already driving to work. I have patients to look in on at the hospital where I have privileges. All my patients know they'll see me at least twice a day: once in the morning as they wake up and again in the evening before my work day is done.

Morning hospital rounds are over and I'm back in the car again, dictating notes into a voice-activated recorder I had installed in the dash of the car, allowing me to record my comments on my hospitalized patients while they're still fresh in my mind. The traffic is mild, and though it's only nine o'clock, the sun is well on its way to its apex in the sky. There'll be time when I get to the office to have a cup of coffee and perhaps a doughnut before my first appointment.

Though my colleagues walk in through a separate entrance, I enjoy walking through the lobby, greeting any of my patients who are waiting to see me. I take the time to enjoy the pleasantries of life and inquire about my patients' families. After all, life is more than just work.

After passing the reception area, I stop to chat with my partners. We have a thriving group practice with many specialties because we're all of a similar mind: we treat our patients and their families in a cooperative, team-oriented environment. With that in mind, our group practice includes at least one doctor, if not more, from a variety of specialties: pediatrics, internal medicine, gynecology, geriatrics, orthopedics, neurology, radiology, and psychiatry. Basically our practice could, in essence, take a patient from the cradle through their twilight years.

Our state-of-the art computer system makes it easy for each physician to access information about the entire family. Likewise, our patients know they can access any one or more physicians in our medical family. We also utilize the Internet to stay in contact with physicians worldwide in an effort to provide the latest treatments our patients deserve and expect.

I love my career more with each passing day, with each smile from a healthy patient or a relieved family member. I greet each day with excitement and satisfaction, knowing I've done my best to enhance the lives of others.

Essay 113: We want to know why you've chosen to pursue a career in medicine. Your essay should be no more than two double-spaced pages.

Ever since I can remember, I have wanted to be a doctor and have set my goals accordingly. I went to a good private college and took all the pre-medical classes, worked as a TA in a biology class, was a registered EMT, and worked at a local hospital during my summer breaks. I am a dedicated student; I am motivated to work hard to achieve my goals; I am compassionate and empathetic; I am willing and anxious to learn; I am analytical and good at problem solving; and I am a good listener. Medicine requires all of these behaviors and traits, but, in reality, I am describing every pre-medical student and his basic achievements. Certainly, there are unusual students who have had unusual opportunities, but what can I say to make you see that I am unique? Through a series of not so dramatic or profound events, I realized that I have that unique something that no one else has to offer. I have myself and every unique part of my personality that sets me apart from any other student.

This became clear to me during a mission trip to Nicaragua. I was sitting with fellow students in an outdoor café waiting for our meal. Three local children covered with dirt, hair tangled and unkempt, moved in closer and closer to our table. However, their approach was halted as our waiter brought our food. Hungry from a day of walking, we heartily attacked our food, ignoring the children. Suddenly, I noticed that the oldest girl had taken something from one of the other customers. The children ran down the street, laughing and thrilled at getting a leftover chicken bone. Reality hit, and the romance vanished. I was in a restaurant in a foreign country, looking at a lake that was so polluted no life could possible survive; locals avoided it, and three innocent children were rejoicing at the prize of someone's leftover chicken bone. What were their chances of survival? I wanted to be a part of helping in real life.

I couldn't help but reflect back to several instances that I thought were more traumatic, more medical, yet certainly more civilized, more palatable. I was an EMT volunteer in the small town where I went to college. At times I longed for the intensity of a real trauma, but sometimes those long two hour rides to the larger hospital said a lot about a situation and gave me insight into how to react to people. One night we had to transfer a seventeen-year-old girl with toxic shock syndrome. I had no great words of wisdom or expertise to offer, but I did have myself to give. I spoke to her the entire trip, assuring her, helping her to stay awake and comforting her.

Another episode occurred when a woman in advanced labor broke the quietness of the emergency room atmosphere where I was working. I grabbed a stretcher since she revealed signs of merconium staining. It was determined that the umbilical cord was wrapped around the baby's neck. Nurses were screaming at her not to push as I muscled the stretcher up to labor and delivery. It was clear that she was terrified and in intense pain. Thoughts raced through my mind about what I could say to her. Since I didn't know anything about being in labor, I just held her hand and told her it was going to be okay. The nurses later thanked me for my help. It was a wonderful feeling!

Yes, my schooling has prepared me to work hard toward my goals using problem solving and analytical skills. Yes, my work has given me clinical exposure to the nature of medical environments. And, yes, my experiences have reinforced my desire, my single-minded commitment to medicine. But more than any of the above, I have realized that I have something unique to offer patients, myself. I know that I can have a significant impact on any patients, my profession, and my surroundings. This is why I want to be a doctor. I have myself to offer. I am determined to make a difference.

Essay 113—Makeover: This essay lacks focus. The best thing the student could do was start over. The student needs to select one experience, and describe it vividly. Was it nighttime or daytime? Was the student alone or with others? What time of year was it? Remember to relate what you saw, heard, felt, tasted, and smelled when you tell a story in an essay. Jot down some thoughts about the event and the effect it had on your life. This essay doesn't necessarily have to indicate that this experience prepared the student for medical school, but should state that this experience helped the student to cope with whatever comes her way.

A ~~calm~~ lull had overtaken the emergency room for the moment. It was Tuesday at about 3:00 ~~in the morning.~~ *a.m.* All the emergencies had been tended to, and the nurses were busy with routine chart work. The doctors were catching up on their patient dictations ~~and~~ I was taking a breather. ~~Outside~~ *The*

I rushed to the lobby to
~~the ER treatment area the~~ calmness was shattered by a woman's screams. ~~The ER charge nurse told~~

A pregnant *was*
~~me to go~~ see what was happening. ~~Entering the lobby area, I saw a~~ woman clutching her ~~pregnant~~

quietly *obviously*
belly, struggling to stand upright, screaming in pain. Her husband was standing by her side, ~~quiet,~~

her
~~yet~~ concerned and confused about what he could do to help his wife. Despite being attended to by

I needed
an ER nurse and a labor and delivery nurse, ~~I knew the immediate need was~~ to get a stretcher.

The *helped* *onto* *a quick examination,*
~~I rushed back and the~~ nurses ~~pushed~~ the woman ~~on~~ the stretcher. After ~~the L&D nurse examined~~

determined
~~her~~ it was ~~evident~~ that the baby was crowning and in distress. When the nurse pulled her glove

The
away, I saw the meconium staining ~~on~~ the glove. ~~I looked back on the woman's face.~~ She was

covered in perspiration and clutching the sheets. Her breathing was heavy in between the moaning

and screaming. The nurses were yelling at her not to push ~~and I sensed the urgency to get her up to~~

, running
~~the labor and delivery floor.~~ I wheeled the stretcher around ~~and we ran~~ down the hall to the

to get to the labor and delivery floor.
elevator. When we reached the third floor, I ran ~~with the stretcher~~ down the hall, pushing the

worried
stretcher. We were moving so fast and around so many ~~multiple~~ sharp corners, ~~I couldn't help but~~

. [Move to beginning of sentence.]
~~worry that~~ I was going to run her into the wall ~~since I was Pushing the stretcher so fast and around~~

, labor and delivery
~~multiple sharp corners.~~ As I rounded the final corner I saw the ~~L&D~~ doctor and nurses waiting for

into a "heads first" position
us. I ~~questioned "head first" and~~ swung the stretcher ~~around as directed.~~ I backed her into the

pinning
room, ~~and it was clear that I had pinned~~ myself at the head of the stretcher next to the bed. As she

was transferred to the bed, I looked up and saw the woman's husband standing in the corner

standing there
attempting to stay out of the way. He looked completely lost holding his wife's overnight bag. My

again on
attention focused ~~back to~~ the woman. ~~I looked directly into her eyes and by the expression on her~~

~~face~~ I could see she was frightened. The nurses were still yelling at her not to push, and her

Knowing

husband was not close enough to comfort her. ~~Aware of the fact that~~ the medical team had to

concentrate on the delivery ~~of the baby~~ and the husband was motionless in the corner, ~~I turned to~~

. Holding   *I reassured her she*

~~focus on her.~~ I grabbed her hand ~~and held~~ it gently but firmly, ~~telling her that it~~ would be okay.

talked   *time*

I ~~continued to talk~~ to her in a calm voice until I was told it was ~~okay~~ for me to leave.

empty

As I slowly rolled the stretcher back to the ER, I reflected on the intensity of the preceding

I had been

moments. What if ~~that was me~~ lying there? How would I have felt? ~~Then I thought about my~~

Had done   *Had I done*

~~reaction to her.~~ ~~Did~~ I ~~do~~ the right thing? ~~Was it~~ enough? If I had to do it over again, would I have

I'd made

reacted in the same manner? I'd recognized the urgency of the situation and ~~Comfortable that~~ my

clearly   *accurately.*   *T*

decisions ~~were clear~~ and ~~accurate I realized the intensity of the situation and~~ ~~t~~he exhilaration of

in this

being involved ~~during the~~ episode bolstered my desire to pursue medicine. ~~I concluded that not~~

enthusiastically

~~only could I handle this, but~~ I anticipated the daily involvement with patients and medical

situations.

[Delete part of this paragraph. It detracts from the focus of the essay.]

~~My interest in medicine was reinforced during a human anatomy and physiology class. It~~

~~fascinated me to see the application of what I was learning to the actual working of a physical body.~~

~~Starting with basic biology to the advanced study of histology, the investigation of the human body~~

~~has been intriguing with new insights gained in every course. I enjoyed teaching the human~~

~~anatomy and physiology lab experiments while I was a TA at college. I loved how the elements of~~

~~an experiment came together to shed light and provide knowledge about our bodies.~~ Although ~~I~~

intrigues me, after   *I realized it was*

~~enjoyed the experimental aspect of medicine~~ working in the ER ~~has made it clear to me that~~ the

,   *necessity of*   *ing*   *that*

human component, the need for compassion and the ~~urgency to~~ make quick, critical decisions

feeds my desire to be a doctor.

The pain and fear of that pregnant woman left me with a lasting memory. The experience gave

me the opportunity for personal growth and accomplishment. I could have left her lying there with

reassure

no one available to calm and ~~assure~~ her. But I didn't. I reacted to the look of fear on her face and
        ^

respond to   *in*   *A career in*   *will*

responded as I would hope a doctor would ~~for~~ me or anyone ~~with the~~ need. ~~I realize that~~ medicine
        ^   ^   ^   ^

and experiences.

offers me a lifetime of opportunities ~~such as this one~~. Just as I faced ~~what I knew was~~ a situation
        ^   -

I'm

requiring immediate action and clear decision making, ~~I know I am~~ prepared to face the challenges
        ^   ^

in my future.

Essay 114: We are interested in knowing in what ways a scientific education in a research-focused environment is a good choice for you. What areas are you particularly interested in studying and why? How did your interests develop? (California Institute of Technology)

When one wants to become a scientist, one must ask "what exactly does a scientist do and why?" The traditional image of scientists that society has is a picture of people in white coats that stay in their pristine laboratory, completely cut off from the rest of the world and reality. I disagree. Scientists are servants of humanity, discovering more about life and our world and how it affects us. They must communicate and relate to others or their newly found knowledge is in vain.

I want to become a scientist, and Caltech provides an environment in which aspiring scientists can flourish. Of course, I have great interests in math and sciences, but the humanities also appeal to me. I love Caltech's core curriculum. It not only cultivates a prowess in the sciences but also in the humanities. This makes Caltech graduates better able to communicate their ideas and relate to people in all walks of life. Personally, I love to read and analyze literature. Caltech's humanities class will give me a chance to do something I enjoy and improve my communication skills.

Another aspect of Caltech that I like is the diversity of the science courses. I know I am interest in the general area of math, computer science and engineering, but my exact field of study isn't clear to me right now. I am currently working on a computer visualization of ballistic penetration with Dr. Thomas Smith, a scientist from Southwest Research Institute in San Antonio. The program is used to predict the interactions of weapon rounds and various materials, such as fabrics and ceramics. Through this project, I am learning much about visualization and computer science as well as physics and mathematics. I would love to take advantage of the premier opportunities Caltech offers in computer science and mathematics. I may want to continue with this project or a related study in a Summer Undergraduate Research Fellowship Program (SURF) in the future.

Essay 114—Makeover: This is a good essay, but it needed to get the reader's attention from the first word. We suggested the student rewrite the essay as if the bullet were coming at him, but then reveal that he was merely watching a video of a ballistic demonstration. This is the resulting essay, which incorporates portions of his essays from other applications.

Bang! In a split second, the bullet whizzed past ~~me~~ and struck its target. Although it was gone in a matter of microseconds, it seemed as if I could see the projectile burrowing slowly into the material before ~~it was~~ pulverized*ing.* I imagined what I would've felt had I been wearing that vest and how thankful I'd have been that the bullet had stopped a few centimeters short of my heart.

As the lights came on, I was brought back to the safety of the Young Engineers and Scientists Program classroom at Southwest Research Institute *(SwRI)*. I couldn't stop thinking about Dr. Thomas Smith's work developing projectile-stopping armors. I later interviewed him to learn more about this incredible man. My exhilaration knew no bounds when Dr. Smith agreed to mentor me for my independent research project. With Dr. Smith's help, I'm developing a computer visualization of ballistic penetration as calculated by the model he and his collaborator devised to determine ~~for~~ long rod penetration, used to predict the interactions of weapon rounds and various materials, such as fabrics and ceramics. I'm creating the program using cutting-edge graphics software called VTK that is used in many other scientific applications. In addition, I'm teaching myself various programming languages including C++, FORTRAN, and Tcl/Tk to create this graphics package. I also collaborate with computer programmers from SwRI to develop the software. This is ~~undoubtedly~~ one of the greatest challenges I've faced, but I love every minute of it.

Through this project, I'm beginning to see how math and science can be applied to solve real world problems. In ~~the~~ *our* "think tank" discussions ~~we have,~~ I'm exposed to current developments in the fields of materials science, computer visualization, and mathematics. Vast opportunities exist

for exploration and experimentation. One of my dreams is to create true artificial intelligence.

Besides all of the scientific conversations, Dr. Smith and I have discussions about Boy Scouts,

literature, music, and other non~~/science~~ *tific* science subjects. Through our discussions, ~~I have~~ *I've* seen that ~~is~~ *it's* not

only possible but favorable to have a broad understanding in both science and liberal arts, as it

facilitates communication ~~an~~ *and* a more balanced way of living and thinking.

I want to become a scientist, and Caltech provides an environment in which aspiring scientists

can flourish. ~~Of course, I have great interests~~ *My primary interest will always be* in math and sciences, ~~but~~ *yet* the humanities also appeal

to me. ~~I love~~ Caltech's core curriculum/ ~~It~~ not only cultivates a prowess in the sciences but also in

the humanities. This makes Caltech graduates better able to communicate their ideas and relate to

people in all walks of life. ~~Personally, I love to read and analyze literature.~~ Caltech's humanities class

will give me a chance to do something I enjoy and *will* improve my communication skills.

Another aspect of Caltech ~~that I like~~ *to which I'm drawn* is the diversity of the science courses. ~~I know I am interest~~ *Though my interests are*

in ~~the general area of~~ math, computer science, and engineering, ~~but my exact field of study isn't~~ *I haven't decided on the exact*

field in which to specialize. I plan

~~clear to me right now. I would love~~ to take advantage of the premier opportunities Caltech offers in

computer science and mathematics. I may want to continue with this project or ~~a~~ *with* related study in a

Summer Undergraduate Research Fellowship Program (SURF) in the future.

After my experience in the YES Program, I'm

~~Because of this experience, I have become strongly~~ attracted to the academic programs at Cal

Tech. Not only can I pursue the liberal *arts* studies that I enjoy in a highly respected program, ~~I~~ *but* I can

simultaneously study engineering at one of the top engineering schools in the nation. Upon

graduation

~~completion,~~ I'll be a "Renaissance Man" able to communicate with others on all wavelengths with a

specialized knowledge in engineering, exactly what I want in an education. For me, this is an

unbeatable combination.

APPENDICES

A. Glossary

B. Other Books of Interest

C. Essay Tracking Charts

D. Write to Us

APPENDIX A

GLOSSARY

The words in *italics* are examples of each term.

Active voice: A verb form that expresses action performed by its subject. ACTIVE: I *chose* to attend this college. PASSIVE: The college I attend *will be chosen* by me.

Adjective: A word modifying a noun. EXAMPLE: *tall* building, *strong* student

Adverb: A word modifying a verb, adverb, or adjective. EXAMPLE: He passed the course *easily*.

Analogy: A likening of two things that have some essential characteristics in common.

Anecdote: A brief account of an event.

Antecedent: A word or phrase to which a pronoun refers.

Apostrophe: A punctuation mark that stands for missing letters or indicates possession. EXAMPLE: *can't, Jennifer's* skates

Appositive: A word or phrase that explains or identifies another word or phrase coming just before it. EXAMPLE: My sister, *who's five years older than me,* attended Texas A&M University.

Assumption: Something that's taken for granted.

Audience: Those for whom a writer is writing.

Bibliography: A list of reference sources, consisting of books, articles, other printed materials, or e-documents.

Clarity: Clearness of thought and expression.

Clauses: A group of words that can act as a noun or a modifier. The difference between a phrase and a clause is that a clause contains a subject and a verb, and a phrase does not. EXAMPLE: This teddy bear, *which I love,* is an antique. (*Which I love* is the clause, and it modifies *teddy bear.*) *Anyone who likes spiders* should stay away from me. (*Anyone who likes spiders* is the clause and the subject of the sentence, so it is called a noun clause.)

Cliché: A word or expression that has lost its power because it's used too often. EXAMPLE: *bright as the sun, straight as an arrow*

Collaborative writing: Writing done by more than one person.

Collective noun: A noun that refers to a group. EXAMPLES: *family, herd*

Colloquial language: Conversational or informal language.

Colon: A punctuation mark used to indicate the amplification of a point or to precede a list. EXAMPLE: *When applying for scholarships, these are the important things to remember: organization, aggressiveness, and persistence.*

Comma: A punctuation mark used to indicate a pause. EXAMPLE: *He opened the door, but he didn't go through it.*

Comma splice: Two independent sentences joined by a comma. EXAMPLE: *Here today, gone tomorrow.*

Compound sentence: A sentence containing two or more independent clauses. EXAMPLE: *It's nearly five-thirty; we can't possibly reach town before dark.*

Compound subject: Two or more nouns used as the subject in a sentence. EXAMPLE: *Bread and butter* were all she served.

Conclusion: The end of a piece of writing, where the main point is repeated or summarized.

Concrete language: Language that is about substances, persons, or things rather than abstractions. ABSTRACT: *It takes a long time to go through the college*

application process. A period of unfavorable weather set in. CONCRETE: *It took me a week to complete the college application. It rained every day for a week.*

Conjunction: A word that connects words or groups of words in a sentence. EXAMPLE: *and, but, yet, however, nevertheless, thus*

Connotation: The meaning associated with a word.

Context, context clue: The words or ideas that surround an unfamiliar word and provide clues to its meaning. Clues may be in the form of examples, definitions, restatements, or explanations.

Credibility: The condition of being believable.

Critical thinking: A careful analysis of information.

Dangling modifier: A modifier that does not clearly modify any word in a sentence. EXAMPLE: *Bicycling to the store,* a car hit Joan. The correct placement of the modifier is as follows: *Bicycling to the store,* Joan was hit by a car.

Deductive order: A sequence of ideas that moves from the general to the specific.

Deductive reasoning: Drawing a specific conclusion from a general premise.

Demonstrative pronoun: A pronoun used to indicate a particular person or thing. EXAMPLE: *these.*

Denotation: A word's literal meaning.

Dependent clause: A clause that cannot stand alone as a sentence (also called a subordinate clause). EXAMPLE: *By working hard to improve my study skills,* I improved my grades.

Endnote: A note that appears at the end of a paper and gives the origin of a quotation or idea the writer used in the paper, if the quotation or idea is not the writer's own. The endnote states the name of the author of the quotation or idea and where it was originally published.

Essay: A written piece, usually fairly short, about one topic.

Explicit: Clearly or directly stated.

Expository writing: Writing that explains or describes, usually a view on a subject.

Fact: Something that is verifiable.

Fiction: Writing that is about imaginary characters or events. Compare **nonfiction**.

Figure of speech: Used to make descriptions more vivid and to bring fresh meaning to writing: metaphors, similes, hyperbole, and personification. Also referred to as "figurative language" or "figurative expression."

Flashback: An interruption in the current sequence of events to return to an earlier event.

Focus: The center or target of a writer's attention.

Footnote: A note that appears at the bottom of the page and gives the origin of a quotation or idea the writer is using, if the quotation or idea is not the writer's own. The footnote states the name of the author of the quotation or idea and where it was originally published.

Formal outline: A concise way to organize and summarize information in terms of main ideas and subordinate details; uses a system of Roman numerals, letters, and numbers to identify topics and subplots.

Hyperbole: Overstatement or exaggeration used to produce a dramatic effect; not meant to be taken literally. EXAMPLE: *The student's application shot to the top of the application pool. The salmon rocketed out of the river.*

Implicit: Suggested or indirectly stated.

Imply: To suggest without directly stating.

Indent: To move in the first word of a paragraph, usually five spaces.

Independent clause: A clause that can stand by itself as a sentence. EXAMPLE: *Jennifer shook the interviewer's hand* and left the room. *David hung up the phone* and walked away.

Inductive order: A sequence of ideas that moves from the specific to the general.

Inductive reasoning: Drawing a general conclusion from a particular fact or group of facts.

Infer: To draw a conclusion based on evidence.

Interjection: Text that is set off from the rest of a sentence and is usually followed by an exclamation point. EXAMPLE: As I raced for the touchdown, I was tackled from behind—*surprise!*—and the play stopped one yard short of the goal line.

Interrogative: A word used to form a sentence that asks a question. EXAMPLE: *What* is your intended major? *What* kind of ice cream would you like?

Literal language: Writing that uses the ordinary meanings rather than figurative meanings of words.

Logic: A system of reasoning or argument.

Main idea: In a piece of writing, the major point being made by the writer. The idea might be clearly stated, or it might be implied.

Metaphor: A figure of speech that emphasizes the common qualities of two unlike things; a metaphor differs from a simile in that the comparison is presented without the use of words that signal a comparison. EXAMPLE: *The interview was a piece of cake.*

Misplaced modifier: A modifier that has not been placed next to the word it modifies in a sentence.

Modifier: A descriptive word or group of words. Adjectives and adverbs are modifiers. Adjectives describe nouns. Adverbs describe verbs or adjectives. EXAMPLE: Mary, a *talented* girl, sang *beautifully.* The **adjective** is *talented,* modifying the noun "girl." The **adverb** is *beautifully,* modifying the verb "sang."

Narrative writing: Writing that tells a story or gives an account of an event.

Nonfiction: Writing that is about real characters, events, or things. Compare **fiction**.

Noun: A word that names something: a person, place, thing, or idea. *Barbara* is the class *valedictorian*. *Flowers* are beautiful. Getting into *college* gave him *satisfaction*.

Objective writing: Writing that is neutral in its point of view; writing that does not favor either side of an issue.

Objectivity: The state of being without bias.

Opinion: A judgment or belief that is open to debate. Editorial articles are opinion articles.

Order of ideas: The sequence in which ideas are presented.

Order of importance: The sequencing of ideas according to their significance.

Outline: An organizational plan for a piece of writing.

Paragraph: A subsection of a written work, comprising one or more sentences, focused on a particular idea.

Parenthesis: A curved punctuation mark used to set off a phrase from the surrounding text. EXAMPLE: Many students think *(erroneously)* they need to apply to only one college or university.

Part of speech: The way a word is used. There are eight parts of speech: noun, pronoun, verb, adverb, adjective, preposition, conjunction, and interjection.

Passive voice: A verb form that expresses action performed on its subject. PASSIVE: The college I attend *will be chosen* by me. ACTIVE: I *chose* to attend this college.

Personification: A figure of speech that gives human qualities to things, objects, or ideas. EXAMPLE: The *book beckoned* to the student. The *daisies nodded their heads* in the summer breeze.

Phrase: A group of words that does not contain both a subject and verb and that acts as a noun or a modifier. EXAMPLE: *Setting goals* is difficult for some students. *Going to great heights* is torture for some. *Walking to class,* Martin hummed a tune. ("Walking to class" describes Martin, so it's a modifying phrase.)

Point of view: Used as a technical term in writing to refer to the person (first, second, or third) in which a piece of writing is presented. Also used to denote the opinion or stance taken by a writer.

Postulate: To make an assumption.

Predicate: A verb or verb phrase in a sentence.

Prefix: A word element found at the beginning of some words; adding a prefix to a word either changes the word's meaning or creates an entirely new word. EXAMPLE: The word *scope* means "see." With the prefixes *micro-, tele-,* and *peri-,* the words become: *microscope, telescope,* and *periscope.*

Premise: A statement that may serve as the foundation of an argument.

Preposition: A word governing a noun or pronoun to form a phrase that modifies another sentence element. EXAMPLES: *to, from, behind. Behind* every dream of going *to* an Ivy League school is a lot of hard work.

Prepositional phrase: A prepositional phrase begins with a preposition and contains a noun and its modifiers. EXAMPLE: No one works best *under* pressure. The student was *between* a rock and a hard place.

Pronouns: Pronouns are words that replace nouns. EXAMPLES: *I, you, he, she, it, we, you* (plural), and *they.* David likes Madelyn because *she* is considerate. Marcia said *she* couldn't wait to graduate. David said *he* would take responsibility. Pronouns must agree with the nouns they replace. *Pat* likes the wild hat *she* made yesterday. Sometimes when *Erika and Holly* go out, *they* buy candy.

Prose: Any writing that is not poetry.

Quotation marks: Punctuation marks used most often to enclose directly quoted material or to indicate dialogue.

Redundancy: Unnecessary repetition of a word or phrase. EXAMPLE: He promised it would *never ever* happen again.

Reflexive pronoun: A personal pronoun in the self or selves form. EXAMPLE: *himself, themselves*

Relative pronoun: A pronoun that relates a clause to its antecedent. INCORRECT: *There were murmurings in the classroom that suggested dissension.* CORRECT: *Murmurings suggested dissension within the classroom.*

Relevance: A measurement of the relatedness of a statement or observation to a larger point.

Research paper: A paper based on research of a particular subject, using a variety of outside sources.

Root: The word element that is the main part of any word. EXAMPLE: micro*scope*

Run-on sentence: Nonstandard joining of independent clauses; two types of run-on sentences are the comma splice and the fused sentence.

Semicolon: A punctuation mark used to separate independent clauses. EXAMPLE: *I visited the university; I loved the dorms.*

Sentence: A word or group of words containing a subject and a verb. EXAMPLES: *John ran. John* is the subject, and *ran* is the verb. Last year, *I played* the lead in our school production of *Oliver! I* is the subject, and *played* is the verb. Although we are three years apart, my younger *sister* and *I are* the best of friends. *Sister* and *I* are the nouns, and *are* is the verb.

Sentence fragment: A dependent clause or a phrase incorrectly used as a complete sentence.

Sequential order: Organization of facts, events, or ideas based on logical, chronological, or spatial order.

Simile: A figure of speech that shows how two unlike items are alike in some way; introduced by words such as *like, as,* or *similar to.* EXAMPLE: The student's activity resume sparkled *like a diamond.* Getting a student to write an essay can be *as painful as pulling teeth.* Going to college is *similar to starting over.*

Simple sentence: An independent clause that stands alone as a sentence without other clauses. EXAMPLE: *John ran.*

Structure: The sequence in which a writer develops his or her point.

Subject: The part of a sentence that performs the action. EXAMPLE: *Mary* ran to the store. *Izaak* worked hard on the essay. Subjects must agree with their verbs: a singular subject requires a singular verb; a plural subject requires a plural verb. CORRECT: *I like music.* INCORRECT: *I likes music.* CORRECT: Peanut butter and jelly are a good combination. INCORRECT: Peanut butter and jelly is a good combination.

Subordinate detail: A piece of information that is less important than another.

Suffix: A word element found at the end of some words; adding a suffix to a word either changes the word's meaning or creates an entirely new word. EXAMPLE: *fix, fixed, fixer, fixable; coax, coaxed, coaxing*

Summary: A concise presentation of a larger body of information.

Supporting detail: Information in a piece of writing that clarifies, illustrates, or elaborates the main idea.

Syllogism: The basic form of deductive reasoning in which a conclusion is drawn from two statements or premises.

Text mapping: A graphic method of organizing and summarizing written information into main ideas and subordinate details. Text mapping is an alternative to making an outline.

Thesis: A point set forth and defended in writing.

Tone: The general quality of the atmosphere of an individual's writing, much like tone of voice. CASUAL: *I'm going to Purdue in the fall. If there's anything I can't stand it's snobbery.* FORMAL: *I will be attending Purdue in the fall. I strongly dislike all forms of snobbery.*

Topic sentence: A sentence, generally at the beginning of a paragraph, that explains the main point of that paragraph.

Validity: An idea's soundness, based on clear logic or facts.

Verb: A word expressing action or a state of being. EXAMPLE: Thomas *works* at the bookstore. Mary *plays* the piano.

APPENDIX B

__ OTHER BOOKS OF INTEREST __

Conner, Ellen, M.A., Joselyn Chadwick-Joshua, Ph.D., George P. Parks Jr., Ed.M., M.A., Robert B. Truscott, M.A., and Clara Wajngurt, Ph.D. *The Best Test Preparation for the TASP*. Austin, TX: Research & Education Association, 1993.

McCune, Sandra K., Nancy J. Wright, Janet Elder, and Katherine Gonnet. *How to Prepare for the TASP*. New York: Barron's Educational Series, 1991.

McKee, Cynthia Ruíz, and Phillip C. McKee Jr. *Cash for College*. New York: Quill Books, 1999.

The Official TASP Test Study Guide. Austin, TX: National Evaluation Systems, Inc., 1993.

Strunk, William, and E. B. White. *The Elements of Style*. New York: Macmillan, 1979.

Zinsser, William. *On Writing Well*. New York: Harper & Row, 1985.

ESSAY TRACKING CHARTS

ESSAY TRACKING CHART 1

Type of Essay	Rough Draft	Finished Draft
Experience		
800–1,000 words in length		
400–500 words in length		
100–200 words in length		
Role Model		
600–800 words in length		
400–500 words in length		
100–200 words in length		
Experiences + Goals		
1,000–1,200 words in length		
400–600 words in length		
100–200 words in length		
Role Model + Goals		
800–1,000 words in length		
400–500 words in length		
100–200 words in length		
Other Topics/Word Counts		

ESSAY TRACKING CHART 2

Place Sent College/ University Scholarship	Date Sent	Experience Total Word Count	Role Model Total Word Count	Goals Total Word Count	Combination Total Word Count	Other Essays

WRITE TO US

HOW TO CONTACT US

We always want to hear from students, families, teachers, counselors, professors, and admissions officers. Tell us about your experiences—success stories and horror stories. We might just put them in a future edition of this book. If you write and share your success stores, we'll post them on our "Page of Fame" on our web site.

We welcome your evaluation of this book. What did you think? Was it comprehensive enough? Was there something we didn't cover?

You can contact us in a variety of ways:

Cynthia Ruíz McKee and Phillip C. McKee Jr.
1633 Babcock Road, PMB 425
San Antonio, TX 78229-4725
Tel: (210) 614-5919
Fax: (210) 614-5937
E-mail: mckee@cashforcollege.com
Web site: http://www.cashforcollege.com

INDEX

Do your essays need help?

Don't know what to write about?

Don't know if it's long enough?

Don't know if your essay is interesting?

Don't know whether you answered the question?

Then maybe you need to send your essays to our newly opened Cash for College™ Essay ER.

The **Cash for College™ Essay ER** can help any student know how to apply just the right amount of pressure on just the right focal points to resuscitate any essay and bring it back to life. Give your essays a fighting chance.

The **Cash for College™ Essay ER** doctors, better known as Cynthia Ruiz McKee and Phillip C. McKee Jr., have developed scholarship application rating systems and know which essays work and which don't. Cynthia and Phil are parents, published authors, and educational consultants who have helped thousands of students win millions of dollars in scholarships to attend the college or university of their choice. Cynthia and Phil know their craft and approach each essay with the skill of a surgeon with a laser scalpel, knowing what to remove, what to alter, and what to save in an essay.

Through Cynthia and Phil's gentle but precise guidance, students:

- Learn what scholarship committees and college admissions officers are looking for
- Learn how to be selective and creative about what they write
- Get an essay ready for scholarship or college applications
- Receive immediate attention and instructions on healing their essays

The McKees have helped students attending Yale, Harvard, MIT, Boston University, Boston College, Stanford, MIT, military academies, University of Texas, University of Texas Honors (Plan II), Texas A&M University, Rice University, Duke University, Trinity University, St. Mary's University, and many more.

Normally $75, with this Coupon Offer, the price for this service is $50 and proof of purchase of *Cash for College's™ Write it Right*. For that fee, Cynthia and Phil will proofread and critique ten essays at any time within a year of signing in. Each student receives an Essay Patient ID Number. Each time an essay is submitted (by fax, e-mail, or mail), the student just provides that number and receives their critique within three days. A family may purchase the Essay Patient ID Number and use it for the whole family.

We also have a program for schools and school districts to register in our Essay ER in which all students in a school or school district can send essays for us to critique. Pricing depends on size of school. Contact us for costs.

Sign up today and give your essays all the TLC they deserve. No need to worry about HMOs or PPOs. You get the specialists when you need them!

Through College Resource Materials, we offer private services, but we don't do anything you couldn't do. We just save you time. When you need butter, do you spend hours churning it or do you go to the grocery or convenience store to buy it? When you need a car, do you purchase it from a dealer or individual, or do you buy a kit and build one? If you value your time, you might want to consider using some of our products or services.

If you're interested in any of our products or services, contact us or log onto our web site. Our web site address is: http://www.cashforcollege.com.

SPECIAL COUPON OFFER
ESSAY ER

Name _____

Address _____

City/State _____

Zip _____ Phone (___) _____

FAX (___) _____ E-mail: _____

Grade Level in School _____

School / College _____

Make $50 money order or check payable to:
College Resource Materials
1633 Babcock Road, PMB 425
San Antonio, TX 78229-4725

Phone: (210) 614-5919, FAX: (210) 614-5937
E-mail: mckee@cashforcollege.com   Website: http://www.cashforcollege.com

Please retain a copy of the completed order form for your records.

Original coupon (copies not accepted) must be redeemed within 60 days of purchase and must be accompanied by the receipt of purchase of this book. To utilize the Special Coupon Offer, send this coupon, the sales receipt, and check or money order to: College Resource Materials, 1633 Babcock Road, PMB 425, San Antonio, TX 78229. Coupon limit, one per customer.